LAFCADIO HEARN:
JAPAN'S GREAT INTERPRETER
A new anthology of his writings 1894-1904

Portrait of Lafcadio Hearn taken in Cincinnati when he was 23 (1873).

Lafcadio Hearn:
Japan's Great Interpreter

A new anthology
of his writings :
1894-1904

Edited by Louis Allen
& Jean Wilson

Japan Library Ltd
Sandgate, Folkestone, Kent

First published 1992 by
JAPAN LIBRARY LTD.
Knoll House, 35 The Crescent,
Sandgate, Folkestone,
Kent CT20 3EE

© Louis Allen (*Introduction*) and
Hirakawa Sukehiro (*Commentaries*) 1992

The Publishers gratefully acknowledge the assistance of
the Great Britain-Sasakawa Foundation
in the publication of this volume.

British Library Cataloguing in Publication Data
A CIP catalogue entry for this book is
available from the British Library

ISBN 1-873410-02-6 (Limp)
      0-904404-48-X (Case)

Distributed in the United States by
The Talman Co. Inc
131 Spring Street, Suite 201E-N
New York, NY 10012

Hearn photographs: courtesy IBM 'Infinity' issue No.88, 1991

Set in Plantin Roman 10 on 11 point
Keywork by Jean Brann and Ann Tiltman
Typesetting by Visual Typesetting, Harrow, Middlesex
Printed and bound in England by BPCC Wheatons Ltd., Exeter.

CONTENTS

Louis Allen

In Memoriam

Louis Allen first encountered the Japanese in Burma in mid 1945. At the age of 19 as an undergraduate reading French at Manchester University he was recruited by the Army into Intelligence and sent to London University's School of Oriental and African Studies to learn Japanese on an intensive 18-month course. His class, a group known as Translators Five, consisted of John 'Roger' Fry, Kenneth Gardner, John Hartley, Jim Follan, Stan Radcliff, Ron Beverton and David Anderson. A remarkable collection of irreverent and talented personalities, their collective story was to be told years later by Sadao Oba in his 1988 book *Senchu Rondon Nihongo Gakko*.

After completing the SOAS course, he was commissioned as a Lieutenant in the Intelligence Corps. His first assignment in the Far East was as a translator at the South-East Asia Translation and Interrogation Centre (SEATIC) in Delhi. However, he soon volunteered to serve close to the front line in Burma. He joined the mobile translation and interrogation section attached to the 4 Corps, Fourteenth Army and was posted to the 17th Indian Division at the Sittang.

He subsequently attained the rank of Captain and was mentioned in despatches. This distinction was earned in the summer of 1945 when, from amongst a pile of soaking battlefield litter captured by a Gurkha patrol, he spotted a Japanese document which he believed might have considerable significance. He immediately translated it straight onto a typewriter. It was in effect the forward break-out plan of the large Japanese force trapped in the Pegu Yomas. It described in detail the routes to be taken by the fleeing Japanese army — east to the Sittang River and to its regrouping with forces in Thailand and from Rangoon. Forewarned, the blocking manoeuvres of the Indian Divisions turned the planned Japanese operation into what has been called the *coup de grace* of the Japanese Imperial Army in Burma.

In the months immediately following the Japanese surrender in August 1945, Louis Allen was engaged as a language officer in liaison work and war crimes investigations at Payagyi Japanese Surrendered Personnel Camp near Pegu in southern Burma. During this period, he interviewed over 600 members of the Japanese forces, from generals to line soldiers. He later was to state many times that this close daily contact with the Japanese, with whom he was able to communicate with considerable fluency, enabled him to see them as human beings rather than the brutal savages of war-time propaganda.

'If you were involved in the early days of the defeat of Malaya, or if you were in Burma before ... the summer of 1944, the Japanese were a hard and ruthless enemy that you feared and took very seriously if you valued your life ... After that ... from late 1944 until the end of the war, my only feeling for the Japanese I saw was one of compassion. I felt sorry for them — I didn't think they could do anything ultimately harmful at all — and the notion of fear had gone completely.'

There is no doubt that this unique combination of his particular contribution to the Burma war campaign and the timing of his arrival left him free of the bitterness and hatred felt by so many among the British and Allied forces who witnessed at first hand the horrors of the worst kinds of Japanese behaviour during the war. Instead, he saw an enormous need for mutual understanding and reconciliation between the former enemies. He began as a soldier of Burma but then went on to spend much of his later life as an assiduous and often passionate student and interpreter of Japanese life and culture.

He returned to Manchester when he was demobbed to complete his French degree and then won a two-year scholarship to the Sorbonne. In 1951 he accepted a post as lecturer in French at Durham University, where he was to remain for the rest of his academic life, gaining the status of Reader in French in 1983. He was later made both Emeritus Reader in French and Honorary Fellow of the Northumbrian Universities East Asian Centre. His profound erudition was allied to his mastery of a vast array of languages and to a constant and life-affirming intellectual curiosity. It was precisely this combination of qualities that inspired and formed the subject-matter of Roy Fuller's poem 'Strange Revelations' which appeared in his anthology *Consolations*. His Durham base, provided by the university, was Dun Cow Cottage where he and his wife, Margaret, settled down and brought up a family of four sons and two daughters. (Great sadness was visited on the family when Margaret died prematurely in 1979 after thirty years of marriage.)

To many of his friends around the world Dun Cow Cottage came to be perceived as a sort of headquarters — an oasis even — for intellectual debate and exchange. For Louis Allen, almost biblical in appearance with his precipitous eyebrows and luxuriant beard and moustache, the roles of teacher and pater familias were utterly instinctive.

Soon after his arrival in Durham he began work on the series of war histories for which he is best remembered: *Japan: The Years of Triumph* (1971), *Sittang: The Last Battle* (1973), *The End of the War in Asia* (1976), *Singapore 1941-42* (1977) and *Burma: The Longest War 1941-45* (1984). These volumes were the result of extensive personal research and first-hand knowledge of the area, together with an ability to read Japanese sources fluently. His conviction that 'you cannot tell a story from one side' to get the true picture of events was the basis of his even-handed and comprehensive approach. *Burma: The Longest War* is widely perceived as a model for military historians in terms of its clarity and the weaving of the stories of both sides into one narrative.

Among his other publications is a collaborative translation of a book in Japanese by Yuji Aida, titled *Prisoner of the British*. It was a best-seller in Japan and Allen considered it important to make it available in English, even though Aida's post-war experience bore no comparison to the treatment suffered by British POWs under the Japanese in wartime. Aida was, in fact, a Japanese Surrendered Person (JSP) at the end of the war. Allen's determination that history should not be forgotten but rather remembered from all points of view won him many friends among ex-servicemen in both Britain and Japan.

Louis Allen was a man of many talents, huge conviction, great humour and amazing energy which found outlets in a wide variety of activities — the principal reason, perhaps, why he never received the recognition his academic ability deserved. He was involved in the advisory board of the BBC for many years, and his part in the *Round Britain Quiz* radio show, first as a participator and then as question-master gave him an opportunity to reach a wider audience, albeit one that revelled in the esoteric and the erudite. He also contributed theatre and literary reviews to *Kaleidoscope*, the Radio 4 arts programme. He was president of the British Association of Japanese Studies and a respected member of the Japan Society, where he was often welcomed as a speaker. His skill as a communicator was renowned and those who had the pleasure of hearing (and watching) him deliver an academic paper or just a general talk will have marvelled at his remarkable gift for speaking without recourse to a single note, including quoting *in extenso* from his chosen references. As well as producing an important body of monographs and reviews for many scholarly periodicals, he also contributed articles on classical and modern Japanese literature to a wide range of publications, including the *Times Literary Supplement*, *The Listener*, *Stand*, and *The Tablet*.

In retirement he remained as active as ever, becoming especially involved in organising, with Hirakubo Masao, exchange visits, beginning in 1989, between British and Japanese war veterans. Sponsored by the Great Britain-

Sasakawa Foundation, the Burma Campaign Fellowship Group, as it became known, was close to his heart and provided an essential person-to-person route towards further reconciliation and enhanced mutual respect. In a lecture to the Japan Society in April 1990, in which he reflected on his contacts with Japan in the post-war period, as well as the first visit of the Burma veterans the previous year, he said:

'I have spoken of my own diffidence about expressing our mission in terms of forgiving and forgetting ... I would insist on *remembering*. What is vital to me ... is that remembering should not be equated with recrimination. There has been plenty of that from both sides in the last fifty years. It must give place to knowledge and understanding. *Onshu wo koete.*'

During his last years he and his family found great support and companionship in Jean Wilson, a friend from his student days at Manchester. She shared his great interest and enthusiasm for Japan and collaborated with him as co-editor of this volume.

It was Louis Allen's pioneering research into the many historic links between the North-East of England and Japan that led him into the deeper study of Lafcadio Hearn who in his early teenage years had attended Ushaw College, near Durham. Hearn shared a common Irish ancestry with Allen, but their fundamental bond was a fascination for Japan and her culture and the desire to share their knowledge. Allen especially respected Hearn's awareness of the deeply spiritual nature of the Japanese. Hearn saw Japanese spirituality threatened by the great engineering triumphs of the nineteenth century, just as today economic successes tend to obscure the inner life of Japan from outsiders.

As an excellent communicator himself, Allen appreciated Hearn's writing skill, his ability to convey his observations on Japanese literature and culture so effectively to a Western audience. 'The Victorian sentimentalist is compensated for by the conscientious reporter', he wrote of Hearn. Allen's own experience of Japan precluded any possibility of sentimentality on his part, yet in his understanding of the importance of greater comprehension between Japan and the West for their mutual survival, Allen stood together with Hearn.

Today, a relief of Lafcadio Hearn stands outside the walls of the new University of Teikyo in Durham City, where Allen spent so many years of his working life.

Louis Allen died on his 69th birthday on 22 December 1991.

Study of Lafcadio Hearn in traditional Japanese dress taken in Matsue in 1891.

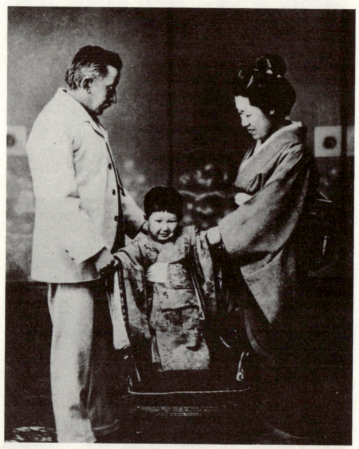

Formal picture of Lafcadio Hearn, his wife Setsu Koizumi and his eldest son Kazuo, 1895.

INTRODUCTION

By LOUIS ALLEN

Lafcadio Hearn was the most gifted and interesting writer on Japan during its emergence into the modern world. He spent the last fourteen years of his life there, married a Japanese woman, took Japanese citizenship and adopted a Japanese name. Yet he remained incurably Western in many respects, his literary background is European, and the medium which kept him alive - in addition to his teaching posts in Japan - were the readers of American literary periodicals. He fell out of fashion during the 1930s and 1940s when the popular image of Japan was almost universally hostile; and as his observations do not arise from any particular sociological method of analysis but are based on the impressions of a sensitive mind, his works were not resurrected when the economic growth of Japan made her society the object of renewed Western attention.

He had a fascinatingly mixed ancestry. His father, Charles Hearn, was a British army surgeon - an Irishman from Trinity College, Dublin, and nominally an Anglican. During a tour of duty in the Ionian Islands in 1848, he was stationed on Cerigo (Cythera) and there married the daughter of one of the local nobles, Rosa Antonia Cassimati. Their half-Irish, half-Greek child was born in 1850 and baptised Patrick Lafcadio, after his birthplace, the Greek island of Lefcadia (Levkas). When he was two, his mother brought him to Dublin while his father was away in the West Indies, and at once antagonised the Anglo-Irish Hearns. Mid-Victorian Dublin respectability must have found her very odd.

'And do you not remember that dark and beautiful face (Hearn wrote many years later to his brother) - with large brown eyes like a wild deer's - that used to bend above your cradle? You do not remember the voice which told you each night to cross your fingers after the old Greek orthodox fashion, and utter the words - "In the name of the Father, and of the Son, and of the Holy Ghost?" She made, or had made, three little wounds upon you when a baby - to place you, according to her childish faith, under the protection of those three powers, but especially that of Him for whom alone the Nineteenth Century still feels some reverence - *the Lord and Giver of Life*.... We were all very dark as children, very passionate, very odd-looking, and wore gold rings in our ears. Have you not the marks yet?'

This maternal memory is linked with what Hearn later fancied were

1

slivers of Mediterranean light from a vanished childhood paradise, the Greece which he had left too early and was never to know again.

Returned from the Crimea in 1856, Charles Hearn found an old girl-friend, Alicia Goslin, now widowed, and it was not long before he had set in train an annulment of his first marriage while Rosa was having his third child back home in Greece:

'One day my father came to my aunt's house to take me out for a walk. He took me into some quiet street, where the houses were very high - with long flights of steps going up to the front door. Then a lady came down to meet us, all white-robed, with very bright hair - quite slender. I thought her beautiful as an angel, perhaps partly because she kissed me and petted me and gave me a beautiful book and a toy gun. But my aunt found it out, and took away the book and the gun, and said that she was a very wicked woman and my father a very wicked man. She was the woman who afterwards became my father's second wife and died in India....'

This piece of Murdstonery had further consequences. Rosa married again, and the Hearn family in Dublin undertook to educate two of the Hearn boys, Lafcadio and his brother Daniel James. In good Empire-building fashion, and in a most suitable spot, Charles Hearn died of malaria in the Gulf of Suez in 1866. By then Lafcadio was being brought up by his father's aunt, Sarah Brenane, whose husband had died without giving her the heir he had longed for. In her mind, the little Lafcadio took the place of this heir, and every kind of attention was focused upon him. Materially, he was coddled and fussed. However, there was one difficulty. Mr Brenane had been a Catholic and Sarah - herself a convert - felt that the boy must be brought up as a Catholic; though she did not believe he ought to be taught the doctrines of the Church, merely imbibe its atmosphere. Those who helped him 'imbibe' it were not always the most fortunate of interpreters.

Cousin Jane, Aunt Sarah's protégé, came to the tall dark house in Rathmines to stay occasionally, 'a tall girl who looked like some of the long angels in my French pictures' he later remembered. She found out that Lafcadio did not know who God was. 'Why should I try to please God more than to please anybody else'? the child asked her. Cousin Jane gave forth in no uncertain terms. She grasped him to her, frightened him by the intensity of her gaze, and began, hardly breathing herself, to tell him who God was, or who her God was. 'You do not know about Heaven and Hell'? she asked. 'I do not remember all the rest of her words; I can recall with distinctness only the following:

'and send you down to Hell to burn alive in fire for ever and ever! Think of it! - always burning, burning, burning! - screaming and burning! screaming and burning! - never to be saved from that pain of fire!... You remember when you burned your finger at the lamp? Think of your whole body burning - always, always, always burning! - for ever and ever.'

In addition to terror, Victorian religion proved to be worse from the child Lafcadio's point of view: it was a destroyer of beauty. A wonderful book he had found in the Dublin house, full of pictures of Greek gods and goddesses, fauns and satyrs, dryads and nymphs, was removed from him by a private tutor and only returned when suitably dealt with.

'Evidently "the breasts of the nymphs in the brake" had been found too charming; dryads, naiads, graces and muses - all had been rendered breastless. And, in most cases, *drawers* had been put upon the gods - even upon the tiny Loves - large baggy bathing-drawers, woven with cross-strokes of a quill-pen, so designed as to conceal all curves of beauty - especially the lines of the long fine thighs.... However, in my case, this barbarism proved of some educational value. It furnished me with many problems of restoration; and I often tried very hard to reproduce in pencil-drawing the obliterated or hidden line.' (*Letters*, ed. Bisland, *Writings*, Vol. XIII, p. 27 in Stevenson, *Lafcadio Hearn*, p. 17).

Clearly, if we are to believe the hindsight of later years, resentful scepticism was already making its way in the soul of this believer.

'Now after I had learned to know and to love the elder gods, the world again began to glow about me. Glooms that had brooded over it slowly thinned away. The terror had not yet gone; but I now wanted only reasons to disbelieve all that I feared and hated....

'I looked for beauty, and everywhere found it; in passing faces - in attitudes and motions - in the poise of plants and trees - in long white clouds - in faint blue lines of far-off hills. At moments the simple pleasure of life would frighten me. But at other times there would come to me a new and strange sadness - a shadowy and inexplicable pain.' (Stevenson, op.cit., p. 18)

His further education was a step away from fulfilment of this desire for beauty. On the advice of an unscrupulous young man who was planning to channel Sarah Brenane's money into his own pockets, the young Lafcadio was sent to a Catholic school at Yvetot near Rouen, the same school from which de Maupassant was expelled a few years after young Hearn had left, and which he describes in the story *Une Surprise*.

'I can never think of the place even now without a shudder. It smelled of prayers the way a fish-market smells of fish. Oh! that dreary school, with its eternal religious ceremonies, its freezing Mass every morning, its periods of meditation, its gospel recitations, and the reading from pious books between meals! Oh those dreary days passed within those cloistering walls!... We lived there in narrow contemplative, unnatural piety and also in a truly meritorious state of filth, for I well remember that the boys were made to wash their feet but three times a year, the night before each vacation. As for baths, they were as unknown as the name of Victor Hugo. Our masters apparently held them in the greatest contempt.' (Stevenson, op.cit., p. 20)

Many years later Hearn was to recall being educated by the Jesuits, in very unfriendly terms. 'You know, I suppose', he wrote to Basil Hall Chamberlain, his first great patron in Japan, 'that my relatives tried once to make a priest of me. My father was an Episcopalian; but after his death in India, I fell into the hands of relatives who sent me to a Jesuit College. By the Jesuit standard, I was a fiend incarnate, and treated accordingly. How I hated them. My impotent resentment used to relieve itself in the imagination of massacres and horrible tortures. I hate them and have nightmares about them still....'

In the autumn of 1863, when he was thirteen, he was sent to St Cuthbert's, Ushaw College, near Durham in the North of England. Ushaw was a proudly secular institution, not a Jesuit one, but it certainly prepared boys for the priesthood, and one wonders whether Hearn's recollection was sufficiently dimmed after thirty years to make him confuse the training at Yvetot with that at Ushaw. Then, as later, it was a seminary as well as a school, and its Victorian manners were, in his memory, the harshly brutal ones of *Tom Brown's Schooldays*. On the other hand, the older Hearn who could remember that 'there is a world of romance in old Romanism' was no doubt recalling the genuine devotional piety of the place, and its richly ceremonial celebrations of the liturgy. He spent four years at Ushaw, and, because of the unpleasantness of his domestic background - his aunt was now totally taken up with a new protégé - he even spent the holidays there. The school was negatively good for the wayward imagination, writes one of his biographers: there were fields nearby for walks, there was a room with books where he was left alone to read while other boys played soccer outside in the sunlight. Games were not compulsory, activities were not organised. 'There was enough unregarded time to form an individuality' (Stevenson, op.cit. p.22). He won a prize in English, but was constantly embroiled in escapades, regarded as both popular and somewhat off balance mentally by his more orthodox friends.

Ushaw has a number of games that are its own, derived from a past that goes deep into French history when the school was in exile in North-Eastern France until the Revolution. In one of these games, 'Giant's Stride', a piece of knotted rope is used, and during one such game, the young Hearn was struck by this rope. He was sixteen at the time. The blow had severe and unpredictable consequences. He lost the sight of one eye, over which scar tissue formed; and the other eye became enlarged with over-use, and began to protrude from its socket. He was at an age when he was intensely sensitive to outward appearances, and the deformation this game caused him was inward as well as outward. His gaiety and ease of manner disappeared when he returned to Ushaw after an operation to save the injured eye. 'He never forgot that he was deformed', his son wrote of him, and he acquired the conviction that he was, as a result, sexually unattractive to women. Since he was deeply and passionately attracted to *them*, the hurt went deeper and deeper with the years. He could show only one side of his face to the camera - this is how he often appears - but in real life it was not so easy. Many years later, in a letter from Japan to a newly discovered half-sister, wondering if her children would ever see him, 'if they see me without previous discipline', he wrote, 'they will be afraid of my ugly face when I come - I send you a photo of one-half of it, the other is not pleasant, I assure you: like the moon, I show only one side of myself.'

The awareness of the way he thought his eyes looked, and the value he attached to the beauty of the eye, is very clear from a letter he wrote in Japan (1894):

'To me the Japanese eye has a beauty which I think Western eyes have not. I have read nasty things written about Japanese eyes until I am tired of reading them. Now let me defend my seemingly monstrous proposition.

'Miss Bird has well said that when one remains long in Japan, one finds one's standard of beauty changing; and the fact is true of other countries than Japan. Any *real* traveller can give similar experiences. When I show beautiful European engravings of young girls or children to Japanese, what do they say? I have done it fifty times, and whenever I was able to get a criticism, it was always the same: - "The faces are nice - all but the eyes: the eyes are too big - the eyes are monstrous." We judge by our conventions. The Orient judges by its own. Who is right?

.... 'The most beautiful pair of eyes I ever saw, a pair that fascinated me a great deal too much, and caused me to do some foolish things in old bachelor days - were Japanese. They were not small, but very characteristically racial; the lashes were very long, and the opening also of the lids - and the feeling they gave one was that of the eyes of a great wonderful bird of prey. There are wonderful eyes in Japan for those who can see.

'The eyelid is so very peculiar that I think its form decides - more than any other characteristic of the Far Eastern races - the existence of two entirely distinct original varieties of mankind. The muscular attachments are quite different, and the lines of the lashes - indeed, the whole outer anatomy.

'One might ask mockingly whether to Japanese eyelids could be applied the Greek term *charitoblepharos* (with eyelids like the Charites - the Graces). I think it could. There is a beauty of the Japanese eyelid, quite rare, but very singular - in which the lid-edge seems double, or at least marvellously grooved - and the effect is a softness and shadowiness difficult to describe.

'However, it seems to me that the chief beauty of a beautiful Japanese eye is in the peculiar anatomical arrangement which characterises it. The ball of the eye is *not* shown - the setting is totally hidden. The brown smooth skin opens quite suddenly and strangely over a moving jewel. Now in the most beautiful Western eyes the set of the ball into the skull is visible - the whole orbed form, and the whole line of the bone-socket - except in special cases. The mechanism is visible. I think that from a perfectly artistic point of view, the veiling of the mechanism is a greater feat on Nature's part....

'I don't mean to make any sweeping general rule. I only mean this: "Compare the most beautiful Japanese or Chinese eye with the most beautiful European eye, and see which suffers by comparison." I believe the true artist would say "neither"; but that which least shows the *machinery* behind it - the osteological and nervous machinery - now appears to me to have the greater charm. I dare say such eyes as I speak of are not common; but beautiful eyes are common in no country that I have ever visited.'

I don't think there can be any doubt that that is the writing of someone who has passionately examined the human eye, and examined it for mechanism and beauty, in the full and bitter knowledge of the destruction of beauty in his own. But before these thoughts were possible, Lafcadio had many vicissitudes to pass through. Losses in speculation on his aunt's behalf meant that the young Hearn's fees could no longer be paid, and he had to leave Ushaw, without any prospect of a university career. He was dispatched to London to live for a while with a woman who had been a family servant, and then, even more summarily, across the Atlantic - he was just 19 - to contact a vague family connection, in the city of Cincinnati, Ohio. A population of mixed New Englanders, Germans, and rootless blacks of the near South is how Hearn's biographer sums up the condition of Cincinnati in the years immediately after the Civil War, when the city had resolutely turned its back upon the past and determined to make money - 'a noisy, energetic centre of trade and industry. It was a whirlpool of opportunity, for death, for disease, neglect, as well as for success in the most blatant and obvious forms.' (Stevenson, op.cit., p. 29).

In this city, the young Hearn slept in the streets, experienced great poverty, took all kinds of makeshift jobs, writing articles and having them published without payment, began to pick up an acquaintance - of all things - with nineteenth-century French fiction, and found the human love he had searched for in Mattie Foley, a young mulatto boarding-house cook. 'Practical, pork-packing Cincinnati' made life possible for Hearn, and turned him into a writer. From occasional pieces he graduated to being a sensational reporter on the Cincinnati *Enquirer*. His themes were police court rounds, saloon brawls, and brutal crime, evoked with spectacular violence of style.

A piece about a particularly horrible murder (9 November, 1874) offers a fruity example of the kind of style he cultivated for the *Enquirer*:

'A tanyard worker named Herman Schilling had been set upon, beaten, stabbed with a pitchfork, stuffed into the furnace of the tannery where he worked, and there cremated. His suspected murderers were quickly found and arrested.' What Hearn seized upon was, naturally enough, the appalling details of the cremation. The fragments of the burned body on the clean white coffin-lining were described. They 'rather resembled great shapeless lumps of half-burnt bituminous coal than aught else at the first hurried glance: and only a closer investigation could enable a strong-stomached observer to detect their ghastly character - masses of crumbling human bones, strung together by half-burnt sinews, or glued one upon another by a hideous adhesion of half-molten flesh, boiled brains and jellied blood mingled with coal. The skull had burst like a shell in the fierce furnace-heat; and the whole upper portion seemed as though it had been *blown out* by the steam from the boiling and bubbling brains....

'The brain had all boiled away, save a small wasted lump at the base of the skull about the size of a lemon. It was crisped and still warm to the touch. On pushing the finger through the crisp, the interior felt about the consistency of human fruit, and the yellow fibres seemed to writhe like worms in the coroner's hands. The eyes were cooked to bubbled crisps in the blackened sockets, and the bones of the nose were gone, leaving a hideous hole.'

But of course the sensational reporter could not stop short at this unspeakable mass of physical detail. There was speculation about the last few seconds of the unfortunate victim:

'His teeth were so terribly clenched that more than one spectator of the hideous skull declared that only the most frightful agony could have set those jaws together. Perhaps, stunned and disabled by the murderous blows of his assailants, the unconscious body of the poor German was forced into the furnace. Perhaps the thrusts of the assassin's pitchfork, wedging him still further into the fiery hell, or the first agony of burning when his bloody garments took fire, revived him to meet the death of flame. Fancy the shrieks for mercy, the mad expostulation, the frightful fight for life, the superhuman struggles for existence - a century of agony crowded into a moment - the shrieks growing feebler - the desperate struggles dying into feeble writhings. And through all the grim murderers, demoniacally pitiless, devilishly desperate, gasping with their exertions to destroy a poor human life, looking on in silent triumph! Peering into the furnace until the skull exploded and the steaming body burst, and the fiery flue hissed like a hundred snakes!'

There is, in spite of 'demoniacally pitiless, devilishly desperate', an undeniable gift for the prose of horror there. But it was clearly time Hearn saw something other of American life than the backstreets of Cincinnati. His relationship with his mulatto had gone seriously wrong. The whites of Cincinnati shunned him because of her, and took it as the last straw that he went through a form of marriage with her. Cincinnati never forgave him this. Even eighty years after all these events, when Elizabeth Stevenson was doing research for her biography of him, the Curator of Rare Books in the Public Library of Cincinnati reminded her, with some disapproval, that Hearn left Cincinnati under a dark cloud. Mattie Foley herself was long past redemption in drink and street brawling when Hearn left her not long after their common-law marriage and moved south, to New Orleans, in October 1877. He was 27.

The South was what he needed, its warmth and air of careless neglect, its French survivals in speech and manner:

'The wealth of a world is here - unworked gold in the ore... the paradise of the South is here, deserted and half in ruins. I never beheld anything so beautiful and so sad. When I saw it first - Sunrise over Louisiana - the tears sprang to my eyes. It was like young death - a dead bride crowned with orange flowers - a dead face that asked for a kiss.'

He made a living by sending pieces on Southern life to a Cincinnati newspaper which paid him sporadically or not at all. His poverty continued, he caught dengue fever, and then at last, from the very depths of misery, he was rescued by a Colonel John Fairfax who employed him on his New Orleans paper *The Item*, in spite of the impression given by the eye from his Ushaw accident.

'That odd, rolling eye of his was the only thing you could see at first - enormous, protruding. After you got used to that eye, you saw that his other features were good, and his face refined....'

New Orleans fostered his talents, and its atmosphere gave him a taste for even more southerly exploration. The period from Summer 1887 until May 1889 he spent in the West Indies, steeping himself in Creole language and superstition, living not merely on the appetite for fresh sensations but also - like the French poet Saint-John Perse two decades later - on the appetite for the exact word and the exact piece of information. Contrary to our usual picture of Hearn - and this is true of the Japanese Hearn, as I hope to show - he did not idealise 'man or nature in Martinique... nothing could be more material than this tropic life'; but it provided him with a subject matter from which he drew more considered work than his journalistic pieces and he began to write, not for Cincinnati, but for New York, and it was to New York that he returned in 1889.

After the lazy islands, the reaction was predictable:

'The moment I get into all this beastly machinery called "New York", I get caught in some belt and whirled around madly in all directions until I have no sense left. This city drives me crazy, or if you prefer, crazier; and I have no peace of mind or rest of body until I get out of it. Nobody can find anybody, nothing seems to be anywhere, everything seems to be mathematics and geometry and enigmatics and riddles and confusion worse confounded: architecture and mechanics run mad.'

After a period in Philadelphia under the aegis of a dominating and resentful eye-specialist, Dr Gould, Hearn took up a suggestion from an art editor at Harper's that he should go to Japan. He had read Edwin Arnold's *Light of Asia*, and Percival Lowell's *Soul of the Far East*, and decided that he would go there and write a travel book.

There was no question of a new discovery of Japan in 1890. It was already, from the tourist viewpoint, a country of well-trodden paths. In fact, only a few years later, a canon of Durham, H. B. Tristram, who wrote a travel book on Japan, apologised in the preface for adding yet another work to the many which had been written on that country. Hearn said much the same thing in his plan to Harpers:

'In attempting a book upon a country so well trodden as Japan, I could not hope - nor would I consider it prudent attempting - to discover totally new things, but only to consider things in a totally new way.... The studied aim would be to create, in the minds of the readers, a vivid impression of *living* in Japan - not simply as an observer but as one taking part in the daily existence of the common people, and thinking with their thoughts.'

It was a country which had already been discovered and re-discovered, not merely by European intellectuals like the Goncourts who had studied it through its wood-block prints without ever having seen it or like the British scholar, Basil Hall Chamberlain, who became the first professor of Japanese language in the new Imperial University of Tokyo; but also by the Boston intelligentsia, or, to include Fenollosa, who originated in Salem, Massachusetts, the New England intelligentsia. The art of Japan and China was fashionable. The Boston museum bought the great collection of Japanese pottery amassed by Edward Morse during his zoological trips to Japanese waters. Fenollosa collected Japanese pictures. William Sturgis Bigelow brought back from Japan twenty-six thousand objects of Japanese art. 'We shall see a little of the life of old Japan', wrote Morse, as he, Fenollosa and Bigelow toured the southern provinces in 1882, 'I shall add a great many specimens to my collection of pottery; Dr Bigelow will secure many forms of swords, guards and lacquer; and Mr Fenollosa will increase his remarkable collection of pictures, so that we shall have in the vicinity of Boston by far the largest collection of Japanese art in the world.' (Van Wyck Brooks, *New England, Indian Summer*, p. 358 et seq.).

By a singular turn of fate, the grandson of the brother of Commodore Perry, whose 'black ships' in Tokyo Bay had opened Japan to the commerce of the world in 1853, spent three years as a professor at Keiō University (1897-1900). Henry Adams and his friend John La Farge, the painter, spent part of their incessant travels in Japan, passing through Hawaii and the South Seas en route for what Van Wyck Brooks calls discreetly an 'education of the senses' and long pow-wows with Samoan nobles. Their journey finally took them to Ceylon where, says Van Wyck Brooks, 'seated like priests or deities in a sacred ox-cart, on chairs upholstered in red, they were dragged through the woods to Anuradhapura. There, among the stone doorways standing in the jungle, monkeys jumped from branch to branch; and Adams sat for half an hour under the shoot of Buddha's bo-tree. Where else could he hope to find Nirvana?'

Where else? Some of his contemporaries had already found it in Japan. Bigelow became a convert to Buddhism, as did Fenollosa, and there were certainly moments for Henry Adams when he found himself very near the truth of human existence in the hills above Nikko or the temples of Kyoto. While La Farge painted, Adams read Dante or rode on pack-horses over the Japanese hills. 'Sometimes he took photographs, or he sat cross-legged on the verandah, overhauling bales of stuffs and lacquers, mounds of books and tons of bronzes, with Bigelow and Fenollosa to guide his choice.' (It was the great era for looting the East of its treasures).

'The friends rejoiced in the sacred groves, where the god Pan might still be living, the holy trees and stones, the little shrines, the old roads between the walls, broken by turrets and bridges. Here were the "soul-informed" rocks of the Greeks and a world that associated spirits with every visible form of the earthly dwelling. The bareness and coldness of the Japanese interiors, which insisted on the idea of doing with little - a noble one, certainly - pleased La Farge; the highest care in workmanship was all that adorned the emperor's palace at Kioto[sic]. How civilised, this emptiness, after the accumulations of Western houses!... For a painter, Japan was a godsend; while, as for Adams, he found in the statue of Kwannon the image of his quest. Here was Nirvana indeed, achieved in eternal calm, with eternal compassion.'

Most of the young Americans who went to Japan were, if they were monied (and most of them were) naturally taken up by the external aspect of Japan and by the fresh revelation of the fine arts. Some of them, like Bigelow, looked further, into Japanese religion; others, like Fenollosa, attempted to link the two. Bigelow studied Buddhism for seven years with a friendly abbot and was received into the Buddhist communion. 'Three or four decades later, dying in Boston', writes Van Wyck Brooks, 'he summoned a Catholic priest and besought him to annihilate his soul. He could not forgive the priest for refusing to do so.' (There are clearly certain things one should not ask of Boston Catholicism.) Bigelow's ashes, with soul still unannihilated, lie beside Fenollosa's on the shores of Lake Biwa.

Of all these predecessors, it was Percival Lowell whom Lafcadio Hearn most admired. A young man of fashion, Lowell had gone to Japan in 1883, drawn by a wish to learn the language. For ten years he studied the life of Japan, built himself a mansion in Tokyo where he lived the life of a Japanese prince, and wrote three books about the Far East. One of these, *The Soul of the Far East*, impressed Hearn profoundly, though, as he got to know Japan better, there were comments in it that he found it in himself to contradict. 'Lowell says the Japanese have no individuality', he wrote to Chamberlain in June 1894, 'I wish he had to teach here for a year, and he would discover some of the most extraordinary individualities he ever saw. There are eccentrics and personalities among the Japanese as with us: only, they show less quickly on the surface. No man can make a sweeping general statement about Japanese character in a negative sense, without finding out his mistake later.' Lowell's theme was that the characteristic of the Japanese mind, (and this was shown in family life, language and art,) was its *impersonality*; and that individuality itself was a transient illusion (the latter a message that Hearn found to be like some of his own ideas).

Fenollosa was sympathetic from another angle. He had taught the Japanese themselves to reverence their ancient art, at a moment when they were likely to throw it out in their hot pursuit of everything western. Literally 'throw it out' in some cases - Fenollosa once found a huge ceramic head of Buddha in a dust heap, and was said to have picked up one of Japan's greatest paintings in the market at Osaka. Gradually, he interested some Japanese nobles in the cause of conservation, and became Commissioner of Fine Arts in 1886 and later Director of the Tokyo Academy and the Imperial Museum.

His theme became Hearn's: the Japanese themselves were in the process of destroying what made them interesting and valuable as a people. Hearn, of course, went further. The bitter anti-Christian resentment that stemmed from his stormy and abandoned childhood soon found a target in Japan. The missionaries were the culprits. In moments of despair about the country's future he would blame the introduction of Christianity: 'There are times I feel so hopeless about everything in Japan', he writes to W. B. Mason from Kyoto in 1892, 'that I would like to leave it if I had no-one else to care for. Especially when I meet insolent clerks who have learned impertinence and Christianity at the Doshisha [a Christian university in Tokyo] - when I see Christian cathedrals - when I find Christian teachers among the Japanese instructors of the higher schools.'

Not that Hearn himself became a Buddhist *tout court*; he found too much to sympathise with in the older faith, Shinto, which Buddhism had first displaced and with which it later co-existed throughout the history of Japan and which was, as Hearn was writing, beginning to be used again in the service of the new imperialism, while Buddhism was left to wither on the branch.

Hearn came to Japan in 1890 and died there in 1904. During this period of fourteen years he wrote voluminously about Japan, but in only one instance did he sit down formally to write anything one could call a treatise, or sequence of argument, about the country of his adoption. That book was *Japan, An attempt at interpretation*, published by Macmillan of New York in 1905. Of its twenty-two chapters, thirteen deal with religion or subjects involved with religious issues, such as the structure of the family. It is interesting that of all the books on modern Japan, this one was singled out for reading by the French sociologist Jean Stoetsel. In his *Jeunesse sans chrysanthème ni sabre*, he put nothing between it and Ruth

Benedict's book (*The Chrysanthemum and the Sword*) of the 1940s. But it is not really typical of Hearn's writing about Japan.

Hearn's method was, almost instinctively, the Japanese one of *zuihitsu*, miscellaneous narrative essays which followed the flow of the pen. There is a tremendous risk in this genre, and he does not escape it - it is the risk of whimsy, and this is occasionally visible even in the titles he chooses for his books:

> *Glimpses of Unfamiliar Japan (1894)*
> *Out of the East: Reveries and Studies in New Japan (1895)*
> *Kokoro [heart]: Hints and Echoes of Japanese Inner Life (1896)*
> *Gleanings in Buddha Fields: Studies of Hand and Soul in the Far East (1897)*
> *Exotics and Retrospectives (1898)*
> *In Ghostly Japan (1899)*
> *Shadowings (1900)*
> *A Japanese Miscellany (1901)*
> *Kotto; Being Japanese Curios, with Sundry Cobwebs (1902)*
> *Kwaidan: Stories and Studies of Strange Things (1904)*
> *The Romance of the Milky Way and other stories (1905)*
> *Japanese Fairy Tales (5 vols. Tokyo 1898-1922)*

In that brilliant little book *The Japanese Tradition in British and American Literature*, Earl Miner asks in mock exasperation how to explain Hearn's enormous popular appeal. His peculiar talent came at a propitious time, is one answer he gives. Progress and Respectability were no longer the gods they had been, and the public mind was sufficiently attuned to the Aesthetic Revolt against them to accept Hearn's version of it in Japan. 'He may have made a great deal of pother about Oriental refinement which treated of realms above the popular mind, but it was all very quaint and pretty. He may have proclaimed the superiority of Buddhism to Christianity and Science, but all of this protest against the ideals of the age was safely off in faraway Japan, and not in London or Boston.' In fact, to be fair, it was *not* all quaint and pretty; and Hearn was very eager to show not that Buddhism was superior to science - that almost *anything* was superior to Christianity he was convinced - but that its insights were very close to what he thought was true science, the evolutionary philosophy of Herbert Spencer, who had convinced him as he had convinced Fenollosa.

Rather than theorise, let us see the kind of article which made up the typical Hearn miscellany: vignettes of travel, for one thing; stories of the supernatural, for another; descriptions of the minutiae of nature as in the insect notes; retellings of Japanese legends; speculations on Buddhist doctrine and Shinto ancestor worship. The article I would like to take as an example of his work is from *Out of the East*, which runs to 27 pages and is divided into five numbered sections. Its source lies in a trip to Nagasaki in the summer of 1893 which he described in a letter to Basil Hall Chamberlain. The letter itself is highly romanticised, as for example this scene of departure from the Urashima Hotel:

> 'Also a very beautiful woman - graceful as a dragon-fly - with a voice like a tinkling of a crystal wind-bell, took care of me, hired *kurumaya*

[rickshaw pullers] gave me a splendid breakfast, and charged me for all the entertainment only forty sen. She understood my Japanese, and talked to me, and I felt like a soul suddenly reborn in the heart of a luminous lotus-flower in the garden of Paradise.... And summer mists bathed sea and hills and all distant things - a world of divinely soft blue, the blue of iridescent mother of pearl....'

Hearn goes along the coast, pulled by his rickshaw-puller in the summer heat until, at the village of Nagahama, or Long Beach, the man declares he can go no further. Along the way he sees endless numbers of birds along the telegraph wires, and thinks of the story of Urashima: a fisherman was bewitched by a sea-maiden, left her to visit the mainland again, found the world had grown four hundred years older in his absence, opened a magic box she had given him, and was at once reduced to hideous old age and death. The background of it all is the sound of drums beaten by the villagers to bring rain from the gods.

His essay-cum-story is constructed on three levels. There is the factual level of his journey, a summer day, a departure from an hotel, and a long rickshaw ride. This factual level is subject to attacks of whimsy: 'The hotel seemed to me a paradise, and the maids thereof celestial beings.' But the courtesy of the hotel now is a pretext for *distanciation* from his own time:

'To find myself at ease once more in *yukata*, seated upon cool, soft matting, waited upon by sweet-voiced girls, and surrounded by things of beauty, was... like a redemption from all the sorrows of the nineteenth century.'

When the farewell comes, he descends into *Mikado*-ese:

'She asked whither I honourably intended to go, that she might order a *kuruma* for me. And I made answer: "To Kumamoto. But the name of your house I much wish to know, that I may always remember it." "My guest-rooms", she said, "are augustly insignificant, and my maidens honourably rude. But the house is called the House of Urashima. And now I go to order a *kuruma*." The music of her voice passed; and I felt enchantment falling all about me - like the thrilling of a ghostly web. For the name was the name of the story of a song that bewitches men.'

Hearn then recounts, in his second section, the legend of the fisherman Urashima, with conscious reminiscences of Washington Irving, for he had told his Japanese students the story of Rip Van Winkle. In the Dragon Kingdom of the sea, where the sea-maiden had taken him, Urashima is given all possible pleasures, but feels heavy at heart when he thinks of his parents waiting for him in their loneliness at home. 'So that at last he prayed his bride to let him go home for a little while only, just to say one word to his father and mother - after which he would hasten back to her.' He does so, but 'The place was at once the same, and yet not the same. The cottage of his fathers had disappeared. There was a village; but the shapes of the houses were all strange, and the trees were strange, and the fields, and even the faces of the people.... Only the voice of the little stream flowing through the settlement, and the forms of the mountains, are still the same. All else was unfamiliar and new.' And he meets an old man who tells him that Urashima Taro was drowned off the sea-coast of the village four hundred years before, and in the graveyard is a monument to him:

'Then he knew himself the victim of some strange illusion, and he took his way back to the beach - always carrying in his hand the box, the gift of the Sea King's daughter. But what was this illusion? And what could be in that box? Or might not that which was in the box be the cause of the illusion? Doubt mastered faith. Recklessly he broke the promise made to his beloved; he loosened the silken cord - he opened the box!

'Instantly, without any sound, there burst from it a cold white spectral vapour that rose in air like a summer cloud, and began to drift away swiftly into the south, over the silent sea. There was nothing else in the box.

'And Urashima then knew that he had destroyed his own happiness - that he could never again return to his beloved, the daughter of the Ocean King. So that he wept and cried out bitterly in his despair.'

[Then the Cincinnati reporter intervenes:]

'Yet for a moment only. In another, he himself was changed. An icy chill shot through all his blood - his teeth fell out; his face shrivelled; his hair turned white as snow; his limbs withered; his strength ebbed; he sank down lifeless on the sand, crushed by the weight of four hundred winters.'

So Hearn sets off along a white road overlooking the shore, in the summer heat:

'What a blue transparency. The universal colour was broken only by the dazzling white of a few high summer clouds, motionlessly curled above one phantom peak in the offing. They threw down upon the water snowy tremulous lights. Midges of ships creeping far away seemed to pull long threads after them - the only sharp lines in all that hazy glory. But what divine clouds! White purified spirits of clouds, resting on their way to the beatitude of Nirvana? Or perhaps the mists escaped from Urashima's box a thousand years ago.'

The rickshaw man sprints on under the telegraph wires and the transparent sunlight, and the sharp rattle of the wheels is drowned by a deep booming, the drums which ask the gods for rain. And Hearn dreamed of the dance he had seen based on the Urashima legend, about a dancing-girl he had seen perform it, about vanished generations of dancing-girls, and inevitably the idea of dust and mortality, and the real dust flung up by the rickshaw-puller's feet. For dust is one of Hearn's symbols. It is the token of the evolutionary process, the factual support brought by the disciple of Herbert Spencer to the speculations of the Buddhist:

'And I wondered how much of it might be old human dust, and whether in the eternal order of things the motion of hearts might be of more consequence than the motion of dust.'

Heat and dust make him stop to drink, and think again about Urashima. The Japanese people who had told him the story had given all their pity to Urashima; but Hearn's pity began to reach out to the abandoned Daughter of the Dragon-King. Urashima had conveniently died without trouble and had had a shrine built to him. 'Why, then, so much pity?'

'Things are quite differently managed in the West. After disobeying Western gods, we have still to remain alive and learn the height and the breadth and the depth of superlative sorrow. We are not allowed to die quite comfortably just at the best possible time: much less are we suffered to become after death small gods in our own right. How can we pity the folly of Urashima when he had lived so long alone with visible gods?'

Where was Urashima's island of unending summer - what was the cloud in the box? 'I cannot answer all those questions', says Hearn, 'I know this only - which is not at all new': - and then modern Japan slips away, and the adult Hearn, with his carapace thickened against insult and indifference, and the memories of the hot Antilles, the bitter, starving streets of Cincinnati, the tall cold rooms, the resounding chapel, and the woods of Ushaw College, and the house in Rathmines, all go:

'I have memory of a place and a magical time in which the Sun and the Moon were larger and brighter than now. Whether it was of this life or of some life before I cannot tell. But I know the sky was very much more blue, and nearer to the world - almost as it seems to become above the masts of a steamer steaming into equatorial summer. The sea was alive, and used to talk, and the wind made me cry out for joy when it touched me. Once or twice during other years, in divine days lived among the peaks, I have dreamed just for a moment that the same wind was blowing - but it was only a remembrance.

'Also in that place the clouds were wonderful, and of colours for which there are no names at all - colours that used to make me hungry and thirsty. I remember, too, that the days were ever so much longer than these days - and that every day there were new wonders and new pleasures for me. And all that country and all that time were softly ruled by One who thought only of ways to make me happy....'

'When day was done, and there fell the great hush of the light before moonrise, she would tell me stories that made me tingle from head to foot with pleasure. I have never heard any other stories half so beautiful. And when the pleasure became too great, she would sing a weird little song which always brought sleep. At last there came a parting day; and she wept, and told me of a charm she had given that I must never, never lose, because it would keep me young, and give me power to return. But I never returned. And the years went; and one day I knew that I had lost the charm, and had become ridiculously old.'

In Nagahama, the Village of the Long Beach, the splashing of water over his rickshaw-puller reminds him of another story, the legend of the woodcutter and his wife who drink of the Fountain of Youth, the woodcutter becoming a young man, and the wife a baby; but the morality of this story seems less satisfactory to Hearn than when he had heard it first, before he had meditated upon the story of Urashima: 'Because by drinking too deeply of life we do not become young'.

The account ends factually, and the reader is brought down, but not completely, out of myth into reality:

'Naked and cool, my *kurumaya* returned, and said that because of the heat he could not finish the promised run of twenty-five miles, but that he had found another runner to take me the rest of the way. For so much as he himself had done, he wanted fifty-five sen.

'It was really very hot - more than 100 degrees I afterwards learned, and far away there throbbed continually, like a pulsation of the heat itself, the sound of great drums beating for rain. And I thought of the daughter of the Dragon King.

'"Seventy-five sen, she told me", I observed; "and that promised to be done has not been done. Nevertheless, seventy-five sen to you shall be given - because I am afraid of the gods."

'And behind a yet unwearied runner I fled away into the enormous blaze - in the direction of the great drums.'

The theme of dust was later to be amplified in an essay bearing that name in *Gleanings in Buddha Fields*. In it, Hearn takes his total distance from the transcendental God of his youth, and the linear time of historical Christianity:

'Is there aught visible, tangible, measurable, that has never been mixed with sentiency? - atom that has never vibrated to pleasure or to pain? - air that has never been cry or speech? - drop that has never been a tear? Assuredly this dust has felt. It has been everything we know; also much that we cannot know. It has been nebula and star, planet and moon, times unspeakable. Deity also has it been - the Sun-God of worlds that circled and worshipped in other aeons. *"Remember Man, thou art but dust"*! - a saying profound only as materialism, which stops short at surfaces. For what is dust? "Remember, Dust, thou hast been Sun, and Sun shalt thou become again!... Thou hast been Light, Life, Love; and into all these, by ceaseless cosmic magic, thou shalt many times be turned again!"

'.... Suns yield up their ghosts of flame; but out of their graves new suns rush into being. Corpses of worlds pass all to some solar funereal pyre; but out of their own ashes they are born again. This earth must die: her seas shall be Saharas. But those seas once existed in the sun; and their dead tides, revived by fire, will pour their thunder upon the coasts of another world. Transmigration - transmutation: these are not fables! What is impossible?... If seas can pass from world to sun, from sun to world again, what of the dust of dead selves - dust of memory and thought? Resurrection there is - but a resurrection more stupendous than any dreamed of by Western creeds. Dead emotions will revive as surely as dead suns and moons. Only, so far as we can just now discern, there will be no return of identical individualities....'

The human soul, for Hearn, was, like the human body, a composite entity, 'a composite of quintillions of souls. We are, each and all, infinite compounds of fragments of anterior lives'. Such a belief, of course, provides a factual explanation for the *rule of the dead* which for him characterised Japanese social life, and which makes it easy for Buddhism and Shinto to co-exist. And the incredibly detailed laws of social behaviour and the sanctions behind them were backed by religion:

'Only religion could have enabled any people to bear such discipline without degenerating into mopes and cowards; and the Japanese never so degenerated: the traditions that compelled self-denial and obedience also cultivated courage, and insisted upon cheerfulness.

The power of the ruler was unlimited because the power of all the dead supported him. "Laws", says Herbert Spencer, "whether written or unwritten, formulate the rule of the dead over the living. In addition to that power which past generations exercise over present generations, by transmitting their natures - bodily and mental - there is the power they exercise through their regulations for public conduct... they imply a tacit ancestor-worship."'

And the hand of the dead was heavy, commented Hearn: 'it is heavy upon the living even today'.

Those words, and the criticism they imply, were written in 1904. In a few months he would be dead. But long before he brooded upon these thoughts, he had gone much further than any other Western intellectual in his identification with the people of Japan. Bigelow and Fenollosa had turned Buddhist, but they remained Americans, just as Chamberlain remained English. Hearn decided to shed the West.

Hearn was happy in his first home in Japan. Until the end of 1891 he lived and taught in Matsue, a little town on the west coast, somewhat isolated and away from the main stream of Japanese industrial development. 'Old Japan' was still present there. Just over twenty miles away lay the shrine of Izumo, one of the most sacred spots in Japanese history and still a centre of pilgrimage, and the nearby village of Kitzuki, with its beach, its tiny shops, and its clean and hospitable inn, was a place to which Hearn often returned. But in spite of its isolation, Matsue was open to western influences; he found the philosophical and scientific gods he himself revered - Darwin and Spencer in particular - were gods in Matsue too.

There were other easements: it was the first time that Hearn, who was to spend the rest of his life as a teacher, found that he had a gift for teaching. His students took to his personal warmth - something they had not expected from a foreign teacher - and he himself began to conform to Japanese custom, wearing *yukata* and sandals in the evening to relax, eating Japanese food and heating his house by the traditional but inadequate means of the hot charcoal *hibachi*, a mere shadow of heat (he wrote to Chamberlain) quite incapable of spreading warmth throughout houses 'as cold as cattle barns'. Of course he caught cold, and his awareness of insecurity, trying to cure himself in this lonely, freezing house, was no doubt a factor in his acceptance of a suggestion from a colleague, Nishida Sentaro, that he should marry a Japanese girl. He was married to Koizumi Setsuko in January 1891. They were never to communicate in anything but ungrammatical Japanese, but she set his affairs in order, and provided him with the blissful experience of fatherhood. And its fears: 'Come into the world with good eyes', he prayed as he watched beside his wife in labour with their first-born son, Kazuo. In an outburst to Chamberlain which echoes every banality about the difference between the sexes in Japan, 'how sweet the Japanese woman is'! he wrote, 'all the possibilities of the race for goodness seem to be concentrated in her.... If this be the result of suppression and oppression - then these are not altogether bad. On the other hand, how diamond-hard the character of the American woman becomes under the idolatry of which she is the subject.'

16

But Setsuko had another effect on him. She had known poverty, and she knew that if he taught English in a bigger city than Matsue, he would be better off. Through Basil Hall Chamberlain, who pulled strings on his behalf in the Ministry of Education, Lafcadio was offered a job in Kumamoto on the southern island of Kyushu, for double the salary.

It was not a good move. The Fifth National College of Kumamoto was a set of large buildings in stone and red brick which might have stood anywhere in the west. Hearn was the only foreign teacher in this impressive place but he found his reception chilly in contrast with the friendship he had known in Matsue. The students were at the competitive stage, but often recalcitrant, the city itself, he thought, was dull and lacked beauty, though it did provide him with one startling incident - a murderer begging forgiveness from the son of his victim - which he later turned into a story. There he completed his first book about Japan, *Glimpses of Unfamiliar Japan* (January 1893), and his first son, Kazuo, was born there. But he continued to find his Kumamoto colleagues indifferent, hostile and unintelligent, and the secret of this seems to lie in the fact that while they were doing their utmost to westernise themselves in their pupils, here was their only western teacher aping Japanese manners and dress, preferring sake and a Japanese pipe to cigars and beer. He was sure they were conspiring against him, and, with that paranoid loathing of missionaries which marks his whole life in Japan, he was convinced 'the missionaries' were behind it.

In the end, the offer of a job in Kobe saved him. He worked as a journalist on the *Kobe Chronicle*, an English language newspaper. Kobe had a prosperous business colony of western merchants, but Hearn did not care to mix with them. On the other hand, what he saw of western mercantile and scientific power in the ships in Kobe harbour impressed him, Englishmen and Americans were his readers, and on their behalf he churned out endless editorials, scribbling away with his nose an inch from the paper until - catastrophe - his eyesight gave out.

In Kobe, too, he had felt a sudden revulsion against the Japanese themselves: 'I've seen how thoroughly detestable Japanese can be', he wrote to Chamberlain, and added later, 'I felt as if I hated Japan unspeakably'. Chamberlain himself was no stranger to these reactions. 'He spoke to me', Lafcadio wrote to another great friend, W. B. Mason, also married to a Japanese wife, 'about the variability of one's feelings towards Japan being like the oscillation of a pendulum, one day swinging towards pessimism and the next to optimism. I have this feeling very often, and I suppose you must have had it many times. But the pessimistic feeling is generally coincident with some experience of New Japan, and the optimistic with something of Old Japan.... But with what hideous rapidity Japan is modernising!... not in costume, or architecture, or habit, but in heart and manner. The emotional nature of the race is changing. Will it ever become beautiful again?' (6 August 1892 *Japanese Letters*, pp. 411-413)

It is the not unfamiliar reaction of someone who gives himself heart and soul to a people not his own, and finds sooner or later that the gift has gone wrong. There is also, perhaps, something else. As a devoted disciple of Herbert Spencer, Hearn believed in progress, and was bound to accept, in the inevitability of history, the emergence of a new Japan. At the same time, as Professor Watanabe Shōichi has pointed out in an essay on Hearn, Spencer and the Japanese, however much Hearn understood the process, intellectually his *nasake* (sympathy, compassion) was directed lovingly towards old Japan, so that in him understanding and sympathy were estranged from each other.

After eyestrain resulting from the frenetic activity of putting a newspaper together, Hearn decided to try and make a more leisurely living by writing articles for the American monthlies. Then, in December 1895, Dr Toyama, the president of the College of Literature in Tokyo University, pressed him to take the Chair of English Language and Literature for which Chamberlain had recommended him. There was a slight complication: to ensure that his Japanese family would be able to retain property rights (which they would lose if they adopted his own British nationality), he took Japanese citizenship in 1895, together with his wife's family name, Koizumi. For his first name he chose Yakumo, to remind him of his happy early days in Japan.

> I am waiting every day for the sanction of the minister to change my name [he wrote to Ellwood Hendrick in September 1895], and I think it will come soon. This will make me Koizumi Yakumo.... 'Eight Clouds' is the meaning of 'Yakumo', and is the first part of the most ancient poem extant in the Japanese language... it is a poetical alternative for Izumo, my beloved province, 'the Place of the Issuing of Clouds', You will understand how the name was chosen.

But the snag was that as a Japanese national, he would normally be given the salary of a Japanese, far less than that paid to foreign teachers.

Fortunately, Dr Toyama did not insist on this, and Hearn accepted the Chair, though he did not view the prospect of living in bustling, modern Tokyo without misgivings:

> For the New Japan is waiting; the great capital so long dreaded, draws me to her vortex at last. And the question I now keep asking myself is whether in that New Japan I can be fortunate enough at happy moments to meet with something of the Old. ('Notes of a Trip to Izumo', *Atlantic Monthly*, Vol. 79, May 1897, p. 687, in Stevenson, *Lafcadio Hearn*, p. 185).

He took his family to live in Ushigome, in a house facing a hill covered with cedars, Kobudera, on which stood a Zen temple, the Jishoin. He and the abbot quickly became friends. And he found friendliness among his students too. Their linguistic standards precluded any very technical criticism of English literature, but his simplicity and enthusiasm caught at their emotions. And he persuaded them that his ultimate purpose was, through them, to help create a modern Japanese literature. 'Except with the sole purpose of making a new Japanese literature', he wrote to one of them, Otani Masanobu, 'I do not sympathise with English or French or German Studies'. (*Writings*, XV, p. 202) His advice on how this should be done anticipates, very curiously, one of the main tenets of surrealism, the use of dreams. 'Trust to your own dream-life, study it carefully, and draw your inspiration from that. For dreams are the primary source of almost everything that is beautiful in literature which treats of what lies beyond mere daily experience.' (*Talks to Writers*, ed. Erskine, New York, 1927, p. 149).

His new status was formally conferred in February 1896. It was, of course, Pinkerton and *Madame Chrysanthème* in reverse: and a challenge to the story of Urashima. No question of making love and saying goodbye. No question of leaving behind the Ocean King's daughter and going home. With all its faults, Japanese life and religion had bewitched Lafcadio Hearn to such an extent that he had to be identified with it as totally as lay within his grasp. He could never speak or read the language properly. His son remembers his tales in poor, halting Japanese, and Hearn himself claimed that no adult could ever master it. But he never relied upon his knowledge of the language for literary inspiration. His western readers credited him with more inventiveness than he really had when they read the stories which were set in his speculative or descriptive essays: for these were real Japanese legends, and he was indebted to Chamberlain and his own students for knowledge of them, sometimes for translation of them. But this did not prevent him being, at that particular moment, the perfect interpreter of a Japan that was, on the surface at any rate, disappearing for ever.

The picture is a proper rectification of the cartoon portrayal of Japan that existed in the minds of British and Americans as a result of *The Mikado* and *Madame Butterfly*. And as far as the Japanese were concerned, he had the same virtue Fenollosa had: he taught them to value what they were in danger of inconsiderately casting off. 'He idealised the people of Japan and their culture, not simply or blindly, but in the terms in which the Japanese themselves like to think they excel', writes Earl Miner. 'A nation which found somewhat to its embarrassment that it was far behind in what the West liked to think was civilisation was naturally happy to find itself praised for what it was, rather than blamed for what it failed to succeed in becoming; and later, in this century, when the Japanese found they had become rather too drably the Westernised nation which they had once sought to be, it was pleasant for them to be able to return to his praise in the hope that what he saw was still basically true, after all. In a sense, the Japanese have fallen prey to a foreign exoticising of themselves.... The West and Japan shared the idea that he had understood Japan as no Westerner ever had before or is likely to again and, in certain rather limited senses, this is true. With the help of a sensitive personality which was akin to Japanese aestheticism, and with the aid of the sentimental image of Japan which the travellers had established before him, he more than any other man gave Japan an appeal that it had never before exercised over the imagination, especially the popular imagination of the West.'

It is a considerable achievement, and it matters little whether we consider Hearn to belong to American literature or to English literature. He wrote most of his life for American periodicals, and his books were published in Boston and New York before they found a public in London. Many of the early experiences which turned him into a writer were experiences of America in the seventies and eighties, and it was this new civilisation which was in his mind whenever he contrasted the frenetic ugly thrustings of the industrial nineteenth century - 'Hell is realised there'

- with the fast disappearing world of Old Japan. He held on to his British nationality for thirty years, and there were moments when he rediscovered the West, in terms that must occur to anyone who has steeped himself in the life of another people and knows that ultimately he must stay outside them. In a moment of exasperation in Kumamoto, he wrote to Chamberlain:

'We are all tired of Kumamoto. I must try to get out of it this year or next year. I am almost certain, however, that I had better go to America for a time. One does not isolate one's self from the Aryan race without paying the penalty. You could not know what it means, unless you had borne it long; the condition is unspeakable.'

Seeing the industry of the West in the foreign settlements of Kobe on a trip from Kumamoto in 1894, he wrote to Chamberlain:

'Coming out of my solitude of nearly five years to stand on the deck of the *Kobe Maru* on the 10th, I felt afraid. I saw myself again among giants. Everything seemed huge, full of force, dignity, massive potentialities divined but vaguely. A sudden sense of the meaning of that civilisation I had been so long decrying and arguing against, and vainly rebelling against, came upon me crushingly.

'The first man I spoke to was an engineer. He and I felt each other at once. He had been like myself a wanderer - had seen Mt Everest from a bungalow in Nepal - and studied many things.

'The twin bits of our race-souls touched at once. What no Japanese could feel, that rough square man knew - and he seemed to me a deity, or a semi-deity - and I felt like one about to worship Western Gods.

'Another day, and I was in touch with England again. How small suddenly my little Japan became! - how lonesome! What a joy to feel the West! What a great thing is the West! What new appreciations of it are born of isolation!'

This difficulty of shedding a spiritual and historical skin was echoed three decades later by another Englishman who had attempted a similar *déracinement*:

'Pray God that men reading the story [wrote T.E. Lawrence at the beginning of *The Seven Pillars of Wisdom*] will not, for love of the glamour of strangeness, go out to prostitute themselves and their talents in serving another race.

'A man who gives himself up to be a possession of aliens leads a Yahoo life, having bartered his soul to a brute-master. He is not of them. He may stand against them, persuade himself of a mission, batter and twist them into something which they, of their own accord, would not have been. Then he is exploiting his own environment to press them out of theirs. Or, after my model, he may imitate them so well that they spuriously invite him back again. Then he is giving away his own environment: pretending to theirs; and pretences are hollow, worthless things. In neither case does he do a thing of himself, nor a thing so clean as to be his own (without thought of conversion), letting them take what action or reaction they please from the silent example.

'In my case, the effort for these years to live in the dress of Arabs, and to imitate their mental foundation, quitted me of my English self, and let me look at the West and its conventions with new eyes: they destroyed it all for me. At the same time, I could not sincerely take on the Arab skin: it was an affectation only.'

The comparison touches at points only, because Lawrence was concerned to dominate, manipulate and use; whereas Lafcadio wanted merely to live beside, and understand. In this sense, though Lawrence's years with the Arabs are only separated from Lafcadio's in Japan by two decades, they represent the last flowering of an old order of imperial supremacy, while Lafcadio, whatever his moments of imitation and disappointment, looks forward to a new age of co-existence. And, unlike Lawrence, he has begotten a child into the other race. After reflecting on the greatness of the West, he added an afterthought:

'.... Then I stopped thinking. For I saw my home and the lights of its household gods - and my boy reaching out his little hands to me - and all the simple charm and love of old Japan. And the fairy-world seized my soul again, very softly and sweetly - as a child might catch a butterfly.'

The penalty of his Japanese citizenship caught up with him in March 1903. When his contract at the University came up for renewal, he was told that he was to be paid from that time on as a Japanese national, in other words at a much reduced rate. Bitterly angry, he resigned. 'After having worked thirteen years for Japan, I have been only driven out of the service, and practically banished from the country', he wrote to Elizabeth Wetman in August 1903. (E. Bisland, *Life and Letters, Writings*, Vol. XV, p. 283, in Stevenson, op.cit., p. 314.) His students were angry, too, and held a meeting to protest against this cavalier treatment of a much-loved professor. One student, Tasawa, proclaimed to the crowded hall, 'The existence of the Imperial University of Tokyo is only known to foreign countries on account of Lafcadio Hearn, the writer. What has the University to be proud of, if he goes?' And when another, Mizuno, more prudent, stood up and advised caution - 'Mr Hearn's one of the best teachers... but it would seem far from necessary that we sacrifice our future by attempting to keep him with us', there were shouts of 'Stop! Traitor! Get out of here'! A delegate was sent from the meeting to call on the director, and when Hearn was told of this, he wept; but the representations had no effect, and another lecturer was appointed in his place. (Yone Noguchi, *Lafcadio Hearn in Japan*, pp.140-145).

Hearn refused to use the students' indignation as a platform from which to defend his rights. He knew it might harm them, and besides, there was another promise in the offing, from the United States, which softened the blow. Cornell University invited him to give a course of lectures on Japanese civilisation. He could not put himself forward as an authority on Japanese history, or any special Japanese subject, he wrote to his friend Elizabeth Bisland Wetman, who seems to have engineered the invitation; the value of his lectures would lie not in any crystallisation of fact but in their ability to suggest.

He began to write his course for Cornell; but the result was not like his usual books. He made a conscious effort to discipline his thoughts into political and sociological analysis, and discovered that, in doing so, he was giving expression to ideas about the changes in Japan and in his views about Japan. When he first arrived, and saw Japanese life on an intimate scale, in the isolation of Matsue, it had seemed spontaneous and free. What he now observed was discipline, the pressure of a tight society upon which weighed the pressure of the powerful dead. One thing survived from his own past: his preoccupation with Japanese religion. 'The real mastery of any European tongue is impossible without a knowledge of European religion.' he wrote ('Difficulties', *Japan: an Interpretation*, P. ') and similarly no just estimate of Japanese literature or society could be made unless the researcher were able not only to understand Japanese beliefs, but to sympathise with them, at least to the extent a classical scholar could enter into the religious world of Euripides, Pindar or Theocritus.

The effort of organising these ideas into literary shape exhausted him. It was no longer the natural flow of the pen, but a difficult attempt to organise himself into a formal pattern acceptable to a different kind of audience. Then the Cornell offer fell through. There was an outbreak of typhus on the Cornell campus, the invitation was cancelled, and Hearn was left high and dry, jobless and without a future. The indication was obvious: the Cornell lectures should become a book. 'I shall anyway sit down', he wrote to Mrs. Wetman, 'and work as hard as Zola' (*Writings*, XV, p. 243-4). To his wife, he confided 'this book will kill me'.

Perhaps it did. He claimed it to be entirely unlike anything yet written, the substantial idea being that Japanese society represented the condition of ancient Greek society a thousand years before Christ. 'I don't like the work of writing a serious treatise on Sociology', he told Mrs. Wetman. 'It requires training beyond my range, and I imagine that the real sociologist, on reading me, must smile.... I ought to keep to the study of birds and cats and insects and flowers and queer small things - and leave the subject of the destiny of empires to men of brains....' (*Life and Letters*, II, p. 500).

Things were not so simple. By the mere fact of having lived in Japan, at the centre and at the periphery, in daily touch with common life at a time when Japan was undergoing a cataclysmic change in her own nature, and having himself intellectually fed on the imagination of Europe and America, Lafcadio was uniquely placed to register the past and look into the Japanese future.

The labour was interrupted by gratifying invitations. Waseda University, a private institution which owed its existence to Okuma Shigenobu, one of the leaders of the Meiji enlightenment, offered Lafcadio classes in English literature. The University of London asked him to give ten lectures on the civilisation of Japan. That was an offer it was unlikely he could ever take up, but he was pleased by it and tinkered with the notion. In the meanwhile, he relaxed briefly with his son Kazuo in the pine woods and bamboo groves in their holiday place at Yaizu, where they stayed until the end of August 1904. By then Japan was at war with Russia, and Lafcadio's students, stern-faced and uniformed, came to bid the *Sensei* (teacher) farewell. Three weeks later he was dead.

He died just in time. In 1904, the Japanese changed the history of the human race by defeating the Empire of all the Russias in a bitter war, involving millions of men. They showed the West that they could beat it at its own game of industrialised munitions and how to throw them about. Just over three decades later they were passing the lesson on to the Americans and the British. Both sides had by then long forgotten what the Japan of Lafcadio Hearn was like. But there are modern Japanese, our own contemporaries, who do not forget.

JAPAN PHYSICAL

Landscapes

Notes Of A Trip To Kyoto

1

It had been intended to celebrate in spring the eleven-hundredth anniversary of the foundation of Kyoto; but the outbreak of pestilence caused postponement of the festival to the autumn, and the celebration began on the 15th of the tenth month. Little festival medals of nickel, made to be pinned to the breast, like military decorations, were for sale at half a yen each. These medals entitled the wearers to special cheap fares on all the Japanese railroad and steamship lines, and to other desirable privileges, such as free entrance to wonderful palaces, gardens, and temples. On the 23rd of October I found myself in possession of a medal, and journeying to Kyoto by the first morning train, which was overcrowded with people eager to witness the great historical processions announced for the 24th and 25th. Many had to travel standing, but the crowd was good-natured and merry. A number of my fellow-passengers were Osaka geisha going to the festival. They diverted themselves by singing songs and by playing *ken* with some male acquaintances, and their kittenish pranks and funny cries kept everybody amused. One had an extraordinary voice, with which she could twitter like a sparrow.

You can always tell by the voices of women conversing anywhere - in a hotel, for example - if there happen to be any geisha among them, because the peculiar timbre given by professional training is immediately recognisable. The wonderful character of that training, however, is fairly manifested only when the really professional tones of the voice are used -

falsetto tones, never touching, but often curiously sweet. Now, the street singers, the poor blind women who sing ballads with the natural voice only, use tones that draw tears. The voice is generally a powerful contralto; *and the deep tones are the tones that touch.* The falsetto tones of the geisha rise into a treble above the natural range of the adult voice, and as penetrating as a bird's. In a banquet-hall full of guests, you can distinctly hear, above all the sound of drums and *samisen* and chatter and laughter, the thin, sweet cry of the geisha playing *ken* -

'Futatsu! futatsu! futatsu'!

- while you may be quite unable to hear the shouted response of the man she plays with -

'Mitsu! mitsu! mitsu'!

2

The first surprise with which Kyoto greeted her visitors was the beauty of her festival decorations. Every street had been prepared for illumination. Before each house had been planted a new lantern-post of unpainted wood, from which a lantern bearing some appropriate design was suspended. There were also national flags and sprigs of pine above each entrance. But the lanterns made the charm of the display. In each section of street they were of the same form, and were fixed at exactly the same height, and were protected from possible bad weather by the same kind of covering. But in different streets the lanterns were different. In some of the wide thoroughfares they were very large; and while in some streets each was sheltered by a little wooden awning, in others every lantern had a Japanese paper umbrella spread and fastened above it.

There was no pageant on the morning of my arrival, and I spent a couple of hours delightfully at the festival exhibition of *kakemono* in the imperial summer palace called Omuro Gosho. Unlike the professional art display which I had seen in the spring, this represented chiefly the work of students; and I found it incomparably more original and attractive. Nearly all the pictures, thousands in number, were for sale, at prices ranging from three to fifty yen; and it was impossible not to buy to the limit of one's purse. There were studies of nature evidently made on the spot: such as a glimpse of hazy autumn rice-fields, with dragonflies darting over the drooping grain; maples crimsoning above a tremendous gorge; ranges of peaks steeped in morning mist; and a peasant's cottage perched on the verge of some dizzy mountain road. Also there were fine bits of realism, such as a cat seizing a mouse in the act of stealing the offerings placed in a Buddhist household shrine.

But I have no intention to try the reader's patience with a description of pictures. I mention my visit to the display only because of something I saw there more interesting than any picture. Near the main entrance was a specimen of handwriting, intended to be mounted as a kakemono later on, and temporarily fixed upon a board about three feet long by

25

eighteen inches wide - a Japanese poem. It was a wonder of calligraphy. Instead of the usual red stamp or seal with which the Japanese calligrapher marks his masterpieces, I saw the red imprint of a tiny, tiny hand - a *living* hand, which had been smeared with crimson printing-ink and deftly pressed upon the paper. I could distinguish those little finger-marks of which Mr Galton has taught us the characteristic importance.

That writing had been done in the presence of His Imperial Majesty by a child of six years - or of five, according to our Western method of computing age from the date of birth. The prime minister, Marquis Ito, saw the miracle, and adopted the little boy, whose present name is therefore Ito Medzui.

Even Japanese observers could scarcely believe the testimony of their own eyes. Few adult calligraphers could surpass that writing. Certainly no Occidental artist, even after years of study, could repeat the feat performed by the brush of that child before the Emperor. Of course such a child can be born but once in a thousand years - to realise, or almost realise, the ancient Chinese legends of divinely-inspired writers.

Still, it was not the beauty of the thing in itself which impressed me, but the weird, extraordinary, indubitable proof it afforded of an inherited memory so vivid as to be almost equal to the recollection of former births. Generations of dead calligraphers revived in the fingers of that tiny hand. The thing was never the work of an individual child five years old, but beyond all question the work of ghosts - the countless ghosts that make the compound ancestral soul. It was proof visible and tangible of psychological and physiological wonders justifying both the Shinto doctrine of ancestor worship and the Buddhist doctrine of pre-existence.

3

After looking at all the pictures I visited the great palace garden, only recently opened to the public. It is called the Garden of the Cavern of the Genii. (At least '*genii*' is about the only word one can use to translate the term *sennin*, for which there is no real English equivalent: the *sennin*, who are supposed to possess immortal life, and to haunt forests or caverns, being Japanese, or rather Chinese mythological transformations of the Indian Rishi.) The garden deserves its name. I felt as if I had indeed entered an enchanted place.

It is a landscape-garden - a Buddhist creation, belonging to what is now simply a palace, but was once a monastery, built as a religious retreat for emperors and princes weary of earthly vanities. The first impression received after passing the gate is that of a grand old English park: the colossal trees, the shorn grass, the broad walks, the fresh sweet scent of verdure, all awaken English memories. But as you proceed farther these memories are slowly effaced, and the true Oriental impression defines: you perceive that the forms of those mighty trees are not European; various and surprising exotic details reveal themselves; and then you are gazing down upon a sheet of water containing high rocks and islets connected by bridges of the strangest shapes. Gradually - only gradually - the immense charm, the weird Buddhist charm of the place, grows and grows upon you; and the sense of its vast antiquity defines to touch that chord of the aesthetic feeling which brings the vibration of awe.

Considered as a human work alone, the garden is a marvel: only the skilled labour of thousands could have joined together the mere bones of it, the prodigious rocky skeleton of its plan. This once shaped and earthed and planted, nature was left alone to finish the wonder. Working through ten centuries, she has surpassed - nay, unspeakably magnified - the dream of the artist. Without exact information, no stranger unfamiliar with the laws and the purpose of Japanese garden-construction could imagine that all this had a human designer some thousand years ago: the effect is that of a section of primeval forest, preserved untouched from the beginning, and walled away from the rest of the world in the heart of the old capital. The rock-faces, the great fantastic roots, the shadowed by-paths, the few ancient graven monoliths, are all cushioned with the moss of ages; and climbing things have developed stems a foot thick, that hang across spaces like monstrous serpents. Parts of the garden vividly recall some aspects of tropical nature in the Antilles - though one misses the palms, the bewildering web and woof of lianas, the reptiles, and the sinister day-silence of a West-Indian forest. The joyous storm of bird life overhead is an astonishment, and proclaims gratefully to the visitor that the wild creatures of this monastic paradise have never been harmed or frightened by man. As I arrived at last, with regret, at the gate of exit, I could not help feeling envious of its keeper: only to be a servant in such a garden were a privilege well worth praying for.

4

Feeling hungry, I told my runner to take me to a restaurant, because the hotel was very far; and the *kuruma* bore me into an obscure street, and halted before a rickety-looking house with some misspelled English painted above the entrance. I remember only the word 'forign'. After taking off my shoes I climbed three flights of breakneck stairs, or rather ladders, to find in the third story a set of rooms furnished in foreign style. The windows were glass; the linen was satisfactory; the only things Japanese were the mattings and a welcome smoking-box. American chromo-lithographs decorated the walls. Nevertheless, I suspected that few foreigners had ever been in the house: it existed by sending out Western cooking, in little tin boxes, to native hotels; and the rooms had doubtless been fitted up for Japanese visitors.

I noticed that the plates, cups, and other utensils bore the monogram of a long-defunct English hotel which used to exist in one of the open ports. The dinner was served by nice-looking girls, who had certainly been trained by somebody accustomed to foreign service; but their innocent curiosity and extreme shyness convinced me that they had never waited upon a real foreigner before. Suddenly, I observed on a table at the other end of the room something resembling a music-box, and covered with a piece of crochet-work! I went to it, and discovered the wreck of a herophone. There were plenty of perforated musical selections. I fixed the crank in place, and tried to extort the music of a German song, entitled 'Five Hundred Thousand Devils'. The herophone gurgled, moaned, roared for a moment, sobbed, roared again, and relapsed into silence. I tried a number of other selections, including 'Les Cloches de Corneville'; but the noises produced were in all cases about the same. Evidently the thing had been bought, together with the monogram-bearing delft and britannia ware, at some auction sale in one of the foreign settlements. There was a queer melancholy in the experience, difficult to express. One must have lived in Japan to understand why the thing appeared so exiled, so pathetically out of place, so utterly misunderstood. Our harmonised Western music means simply so much noise to the average Japanese ear; and I felt quite sure that the internal condition of the herophone remained unknown to its Oriental proprietor.

An equally singular but more pleasant experience awaited me on the road back to the hotel. I halted at a second-hand furniture shop to look at some curiosities, and perceived, among a lot of old books, a big volume bearing in letters of much-tarnished gold the title, *Atlantic Monthly*. Looking closer, I saw 'Vol. V. Boston: Ticknor & Fields. 1860'. Volumes of The Atlantic of 1860 are not common anywhere. I asked the price; and the Japanese shopkeeper said fifty sen, because it was 'a very large book'. I was much too pleased to think of bargaining with him, and secured the prize. I looked through its stained pages for old friends, and found them - all anonymous in 1865, many world-famous in 1895. There were instalments of *Elsie Venner*, under the title of 'The Professor's Story'; chapters of *Roba di Roma*; a poem called 'Pythagoras', but since renamed 'Metempsychosis', as lovers of Thomas Bailey Aldrich are doubtless aware; the personal narrative of a filibuster with Walker in Nicaragua; admirable papers upon the Maroons of Jamaica and the Maroons of Surinam; and, among other precious things, an essay on Japan, opening with the significant sentence: 'The arrival in this country of an embassy from Japan, the first political delegation ever vouchsafed to a foreign nation by that reticent and jealous people, is now a topic of universal interest.' A little further on, some popular misapprehensions of the period were thus corrected: 'Although now known to be entirely distinct, the Chinese and Japanese... were for a long time looked upon as kindred races, and esteemed alike.... We find that while, on close examination, the imagined attractions of China disappear, those of Japan become more definite.' Any Japanese of this self-assertive twenty-eighth year of Meiji could scarcely find fault with The Atlantic's estimate of his country thirty-five years ago: 'Its commanding position, its wealth, its commercial resources, and the quick intelligence of its people - not at all inferior to that of the people of the West, although naturally restricted in its development - give to Japan... an importance far above that of any other eastern country.' The only error of this generous estimate was an error centuries old - the delusion of Japan's wealth. What made me feel a little ancient was to recognise in the quaint spellings Ziogoon, Tycoon, Sintoo, Kiusiu, Fide-yosi, Nobunanga - spellings of the old Dutch and old Jesuit writers - the modern and familiar *Shōgun, Taikun, Shinto, Kyushu, Hideyoshi* and *Nobunaga*.

I passed the evening wandering through the illuminated streets, and visited some of the numberless shows. I saw a young man writing Buddhist texts and drawing horses with his feet; the extraordinary fact about the work being that the texts were written backwards - from the bottom of the column up, just as an ordinary calligrapher would write them from the top of the column down - and the pictures of horses were always commenced with the tail. I saw a kind of amphitheatre, with an aquarium in lieu of arena, where mermaids swam and sang Japanese songs. I saw maidens 'made by glamour out of flowers' by a Japanese cultivator of chrysanthemums. And between whiles I peeped into the toy-shops, full of novelties. What there especially struck me was the display of that astounding ingenuity by which Japanese inventors are able to reach, at a cost too small to name, precisely the same results as those exhibited in our expensive mechanical toys. A group of cocks and hens made of paper were set to pecking imaginary grain out of a basket by the pressure of a bamboo spring - the whole thing costing half a cent. An artificial mouse ran about, doubling and scurrying, as if trying to slip under mats or into chinks: it cost only one cent, and was made with a bit of coloured paper, a spool of baked clay, and a long thread; you had only to pull the thread, and the mouse began to run. Butterflies of paper, moved by an equally simple device, began to fly when thrown into the air. An artificial cuttlefish began to wriggle all its tentacles when you blew into a little rush tube fixed under its head.

When I decided to return, the lanterns were out, the shops were closing; and the streets darkened about me long before I reached the hotel. After the great glow of the illumination, the witchcrafts of the shows, the merry tumult, the sea-like sound of wooden sandals, this sudden coming of blankness and silence made me feel as if the previous experience had been unreal - an illusion of light and colour and noise made just to deceive, as in stories of goblin foxes. But the quick vanishing of all that composes a Japanese festival-night really lends a keener edge to the pleasure of remembrance: there is no slow fading out of the phantasmagoria, and its memory is thus kept free from the least tinge of melancholy.

5

While I was thinking about the fugitive charm of Japanese amusements, the question put itself, Are not all pleasures keen in proportion to their evanescence? Proof of the affirmative would lend strong support to the Buddhist theory of the nature of pleasure. We know that mental enjoyments are powerful in proportion to the complexity of the feelings and ideas composing them; and the most complex feelings would therefore seem to be of necessity the briefest. At all events, Japanese popular pleasures have the double peculiarity of being evanescent and complex, not merely because of their delicacy and their multiplicity of detail, but because this delicacy and multiplicity are adventitious, depending upon temporary conditions and combinations. Among such conditions are the seasons of flowering and of fading, hours of sunshine or full moon, a change of place, a shifting of light and shade. Among combinations are the fugitive holiday manifestations of the race genius: fragilities utilised to create illusion; dreams made visible; memories revived in symbols, images, ideographs, dashes of colour, fragments of melody; countless minute appeals both to individual experience and to national sentiment. And the emotional result remains incommunicable to Western minds, because the myriad little details and suggestions producing it belong to a world incomprehensible without years of familiarity - a world of traditions, beliefs, superstitions, feelings, ideas, about which foreigners, as a general rule, know nothing. Even by the few who do know that world, the nameless delicious sensation, the great vague wave of pleasure excited by the spectacle of Japanese enjoyment, can only be described as *the feeling of Japan*.

A sociological fact of interest is suggested by the amazing cheapness of these pleasures. The charm of Japanese life presents us with the extraordinary phenomenon of poverty as an influence in the development of aesthetic sentiment, or at least as a factor in deciding the direction and expansion of that development. But for poverty, the race could not have discovered, ages ago, the secret of making pleasure the commonest instead of the costliest of experiences - the divine art of creating the beautiful out of nothing!

One explanation of this cheapness is the capacity of the people to find in everything natural - in landscapes, mists, clouds, sunsets - in the sight of birds, insects, and flowers - a much keener pleasure than we, as the vividness of their artistic presentations of visual experience bears witness. Another explanation is that the national religions and the old-fashioned education have so developed imaginative power that it can be stirred into an activity of delight by anything, however trifling, able to suggest the traditions or the legends of the past.

Perhaps Japanese cheap pleasures might be broadly divided into those of time and place furnished by nature with the help of man, and those of time and place invented by man at the suggestion of nature. The former class can be found in every province, and yearly multiply. Some locality is chosen on hill or coast, by lake or river: gardens are made, trees planted, resting-houses built to command the finest points of view; and the wild site is presently transformed into a place of pilgrimage for pleasure-seekers. One spot is famed for cherry-trees, another for maples, another for wistaria: and each of the seasons - even snowy winter - helps to make the particular beauty of some resort. The sites of the most celebrated temples, or at least of the greater number of them, were thus selected - always where the beauty of nature could inspire and aid the work of the religious architect, and where it still has power to make many a one wish that he could become a Buddhist or Shinto priest. Religion, indeed, is everywhere in Japan associated with famous scenery: with landscapes, cascades, peaks, rocks, islands; with the best places from which to view the blossoming of flowers, the reflection of the autumn moon on water, or the sparkling of fireflies on summer nights.

Decorations, illuminations, street displays of every sort, but especially those of holy days, compose a large part of the pleasures of city life which all can share. The appeals represent the labour, perhaps, of tens of thousands of hands and brains; but each individual contributor to the public effort works according to his particular thought and taste, even while obeying old rules, so that the total ultimate result is a wondrous, a bewildering, an incalculable variety. Anybody can contribute to such an occasion; and everybody does, for the cheapest material is used. Paper, straw, or stone makes no real difference: the art sense is superbly independent of the material. What shapes that material is perfect comprehension of something natural, something real. Whether a blossom made of chicken feathers, a clay turtle or duck or sparrow, a pasteboard cricket or mantis or frog, the idea is fully conceived and exactly realised. Spiders of mud seem to be spinning webs, butterflies of paper delude the eye. No models are needed to work from; - or rather, the model in every case is only the precise memory of the object or living fact. I asked at a doll-maker's for twenty tiny paper dolls, each with a different coiffure - the whole set to represent the principal Kyoto styles of dressing women's hair. A girl went to work with white paper, paint, paste, thin slips of pine; and the dolls were finished in about the same time that an artist would have taken to draw a similar number of such figures. The actual time needed was only enough for the necessary digital movements - not for correcting, comparing, improving: the image in the brain realised itself as fast as the slender hands could work. Thus most of the wonders of festival nights are created: toys thrown into existence with a twist of the fingers, old rags turned into figured draperies with a few motions of the brush, pictures made with sand. The same power of enchantment puts human grace under contribution. Children who on other occasions would attract no attention are converted into fairies by a few deft touches of paint and powder, and costumes devised for artificial light. Artistic sense of line and colour suffices for any transformation. The tones of decoration are never of chance, but of knowledge: even the lantern illuminations prove this fact, certain tints only being used in combination. But the whole exhibition is as evanescent as it is wonderful. It vanishes much too quickly to be found fault with. It is a mirage that leaves you marvelling and dreaming for a month after having seen it.

Perhaps one inexhaustible source of the contentment, the simple happiness, belonging to Japanese common life is to be found in this universal cheapness of pleasure. The delight of the eyes is for everybody. Not the seasons only nor the festivals furnish enjoyment: almost any quaint street, any truly Japanese interior, can give real pleasure to the poorest servant who works without wages. The beautiful, or the suggestion of the beautiful, is free as air. Besides, no man or woman can be too poor to own something pretty: no child need be without delightful toys. Conditions in the Occident are otherwise. In our great cities, beauty is for the rich; bare walls and foul pavements and smoky skies for our poor, and the tumult of hideous machinery - a hell of eternal ugliness and joylessness invented by our civilisation to punish the atrocious crime of being unfortunate, or weak, or stupid, or overconfident in the morality of one's fellow-man.

6

When I went out, next morning, to view the great procession, the streets were packed so full of people that it seemed impossible for anybody to go anywhere. Nevertheless, all were moving, or rather circulating; there was a universal gliding and slipping, as of fish in a shoal. I find no difficulty in getting through the apparently solid press of heads and shoulders to the house of a friendly merchant, about half a mile away. How any crowd could be packed so closely, and yet move so freely, is a riddle to which Japanese character alone can furnish the key. I was not once rudely jostled. But Japanese crowds are not all alike: there are some through which an attempt to pass would be attended with unpleasant consequences. Of course the yielding fluidity of any concourse is in proportion to its gentleness; but the amount of that gentleness in Japan varies greatly according to locality. In the central and eastern provinces the kindliness of a crowd seems to be proportionate to its inexperience of 'the new civilisation'. This vast gathering, of probably not less than a million persons, was astonishingly good-natured and good-humoured, because the majority of those composing it were simple country folk. When the police finally made a lane for the procession, the multitude at once arranged itself in the least egotistical manner possible - little children to the front, adults to the rear.

Though announced for nine o'clock, the procession did not appear till nearly eleven; and the long waiting in those densely packed streets must have been a strain even upon Buddhist patience. I was kindly given a kneeling-cushion in the front room of the merchant's house; but although the cushion was of the softest and the courtesy shown me of the sweetest, I became weary of the immobile posture at last, and went out into the crowd, where I could vary the experience of waiting by standing first on one foot, and then on the other. Before thus deserting my post, however, I had the privilege of seeing some very charming Kyoto ladies, including a princess, among the merchant's guests. Kyoto is famous for the beauty of its women; and the most charming Japanese woman I ever saw was in that house - not the princess, but the shy young bride of the merchant's eldest son. That the proverb about beauty being only skin-deep 'is but a skin-deep saying' Herbert Spencer has amply proved by the laws of physiology; and the same laws show that grace has a much more profound significance than beauty. The charm of the bride was just that rare form of grace which represents the economy of force in the whole framework of the physical structure - the grace that startles when first seen, and appears more and more wonderful every time it is again looked at. It is very seldom indeed that one sees in Japan a pretty woman who would look equally pretty in another than her own beautiful national attire. What we usually call grace in Japanese women is daintiness of form and manner rather than what a Greek would have termed grace. In this instance, one felt assured that long, light, slender, fine, faultlessly knit figure would ennoble any costume: there was just that suggestion of pliant elegance which the sight of a young bamboo gives when the wind is blowing.

To describe the procession in detail would needlessly tire the reader:

and I shall venture only a few general remarks. The purpose of the pageant was to represent the various official and military styles of dress worn during the great periods of the history of Kyoto, from the time of its foundation in the eighth century to the present era of Meiji, and also the chief military personages of that history. At least two thousand persons marched in the procession, figuring *daimyō*, *kuge*, *hatamoto*, samurai, retainers, carriers, musicians, and dancers. The dancers were impersonated by *geisha*: and some were attired so as to look like butterflies with big gaudy wings. All the armour and the weapons, the ancient head-dresses and robes, were veritable relics of the past, lent for the occasion by old families, by professional curio-dealers, and by private collectors. The great captains - Oda Nobunaga, Kato Kiyomasa, Iyeyasu, Hideyoshi - were represented according to tradition; a really monkey-faced man having been found to play the part of the famous Taiko.

While these visions of dead centuries were passing by, the people kept perfectly silent - which fact, strange as the statement may seem to Western readers, indicated extreme pleasure. It is not really in accordance with national sentiment to express applause by noisy demonstration - by shouting and clapping of hands, for example. Even the military cheer is an importation; and the tendency to boisterous demonstrativeness in Tokyo is probably as factitious as it is modern. I remember two impressive silences in Kobe during 1895. The first was on the occasion of an imperial visit. There was a vast crowd; the foremost ranks knelt down as the Emperor passed; but there was not even a whisper. The second remarkable silence was on the return of the victorious troops from China, who marched under the triumphal arches erected to welcome them without hearing a syllable from the people. I asked why, and was answered, 'We Japanese think we can better express our feelings by silence'. I may here observe, also, that the sinister silence of the Japanese armies before some of the late engagements terrified the clamorous Chinese much more than the first opening of the batteries. Despite exceptions, it may be stated as a general truth that the deeper the emotion, whether of pleasure or of pain, and the more solemn or heroic the occasion, in Japan, the more naturally silent those who feel or act.

Some foreign spectators criticised the display as spiritless, and commented on the unheroic port of the great captains and the undisguised fatigue of their followers, oppressed under a scorching sun by the unaccustomed weight of armour. But to the Japanese all this only made the pageant seem more real; and I fully agreed with them. As a matter of fact, the greatest heroes of military history have appeared at their best in exceptional moments only; the stoutest veterans have known fatigue; and undoubtedly Nobunaga and Hideyoshi and Kato Kiyomasa must have more than once looked just as dusty, and ridden or marched just as wearily, as their representatives in the Kyoto procession. No merely theatrical idealism clouds, for any educated Japanese, the sense of the humanity of his country's greatest men: on the contrary, it is the historical evidence of that ordinary humanity that most endears them to the common heart, and makes by contrast more admirable and exemplary all of the inner life which was not ordinary.

After the procession I went to the Dai-Kioku-Den, the magnificent memorial Shinto temple built by the government, and described in a former book. On displaying my medal I was allowed to pay reverence to the spirit of good Kwammu-Tenno, and to drink a little rice wine in his honour, out of a new wine-cup of pure white clay presented by a lovely child - *miko*. After the libation, the little priestess packed the white cup into a neat wooden box and bade me take it home for a souvenir; one new cup being presented to every purchaser of a medal.

Such small gifts and memories make up much of the unique pleasure of Japanese travel. In almost any town or village you can buy for a souvenir some pretty or curious thing made only in that one place, and not to be found elsewhere. Again, in many parts of the interior a trifling generosity is certain to be acknowledged by a present, which, however cheap, will seldom fail to prove a surprise and a pleasure. Of all the things which I picked up here and there, in travelling about the country, the prettiest and the most beloved are queer little presents thus obtained.

7

I wanted, before leaving Kyoto, to visit the tomb of Yuko Hatakeyama. After having vainly inquired of several persons where she was buried, it occurred to me to ask a Buddhist priest who had come to the hotel on some parochial business. He answered at once, 'In the cemetery of Makkeiji'. Makkeiji was a temple not mentioned in guide-books, and situated somewhere at the outskirts of the city. I took a *kuruma* forthwith, and found myself at the temple gate after about half an hour's run.

A priest, to whom I announced the purpose of my visit, conducted me to the cemetery - a very large one - and pointed out the grave. The sun of a cloudless autumn day flooded everything with light, and tinged with spectral gold the face of a monument on which I saw, in beautiful large characters very deeply cut, the girl's name, with the Buddhist prefix *retsujo*, signifying chaste and true:

RETSUJO HATAKEYAMA YUKO HAKA

The grave was well kept, and the grass had been recently trimmed. A little wooden awning erected in front of the stone sheltered the offerings of flowers and sprays of shikimi, and a cup of fresh water. I did sincere reverence to the heroic and unselfish spirit, and pronounced the customary formula. Some other visitors, I noticed, saluted the spirit after the Shinto manner. The tombstones were so thickly crowded about the spot that, in order to see the back of the monument, I found I should have to commit the rudeness of stepping on the grave. But I felt sure she would forgive me; so, treading reverently, I passed round, and copied the inscription: '*Yuko, of Nagasagori, Kamagawamachi... from day of birth always good... Meiji, the twenty-fourth year, the fifth month, the twentieth day... cause of sorrow the country having... the Kyoto government-house to went... and her own throat cut... twenty and seven years... Tani Tetsuomi made... Kyoto-folk-by erected this stone is.*' The Buddhist Kaimyo read, '*Gi-yu-in-ton-shi-chu-myo-kyo*' - apparently signifying, 'Right-meaning the valiant woman,

34

instantly attaining to the admirable doctrine of loyalty'.

In the temple, the priest showed me the relics and mementos of the tragedy: a small Japanese razor, blood-crusted, with the once white soft paper thickly wrapped round its handle caked into one hard red mass; the cheap purse; the girdle and clothing, blood-stiffened (all except the kimono, washed by order of the police before having been given to the temple); letters and memoranda; photographs, which I secured, of Yuko and her tomb; also a photograph of the gathering in the cemetery, where the funeral rites were performed by Shinto priests. This fact interested me; for although condoned by Buddhism, the suicide could not have been regarded in the same light by the two faiths. The clothing was coarse and cheap: the girl had pawned her best effects to cover the expenses of her journey and her burial. I bought a little book containing the story of her life and death, copies of her last letters, poems written about her by various persons - some of very high rank - and a clumsy portrait. In the photographs of Yuko and her relatives there was nothing remarkable: such types you can meet with every day and anywhere in Japan. The interest of the book was psychological only, as regarded both the author and the subject. The printed letters of Yuko revealed that strange state of Japanese exaltation in which the mind remains capable of giving all possible attention to the most trivial matters of fact, while the terrible purpose never slackens. The memoranda gave like witness:

> *Meiji twenty-fourth year, fifth month, eighteenth day.*
> 5 sen to kurumaya from Nihonbashi to Uyeno. *Nineteenth day.*
> 5 yen to kurumaya to Asakusa Umamachi. 1 sen 5 rin for sharpening something to hair-dresser in Shitaya. 10 yen received from Sano, the pawnbroker in Baba. 20 sen for train to Shincho.
> 1 yen 2 sen for train from Hama to Shidzuoka. *Twentieth day.*
> 2 yen 9 sen for train from Shidzuoka to Hama. 6 sen for postage-stamps for two letters. 14 sen in Kiyomidzu. 12 sen 5 rin for umbrella given to kurumaya.

But in strange contrast to the methodical faculty thus manifested was the poetry of a farewell letter, containing such thoughts as these:

'The eighty-eighth night' [that is, from the festival of the Setsubun] 'having passed like a dream, ice changed itself into clear drops, and snow gave place to rain. Then cherry-blossoms came to please everybody; but now, poor things! they begin to fall even before the wind touches them. Again a little while, and the wind will make them fly through the bright air in the pure spring weather. Yet it may be that the hearts of those who love me will not be bright, will feel no pleasant spring. The season of rains will come next and there will be no joy in their hearts... Oh! what shall I do? There has been no moment in which I have not thought of you.... But all ice, all snow, becomes at last free water; the incense buds of the *kiku* will open even in frost. I pray you, think later about these things.... Even now, for me, is the time of frost, the time of *kiku* buds: if only they can blossom, perhaps I shall please you much. Placed in this world of sorrow, but not to stay, is the destiny of all. I beseech you, think me not unfilial; say to none that you have lost me, that I have passed into the darkness. Rather wait and hope for the fortunate time that shall come.'

The editor of the pamphlet betrayed rather too much of the Oriental manner of judging woman, even while showering generous praise upon one typical woman. In a letter to the authorities Yuko had spoken of a family claim, and this was criticised as a feminine weakness. She had, indeed, achieved the extinction of personal selfishness, but she had been 'very foolish' to speak about her family. In some other ways the book was disappointing. Under the raw, strong light of its commonplace revelations, my little sketch, 'Yuko', written in 1894, seemed for the moment much too romantic. And yet the real poetry of the event remained unlessened - the pure ideal that impelled a girl to take her own life merely to give proof of the love and loyalty of a nation. No small, mean, dry facts could ever belittle that large fact.

The sacrifice had stirred the feelings of the nation much more than it had touched my own. Thousands of photographs of Yuko and thousands of copies of the little book about her were sold. Multitudes visited her tomb and made offerings there, and gazed with tender reverence at the relics of Makkeiji; and all this, I thought, for the best of reasons. If commonplace facts are repellent to what we are pleased, in the West, to call 'refined feeling', it is proof that the refinement is factitious and the feeling shallow. To the Japanese, who recognise that the truth of beauty belongs to the inner being, commonplace details are precious: they help to accentuate and verify the conception of a heroism. Those poor blood-stained trifles - the coarse honest robes and girdle, the little cheap purse, the memoranda of a visit to the pawnbroker, the glimpses of plain, humble, every-day humanity shown by the letters and the photographs and the infinitesimal precision of police records - all serve, like so much ocular evidence, to perfect the generous comprehension of the feeling that made the fact. Had Yuko been the most beautiful person in Japan, and her people of the highest rank, the meaning of her sacrifice would have been far less intimately felt. In actual life, as a general rule, it is the common, not the uncommon person who does noble things; and the people, seeing best by the aid of ordinary facts, what is heroic in one of their own class, feel themselves honoured. Many of us in the West will have to learn our ethics over again from the common people. Our cultivated classes have lived so long in an atmosphere of false idealism, mere conventional humbug, that the real, warm, honest human emotions seem to them vulgar; and the natural and inevitable punishment is inability to see, to hear, to feel, and to think. There is more truth in the little verse poor Yuko wrote on the back of her mirror than in most of our conventional idealism:

'By one keeping the heart free from stain, virtue and right and wrong are seen clearly as forms in a mirror.'

8

I returned by another way, through a quarter which I had never seen before - all temples. A district of great spaces - vast and beautiful and hushed as by enchantment. No dwellings or shops. Pale yellow walls only, sloping back from the roadway on both sides, like fortress walls, but coped with a coping or rooflet of blue tiles; and above these yellow sloping walls (pierced with elfish gates at long, long intervals), great soft hilly masses of foliage - cedar and pine and bamboo - with superbly curved roofs sweeping up through them. Each vista of those silent streets of temples, bathed in the gold of the autumn afternoon, gave me just such a thrill of pleasure as one feels on finding in some poem the perfect utterance of a thought one has tried for years in vain to express.

Yet what was the charm made with? The wonderful walls were but painted mud; the gates and the temples only frames of wood supporting tiles: the shrubbery, the stonework, the lotus-ponds, mere landscape-gardening. Nothing solid, nothing enduring; but a combination so beautiful of lines and colours and shadows that no speech could paint it. Nay! even were those earthen walls turned into lemon-coloured marble, and their tiling into amethyst; even were the material of the temples transformed into substance precious as that of the palace described in the Sutra of the Great King of Glory - still the aesthetic suggestion, the dreamy repose, the mellow loveliness and softness of the scene, could not be in the least enhanced. Perhaps it is just because the material of such creation is so frail that its art is so marvellous. The most wonderful architecture, the most entrancing landscapes, are formed with substance the most imponderable - the substance of clouds.

But those who think of beauty only in connection with costliness, with stability, with 'firm reality', should never look for it in this land - well called the Land of Sunrise, for sunrise is the hour of illusions. Nothing is more lovely than a Japanese village among the hills or by the coast when seen just after sunrise, through the slowly lifting blue mists of a spring or autumn morning. But for the matter-of-fact observer, the enchantment passes with the vapours: in the raw, clear light he can find no palaces of amethyst, no sails of gold, but only flimsy sheds of wood and thatch and the unpainted queerness of wooden junks.

So perhaps it is with all that makes life beautiful in any land. To view men or nature with delight, we must see them through illusions, subjective or objective. How they appear to us depends upon the ethical conditions within us. Nevertheless, the real and the unreal are equally illusive in themselves. The vulgar and the rare, the seemingly transient and the seemingly enduring, are all alike mere ghostliness. Happiest he who, from birth to death, sees ever through some beautiful haze of the soul - best of all that haze of love which, like the radiance of this Orient day, turns common things to gold.

A Pilgrimage To Enoshima

1

KAMAKURA

A long, straggling country village, between low-wooded hills, with a canal passing through it. Old Japanese cottages, dingy, neutral-tinted, with roofs of thatch, very steeply sloping, above their wooden walls and paper *shōji*. Green patches on all the roof-slopes, some sort of grass; and on the very summits, on the ridges, luxurious growths of *yaneshōbu*,[1] the roof-plant, bearing pretty purple flowers. In the lukewarm air a mingling of Japanese odours, smells of sake, smells of seaweed soup, smells of *daikon*, the strong native radish; and dominating all, a sweet, thick, heavy scent of incense - incense from the shrines of gods.

Akira has hired two *jinricksha* for our pilgrimage; a speckless azure sky arches the world; and the land lies glorified in the joy of sunshine. And yet a sense of melancholy, of desolation unspeakable, weighs upon me as we roll along the bank of the tiny stream, between the mouldering lines of wretched little homes with grass growing on their roofs. For this mouldering hamlet represents all that remains of the million-peopled streets of Yoritomo's capital, the mighty city of the shogunate, the ancient seat of feudal power, whither came the envoys of Kublai Khan demanding tribute, to lose their heads for their temerity. And only some of the unnumbered temples of the once magnificent city now remain, saved from the conflagrations of the fifteenth and sixteenth centuries, doubtless because built in high places, or because isolated from the maze of burning streets by vast courts and groves. Here still dwell the ancient gods in the great silence of their decaying temples, without worshippers, without revenues, surrounded by desolations of rice-fields, where the chanting of frogs replaces the sea-like murmur of the city that was and is not.

2

The first great temple, Engakuji, invites us to cross the canal by a little bridge facing its outward gate - a roofed gate with fine Chinese lines, but without carving. Passing it, we ascend a long, imposing succession of broad steps, leading up through a magnificent grove to a terrace, where we reach the second gate. This gate is a surprise; a stupendous structure of two storeys, with huge sweeping curves of roof and enormous gables, antique, Chinese, magnificent. It is more than four hundred years old, but seems scarcely affected by the wearing of the centuries. The whole of the ponderous and complicated upper structure is sustained upon an open-work of round, plain pillars and cross-beams; the vast eaves are full of bird-nests; and the storm of twittering from the roofs is like a rushing of water. Immense the work is, and imposing in its aspect of settled power; but, in its way, it has great severity: there are no carvings, no gargoyles, no dragons; and yet the maze of projecting timbers below the eaves will both excite and delude expectation, so strangely does it suggest the grotesqueries and fantasticalities of another art. You look everywhere for the heads of lions, elephants, dragons, and see only the four-angled ends of beams, and feel rather astonished than disappointed. The majesty of the edifice could not have been strengthened by any such carving.

After the gate another long series of wide steps, and more trees, millennial, thick-shadowing, and then the terrace of the temple itself, with two beautiful stone lanterns (*tōrō*) at its entrance. The architecture of the temple resembles that of the gate, although on a lesser scale. Over the doors is a tablet with Chinese characters, signifying, 'Great, Pure, Clear, Shining Treasure'. But the heavy framework of wooden bars closes the sanctuary, and there is no one to let us in. Peering between the bars I see, in a sort of twilight, first a pavement of squares of marble, then an aisle of massive wooden pillars upholding the dim lofty roof, and at the farther end, between the pillars, Shaka, colossal, black-visaged, gold-robed, enthroned upon a giant lotus fully forty feet in circumference. At his right hand some white mysterious figure stands, holding an incense-box; at his left, another white figure is praying with clasped hands. Both are of superhuman stature. But it is too dark within the edifice to discern who they may be - whether disciples of the Buddha, or divinities, or figures of saints.

Beyond this temple extends an immense grove of trees, ancient cedars and pines, with splendid bamboos thickly planted between them, rising perpendicularly as masts to mix their plumes with the foliage of the giants: the effect is tropical, magnificent. Through this shadowing, a flight of broad stone steps slant up gently to some yet older shrine. And ascending them we reach another portal, smaller than the imposing Chinese structure through which we already passed, but wonderful, weird, full of dragons, dragons of a form which sculptors no longer carve, which they have even forgotten how to make, winged dragons rising from a storm-whirl of waters or thereinto descending. The dragon upon the panel of the left gate has her mouth closed; the jaws of the dragon on the panel of the right gate are open and menacing. Female and male they are, like the lions of Buddha. And the whirls of the eddying water, and the crests of the billowing, stand out from the panel in astonishing boldness of relief, in loops and curlings of grey wood time-seasoned to the hardness of stone.

The little temple beyond contains no celebrated image, but a *shari* only, or relic of Buddha, brought from India. And I cannot see it, having no time to wait until the absent keeper of the *shari* can be found.

3

'Now we shall go to look at the big bell', says Akira.

We turn to the left as we descend along a path cut between hills faced for the height of seven or eight feet with protection-walls made green by moss; and reach a flight of extraordinary dilapidated steps, with grass springing between their every joint and break - steps so worn down and displaced by countless feet that they have become ruins, painful and even dangerous to mount. We reach the summit, however, without mishap, and find ourselves before a little temple, on the steps of which an old priest awaits us, with smiling bow of welcome. We return his salutation; but ere entering the temple turn to look at the *tsurigane* on the right - the famous bell.

Under a lofty open shed, with a tilted Chinese roof, the great bell is hung. I should judge it to be fully nine feet high, and about five feet in diameter, with lips about eight inches thick. The shape of it is not like that of our bells, which broaden toward the lips; this has the same diameter through all its height, and it is covered with Buddhist texts cut into the smooth metal of it. It is rung by means of a heavy swinging beam, suspended from the roof by chains, and moved like a battering-ram. There are loops of palm-fibre rope attached to this beam to pull it by; and when you pull hard enough, so as to give it a good swing, it strikes a moulding like a lotus-flower on the side of the bell. This it must have done many hundred times; for the square, flat end of it, though showing the grain of a very dense wood, has been battered into a convex disk with ragged protruding edges, like the surface of a long-used printer's mallet.

A priest makes a sign to me to ring the bell. I first touch the great lips with my hand very lightly; and a musical murmur comes from them. Then I set the beam swinging strongly; and a sound deep as thunder, rich as the bass of a mighty organ - a sound enormous, extraordinary, yet beautiful - rolls over the hills and away. Then swiftly follows another and lesser and sweeter billowing of tone; then another; then an eddying of waves of echoes. Only once was it struck, the astounding bell; yet it continues to sob and moan for at least ten minutes!

And the age of this bell is six hundred and fifty years.[2]

In the little temple nearby, the priest shows us a series of curious paintings, representing the six-hundredth anniversary of the casting of the bell. (For this is a sacred bell, and the spirit of a god is believed to dwell within it.) Otherwise the temple has little of interest. There are some *kakemono* representing Iyeyasu and his retainers; and on either side of the door, separating the inner from the outward sanctuary, there are life-size images of Japanese warriors in antique costume. On the altars of the inner shrine are small images, grouped upon a miniature landscape-work of painted wood - the Jiugo-Dōji, or Fifteen Youths - the Sons of the Goddess Benten. There are *gohei* before the shrine, and a mirror upon it; emblems of Shinto. The sanctuary has changed hands in the great transfer of Buddhist temples to the State religion.

In nearly every celebrated temple little Japanese prints are sold, containing the history of the shrine, and its miraculous legends. I find several such things on sale at the door of the temple, and in one of them, ornamented with a curious engraving of the bell, I discover, with Akira's aid, the following traditions:

4

In the twelfth year of Bummei, this bell rang itself. And one who laughed on being told of the miracle, met with misfortune; and another, who believed, thereafter prospered, and obtained all his desires.

Now, in that time there died in the village of Tamanawa a sick man whose name was Ono-no-Kimi; and Ono-no-Kimi descended to the region of the dead, and went before the Judgment-Seat of Emma-Ō. And Emma, Judge of Souls, said to him, 'You come too soon! The measure of life allotted you in the *Shaba*-world has not yet been exhausted. Go back at once.' But Ono-no-Kimi pleaded, saying, 'How may I go back, not knowing my way through the darkness?' And Emma answered him, 'You can find your way back by listening to the sound of the bell of Engakuji, which is heard in the *Nan-en-budi*-world, going south.' And Ono-no-Kimi went south, and heard the bell, and found his way through the darknesses, and revived in the *Shaba*-world.

Also in those days there appeared in many provinces a Buddhist priest of giant stature, whom none remembered to have seen before, and whose name no man knew, travelling through the land, and everywhere exhorting the people to pray before the bell of Engakuji. And it was at last discovered that the giant pilgrim was the holy bell itself, transformed by supernatural power into the form of a priest. And after these things had happened, many prayed before the bell, and obtained their wishes.

5

'Oh! there is something still to see', my guide exclaims as we reach the great Chinese gate again; and he leads the way across the grounds by another path to a little hill, previously hidden from view by trees. The face of the hill, a mass of soft stone perhaps one hundred feet high, is hollowed out into chambers, full of images. These look like burial-caves; and the images seem funereal monuments. There are two stories of chambers - three above, two below; and the former are connected with the latter by a narrow interior stairway cut through the living rock. And all around the dripping walls of these chambers on pedestals are grey slabs, shaped exactly like the *haka* in Buddhist cemeteries, and chiselled with figures of divinities in highrelief. All have glory-disks: some are naive and sincere like the work of our own medieval image-makers. Several are not unfamiliar. I have seen before, in the cemetery of Kuboyama, this kneeling woman with countless shadowy hands; and this figure tiara-coiffed, slumbering with one knee raised, and cheek pillowed upon the left hand - the placid and pathetic symbol of the perpetual rest. Others, like Madonnas, hold lotus-flowers, and their feet rest upon the coils of a serpent. I cannot see them all, for the rock roof of one chamber has fallen in; and a sunbeam entering the ruin reveals a host of inaccessible sculptures half buried in rubbish.

But no! - this grotto-work is not for the dead; and these are not *haka*, as I imagined, but only images of the Goddess of Mercy. These chambers are chapels; and these sculptures are the Engakuji-no-hyaku-Kwannon, 'the Hundred Kwannons of Engakuji'. And I see in the upper chamber above the stairs a granite tablet in a rock-niche, chiselled with an inscription in Sanscrit transliterated into Chinese characters, 'Adoration to the great merciful Kwan-ze-on, who looketh down above the sound of prayer.'[3]

6

Entering the grounds of the next temple, the Temple of Kenchōji, through the 'Gate of the Forest of Contemplative Words', and the 'Gate of the Great Mountain of Wealth', one might almost fancy one's self re-entering, by some queer mistake, the grounds of Engakuji. For the third gate before us, and the imposing temple beyond it, constructed upon the same models as those of the structures previously visited, were also the work of the same architect. Passing this third gate - colossal, severe, superb - we come to a fountain of bronze before the temple doors, an immense and beautiful lotus-leaf of metal, forming a broad shallow basin kept full to the brim by a jet in its midst.

This temple also is paved with black and white square slabs, and we can enter it with our shoes. Outside it is plain and solemn as that of Engakuji; but the interior offers a more extraordinary spectacle of faded splendour. In lieu of the black Shaka throned against a background of flamelets, is a colossal Jizō-Sama, with a nimbus of fire - a single gilded circle large as a wagon-wheel, breaking into fire-tongues at three points. He is seated upon an enormous lotus of tarnished gold - over the lofty edge of which the skirt of his robe trails down. Behind him, standing on ascending tiers of golden steps, are glimmering hosts of miniature figures of him, reflections, multiplications of him, ranged there by ranks of hundreds - the Thousand Jizō. From the ceiling above him droop the dingy splendours of a sort of dais-work, a streaming circle of pendants like a fringe, shimmering faintly through the webbed dust of centuries. And the ceiling itself must once have been a marvel; all beamed in caissons, each caisson containing, upon a gold ground, the painted figure of a flying bird. Formerly the eight great pillars supporting the roof were also covered with gilding; but only a few traces of it linger still upon their worm-pierced surfaces, and about the bases of their capitals. And there are wonderful friezes above the doors, from which all colour has long since faded away, marvellous grey old carvings in relief; floating figures of *tennin*, or heavenly spirits playing upon flutes and *biwa*.

There is a chamber separated by a heavy wooden screen from the aisle on the right; and the priest in charge of the building slides the screen aside, and bids us enter. In this chamber is a drum elevated upon a brazen stand - the hugest I ever saw, fully eighteen feet in circumference. Beside it hangs a big bell, covered with Buddhist texts. I am sorry to learn that it is prohibited to sound the great drum. There is nothing else to see except some dingy paper lanterns figured with the svastika, the sacred Buddhist symbol called by the Japanese *manji*.

7

Akira tells me that in the book called *Jizō-kyō-Kosui*, this legend is related of the great statue of Jizō in this same ancient temple of Kenchōji.

Formerly there lived at Kamakura the wife of a *rōnin*[4] named Soga Sadayoshi. She lived by feeding silkworms and gathering the silk. She used often to visit the temple of Kenchōji; and one very cold day that she went there, she thought that the image of Jizō looked like one suffering from cold; and she resolved to make a cap to keep the god's head warm - such a cap as the people of the country wear in cold weather. And she went home and made the cap and covered the god's head with it, saying, 'Would I were rich enough to give thee a warm covering for all thine august body; but, alas! I am poor, and even this which I offer thee is unworthy of they divine acceptance.'

Now this woman very suddenly died in the fiftieth year of her age, in the twelfth month of the fifth year of the period called Chisho. But her body remained warm for three days, so that her relatives would not suffer her to be taken to the burning-ground. And on the evening of the third day she came to life again.

Then she related that on the day of her death she had gone before the judgement-seat of Emma, king and judge of the dead. And Emma, seeing her, became wroth, and said to her: 'You have been a wicked woman, and have scorned the teaching of the Buddha. All your life you have passed in destroying the lives of silkworms by putting them into heated water. Now you shall go to the Kwakkto-Jigoku, and there burn until your sins shall be expiated.' Forthwith she was seized and dragged by demons to a great pot filled with molten metal, and thrown into the pot, and she cried out horribly. And suddenly Jizō-Sama descended into the molten metal beside her, and the metal became like a flowing of oil and ceased to burn; and Jizō put his arms about her and lifted her out. And he went with her before King Emma, and asked that she should be pardoned for his sake, forasmuch as she had become related to him by one act of goodness. So she found pardon, and returned to the Shaba-world.

'Akira', I ask, 'it cannot then be lawful, according to Buddhism, for any one to wear silk?'

'Assuredly not', replies Akira; 'and by the law of Buddha priests are expressly forbidden to wear silk. Nevertheless', he adds with that quiet smile of his, in which I am beginning to discern suggestions of sarcasm, 'nearly all the priests wear silk.'

8

Akira also tells me this:

It is related in the seventh volume of the book *Kama-kurashi* that there was formerly at Kamakura a temple called Emmeiji, in which there was enshrined a famous statue of Jizō, called Hadaka-Jizō, or Naked Jizō. The statue was indeed naked, but clothes were put upon it; and it stood upright with its feet upon a chessboard. Now, when pilgrims came to the temple and paid a certain fee, the priest of the temple would remove the clothes of the statue; and then all could see that, though the face was the face of Jizō, the body was the body of a woman.

Now this was the origin of the famous image of Hadaka-Jizō standing upon the chessboard. On one occasion the great prince Taira-no-Tokyori was playing chess with his wife in the presence of many guests. And he made her agree, after they had played several games, that whosoever should lose the next game would have to stand naked on the chessboard. And in the next game they played his wife lost. And she prayed to Jizō to save her from the shame of appearing naked. And Jizō came in answer to her prayer and stood upon the chessboard, and disrobed himself, and changed his body suddenly into the body of a woman.

9

As we travel on, the road curves and narrows between higher elevations, and becomes more sombre. '*Oi! mat*'! my Buddhist guide calls softly to the runners; and our two vehicles halt in a band of sunshine, descending, through an opening in the foliage of immense trees, over a flight of ancient mossy steps. 'Here', says my friend, 'is the temple of the King of Death: it is called Emma-Dō; and it is a temple of the Zen sect - Zen Oji. And it is more than seven hundred years old, and there is a famous statue in it.'

We ascend to a small, narrow court in which the edifice stands. At the head of the steps, to the right, is a stone tablet, very old, with characters cut at least an inch deep into the granite of it, Chinese characters signifying, 'This is the Temple of Emma, King'.

The temple resembles outwardly and inwardly the others we have visited, and, like those of Shaka and of the colossal Jizō of Kamakura, has a paved floor, so that we are not obliged to remove our shoes on entering. Everything is worn, dim, vaguely grey; there is a pungent scent of mouldiness; the paint has long ago peeled away from the naked wood of the pillars. Throned to right and left against the high walls tower nine grim figures - five on one side, four on the other - wearing strange crowns with trumpet-shaped ornaments; figures hoary with centuries, and so like to the icon of Emma, which I saw at Kuboyama, that I ask, 'Are all these Emma'?! 'Oh, no'! my guide answers; 'these are his attendants only - the Jiu-Ō, the Ten Kings'. 'But there are only nine'? I query. 'Nine, and Emma completes the number. You have not yet seen Emma.'

Where is he? I see at the farther end of the chamber an altar elevated upon a platform approached by wooden steps; but there is no image, only the usual altar furniture of gilded bronze and lacquer-ware. Behind the altar I see only a curtain about six feet square - a curtain once dark red, now almost without any definite hue - probably veiling some alcove. A temple guardian approaches, and invites us to ascend the platform. I remove my shoes before mounting upon the matted surface, and follow the guardian behind the altar, in front of the curtain. He makes me a sign to look, and lifts the veil with a long rod. And suddenly, out of the blackness of some mysterious profundity masked by that sombre curtain, there glowers upon me an apparition at the sight of which I involuntarily start back - a monstrosity exceeding all anticipation - a Face.[5]

A Face tremendous, menacing, frightful, dull red, as with the redness of heated iron cooling into grey. The first shock of the vision is no doubt partly due to the somewhat theatrical manner in which the work is suddenly revealed out of darkness by the lifting of the curtain. But as the surprise passes I begin to recognise the immense energy of the conception - to look for the secret of the grim artist. The wonder of the creation is not in the tiger frown, nor in the violence of the terrific mouth, nor in the fury and ghastly colour of the head as a whole: it is in the eyes - eyes of nightmare.

10

Now this weird old temple has its legend.

Seven hundred years ago, 'tis said, there died the great image-maker, the great *bushi*, Unke-Sosei. And Unke-Sosei signifies 'Unke who returned from the dead'. For when he came before Emma, the judge of Souls, Emma said to him: 'Living, thou madest no image of me. Go back unto earth and make one, now that thou hast looked upon me.' And Unke found himself suddenly restored to the world of men; and they that had known him before, astonished to see him alive again, called him Unke-Sosei. And Unke-Sosei, bearing with him always the memory of the countenance of Emma, wrought this image of him, which still inspires fear in all who behold it; and he made also the images of the grim Jiu-Ō, the Ten Kings obeying Emma, which sit throned about the temple.

I want to buy a picture of Emma, and make my wish known to the temple guardian. Oh, yes, I may buy a picture of Emma, but I must first see the *oni*. I follow the guardian out of the temple, down the mossy steps, and across the village highway into a little Japanese cottage, where I take my seat upon the floor. The guardian disappears behind a screen, and presently returns dragging with him the *oni* - the image of a demon, naked, blood-red, indescribably ugly. The *oni* is about three feet high. He stands in an attitude of menace, brandishing a club. He has a head shaped something like the head of a bulldog, with brazen eyes; and his feet are like the feet of a lion. Very gravely the guardian turns the grotesquery round and round, that I may admire its every aspect; while a naïve crowd collects before the open door to look at the stranger and the demon.

Then the guardian finds me a rude woodcut of Emma, with a sacred inscription printed upon it; and as soon as I have paid for it, he proceeds to stamp the paper with the seal of the temple. The seal he keeps in a wonderful lacquered box, covered with many wrappings of soft leather. These having been removed, I inspect the seal - an oblong, vermilion-red polished stone, with the design cut in intaglio upon it. He moistens the surface with red ink, presses it upon the corner of the paper bearing the grim picture, and the authenticity of my strange purchase is established for ever.

11

You do not see the Dai-Butsu as you enter the grounds of his long-vanished temple, and proceed along a paved path across stretches of lawn; great trees hide him. But very suddenly, at a turn, he comes into full view and you start! No matter how many photographs of the colossus you may have already seen, this first vision of the reality is an astonishment. Then you imagine that you are already too near, though the image is at least a hundred yards away. As for me, I retire at once thirty or forty yards back, to get a better view. And the *jinricksha* man runs after me, laughing and gesticulating, thinking that I imagine the image alive and am afraid of it.

But, even were that shape alive, none could be afraid of it. The gentleness, the dreamy passionlessness of those features, the immense repose of the whole figure, are full of beauty and charm. And, contrary to all expectation, the nearer you approach the giant Buddha, the greater this charm becomes. You look up into the solemnly beautiful face, into the half-closed eyes that seem to watch you through their eyelids of bronze as gently as those of a child; and you feel that the image typifies all that is tender and calm in the Soul of the East. Yet you feel also that only Japanese thought could have created it. Its beauty, its dignity, its perfect repose, reflect the higher life of the race that imagined it; and, though doubtless inspired by some Indian model, as the treatment of the hair and various symbolic marks reveal, the art is Japanese.

So mighty and beautiful the work is, that you will not for some time notice the magnificent lotus-plants of bronze, fully fifteen feet high, planted before the figure, on either side of the great tripod in which incense-rods are burning.

Through an orifice in the right side of the enormous lotus-blossom on which the Buddha is seated, you can enter into the statue. The interior contains a little shrine of Kwannon, and a statue of the priest Yuten, and a stone tablet bearing in Chinese characters the sacred formula, *Namu Amida Butsu.*

A ladder enables the pilgrim to ascend into the interior of the colossus as high as the shoulders, in which are two little windows commanding a wide prospect of the grounds; while a priest, who acts as guide, states the age of the statue to be six hundred and thirty years, and asks for some small contribution to aid in the erection of a new temple to shelter it from the weather.

For this Buddha once had a temple. A tidal wave following an earthquake swept walls and roof away, but left the mighty Amida unmoved, still meditating upon his lotus.

12

And we arrive before the far-famed Kamakura temple of Kwannon - Kwannon, who yielded up her right to the Eternal Peace that she might save the soul of men, and renounced Nirvana to suffer with humanity for other myriad million ages - Kwannon, the Goddess of Pity and of Mercy.

I climb three flights of steps leading to the temple, and a young girl, seated at the threshold, rises to greet us. Then she disappears within the temple to summon the guardian priest, a venerable man, white-robed, who makes me a sign to enter.

The temple is large as any that I have yet seen, and, like the others, grey with the wearing of six hundred years. From the roof there hang down votive offerings, inscriptions, and lanterns in multitude, painted with various pleasing colours. Almost opposite to the entrance is a singular statue, a seated figure, of human dimensions and most human aspect, looking upon us with small weird eyes set in a wondrously wrinkled face. This face was originally painted flesh-tint, and the robes of the image pale blue; but now the whole is uniformly grey with age and dust, and its colourlessness harmonises so well with the senility of the figure that one

46

is almost ready to believe one's self gazing at a living mendicant pilgrim. It is Benzuru, the same personage whose famous image at Asakusa has been made featureless by the wearing touch of countless pilgrim-figures. To left and right of the entrance are the Ni-Ō, enormously muscled, furious of aspect; their crimson bodies are speckled with a white scum of paper pellets spat at them by worshippers. Above the altar is a small but very pleasing image of Kwannon with her entire figure relieved against an oblong halo of gold, imitating the flickering of flame.

But this is not the image for which the temple is famed; there is another to be seen upon certain conditions. The old priest presents me with a petition, written in excellent and eloquent English, praying visitors to contribute something to the maintenance of the temple and its pontiff, and appealing to those of another faith to remember that 'any belief which can make men kindly and good is worthy of respect'. I contribute my mite, and I ask to see the great Kwannon.

Then the old priest lights a lantern, and leads the way, through a low doorway on the left of the altar, into the interior of the temple, into some very lofty darkness. I follow him cautiously awhile, discerning nothing whatever but the flicker of the lantern; then we halt before something which gleams. A moment, and my eyes, becoming more accustomed to the darkness, begin to distinguish outlines; the gleaming object defines itself gradually as a Foot, an immense golden Foot, and I perceive the hem of a golden robe undulating over the instep. Now the other foot appears; the figure is certainly standing. I can perceive that we are in a narrow but also very lofty chamber, and that out of some mysterious blackness overhead ropes are dangling down into the circle of lantern-light illuminating the golden feet. The priest lights two more lanterns, and suspends them upon hooks attached to a pair of pendent ropes about a yard apart; then he pulls up both together slowly. More of the golden robe is revealed as the lanterns ascend, swinging on their way; then the outlines of two mighty knees; then the curving of columnar thighs under chiselled drapery, and, as with the still waving ascent of the lanterns the golden Vision towers ever higher through the gloom, expectation intensifies. There is no sound but the sound of the invisible pulleys overhead, which squeak like bats. Now above the golden girdle, the suggestion of a bosom. Then the glowing of a golden hand uplifted in benediction. Then another golden hand holding a lotus. And at last a Face, golden, smiling with eternal youth and infinite tenderness, the face of Kwannon.

So revealed out of the consecrated darkness, this ideal of divine feminity - creation of a forgotten art and time - is more than impressive. I can scarcely call the emotion which it produces admiration; it is rather reverence.

But the lanterns, which paused awhile at the level of the beautiful face, now ascend still higher, with a fresh squeaking of pulleys. And lo! the tiara of the divinity appears with strangest symbolism. It is a pyramid of heads, of faces - charming faces of maidens, miniature faces of Kwannon herself.

For this is the Kwannon of the Eleven Faces - Jiu-ichi-men-Kwannon.

13

Most sacred this statue is held; and this is its legend.

In the reign of Emperor Gensei, there lived in the province of Yamato a Buddhist priest, Tokudo Shōnin, who had been in a previous birth Hoki Bosatsu, but had been reborn among common men to save their souls. Now at that time, in a valley in Yamato, Tokudo Shōnin, walking by night, saw a wonderful radiance; and going towards it found that it came from the trunk of a great fallen tree, a *kusunoki*, or camphor-tree. A delicious perfume came from the tree, and the shining of it was like the shining of the moon. And by these signs Tokudo Shōnin knew that the wood was holy; and he bethought him that he should have the statue of Kwannon carved from it. And he recited a sutra, and repeated the Nenbutsu, praying for inspiration; and even while he prayed there came and stood before him an aged man and an aged woman; and these said to him, 'We know that your desire is to have the image of Kwannon-Sama carved from this tree with the help of Heaven; continue therefore, to pray, and we shall carve the statue.'

And Tokudo Shōnin did as they bade him; and he saw them easily split the vast trunk into two equal parts, and begin to carve each of the parts into an image. And he saw them so labour for three days; and on the third day the work was done - and he saw the two marvellous statues of Kwannon made perfect before him. And he said to the strangers: 'Tell me, I pray you, by what names you are known.' Then the old man answered: 'I am Kasuga Myōjin.' And the woman answered: 'I am called Ten-shō-kō-dai-jin; I am the Goddess of the Sun.' And as they spoke both became transfigured and ascended to heaven and vanished from the sight of Tokudo Shōnin.[6]

And the Emperor, hearing of these happenings, sent his representative to Yamato to make offerings, and to have a temple built. Also the great priest, Gyōgi-Bosatsu, came and consecrated the images, and dedicated the temple which by order of the Emperor was built. And one of the statues he placed in the temple, enshrining it, and commanding it: 'Stay thou here always to save all living creatures'! But the other statue he cast into the sea, saying to it: 'Go thou whithersoever it is best, to save all the living'.

Now the statue floated to Kamakura. And there arriving by night it shed a great radiance all about it as if there were sunshine upon the sea; and the fishermen of Kamakura were awakened by the great light; and they went out in boats, and found the statue floating and brought it to shore. And the Emperor ordered that a temple should be built for it, the temple called Shin-haseidera, on the mountain called Kaiko-San, at Kamakura.

14

As we leave the temple of Kwannon behind us, there are no more dwellings visible along the road; the green slopes to left and right become steeper, and the shadows of the great trees deepen over us. But still, at intervals, some flight of venerable mossy steps, a carven Buddhist gateway, or a lofty *torii*, signals the presence of sanctuaries we have no time to visit: countless crumbling shrines are all around us, dumb witnesses to the antique splendour and vastness of the dead capital; and everywhere, mingled with perfume of blossoms, hovers the sweet, resinous smell of Japanese incense. Betimes we pass a scattered multitude of sculptured stones, like segments of four-sided pillars - old *haka*, the forgotten tombs of a long-abandoned cemetery; or the solitary image of some Buddhist deity - a dreaming Amida or faintly smiling Kwannon. All are ancient, time-discoloured, mutilated; a few have been weather-worn into unrecognisability. I halt a moment to contemplate something pathetic, a group of six images of the charming divinity who cares for the ghosts of little children - the Roku-Jizō. Oh, how chipped and scurfed and mossed they are! Five stand buried almost up to their shoulders in a heaping of little stones, testifying to the prayers of generations; and votive *yodarekake*, infant bibs of divers colours, have been put about the necks of these for the love of children lost. But one of the gentle gods' images lies shattered and overthrown in its own scattered pebble-pile - broken perhaps by some passing wagon.

15

The road slopes before us as we go, sinks down between cliffs steep as the walls of a canyon, and curves. Suddenly, we emerge from the cliffs, and reach the sea. It is blue like the unclouded sky - a soft dreamy blue.

And our path turns sharply to the right, and winds along cliff-summits overlooking a broad beach of dun-coloured sand; and the sea wind blows deliciously with a sweet saline scent, urging the lungs to fill themselves to the very utmost; and far away before me, I perceive a beautiful high green mass, an island foliage-covered, rising out of the water about a quarter of a mile from the mainland - Enoshima, the holy island, sacred to the goddess of the sea, the goddess of beauty. I can already distinguish a tiny town, grey-sprinkling its steep slope. Evidently it can be reached today on foot, for the tide is out, and has left bare a long broad reach of sand, extending to it, from the opposite village which we are approaching, like a causeway.

At Katase, the little settlement facing the island, we must leave our *jinricksha* and walk; the dunes between the village and the beach are too deep to pull the vehicle over. Scores of other *jinricksha* are waiting here in the little narrow street for pilgrims who have preceded me. But today, I am told, I am the only European who visits the shrine of Benten.

Our two men lead the way over the dunes, and we soon descend upon damp firm sand.

As we near the island the architectural details of the little town define delightfully through the faint sea-haze - curved bluish sweeps of fantastic roofs, angles of airy balconies, high-peaked curious gables, all above a fluttering of queerly shaped banners covered with mysterious lettering. We pass the sand-flats; and the ever-open Portal of the Sea-city, the City of the Dragon-goddess is before us, a beautiful *torii*. All of bronze it is, with *shimenawa* of bronze above it, and a brazen tablet inscribed with characters declaring: *'This is the Palace of the Goddess of Enoshima'*. About the bases of the ponderous pillars are strange designs in *relievo*, eddyings of waves with tortoises struggling in the flow. This is really the gate of the city facing the shrine of Benten by the land approach; but it is only the third torii of the imposing series through Katase: we did not see the others, having come by way of the coast.

And lo! we are in Enoshima. High before us slopes the single street, a street of broad steps, a street shadowy, full of multi-coloured flags and dark blue drapery dashed with white fantasticalities, which are words, fluttered by the sea wind. It is lined with taverns and miniature shops and at every one I must pause to look; and to dare to look at anything in Japan is to want to buy it. So I buy, and buy, and buy!

For verily 'tis the City of Mother-of-Pearl, this Enoshima. In every shop, behind the lettered draperies there are miracles of shell-work for sale at absurdly small prices. The glazed cases laid flat upon the matted platforms, the shelved cabinets set against the walls, are all opalescent with nacreous things - extraordinary surprises, incredible ingenuities; strings of mother-of-pearl fish, strings of mother-of-pearl birds, all shimmering with rainbow colours. There are little kittens of mother-of-pearl, and little foxes of mother-of-pearl, and little puppies of mother-of-pearl, and girls' hair-combs, and cigarette-holders, and pipes too beautiful to use. There are little tortoises, not larger than a shilling, made of shells, that, when you touch them, however lightly, begin to move head, legs, and tail, all at the same time, alternately withdrawing or protruding their limbs so much like real tortoises as to give one a shock of surprise. There are storks and birds, and beetles and butterflies, and crabs and lobsters, made so cunningly of shells, that only touch convinces you they are not alive. There are bees of shell, poised on flowers of the same material - poised on wire in such a way that they seem to buzz if moved only with the tip of a feather. There is shell-work jewellery indescribable, things that Japanese girls love, enchantments in mother-of-pearl, hair-pins carven in a hundred forms, brooches, necklaces. And there are photographs of Enoshima.

16

This curious street ends at another *torii*, a wooden *torii*, with a steeper flight of stone steps ascending to it. At the foot of the steps are votive stone lamps and a little well, and a stone tank at which all pilgrims wash their hands and rinse their mouths before approaching the temples of the gods. And hanging beside the tank are bright blue towels, with large white Chinese characters upon them. I ask Akira what these characters signify:

'Ho-Keng is the sound of the characters in the Chinese; but in Japanese the same characters are pronounced *Kenji-tatematsuru*, and signify that those towels are mostly humbly offered to Benten. They are what you call votive offerings. And there are many kinds of votive offerings made to famous shrines. Some people give towels, some give pictures, some give vases; some offer lanterns of paper, or bronze, or stone. It is common to

promise such offerings when making petitions to the gods; and it is usual to promise a *torii*. The *torii* may be small or great according to the wealth of him who gives it; the very rich pilgrim may offer to the gods a *torii* of metal, such as that below, which is the Gate of Enoshima.'

'Akira, do the Japanese always keep their vows to the gods?'

Akira smiles a sweet smile, and answers:

'There was a man who promised to build a *torii* of good metal if his prayers were granted. And he obtained all that he desired. And then he built a *torii* with three exceedingly small needles.'

17

Ascending the steps, we reach a terrace, overlooking all the city roofs. There are Buddhist lions of stone and stone lanterns, mossed and chipped, on either side the *torii*; and the background of the terrace is the sacred hill, covered with foliage. To the left is a balustrade of stone, old and green, surrounding a shallow pool covered with scum of water-weed. And on the farther bank above it, out of the bushes, protrudes a strangely shaped stone slab, poised on edge, and covered with Chinese characters. It is a sacred stone, and is believed to have the form of a great frog, *gama*; wherefore it is called Gama-ishi, the Frog-stone. Here and there along the edge of the terrace are other graven monuments, one of which is the offering of certain pilgrims who visited the shrine of the sea-goddess one hundred times. On the right other flights of steps lead to loftier terraces; and an old man, who sits at the foot of them, making bird-cages of bamboo, offers himself as guide.

We follow him to the next terrace, where there is a school for the children of Enoshima, and another sacred stone, huge and shapeless: Fuku-ishi, the Stone of Good Fortune. In old times pilgrims who rubbed their hands upon it believed they would thereby gain riches; and the stone is polished and worn by the touch of innumerable palms.

More steps and more green-mossed lions and lanterns, and another terrace with a little temple in its midst, the first shrine of Benten. Before it a few stunted palm-trees are growing. There is nothing in the shrine of interest, only Shinto emblems. But there is another well beside it with other votive towels, and there is another mysterious monument, a stone shrine brought from China six hundred years ago. Perhaps it contained some far-famed statue before this place of pilgrimage was given over to the priests of Shinto. There is nothing in it now; the monolith slab forming the back of it has been fractured by the falling of rocks from the cliff above; and the inscription cut therein has been almost effaced by some kind of scum. Akira reads '*Dai-Nippon-goku-Enoshima-no-reiseki-ken...*'; the rest is undecipherable. He says there is a statue in the neighbouring temple, but it is exhibited only once a year, on the fifteenth day of the seventh month.

Leaving the court by a rising path to the left, we proceed along the verge of a cliff overlooking the sea. Perched upon this verge are pretty tea-houses, all widely open to the sea wind, so that, looking through them, over their matted floors and lacquered balconies one sees the ocean as in a picture-frame, and the pale clear horizon specked with snowy sails, and a faint blue-peaked shape also, like a phantom island, the far vapoury silhouette of Ōshima. Then we find another *torii*, and other steps leading to a terrace almost black with shade of enormous evergreen trees, and surrounded on the sea side by another stone balustrade, velveted with moss. On the right more steps, another *torii*, another terrace; and more mossed green lions and stone lamps; and a monument inscribed with the record of the change whereby Enoshima passed away from Buddhism to become Shinto. Beyond, in the centre of another plateau, the second shrine of Benten.

But there is no Benten! Benten has been hidden away by Shinto hands. The second shrine is void as the first. Nevertheless, in a building to the left of the temple, strange relics are exhibited. Feudal armour; suits of plate and chain-mail; helmets with visors which are demoniac masks of iron; helmets crested with dragons of gold; two-handed swords worthy of giants; and enormous arrows, more than five feet long, with shafts nearly an inch in diameter. One has a crescent head about nine inches from horn to horn, the interior edge of the crescent being sharp as a knife. Such a missile would take off a man's head; and I can scarcely believe Akira's assurance that such ponderous arrows were shot from a bow by hand only. There is a specimen of the writing of Nichiren, the great Buddhist priest - gold characters on a blue ground; and there is, in a lacquered shrine, a gilded dragon said to have been made by that still greater priest and writer and master-wizard, Kōbōdaishi.

A path shaded by overarching trees leads from this plateau to the third shrine. We pass a *torii* and beyond it come to a stone monument covered with figures of monkeys chiselled in relief. What the signification of this monument is, even our guide cannot explain. Then another *torii*. It is of wood; but I am told it replaces one of metal, stolen in the night by thieves. Wonderful thieves! that *torii* must have weighed at least a ton! More stone lanterns; then an immense court, on the very summit of the mountain, and there, in its midst, the third and chief temple of Benten. And before the temple is a large vacant space surrounded by a fence in such manner as to render the shrine totally inaccessible. Vanity and vexation of spirit!

There is, however, a little *haiden*, or place of prayer, with nothing in it but a money-box and a bell, before the fence, and facing the temple steps. Here the pilgrims make their offerings and pray. Only a small raised platform covered with a Chinese roof supported upon four plain posts, the back of the structure being closed by a lattice about breast high. From this praying-station we can look into the temple of Benten, and see that Benten is not there.

But I perceive that the ceiling is arranged in caissons; and in a central caisson I discover a very curious painting, a foreshortened tortoise, gazing down at me. And while I am looking at it I hear Akira and the guide laughing; and the latter exclaims, '*Benten-Sama*'!

A beautiful little damask snake is undulating up the lattice-work, poking its head through betimes to look at us. It does not seem in the least afraid, nor has it much reason to be, seeing that its kind are deemed the servants and confidants of Benten. Sometimes the great goddess herself assumes the serpent form; perhaps she has come to see us.

Nearby is a singular stone, set on a pedestal in the court. It has the form of the body of a tortoise, and markings like those of the creature's shell; and it is held a sacred thing, and is called the Tortoise-stone. But I fear exceedingly that in all this place we shall find nothing save stones and serpents!

18

Now we are going to visit the Dragon cavern, not so called, Akira says, because the Dragon of Benten ever dwelt therein, but because the shape of the cavern is the shape of a dragon. The path descends towards the opposite side of the island, and suddenly breaks into a flight of steps cut out of the pale hard rock - exceedingly steep, and worn, and slippery, and perilous - overlooking the sea. A vision of low pale rocks, and surf bursting among them, and a *tōrō* or votive stone lamp in the centre of them, all seen as in a bird's-eye view, over the verge of an awful precipice. I see also deep, round holes in one of the rocks. There used to be a tea-house below; and the wooden pillars supporting it were fitted into those holes.

I descend with caution; the Japanese seldom slip in their straw sandals, but I can only proceed with the aid of the guide. At almost every step I slip. Surely these steps could never have been thus worn away by the straw sandals of pilgrims who came to see only stones and serpents!

At last we reach a plank gallery carried along the face of the cliff above the rocks and pools, and following it round a projection of the cliff enter the sacred cave. The light dims as we advance; and the sea-waves, running after us into the gloom, make a stupefying roar, multiplied by the extraordinary echo. Looking back, I see the mouth of the cavern like a prodigious sharply angled rent in blackness, showing a fragment of azure sky.

We reach a shrine with no deity in it, pay a fee; and lamps being lighted and given to each of us, we proceed to explore a series of underground passages. So black they are that even with the light of three lamps, I can at first see nothing. In a while, however, I can distinguish stone figures in relief, chiselled on slabs like those I saw in the Buddhist graveyard. These are placed at regular intervals along the rock walls. The guide approaches his light to the face of each one, and utters a name, 'Daikoku-Sama', 'Fudō-Sama', 'Kwannon-Sama'. Sometimes in lieu of a statue there is an empty shrine only, with a money-box before it; and these void shrines have names of Shinto gods, 'Daijingu', 'Hachiman', 'Inari-Sama'. All the statues are black, or seem black in the yellow lamplight, and sparkle as if frosted. I feel as if I were in some mortuary pit, some subterranean burial-place of dead gods. Interminable the corridor appears; yet there is at last an end - an end with a shrine in it - where the rocky ceiling descends so low that to reach the shrine one must go down on hands and knees. And there is nothing in the shrine. This is the Tail of the Dragon.

We do not return to the light at once, but enter into other lateral black corridors - the Wings of the Dragon. More sable effigies of dispossessed gods; more empty shrines; more stone faces covered with saltpetre; and more money-boxes, possible only to reach by stooping, where more offerings should be made. And there is no Benten, either of wood or stone.

I am glad to return to the light. Here our guide strips naked, and suddenly leaps head foremost into a black deep swirling current between rocks. Five minutes later he reappears, and clambering out lays at my feet a living, squirming sea-snail and an enormous shrimp. Then he resumes his robe, and we reascend the mountain.

19

'And this', the reader may say - 'this is all that you went forth to see: a *torii*, some shells, a small damask snake, some stones?'

It is true. And nevertheless I know that I am bewitched. There is a charm indefinable about the place - that sort of charm which comes with a little ghostly thrill never to be forgotten.

Not of strange sights alone is this charm made, but of numberless subtle sensations and ideas interwoven and interblended: the sweet sharp scents of grove and sea; the blood-brightening, vivifying touch of the free wind; the dumb appeal of ancient mystic mossy things; vague reverence evoked by knowledge of treading soil called holy for a thousand years; and a sense of sympathy, as a human duty, compelled by the vision of steps of rock worn down into shapelessness by the pilgrim feet of vanished generations.

And other memories ineffaceable: the first sight of the sea-girt City of Pearl through a fairy veil of haze; the windy approach to the lovely island over the velvety soundless brown stretch of sand; the weird majesty of the giant gate of bronze; the queer, high-sloping, fantastic, quaintly gabled street, flinging down sharp shadows of aerial balconies; the flutter of coloured draperies in the sea wind, and of flags with their riddles of lettering; the pearly glimmering of the astonishing shops.

And impressions of the enormous day - the day of the Land of the Gods - a loftier day than ever our summers know; and the glory of the view from those green sacred silent heights between sea and sun; and the remembrance of the sky, a sky spiritual as holiness, a sky with clouds ghost-pure and white as the light itself - seeming, indeed, not clouds but dreams, or souls of Bodhisattvas about to melt for ever into some blue Nirvana.

And the romance of Benten, too - the Deity of Beauty, the Divinity of Love, the Goddess of Eloquence. Rightly is she likewise named Goddess of the Sea. For is not the Sea most ancient and most excellent of Speakers, the eternal Poet, chanter of that mystic hymn whose rhythm shakes the world, whose mighty syllables no man may learn?

20

We return by another route.

For a while the way winds through a long narrow winding valley between wooded hills: the whole extent of bottom-land is occupied by rice-farms; the air has a humid coolness, and one hears only the chanting of frogs, like a clattering of countless castanets, as the jinricksha jolts over the rugged elevated paths separating the flooded rice-fields.

As we skirt the foot of a wooded hill upon the right, my Japanese comrade signals to our runners to halt, and himself dismounting, points to the blue peaked roof of a little temple high-perched on the green slope. 'Is it really worth while to climb up there in the sun?' I ask. 'Oh, yes'! he answers: 'it is the temple of Kishibojin - Kishibojin, the Mother of Demons!'

We ascend a flight of broad stone steps, meet the Buddhist guardian lions at the summit, and enter the little court in which the temple stands. An elderly woman, with a child clinging to her robe, comes from the adjoining building to open the screens for us; and taking off our footgear we enter the temple. Without, the edifice looked old and dingy; but within all is neat and pretty. The June sun, pouring through the open *shōji*, illuminates an artistic confusion of brasses gracefully shaped and multi-coloured things - images, lanterns, paintings, gilded inscriptions, pendent scrolls. There are three altars.

Above the centre altar Amida Buddha sits enthroned on his mystic golden lotus in the attitude of the Teacher. On the altar to the right gleams a shrine of five miniature golden steps where little images stand in rows, tier above tier, some seated, some erect, male and female, attired like goddesses or like *daimyō*: the Sanjiubanjin, or Thirty Guardians. Below, on the facade of the altar, is the figure of a hero slaying a monster. On the altar to the left is the shrine of the Mother-of-Demons.

Her story is a legend of horror. For some sin committed in a previous birth, she was born a demon, devouring her own children. But being saved by the teaching of Buddha, she became a divine being, especially loving and protecting infants; and Japanese mothers pray to her for their little ones, and wives pray to her for beautiful boys.

The face of Kishibojin[7] is the face of a comely woman. But her eyes are weird. In her right hand she bears a lotus-blossom; with her left she supports in a fold of her robe, against her half-veiled breast, a naked baby. At the foot of her shrine stands Jizō-Sama, leaning upon his *shakujō*. But the altar and its images do not form the startling feature of the temple-interior. What impresses the visitor in a totally novel way are the votive offerings. High before the shrine, suspended from strings stretched taut between tall poles of bamboo, are scores, no, hundreds, of pretty tiny dresses - Japanese baby-dresses of many colours. Most are made of poor material, for these are the thank-offerings of very poor simple women, poor country mothers, whose prayers to Kishibojin for the blessing of children have been heard.

And the sight of all those little dresses, each telling so naïvely its story of joy and pain - those tiny *kimonos* shaped and sewn by docile patient

patient fingers of humble mothers - touches irresistibly, like some unexpected revelation of the universal mother-love. And the tenderness of all the simple hearts that have testified thus to faith and thankfulness seems to thrill all about me softly, like a caress of summer wind.

Outside the world appears to have suddenly grown beautiful; the light is sweeter; it seems to me there is a new charm even in the azure of the eternal day.

21

Then, having traversed the valley, we reach a main road so level and so magnificently shaded by huge old trees that I could believe myself in an English lane - a lane in Kent or Surrey, perhaps - but for some exotic detail breaking the illusion at intervals; a *torii*, towering before temple-steps descending to the highway, or a signboard lettered with Chinese characters, or the wayside shrine of some unknown god.

All at once I observe by the roadside some unfamiliar sculptures in relief, a row of chiselled slabs protected by a little bamboo shed; and I dismount to look at them, supposing them to be funereal monuments. They are so old that the lines of their sculpturing are half obliterated; their feet are covered with moss, and their visages are half effaced. But I can discern that these are not *haka*, but six images of one divinity; and my guide knows him - Kōshin, the God of Roads. So chipped and covered with scurf he is, that the upper portion of his form has become indefinably vague; his attributes have been worn away. But below his feet, on several slabs, chiselled cunningly, I can still distinguish the figures of the Three Apes, his messengers. And some pious soul has left before one image a humble votive offering, the picture of a black cock and a white hen, painted upon a wooden shingle. It must have been left here very long ago; the wood has become almost black, and the painting has been damaged by weather and by droppings of birds. There are no stones piled at the feet of these images, as before the images of Jizō; they seem like things forgotten, crusted over by the neglect of generations - archaic gods who have lost their worshippers.

But my guide tells me, 'The Temple of Kōshin is near, in the village of Fujisawa.' Assuredly I must visit it.

22

The temple of Kōshin is situated in the middle of the village, in a court opening upon the main street. A very old wooden temple it is, unpainted, dilapidated, grey with the greyness of all forgotten and weather-beaten things. It is some time before the guardian of the temple can be found, to open the doors. For this temple has doors in lieu of *shōji*, old doors that moan sleepily at being turned upon their hinges. And it is not necessary to remove one's shoes; the floor is matless, covered with dust, and squeaks under the unaccustomed weight of entering feet. All within is crumbling, mouldering, worn; the shrine has no image, only Shinto emblems, some poor paper lanterns whose once bright colours have vanished under a coating of dust, some vague inscriptions. I see the circular frame of a metal mirror; but the mirror itself is gone. Whither? The guardian says: 'No priest lives now in this temple; and thieves might come in the night to steal the mirror; so we have hidden it away.' I ask about the image of Kōshin. He answers it is exposed but once in every sixty-one years, so I cannot see it; but there are other statues of the god in the temple court.

I go to look at them: a row of images, much like those upon the public highway, but better preserved. One figure of Kōshin, however, is different from the others I have seen - apparently made after some Hindoo model, judging by the Indian coiffure, mitre-shaped and lofty. The god has three eyes; one in the centre of his forehead, opening perpendicularly instead of horizontally. He has six arms. With one hand he supports a monkey; with another he grasps a serpent; and the other hands hold out symbolic things - a wheel, a sword, a rosary, a sceptre. And serpents are coiled about his wrists and about his ankles; and under his feet is a monstrous head, the head of a demon, Amanjako, sometimes called Utatesa ('Sadness'). Upon the pedestal below the Three Apes are carven; and the face of an ape appears also upon the front of the god's tiara.

I see also tablets of stone, graven only with the god's name, votive offerings. And nearby, in a tiny wooden shrine, is the figure of the Earth-god, Kenrojinjin, grey, primeval, vaguely wrought, holding in one hand a spear, in the other a vessel containing something indistinguishable.

23

Perhaps to uninitiated eyes these many-headed, many-handed gods at first may seem - as they seem always in the sight of Christian bigotry - only monstrous. But when the knowledge of their meaning comes to one who feels the divine in all religions, then they will be found to make appeal to the higher aestheticism, to the sense of moral beauty, with a force never to be divined by minds knowing nothing of the Orient and its thought. To me the image of Kwannon of the Thousand Hands is not less admirable than any other representation of human loveliness idealised bearing her name - the Peerless, the Majestic, the Peace-Giving, or even White Sui-Getsu, who sails the moonlit waters in her rosy boat made of a single lotus-petal; and in the triple-headed Shaka I discern and revere the mighty power of that Truth whereby, as by a conjunction of suns, the Three Worlds have been illuminated.

But vain to seek to memorise the names and attributes of all the gods; they seem, self-multiplying, to mock the seeker; Kwannon the Merciful is revealed as the Hundred Kwannon; the Six Jizō become the Thousand. And as they multiply before research, they vary and change: less multiform, less complex, less elusive the moving of waters than the visions of this Oriental faith. Into it, as into a fathomless sea, mythology after mythology from India and China and the farther East has sunk and been absorbed; and the stranger, peering into its deeps, finds himself, as in the tale of Undine, contemplating a flood in whose every surge rises and vanishes a Face, weird or beautiful or terrible - a most ancient shoreless sea of forms incomprehensibly interchanging and intermingling, but symbolising the protean magic of that infinite Unknown that shapes and re-shapes for ever all cosmic being.

24

I wonder if I can buy a picture of Kōshin. In most Japanese temples little pictures of the tutelar deity are sold to pilgrims, cheap prints on thin paper. But the temple guardian here tells me, with a gesture of despair, that there are no pictures of Kōshin for sale; there is only an old *kakemono* on which the god is represented. If I would like to see it he will go home and get it for me. I beg him to do me the favour; and he hurries into the street.

While awaiting his return, I continue to examine the queer old statues, with a feeling of mingled melancholy and pleasure. To have studied and loved an ancient faith only through the labours of palaeographers and archaeologists, and as something astronomically remote from one's own existence, and then suddenly in after years to find the same faith a part of one's human environment - to feel that its mythology, though senescent, is *alive* all around you - is almost to realise the dream of the Romantics, to have the sensation of returning through twenty centuries into the life of a happier world. For these quaint Gods of Roads and Gods of Earth are really living still, though so worn and mossed and feebly worshipped. In this brief moment, at least, I am really in the Elder World, perhaps just at that epoch of it when the primal faith is growing a little old-fashioned, crumbling slowly before the corrosive influence of a new philosophy; and I know myself a pagan still, loving these simple old gods, these gods of a people's childhood.

And they need some human love, these naïve, innocent, ugly gods. The beautiful divinities will live for ever by that sweetness of womanhood idealised in the Buddhist art of them: eternal are Kwannon and Benten; they need no help of man; they will compel reverence when the great temples shall all have become voiceless and priestless as this shrine of Kōshin is. But these kind, queer, artless, mouldering gods, who have given ease to so many troubled minds, who have gladdened so many simple hearts, who have heard so many innocent prayers - how gladly would I prolong their beneficent lives in spite of the so-called 'laws of progress' and the irrefutable philosophy of evolution!

The guardian returns, bringing with him a *kakemono*, very small, very dusty, and so yellow-stained by time that it might be a thousand years old. But I am disappointed as I unroll it; there is only a very common print of the god within - all outline. And while I am looking at it, I become for the first time conscious that a crowd has gathered about me - tanned, kindly-faced labourers from the fields, and mothers with their babies on their backs, and schoolchildren, and *jinricksha* men, all wondering that a stranger should be thus interested in their gods. And although the pressure about me is very, very gentle, like a pressure of tepid water for gentleness, I feel a little embarrassed. I give back the old *kakemono* to the guardian, make my offering to the god, and take my leave of Koshin and his good servant.

All the kind oblique eyes follow me as I go. And something like a feeling of remorse seizes me at thus abruptly abandoning the void, dusty, crumbling temple, with its mirrorless altar and its colourless lanterns, and the decaying sculptures of its neglected court, and its kindly guardian whom I see still watching my retreating steps, with the yellow *kakemono* in his hand. The whistle of a locomotive warns me that I shall just have time to catch the train. For Western civilisation has invaded all this primitive peace, with its webs of steel, with its ways of iron. This is not of thy roads, O Kōshin! - the old gods are dying along its ash-strewn verge!

Footnotes:

1. *Yane*, 'roof'; *shōbu*, 'sweet-flag' (Acorus calamus).
2. At the time this paper was written, nearly three years ago, I had not seen the mighty bells at Kyoto and at Nara.
       The largest bell in Japan is suspended in the grounds of the grand Jōdo temple of Chion-in, at Kyoto. Visitors are not allowed to sound it. It was cast in 1633. It weighs seventy-four tons, and requires, they say, twenty-five men to ring it properly. Next in size ranks the bell of the Daibutsu temple in Kyoto, which visitors are allowed to ring on payment of a small sum. It was cast in 1615, and weighs sixty-three tons. The wonderful bell of Tōdaiji at Nara, although ranking only third, is perhaps the most interesting of all. It is thirteen feet six inches high, and nine feet in diameter; and its inferiority to the Kyoto bells is not in visible dimensions so much as in weight and thickness. It weighs thirty-seven tons. It was cast in 733, and is therefore one thousand one hundred and sixty years old. Visitors pay one cent to sound it once.
3. In Sanscrit, Avalokitesvara. The Japanese Kwannon, or Kwan-ze-on, is identical in origin with the Chinese virgin-goddess Kwanyin adopted by Buddhism as an incarnation of the Indian Avalokitesvara. (See Eitel's *Handbook of Chinese Buddhism*.) But the Japanese Kwannon has lost all Chinese characteristics - has become artistically an idealisation of all that is sweet and beautiful in the woman of Japan.
4. Let the reader consult Mitford's admirable *Tales of Old Japan* for the full meaning of the term *rōnin*.
5. There is a delicious Japanese proverb, the full humour of which is only to be appreciated by one familiar with the artistic representations of the divinities referred to:

Karutoki no Jizō-gao,
Nasutoki no Emma-gao.
['Borrowing-time, the face of Jizō;
Repaying-time, the face of Emma.']

6. This old legend has peculiar interest as an example of the efforts made by Buddhism to absorb the Shinto divinities, as it had already absorbed those of India and of China. These efforts were, to a great extent, successful prior to the disestablishment of Buddhism and the revival of Shinto as the State religion. But in Izumo, and other parts of Western Japan, Shinto has always remained dominant, and has even appropriated and amalgamated much belonging to Buddhism.
7. In Sanscrit *'Harītī'*. - *Karitei-Bo* is the Japanese name for one form of Kishibojin.

People

Of Women's Hair

1

The hair of the younger daughter of the family is very long; and it is a spectacle of no small interest to see it dressed. It is dressed once in every three days; and the operation, which costs four sen, is acknowledged to require one hour. As a matter of fact it requires nearly two. The hairdresser (*kamiyui*) first sends her maiden apprentice, who cleans the hair, washes it, perfumes it, and combs it with extraordinary combs of at least five different kinds. So thoroughly is the hair cleansed that it remains for three days, or even four, immaculate beyond our Occidental conception of things. In the morning, during the dusting time, it is carefully covered with a handkerchief or a little blue towel; and the curious Japanese wooden pillow, which supports the neck, not the head, renders it possible to sleep at ease without disarranging the marvellous structure.[1]

After the apprentice has finished her part of the work, the hairdresser herself appears, and begins to build the coiffure. For this task she uses, besides the extraordinary variety of combs, fine loops of gilt thread or coloured paper twine, dainty bits of deliciously tinted crape-silk, delicate steel springs, and curious little basket-shaped things over which the hair is moulded into the required forms before being fixed in place.

The *kamiyui* also brings razors with her; for the Japanese girl is shaved - cheeks, ears, brows, chin, even nose! What is there to shave? Only that peachy floss which is the velvet of the finest human skin, but which Japanese taste removes. There is, however, another use for the razor. All maidens bear the signs of their maidenhood in the form of a little round spot, about an inch in diameter, shaven clean upon the very top of the head. This is only partially concealed by a band of hair brought back from the forehead across it, and fastened to the back hair. The girl-baby's head is totally shaved. When a few years old the little creature's hair is allowed to grow except at the top of the head, where a large tonsure is maintained. But the size of the tonsure diminishes year by year, until it shrinks after childhood to the small spot above described; and this, too, vanishes after marriage, when a still more complicated fashion of wearing the hair is adopted.

2

Such absolutely straight dark hair as that of most Japanese women might seem, to Occidental ideas at least, ill-suited to the highest possibilities of the art of the *coiffeuse*.[2] But the skill of the *kamiyui* has made it tractable to every aesthetic whim. Ringlets, indeed, are unknown, and curling irons. But what wonderful and beautiful shapes the hair of the girl is made to assume: volutes, jets, whirls, eddyings, foliations, each passing into the other blandly as a linking of brush-strokes in the writing of a Chinese master! Far beyond the skill of the Parisian *coiffeuse* is the art of the *kamiyui*. From the mythical era[3] of the race, Japanese ingenuity has exhausted itself in the invention and the improvement of pretty devices for the dressing of woman's hair; and probably there have never been so many beautiful fashions of wearing it in any other country as there have been in Japan. These have changed through the centuries; sometimes becoming wondrously intricate of design, sometimes exquisitely simple - as in that gracious custom, recorded for us in so many quaint drawings, of allowing the long black tresses to flow unconfined below the waist.[4] But every mode of which we have any pictorial record had its own striking charm. Indian, Chinese, Malayan, Korean ideas of beauty appropriated and transfigured by the finer native conceptions of comeliness. Buddhism, too, which so profoundly influenced all Japanese art and thought, may possibly have influenced fashions of wearing the hair; for its female divinities appear with the most beautiful coiffures. Notice the hair of a Kwannon or a Benten, and the tresses of the Tennin - those angel-maidens who float in azure upon the ceilings of the great temples.

3

The particular attractiveness of the modern styles is the way in which the hair is made to serve as an elaborate nimbus for the features, giving delightful relief to whatever of fairness or sweetness the young face may possess. Then behind this charming black aureole is a riddle of graceful loopings and weavings whereof neither the beginning nor the ending can possibly be discerned. Only the *kamiyui* knows the key to that riddle. And the whole is held in place with curious ornamental combs, and shot through with long fine pins of gold, silver, nacre, transparent tortoise-shell, or lacquered wood, with cunningly carven heads.[5]

4

Not less than fourteen different ways of dressing the hair are practised by the *coiffeuses* of Izumo; but doubtless in the capital, and in some of the larger cities of eastern Japan, the art is much more elaborately developed. The hairdressers go from house to house to exercise their calling, visiting their clients upon fixed days at certain regular hours. The hair of little girls from seven to eight years old is in Matsue dressed usually after the style called *O-tabako-bon*, unless it be simply 'banged'. In the *O-tabako-bon* ('honourable smoking-box' style) the hair is cut to the length of about four inches all round except above the forehead, where it is clipped a little shorter; and on the summit of the head it is allowed to grow longer and is gathered up into a peculiarly shaped knot, which justifies the curious name of the coiffure. As soon as the girl becomes old enough to go to a female public day-school, her hair is dressed in the pretty, simple style called *katsurashita*, or perhaps in the new, ugly, semi-foreign 'bundle-style' called *sokuhatsu*, which has become the regulation fashion in boarding-schools. For the daughters of the poor, and even for most of those of the middle classes, the public-school period is rather brief; their studies usually cease a few years before they are marriageable, and girls marry very early in Japan. The maiden's first elaborate coiffure is arranged for her when she reaches the age of fourteen or fifteen at earliest. From twelve to fourteen her hair is dressed in the fashion called *omoyedzuki*; then the style is changed to the beautiful coiffure called *jorōwage*. There are various forms of this style, more or less complex. A couple of years later, the 'new-butterfly' style, or the *shimada*, also called *takawage*. The *shinjōchō* style is common, is worn by women of various ages, and is not considered very genteel. The *shimada*, exquisitely elaborate, is; but the more respectable the family, the smaller the form of this coiffure; geisha and *jorō* wear a larger and loftier variety of it, which properly answers to the name *takawage*, or 'high coiffure'. Between eighteen and twenty years of age the maiden again exchanges this style for another termed *tenjingaeshi*; between twenty and twenty-four years of age she adopts the fashion called *mitsuwage*, or the 'triple coiffure' of three loops; and a somewhat similar but still more complicated coiffure, called *mitsuwakudzushi* is worn by young women of from twenty-five to twenty-eight. Up to that age every change in the fashion of wearing the hair has been in the direction of elaborateness and complexity. But after twenty-eight a Japanese woman is no longer considered young, and there is only one more coiffure for her - the *mochiriwage* or *bobai*, the simple and rather ugly style adopted by old women.

But the girl who marries wears her hair in a fashion quite different from any of the preceding. The most beautiful, the most elaborate, and the most costly of all modes is the bride's coiffure, called *hanayome*, a word literally signifying 'flower-wife'. The structure is dainty as its name, and must be seen to be artistically appreciated. Afterwards the wife wears her hair in the styles called *kumesa* or *maruwage*, another name for which is *katsuyama*. The *kumesa* style is not genteel, and is the coiffure of the poor; the *maruwage* or *katsuyama* is refined. In former times the *samurai* women wore their hair in two particular styles: the maiden's coiffure was *ichōgaeshi*, and that of the married folk *katahajishi*. It is still possible to see in Matsue a few *katahajishi* coiffures.

5

The family *kamiyui*, O-Koto-San, the most skilful of her craft in Izumo, is a little woman of about thirty, still quite attractive. About her neck there are three soft pretty lines, forming what connoisseurs of beauty term 'the necklace of Venus'. This is a rare charm; but it once nearly proved the ruin of Koto. The story is a curious one.

Koto had a rival at the beginning of her professional career - a woman of considerable skill as a *coiffeuse*, but of malignant disposition, named Jin. Jin gradually lost all her respectable custom, and little Koto became the fashionable hairdresser. But her old rival, filled with jealous hate, invented a wicked story about Koto, and the story found root in the rich soil of old Izumo superstition, and grew fantastically. The idea of it had been suggested to Jin's cunning mind by those three soft lines about Koto's neck. She declared that Koto had a '*NUKEKUBI*'.

What is a *nukekubi*? *Kubi* signifies either the neck or head. *Nukeru* means to creep, to skulk, to prowl, to slip away stealthily. To have a *nukekubi* is to have a head that detaches itself from the body, and prowls about at night - by itself.

Koto has been twice married, and her second match was a happy one. But her first husband caused her much trouble, and ran away from her at last, in company with some worthless woman. Nothing was ever heard of him afterwards - so that Jin thought it quite safe to invent a nightmare-story to account for his disappearance. She said that he abandoned Koto because, on awaking one night, he saw his young wife's head rise from the pillow, and her neck lengthen like a great white serpent, while the rest of her body remained motionless. He saw the head, supported by the ever lengthening neck, enter the farther apartment and drink all the oil in the lamps, and then return to the pillow slowly - the neck simultaneously contracting. 'Then he rose up and fled away from the house in great fear', said Jin.

As one story begets another, all sorts of queer rumours soon began to circulate about poor Koto. There was a tale that some police-officer, late at night, saw a woman's head without a body, nibbling fruit from a tree overhanging some garden-wall; and that, knowing it to be a *nukekubi*, he struck it with the flat of his sword. It shrank away as swiftly as a bat flies, but not before he had been able to recognise the face of the *kamiyui*. 'Oh! it is quite true'! declared Jin, the morning after the alleged occurence; 'and if you don't believe it, send word to Koto that you want to see her. She can't go out: her face is all swelled up.' Now the last statement was fact, for Koto had a very severe toothache at that time - and the fact helped the falsehood. And the story found its way to the local newspaper, which published it - only as a strange example of popular credulity; and Jin said, 'Am I a teller of the truth? See, the paper has printed it'!

Wherefore crowds of curious people gathered before Koto's little house, and made her life such a burden to her that her husband had to watch her constantly to keep her from killing herself. Fortunately she had good friends in the family of the Governor, where she had been employed for years as *coiffeuse* and the Governor, hearing of the wickedness, wrote a public denunciation of it, and set his name to it, and printed it. Now the people of Matsue reverenced their old *samurai* Governor as if he were a god, and believed his least word; and seeing what he had written, they became ashamed, and also denounced the lie and the liar; and the little hairdresser soon became more prosperous than before through popular sympathy.

Some of the most extraordinary beliefs of old days are kept alive in Izumo and elsewhere by what are called in America 'traveling side-shows'; and the inexperienced foreigner could never imagine the possibilities of a Japanese side-show. On certain great holidays the showmen make their appearance, put up their ephemeral theatres of rush-matting and bamboos in some temple court, surfeit expectation by the most incredible surprises, and then vanish as suddenly as they came. The Skeleton of a Devil, the Claws of a Goblin, and 'a Rat as large as a sheep', were some of the least extraordinary displays which I saw. The Goblin's Claws were remarkably fine shark's teeth; the Devil's Skeleton had belonged to an orang-outang - all except the horns ingeniously attached to the skull; and the wondrous Rat I discovered to be a tame kangaroo. What I could not fully understand was the exhibition of a *nukekubi*, in which a young woman stretched her neck, apparently, to a length of about two feet, making ghastly faces during the performance.

6

There are also some strange old superstitions about women's hair.

The myth of Medusa has many a counterpart in Japanese folk-lore: the subject of such tales being always some wondrously beautiful girl, whose hair turns to snakes only at night, and who is discovered at last to be either a dragon or a dragon's daughter. But in ancient times it was believed that the hair of any young woman might, under certain trying circumstances, change into serpents. For instance: under the influence of long-repressed jealousy.

There were many men of wealth who, in the days of Old Japan, kept their concubines (*mekaké* or *aishō*) under the same roof with their legitimate wives (*okusama*.) And it is told that, although the severest patriarchal discipline might compel the *mekaké* and the *okusama* to live together in perfect seeming harmony by day, their secret hate would reveal itself by night in the transformation of their hair. The long black tresses of each would uncoil and hiss and strive to devour those of the other; and even the mirrors of the sleepers would dash themselves together - for, saith an ancient proverb, *kagami onna-no tamashii* - 'a Mirror is the Soul of a Woman'.[7] And there is a famous tradition of one Kato Sayemon Shigenji, who beheld in the night the hair of his wife and the hair of his concubine, changed into vipers, writhing together and hissing and biting. Then Kato Sayemon grieved much for that secret bitterness of hatred which thus existed through his fault; and he shaved his head and became a priest in the great Buddhist monastery of Koya-San, where he dwelt until the day of his death under the name of Karukaya.

7

The hair of dead women is arranged in the manner called *tabanegami*, somewhat resembling the *shimada* extremely simplified, and without ornaments of any kind. The name *tabanegami* signifies hair tied into a bunch, like a sheaf of rice. This style must also be worn by women during the period of mourning.

Ghosts, nevertheless, are represented with hair loose and long, falling weirdly over the face. And no doubt because of the melancholy suggestiveness of its drooping branches, the willow is believed to be the favourite tree of ghosts. Thereunder, 'tis said, they mourn in the night, mingling their shadowy hair with the long dishevelled tresses of the tree.

Tradition says that Okyo Maruyama was the first Japanese artist who drew a ghost. The Shōgun, having invited him to his palace, said: 'Make a picture of a ghost for me'. Ōkyo promised to do so; but he was puzzled how to execute the order satisfactorily. A few days later, hearing that one of his aunts was very ill, he visited her. She was so emaciated that she looked like one already long dead. As he watched by her bedside, a ghastly inspiration came to him: he drew the fleshless face and long dishevelled hair, and created from that hasty sketch a ghost that surpassed all the Shōgun's expectations. Afterwards Ōkyo became very famous as a painter of ghosts.

Japanese ghosts are always represented as diaphanous, and preternaturally tall - only the upper part of the figure being distinctly outlined, and the lower part fading utterly away. As the Japanese say, 'a ghost has no feet'. Its appearance is like an exhalation, which becomes visible only at a certain distance above the ground; and it wavers and lengthens and undulates in the conceptions of artists, like a vapour moved by wind. Occasionally phantom women figure in picture-books in the likeness of living women; but these are not true ghosts. They are fox-women or other goblins; and their supernatural character is suggested by a peculiar expression of the eyes and a certain impossible elfish grace.

Little children in Japan, like little children in all countries, keenly enjoy the pleasure of fear; and they have many games in which such pleasure forms the chief attraction. Among these is *O-bake-goto*, or Ghost-play. Some nurse-girl or elder sister loosens her hair in front, so as to let it fall over her face, and pursues the little folk with moans and weird gestures, miming all the attitudes of the ghosts of the picture-books.

8

As the hair of the Japanese woman is her richest ornament, it is of all her possessions that which she would most suffer to lose; and in other days the man too manly to kill an erring wife deemed it vengeance enough to turn her away with all her hair shorn off. Only the greatest faith or the deepest love can prompt a woman to the voluntary sacrifice of her entire *chevelure*, though partial sacrifices, offerings of one or two long thick cuttings, may be seen suspended before many an Izumo shrine.

What faith can do in the way of such sacrifice, he best knows who has seen the great cables, woven of women's hair, that hang in the vast Hongwanji temple at Kyoto. And love is stronger than faith, though much less demonstrative. According to ancient custom a wife bereaved sacrifices a portion of her hair to be placed in the coffin of her husband, and buried with him. The quantity is not fixed: in the majority of cases it is very small, so that the appearance of the coiffure is thereby nowise affected. But she who resolves to remain forever loyal to the memory of the lost yields up all. With her own hand she cuts off her hair, and lays the whole glossy sacrifice - emblem of her youth and beauty - upon the knees of the dead.

It is never suffered to grow again.

Footnotes:

1. Formerly both sexes used the same pillow for the same reason. The long hair of a samurai youth, tied up in an elaborate knot, required much time to arrange. Since it has become the almost universal custom to wear the hair short, the men have adopted a pillow shaped like a small bolster.

2. It is an error to suppose that all Japanese have blue-black hair. There are two distinct racial types. In one the hair is a deep brown instead of a pure black, and is also softer and finer. Rarely, but very rarely, one may see a Japanese *chevelure* having a natural tendency to ripple. For curious reasons, which cannot be stated here, an Izumo woman is very much ashamed of having wavy hair - more ashamed than she would be of a natural deformity.

3. Even in the time of the writing of the *Kojiki* the art of arranging the hair must have been somewhat developed. See Professor Chamberlain's introduction to translation, p. xxxi.; also vol. i. section ix.; vol. vii. section xii.; vol. ix. section xviii., *et passim*.

4. An art expert can decide the age of an unsigned kakemono or other work of art in which human figures appear, by the style of the coiffure of the female personages.

5. The principal and indispensable hair-pin (*kanzashi*), usually about seven inches long, is split, and its well-tempered double shaft can be used like a small pair of chopsticks for picking up small things. The head is terminated by a tiny spoon-shaped projection, which has a special purpose in the Japanese toilette.

6. The *shinjōchō* is also called *Ichōgaeshi* by old people, although the original *Ichōgaeshi* was somewhat different. The samurai girls used to wear their hair in the true *Ichōgaeshi* manner; the name is derived from the ichō-tree (*Salisburia andiantifolia*), whose leaves have a queer shape, almost like that of a duck's foot. Certain bands of the hair in this coiffure bore a resemblance in form to ichō-leaves.

7. The old Japanese mirrors were made of metal, and were extremely beautiful. *Kagami ga kumoru to tamashii ga kumoru* ('When the Mirror is dim, the Soul is unclean') is another curious proverb relating to mirrors. Perhaps the most beautiful and touching story of a mirror in any language is that called '*Matsuyama-no-kagami*', which has been translated by Mrs James.

Of A Dancing-Girl

Nothing is more silent than the beginning of a Japanese banquet; and no one, except a native, who observes the opening scene could possibly imagine the tumultuous ending.

The robed guests take their places, quite noiselessly and without speech, upon the kneeling-cushions. The lacquered services are laid upon the matting before them by maidens whose bare feet make no sound. For a while there is only smiling and flitting, as in dreams. You are not likely to hear any voices from without, as a banqueting-house is usually secluded from the street by spacious gardens. At last the master of ceremonies, host or provider, breaks the hush with the consecrated formula: '*O-somatsu degozarimasu ga! - dōzo o-hashi*'! whereat all present bow silently, take up their *hashi* (chopsticks). and fall to. But *hashi*, deftly used, cannot be heard at all. The maidens pour warm sake into the cup of each guest without making the least sound; and it is not until several dishes have been emptied, and several cups of sake absorbed, that tongues are loosened.

Then, all at once, with a little burst of laughter, a number of young girls enter, make the customary prostration of greeting, glide into the open space between the ranks of the guests and begin to serve the wine with a grace and dexterity of which no common maid is capable. They are pretty; they are clad in very costly robes of silk; they are girdled like queens; and the beautifully dressed hair of each is decked with mock flowers, with wonderful combs and pins, and with curious ornaments of gold. They greet the stranger as if they had always known him; they jest, laugh, and utter funny little cries. These are the *geisha*,[1] or dancing-girls, hired for the banquet.

Samisen[2] tinkle. The dancers withdraw to a clear space at the farther end of the banqueting-hall, always vast enough to admit of many more guests than ever assemble upon common occasions. Some form the orchestra, under the direction of a woman of uncertain age; there are several *samisen*, and a tiny drum played by a child. Others, singly or in pairs, perform the dance. It may be swift and merry, consisting wholly of graceful posturing - two girls dancing together with such coincidence of step and gesture as only years of training could render possible. But more frequently it is rather like acting than like what we Occidentals call dancing - acting accompanied with extraordinary waving of sleeves and fans, and with a play of eyes and features, sweet, subtle, subdued, wholly Oriental. There are more voluptuous dances known to *geisha*, but upon ordinary occasions and before refined audiences they portray beautiful old Japanese traditions, like the legend of the fisher Urashima, beloved by the Sea God's daughter; and at intervals they sing ancient Chinese poems, expressing a natural emotion with delicious vividness by a few exquisite words. And always they pour the wine - that warm, pale yellow, drowsy wine which fills the veins with soft contentment, making a faint sense of ecstasy, through which, as through some poppied sleep, the commonplace becomes wondrous and blissful, and the *geisha* Maids of Paradise, and the world much sweeter than, in the natural order of things, it could ever possibly be.

The banquet, at first so silent, slowly changes to a merry tumult. The company break ranks, form groups; and from group to group the girls pass, laughing, prattling - still pouring *saké* into the cups which are being exchanged and emptied with low bows.[3] Men begin to sing old *samurai* songs, old Chinese poems. One or two even dance. A *geisha* tucks her robe well up to her knees; and the *samisen* strike up the quick melody, '*Kompira funé-funé*'. As the music plays, she begins to run lightly and swiftly in a figure of eight, and a young man, carrying a *saké* bottle and cup, also runs in the same figure of eight. If the two meet on a line, the one through whose error the meeting happens must drink a cup of *saké*. The music becomes quicker and quicker and the runners run faster and faster, for they must keep time to the melody; and the *geisha* wins. In another part of the room, guests and *geisha* are playing *ken*. They sing as they play, facing each other, and clap their hands, and fling out their fingers at intervals with little cries; and the *samisen* keep time.

Choito - don-don! Otagaidané; Choito - don-don! Oidemashitané; Choito - don-don! Shimaimashitané.

Now, to play *ken* with a *geisha* requires a perfectly cool head, a quick eye, and much practice. Having been trained from childhood to play all kinds of *ken* - and there are many - she generally loses only for politeness, when she loses at all. The signs of the most common *ken* are a Man, a Fox, and a Gun. If the *geisha* makes the sign of the Gun, you must instantly, and in exact time to the music, make the sign of the Fox, who cannot use the Gun. For if you make the sign of the Man, then she will answer with the sign of the Fox, who can deceive the Man, and you lose. And if she make the sign of the Fox first, then you should make the sign of the Gun, by which the Fox can be killed. But all the while you must watch her bright eyes and supple hands. These are pretty; and if you suffer yourself, just for one fraction of a second, to think how pretty they are, you are bewitched and vanquished.

Notwithstanding all this apparent comradeship, a certain rigid decorum between guest and *geisha* is invariably preserved at a Japanese banquet. However flushed with wine a guest may have become, you will never see him attempt to caress a girl; he never forgets that she appears at the festivities only as a human flower, to be looked at, not to be touched. The familiarity which foreign tourists in Japan frequently permit themselves with *geisha* or with waiter-girls, though endured with smiling patience, is really much disliked, and considered by native observers an evidence of extreme vulgarity.

For a time the merriment grows; but as midnight draws near, the guests begin to slip away, one by one, unnoticed. Then the din gradually dies down, the music stops; and at last the *geisha*, having escorted the latest of the feasters to the door, with laughing cries of *sayonara*, can sit down alone to break their long fast in the deserted hall.

Such is the *geisha*'s rôle. But what is the mystery of her? What are her thoughts, her emotions, her secret self? What is her veritable existence beyond the night circle of the banquet lights, far from the illusion formed around her by the mist of wine? Is she always as mischievous as she seems while her voice ripples out with mocking sweetness the words of the ancient song?

> *Kimi to neyaru ka, go sengoku toruka?*
> *Nanno gosengoku kimi to neyo?*[4]

Or might we think her capable of keeping that passionate promise she utters so deliciously?

> *Omae shindara tera ewa yaranu!*
> *Yaete konishite sake de nomu.*[5]

'Why, as for that', a friend tells me, 'there was O-Kama of Osaka who realised the song only last year. For she, having collected from the funeral pile the ashes of her lover, mingled them with sake, and at a banquet drank them, in the presence of many guests.' In the presence of many guests! Alas for romance!

Always in the dwelling which a band of *geisha* occupy there is a strange image placed in the alcove. Sometimes it is of clay, rarely of gold, most commonly of porcelain. It is reverenced: offerings are made to it, sweetmeats and rice bread and wine; incense smoulders in front of it, and a lamp is burned before it. It is the image of a kitten erect, one paw outstretched as if inviting - whence its name, 'the Beckoning Kitten'.[6] It is the *genius loci*: it brings good fortune, the patronage of the rich, the favour of banquet-givers. Now, they who know the soul of the *geisha* aver that the semblance of the image is the semblance of herself - playful and pretty, soft and young, lithe and caressing, and cruel as a devouring fire.

Worse, also, than this they have said of her: that in her shadow treads the God of Poverty, and that the Fox-women are her sisters; that she is the ruin of youth, the waster of fortunes, the destroyer of families; that she knows love only as the source of the follies which are her gain, and grows rich upon the substance of men whose graves she has made; that she is the most consummate of pretty hypocrites, the most dangerous of schemers, the most insatiable of mercenaries, the most pitiless of mistresses. This cannot all be true. Yet thus much is true - that, like the kitten, the *geisha* is by profession a creature of prey. There are many really lovable kittens. Even so there must be really delightful dancing-girls.

The *geisha* is only what she has been made in answer to foolish human desire for the illusion of love mixed with youth and grace, but without regrets or responsibilities: wherefore she has been taught, besides *ken*, to play at hearts. Now, the eternal law is that people may play with impunity at any game in this unhappy world except three, which are called Life, Love, and Death. Those the gods have reserved to themselves, because nobody else can learn to play them without doing mischief. Therefore, to play with a *geisha* any game much more serious than *ken*, or at least *go*, is displeasing to the gods.

The girl begins her career as a slave, a pretty child bought from miserably poor parents under a contract according to which her services may be claimed by the purchasers for eighteen, twenty, or even twenty-five years. She is fed, clothed, and trained in a house occupied only by *geisha*; and she passes the rest of her childhood under severe descipline. She is taught etiquette, grace, polite speech; she has daily lessons in dancing; and she is obliged to learn by heart a multitude of songs with their airs. Also she must learn games, the service of banquets and weddings, the art of dressing and looking beautiful. Whatever physical gifts she may have are carefully cultivated. Afterwards she is taught to handle musical instruments: first, the little drum (*tsudzumi*), which cannot besounded at all without considerable practice; then she learns to play the *samisen* a little, with a plectrum of tortoise-shell or ivory. At eight or nine years of age she attends banquets, chiefly as a drum-player. She is then the most charming little creature imaginable, and already knows how to fill your wine-cup exactly full, with a single toss of the bottle and without spilling a drop, between two taps of her drum.

Thereafter her discipline becomes more cruel. Her voice may be flexible enough, but lacks the requisite strength. In the iciest hours of winter nights, she must ascend to the roof of her dwelling-house, and there sing and play till the blood oozes from her fingers and the voice dies in her throat. The desired result is an atrocious cold. After a period of hoarse whispering, her voice changes its tone and strengthens. She is ready to become a public singer and dancer.

In this capacity she usually makes her first appearance at the age of twelve or thirteen. If pretty and skilful, her services will be much in demand, and her time paid for at the rate of twenty to twenty-five sen per hour. Then only do her purchasers begin to reimburse themselves for the time, expense, and trouble of her training; and they are not apt to be generous. For many years more, all that she earns must pass into their hands. She can own nothing, not even her clothes.

At seventeen or eighteen she has made her artistic reputation. She has been at many hundreds of entertainments, and knows by sight all the important personages of her city, the character of each, the history of all. Her life has been chiefly a night life; rarely has she seen the sun rise since she became a dancer. She has learned to drink wine without ever losing her head, and to fast for seven or eight hours without ever feeling the worse. She has had many lovers. To a certain extent she is free to smile upon whom she pleases; but she has been well taught, above all else to use her power of charm for her own advantage. She hopes to find Somebody able and willing to buy her freedom - which Somebody would almost certainly thereafter discover many new and excellent meanings in those Buddhist texts that tell about the foolishness of love and the impermanency of all human relationships.

At this point of her career we may leave the *geisha*: thereafter her story is apt to prove unpleasant, unless she die young. Should that happen, she will have the obsequies of her class, and her memory will be preserved by divers curious rites.

Some time, perhaps, while wandering through Japanese streets at night, you hear sounds of music, a tinkling of *samisen* floating through the great gateway of a Buddhist temple, together with shrill voices of singing-girls; which may seem to you a strange happening. And the deep court is thronged with people looking and listening. Then, making your way through the press to the temple steps, you see two *geisha* seated upon the matting within, playing and singing, and a third dancing before a little table. Upon the table is an *ihai*, or mortuary tablet: in front of the tablet burns a little lamp, and incense in a cup of bronze; a small repast has been placed there, fruits and dainties - such a repast as, upon festival occasions, it is the custom to offer to the dead. You learn that the *kaimyō* upon the tablet is that of a *geisha*; and that the comrades of the dead girl assemble in the temple on certain days to gladden her spirit with songs and dances. Then whosoever pleases may attend the ceremony free of charge....

Footnotes:

1. The Kyoto word is *maiko*.
2. Guitars of three strings.
3. It is sometimes customary for guests to exchange cups, after duly rinsing them. It is always a compliment to ask for your friend's cup.
4. 'Once more to rest beside her, or keep five thousand *koku*? What care I for *koku*? Let me be with her!'
   There lived in ancient times a *hatamoto* called Fuji-eda Geki, a vassal of the Shōgun. He had an income of five thousand *koku* of rice, a great income in those days. But he fell in love with an inmate of the Yoshiwara, named Ayaginu, and wished to marry her. When his master bade the vassal choose between his fortune and his passion, the lovers fled secretly to a farmer's house, and there committed suicide together. And the above song was made about them. It is still sung.
5. 'Dear, shouldst thou die, grave shall hold thee never! I thy body's ashes, mixed with wine, will drink.'
6. Maneki-Neko.

The Japanese Smile

...One of my Yokohama friends - a thoroughly lovable man, who had passed more than half his life in the open ports of the East - said to me, just before my departure for the interior: 'Since you are going to study Japanese life, perhaps you will be able to find out something for me. I *can't* understand the Japanese smile. Let me tell you one experience out of many. One day, as I was driving down from the Bluff, I saw an empty *kuruma* coming up on the wrong side of the curve. I could not have pulled up in time if I had tried; but I didn't try, because I didn't think there was any particular danger. I only yelled to the man in Japanese to get to the other side of the road; instead of which he simply backed his *kuruma* against a wall on the lower side of the curve, with the shafts outwards. At the rate I was going, there wasn't room even to swerve; and the next minute one of the shafts of that *kuruma* was in my horse's shoulder. The man wasn't hurt at all. When I saw the way my horse was bleeding, I quite lost my temper, and struck the man over the head with the butt of my whip. He looked right into my face and smiled, and then bowed. I can see that smile now. I felt as if I had been knocked down. The smile utterly nonplussed me - killed all my anger instantly. Mind you, it was a polite smile. But what did it mean? Why the devil did the man smile? I can't understand it.'

Neither, at that time, could I; but the meaning of much more mysterious smiles has since been revealed to me. A Japanese can smile in the teeth of death, and usually does. But he then smiles for the same reason that he smiles at other times. There is neither defiance nor hypocrisy in the smile; nor is it to be confounded with that smile of sickly resignation which we are apt to associate with weakness of character. It is an elaborate and long-cultivated etiquette. It is also a silent language. But any effort to interpret it according to Western notions of physiognomical expression would be just about as successful as an attempt to interpret Chinese ideographs by their real or fancied resemblance to shapes of familiar things.

First impressions, being largely instinctive, are scientifically recognised as partly trustworthy; and the very first impression produced by the Japanese smile is not far from the truth. The stranger cannot fail to notice the generally happy and smiling character of the native faces; and this first impression is, in most cases, wonderfully pleasant. The Japanese smile at first charms. It is only at a later day, when one has observed the same smile under extraordinary circumstances - in moments of pain, shame, disappointment - that one becomes suspicious of it. Its apparent inopportuneness may even, on certain occasions, cause violent anger. Indeed, many of the difficulties between foreign residents and their native servants have been due to the smile. Any man who believes in the British tradition that a good servant must be solemn is not likely to endure with patience the smile of his 'boy'. At present, however, this particular phase of Western eccentricity is becoming more fully recognised by the Japanese; they are beginning to learn that the average English-speaking foreigner hates smiling, and is apt to consider it insulting; wherefore Japanese employees at the open ports have generally ceased to smile, and have assumed an air of sullenness.

At this moment there comes to me the recollection of a queer story told by a lady of Yokohama about one of her Japanese servants. 'My Japanese nurse came to me the other day, smiling as if something very pleasant had happened, and said that her husband was dead, and that she wanted permission to attend his funeral. I told her she could go. It seems they burned the man's body. Well, in the evening she returned, and showed me a vase containing some ashes of bones (I saw a tooth among them); and she said: "That is my husband". And she actually *laughed* as she said it! Did you ever hear of such disgusting creatures?'

It would have been quite impossible to convince the narrator of this incident that the demeanour of her servant, instead of being heartless, might have been heroic, and capable of a very touching interpretation. Even one not a Philistine might be deceived in such a case by appearances. But quite a number of the foreign residents of the open ports are pure Philistines, and never try to look below the surface of the life around them, except as hostile critics. My Yokohama friend who told me the story about the *kurumaya* was quite differently disposed: he recognised the error of judging by appearances.

2

Miscomprehension of the Japanese smile has more than once led to extremely unpleasant results, as happened in the case of T-, a Yokohama merchant of former days. T- had employed in some capacity (I think partly as a teacher of Japanese) a nice old *samurai*, who wore, according to the fashion of the era, a queue and two swords. The English and the Japanese do not understand each other very well now; but at the period in question they understood each other much less. The Japanese servants at first acted in foreign employ precisely as they would have acted in the service of distinguished Japanese;[1] and this innocent mistake provoked a good deal of abuse and cruelty. Finally the discovery was made that to treat Japanese like West Indian negroes might be very dangerous. A certain number of foreigners were killed, with good moral consequences.

But I am digressing. T- was rather pleased with his old *samurai*, though quite unable to understand his Oriental politeness, his prostrations, or the meaning of the small gifts which he presented occasionally, with an exquisite courtesy entirely wasted upon T-. One day he came to ask a favour. (I think it was the eve of the Japanese New Year, when everybody needs money, for reasons not here to be dwelt upon.) The favour was that T- would lend him a little money upon one of his swords, the long one. It was a very beautiful weapon, and the merchant saw that it was also very valuable, and lent the money without hesitation. Some weeks later the old man was able to redeem his sword.

What caused the beginning of the subsequent unpleasantness nobody now remembers. Perhaps T-'s nerves got out of order. At all events, one day he became very angry with the old man, who submitted to the expression of his wrath with bows and smiles. This made him still more angry, and he used some extremely bad language; but the old man still bowed and smiled; wherefore he was ordered to leave the house. But the old man continued to smile, at which T-, losing all self-control, struck him. And then T- suddenly became afraid, for the long sword instantly leaped from its sheath, and swirled above him; and the old man ceased to seem old. Now, in the grasp of anyone who knows how to use it, the razor-edged blade of a Japanese sword wielded with both hands can take a head off with extreme facility. But, to T-'s astonishment, the old *samurai*, almost in the same moment, returned the blade to its sheath with the skill of a practised swordsman, turned upon his heel, and withdrew.

Then T- wondered, and sat down to think. He began to remember some nice things about the old man - the many kindnesses unasked and unpaid, the curious little gifts, the impeccable honesty. T- began to feel ashamed. He tried to console himself with the thought: 'Well, it was his own fault; he had no right to laugh at me when he knew I was angry'. Indeed, T- even resolved to make amends when an opportunity should offer.

But no opportunity ever came, because on the same evening the old man performed *hara-kiri*, after the manner of a *samurai* . He left a very beautifully written letter explaining his reasons. For a samurai to receive an unjust blow without avenging it was a shame not to be borne. He had received such a blow. Under any other circumstances he might have avenged it. But the circumstances were, in this instance, of a very peculiar kind. His code of honour forbade him to use his sword upon the man to whom he had pledged it once for money, in an hour of need. And being thus unable to use his sword, there remained for him only the alternative of an honourable suicide.

In order to render this story less disagreeable, the reader may suppose that T- was really very sorry, and behaved generously to the family of the old man. What he must not suppose is that T- was ever able to imagine why the old man had smiled the smile which led to the outrage and the tragedy.

3

To comprehend the Japanese smile, one must be able to enter a little into the ancient, natural, and popular life of Japan. From the modernised upper classes nothing is to be learned. The deeper signification of race differences is being daily more and more illustrated in the effects of the higher education. Instead of creating any community of feeling, it appears only to widen the distance between the Occidental and the Oriental. Some foreign observers have declared that it does this by enormously developing certain latent peculiarities - among others an inherent materialism little perceptible among the common people. This explanation is one I cannot quite agree with; but it is at least undeniable that, the more highly he is cultivated, according to Western methods, the farther is the Japanese psychologically removed from us. Under the new education, his character seems to crystallise into something of singular hardness, and to Western observation, at least, of singular opacity. Emotionally, the Japanese child appears incomparably closer to us than the Japanese mathematician, the peasant than the statesman. Between the most elevated class of thoroughly modernised Japanese and the Western thinker anything akin to intellectual sympathy is non-existent: it is replaced on the native side by a cold and faultless politeness. Those influences which in other lands appear most potent to develop the higher emotions seem here to have the extraordinary effect of suppressing them. We are accustomed abroad to associate emotional sensibility with intellectual expansion: it would be a grievous error to apply this rule in Japan. Even the foreign teacher in an ordinary school can feel, year by year, his pupils drifting farther away from him, as they pass from class to class; in various higher educational institutions, the separation widens yet more rapidly, so that, prior to graduation, students may become to their professor little more than casual acquaintances. The enigma is perhaps, to some extent, a physiological one, requiring scientific explanation; but its solution must first be sought in ancestral habits of life and of imagination. It can be fully discussed only when its natural causes are understood; and these, we may be sure, are not simple. By some observers it is asserted that because the higher education in Japan has not yet had the effect of stimulating the higher emotions to the Occidental pitch, its developing power cannot have been exerted uniformly and wisely, but in special directions only, at the cost of character. Yet this theory involves the unwarrantable assumption that character can be created by education; and it ignores the fact that the best results are obtained by affording opportunity for the exercise of pre-existing inclination rather than by any system of teaching.

The causes of the phenomenon must be looked for in the race character; and whatever the higher education may accomplish in the remote future, it can scarcely be expected to transform nature. But does it at present atrophy certain finer tendencies? I think that it unavoidably does, for the simple reason that, under existing conditions, the moral and mental powers are overtasked by its requirements. All that wonderful national spirit of duty, of patience, of self-sacrifice, anciently directed to social, moral, or religious idealism, must, under the discipline of the higher training, be concentrated upon an end which not only demands, but exhausts its fullest exercise. For that end, to be accomplished at all, must be accomplished in the face of difficulties that the Western student rarely encounters, and could scarcely be made even to understand. All those moral qualities which made the old Japanese character admirable are certainly the same which make the modern Japanese student the most indefatigable, the most docile, the most ambitious in the world. But they are also qualities which urge him to efforts in excess of his natural powers, with the frequent result of mental and moral enervation. The nation has entered upon a period of intellectual overstrain. Consciously or unconsciously, in obedience to sudden necessity, Japan has undertaken nothing less than the tremendous task of forcing mental expansion up to the highest existing standard; and this means forcing the development of the nervous system. For the desired intellectual change, to be accomplished within a few generations, must involve a physiological change never to be effected without terrible cost. In other words, Japan has attempted too much; yet under the circumstances she could not have attempted less. Happily, even among the poorest of her poor the educational policy of the government is seconded with an astonishing zeal; the entire nation has plunged into study with a fervour of which it is utterly impossible to convey any adequate conception in this little essay. Yet I may cite a touching example. Immediately after the frightful earthquake of 1891, the children of the ruined cities of Gifu and Aichi, crouching among the ashes of their homes, cold and hungry and shelterless, surrounded by horror and misery unspeakable, still continued their small studies, using tiles of their own burnt dwellings in lieu of slates, and bits of lime for chalk, even while the earth still trembled beneath them.[2] What future miracles may justly be expected from the amazing power of purpose such a fact reveals!

But it is true that as yet the results of the higher training have not been altogether happy. Among the Japanese of the old regime one encounters a courtesy, an unselfishness, a grace of pure goodness, impossible to overpraise. Among the modernised of the new generation these have almost disappeared. One meets a class of young men who ridicule the old times and the old ways without having been able to elevate themselves above the vulgarism of imitation and the commonplaces of shallow scepticism. What has become of the noble and charming qualities they must have inherited from their fathers? Is it not possible that the best of those qualities have been transmuted into more effort - an effort so excessive as to have exhausted character, leaving it without weight or balance?

It is to the still fluid, mobile, natural existence of the common people that one must look for the meaning of some apparent differences in the race feeling and emotional expression of the West and the Far East. With those gentle, kindly, sweet-hearted folk, who smile at life, love, and death alike, it is possible to enjoy community of feeling in simple, natural things; and by familiarity and sympathy we can learn why they smile.

The Japanese child is born with this happy tendency, which is fostered through all the period of home education. But it is cultivated with the same exquisiteness that is shown in the cultivation of the natural tendencies of a garden plant. The smile is taught like the bow; like the prostration; like that little sibilant sucking-in of the breath which follows, as a token of pleasure, the salutation to a superior; like all the elaborate and beautiful etiquette of the old courtesy. Laughter is not encouraged, for obvious reasons. But the smile is to be used upon all pleasant occasions, when speaking to a superior or to an equal, and even upon occasions which are not pleasant; it is a part of deportment. The most agreeable face is the smiling face; and to present always the most agreeable face possible to parents, relatives, teachers, friends, well-wishers, is a rule of life. And furthermore, it is a rule of life to turn constantly to the outer world a mien of happiness, to convey to others as far as possible a pleasant impression. Even though the heart is breaking, it is a social duty to smile bravely. On the other hand, to look serious or unhappy is rude, because this may cause anxiety or pain to those who love us; it is likewise foolish, since it may excite unkindly curiosity on the part of those who love us not. Cultivated from childhood as a duty, the smile soon becomes instinctive. In the mind of the poorest peasant lives the conviction that to exhibit the expression of one's personal sorrow or pain or anger is rarely useful, and always unkind. Hence, although natural grief must have, in Japan as elsewhere, its natural issue, an uncontrollable burst of tears in the presence of superiors or guests is an impoliteness; and the first words of even the most unlettered country woman, after the nerves give way in such a circumstance, are invariably: 'Pardon my selfishness in that I have been so rude'! The reasons for the smile, be it also observed, are not only moral; they are to some extent aesthetic; they partly represent the same idea which regulated the expression of suffering in Greek art. But they are much more moral than aesthetic, as we shall presently observe.

From this primary etiquette of the smile there has been developed a secondary etiquette, the observance of which has frequently impelled foreigners to form the most cruel misjudgements as to Japanese sensibility.

It is the native custom that whenever a painful or shocking fact *must* be told, the announcement should be made, by the sufferer, with a smile.[3] The graver the subject, the more accentuated the smile; and when the matter is very unpleasant to the person speaking of it, the smile often changes to a low, soft laugh. However bitterly the mother who has lost her first-born may have wept at the funeral, it is probable that, if in your service, she will tell of her bereavement with a smile: like the preacher, she holds that there is a time to weep and a time to laugh. It was long before I myself could understand how it was possible for those whom I believed to have loved a person recently dead to announce to me that death with a laugh. Yet the laugh was politeness carried to the utmost point of self-abnegation. It signified: 'This you might honourably think to be an unhappy event; pray do not suffer Your Superiority to feel concern about so inferior a matter, and pardon the necessity which causes us to outrage politeness by speaking about such an affair at all.'

The key to the mystery of the most unaccountable smiles is Japanese politeness. The servant sentenced to dismissal for a fault prostrates himself, and asks for pardon with a smile. That smile indicates the very reverse of callousness or insolence: 'Be assured that I am satisfied with the great justice of your honourable sentence, and that I am now aware of the gravity of my fault. Yet my sorrow and my necessity have caused me to indulge the unreasonable hope that I may be forgiven for my great rudeness in asking pardon.' The youth or girl beyond the age of childish tears, when punished for some error, receives the punishment with a smile which means: 'No evil feeling arises in my heart; much worse than this my fault has deserved'. And the *kurumaya* cut by the whip of my Yokohama friend smiled for a similar reason, as my friend must have intuitively felt, since the smile at once disarmed him: 'I was very wrong, and you are right to be angry: I deserve to be struck, and therefore feel no resentment'.

But it should be understood that the poorest and humblest Japanese is rarely submissive under injustice. His apparent docility is due chiefly to his moral sense. The foreigner who strikes a native for sport may have reason to find that he has made a serious mistake. The Japanese are not to be trifled with; and brutal attempts to trifle with them have cost several worthless lives.

Even after the foregoing explanations, the incident of the Japanese nurse may still seem incomprehensible; but this, I feel quite sure, is because the narrator either suppressed or overlooked certain facts in the case. In the first half of the story, all is perfectly clear. When announcing her husband's death, the young servant smiled, in accordance with the native formality already referred to. What is quite incredible is that, of her own accord, she should have invited the attention of her mistress to the contents of the vase, or funeral urn. If she knew enough of Japanese politeness to smile in announcing her husband's death, she must certainly have known enough to prevent her from perpetrating such an error. She could have shown the vase and its contents only in obedience to some real or fancied command; and when so doing, it is more than possible she may have uttered the low, soft laugh which accompanies either the unavoidable performance of a painful duty, or the enforced utterance of a painful statement. My own opinion is that she was obliged to gratify a wanton curiosity. Her smile or laugh would then have signified: 'Do not suffer your honourable feelings to be shocked upon my unworthy account; it is indeed very rude of me, even at your honourable request to mention so contemptible a thing as my sorrow.'

4

But the Japanese smile must not be imagined as a kind of *sourire figé*, worn perpetually as a soul-mask. Like other matters of deportment, it is regulated by an etiquette which varies in different classes of society. As a rule, the old samurai were not given to smiling upon all occasions; they reserved their amiability for superiors and intimates, and would seem to have maintained towards inferiors an austere reserve. The dignity of the Shinto priesthood has become proverbial; and for centuries the gravity of the Confucian code was mirrored in the decorum of magistrates and officials. From ancient times the nobility affected a still loftier reserve; and the solemnity of rank deepened through all the hierarchies up to that awful state surrounding the Tenshi-Sama, upon whose face no living man might look. But in private life the demeanour of the highest had its amiable relaxation; and even today, with some hopelessly modernised exceptions, the noble, the judge, the high priest, the august minister, the military officer, will resume at home, in the intervals of duty, the charming habits of the antique courtesy.

The smile which illuminates conversation is in itself but a small detail of that courtesy; but the sentiment which it symbolises certainly comprises the larger part. If you happen to have a cultivated Japanese friend who has remained in all things truly Japanese, whose character has remained untouched by the new egotism and by foreign influences, you will probably be able to study in him the particular social traits of the whole people - traits in his case exquisitely accentuated and polished. You will observe that, as a rule, he never speaks of himself, and that, in reply to searching personal questions, he will answer as vaguely and briefly as possible, with a polite bow of thanks. But, on the other hand, he will ask many questions about yourself; your opinions, your ideas, even trifling details of your daily life, appear to have deep interest for him; and you will probably have occasion to note that he never forgets anything which he has learned concerning you. Yet there are certain rigid limits to his kindly curiosity, and perhaps even to his observation: he will never refer to any disagreeable or painful matter, and he will seem to remain blind to eccentricities or small weaknesses, if you have any. To your face he will never praise you; but he will never laugh at you nor criticise you. Indeed, you will find that he never criticises persons, but only actions in their results. As a private adviser, he will not even directly criticise a plan of which he disapproves, but is apt to suggest a new one in some such guarded language as: 'Perhaps it might be more to your immediate interest to do thus and so'. When obliged to speak of others, he will refer to them in a curious indirect fashion, by citing and combining a number of incidents sufficiently characteristic to form a picture. But in that event the incidents narrated will almost certainly be of a nature to awaken interest, and to create a favourable impression. This indirect way of conveying information is essentially Confucian. 'Even when you have no doubts', says the Li-Ki, 'do not let what you say appear as your own view'. And it is quite probable that you will notice many other traits in your friend requiring some knowledge of the Chinese classics to understand. But no such knowledge is necessary to convince you of his exquisite consideration for others, and his studied suppression of self. Among no other civilised people is the secret of happy living so thoroughly comprehended as among the Japanese; by no other race is the truth so widely understood that our pleasure in life must depend upon the happiness of those about us, and consequently upon the cultivation in ourselves of unselfishness and of patience. For which reason, in Japanese society, sarcasm, irony, cruel wit, are not indulged. I might almost say that they have no existence in refined life. A personal failing is not made the subject of ridicule or reproach; an eccentricity is not commented upon; an involuntary mistake excites no laughter.

Stiffened somewhat by the Chinese conservatism of the old conditions it is true that this ethical system was maintained to the extreme of giving fixity to ideas, and at the cost of individuality. And yet, if regulated by a broader comprehension of social requirements, if expanded by scientific understanding of the freedom essential to intellectual evolution, the very same moral policy is that through which the highest and happiest results may be obtained. But as actually practised it was not favourable to originality; it rather tended to enforce that amiable mediocrity of opinion and imagination which still prevails. Wherefore a foreign dweller in the interior cannot but long sometimes for the sharp, erratic inequalities of Western life, with its larger joys and pains and its more comprehensive sympathies. But sometimes only, for the intellectual loss is really more than compensated by the social charm; and there can remain no doubt in the mind of one who even partly understands the Japanese, that they are still the best people in the world to live among....

Footnotes:

1. The reader will find it well worth his while to consult the chapter entitled 'Domestic Service', in Miss Bacon's *Japanese Girls and Women*, for an interesting and just presentation of the practical side of the subject, as relating to servants of both sexes. The poetical side, however, is not treated of - perhaps because intimately connected with religious beliefs which one writing from the Christian standpoint could not be expected to consider sympathetically. Domestic service in ancient Japan was both transfigured and regulated by religion; and the force of the religious sentiment concerning it may be divined from the Buddhist saying, still current:

> Oya-ko wa is-se,
> Fūfu wa ni-se,
> Shujū wa san-se.

The relation of parent and child endures for the space of one life only; that of husband and wife for the space of two lives; but the relation between master and servant continues for the period of three existences.
2. The shocks continued, though with lessening frequency and violence, for more than six months after the cataclysm.
3. Of course the converse is the rule in condoling with the sufferer.

JAPAN
PSYCHOLOGICAL

The Genius Of Japanese Civilisation

1

Without losing a single ship or a single battle, Japan has broken down the power of China, made a new Korea, enlarged her own territory, and changed the whole political face of the East. Astonishing as this has seemed politically, it is much more astonishing psychologically; for it represents the result of a vast play of capacities with which the race had never been credited abroad - capacities of a very high order. The psychologist knows that the so-called 'adoption of Western civilisation' within a time of thirty years cannot mean the addition to the Japanese brain of any organs or powers previously absent from it. He knows that it cannot mean any sudden change in the mental or moral character of the race. Such changes are not made in a generation. Transmitted civilisation works much more slowly, requiring even hundreds of years to produce certain permanent psychological results.

It is in this light that Japan appears the most extraordinary country in the world; and the most wonderful thing in the whole episode of her 'Occidentalisation' is that the race brain could bear so heavy a shock. Nevertheless, though the fact be unique in human history, what does it really mean? Nothing more than rearrangement of a part of the pre-existing machinery of thought. Even that, for thousands of brave young minds, was death. The adoption of Western civilisation was not nearly such an easy matter as unthinking persons imagined. And it is quite evident that the mental readjustments, effected at a cost which remains to be told, have given good results only along directions in which the race had always shown capacities of special kinds. Thus, the appliances of Western industrial invention have worked admirably in Japanese hands - have produced excellent results in those crafts at which the nation had been skilful, in other and quainter ways, for ages. There has been no transformation, nothing more than the turning of old abilities into new and larger channels. The scientific professions tell the same story. For certain forms of science, such as medicine, surgery (there are no better surgeons in the world than the Japanese), chemistry, microscopy, the Japanese genius is naturally adapted; and in all these it has done work already heard of round the world. In war and statecraft it has shown wonderful power; but throughout their history the Japanese have been characterised by great military and political capacity. Nothing remarkable has been done, however, in directions foreign to the national genius. In the study, for example, of Western music, Western art, Western literature, time would seem to have been simply wasted.[1] These things make appeal extraordinary to emotional life with us; they make no such appeal to Japanese emotional life. Every serious thinker knows that emotional transformation of the individual through education is impossible. To imagine that the emotional character of an Oriental race could be transformed in the short space of thirty years, by the contact of Occidental ideas, is absurd. Emotional life, which is older than intellectual life, and deeper, can no more be altered suddenly by a change of *milieu* than the surface of a mirror can be changed by passing reflections. All that Japan has been able to do so miraculously well has been done without any self-transformation; and those who imagine her emotionally closer to us today than she may have been thirty years ago ignore facts of science which admit of no argument.

Sympathy is limited by comprehension. We may sympathise to the same degree that we understand. One may imagine that he sympathises with a Japanese or a Chinese; but the sympathy can never be real to more than a small extent outside of the simplest phases of common emotional life - those phases in which child and man are at one. The more complex feelings of the Oriental have been composed by combinations of experiences, ancestral and individual, which have had no really precise correspondence in Western life, and which we can therefore not fully know. For converse reasons, the Japanese cannot, even though they would, give Europeans their best sympathy.

But while it remains impossible for the man of the West to discern the true colour of Japanese life, either intellectual or emotional (since the one is woven into the other), it is equally impossible for him to escape the conviction that, compared with his own, it is very small. It is dainty; it holds delicate potentialities of rarest interest and value; but it is otherwise so small that Western life, by contrast with it, seems almost supernatural. For we must judge visible and measurable manifestations. So judging, what a contrast between the emotional and intellectual worlds of West and East! Far less striking that between the frail wooden streets of the Japanese capital and the tremendous solidity of a thoroughfare in Paris or London. When one compares the utterances which West and East have given to their dreams, their aspirations, their sensations - a Gothic cathedral with a Shinto temple, an opera by Verdi or a trilogy by Wagner with a performance of *geisha*, a European epic with a Japanese poem - how incalculable the difference in emotional volume, in imaginative power, in artistic synthesis! True, our music is an essentially modern art; but in looking back through all our past the difference in creative force is scarcely less marked - not surely in the period of Roman magnificence, of marble amphitheatres and of aqueducts spanning provinces, nor in the Greek period of the divine in sculpture and of the supreme in literature.

And this leads to the subject of another wonderful fact in the sudden development of Japanese power. Where are the outward material signs of that immense new force she has been showing both in productivity and in war? Nowhere! That which we miss in her emotional and intellectual life is missing also from her industrial and commercial life - largeness! The land remains what it was before; its face has scarcely been modified by all the changes of Meiji. The miniature railway and telegraph poles, the bridges and tunnels, might almost escape notice in the ancient green of the landscapes. In all the cities, with the exception of the open ports and their little foreign settlements, there exists hardly a street vista suggesting the teaching of Western ideas. You might journey two hundred miles through the interior of the country, looking in vain for large manifestations of the new civilisation. In no place do you find commerce exhibiting its ambition in gigantic warehouses, or industry expanding its machinery under acres of roofing. A Japanese city is still, as it was ten centuries ago, little more than a wilderness of wooden sheds - picturesque, indeed, as paper lanterns are, but scarcely less frail. And there is no great stir and noise anywhere, no heavy traffic, no booming and rumbling, no furious haste. In Tokyo itself you may enjoy, if you wish, the peace of a country village. This want of visible or audible signs of the new-found force which is now menacing the markets of the West and changing the maps of the Far East gives one a queer, I might even say a weird feeling. It is almost the sensation received when, after climbing through miles of silence to reach some Shinto shrine, you find voidness only and solitude - an elfish, empty little wooden structure, mouldering in shadows a thousand years old. The strength of Japan, like the strength of her ancient faith, needs little material display: both exist where the deepest real power of any great people exists - in the Race Ghost.

2

As I muse, the remembrance of a great city comes back to me, a city walled up to the sky and roaring like the sea. The memory of that roar returns first; then the vision defines: a chasm, which is a street, between mountains, which are houses. I am tired, because I have walked many miles between those precipices of masonry, and have trodden no earth, only slabs of rock, and have heard nothing but thunder of tumult. Deep below those huge pavements I know there is a cavernous world tremendous: systems underlying systems of ways contrived for water and steam and fire. On either hand tower facades pierced by scores of tiers of windows, cliffs of architecture shutting out the sun. Above, the pale blue streak of sky is cut by a maze of spidery lines, an infinite cobweb of electric wires.

In that block on the right there dwell nine thousand souls; the tenants of the edifice facing it pay the annual rent of a million dollars. Seven millions scarcely covered the cost of those bulks overshadowing the square beyond - and there are miles of such. Stairways of steel and cement, of brass and stone, with costliest balustrades, ascend through the decades and double-decades of stories; but no foot treads them. By water-power, or steam, by electricity, men go up and down; the heights are too dizzy, the distances too great, for the use of the limbs. My friend who pays rent of five thousand dollars for his rooms in the fourteenth story of a monstrosity not far off has never trodden his stairway. I am walking forcuriosity alone; with a serious purpose I should not walk: the spaces are too broad, the time is too precious, for such slow exertion - men travel from district to district, from house to office, by steam. Heights are too great for the voice to traverse; orders are given and obeyed by machinery. By electricity far-away doors are opened; with one touch a hundred rooms are lighted or heated.

And all this enormity is hard, grim, dumb; it is the enormity of mathematical power applied to utilitarian ends of solidity and durability. These leagues of palaces, of warehouses, of business structures, of buildings describable and indescribable, are not beautiful, but sinister. One feels depressed by the mere sensation of the enormous life which created them, life without sympathy; of their prodigious manifestation of power, power without pity. They are the architectural utterance of the new industrial age. And there is no halt in the thunder of wheels, in the storm of the hoofs and of human feet. To ask a question, one must shout into the ear of the questioned; to see, to understand, to move in that high-pressure medium, needs experience. The unaccustomed feels the sensation of being in a panic, in a tempest, in a cyclone. Yet all this is order.

The monster streets leap rivers, span seaways, with bridges of stone, bridges of steel. Far as the eye can reach, a bewilderment of masts, a web-work of rigging, conceals the shores, which are cliffs of masonry. Trees in a forest stand less thickly, branches in a forest mingle less closely, than the masts and spars of that immeasurable maze. Yet all is order.

3

Generally speaking, we construct for endurance, the Japanese for impermanency. Few things for common use are made in Japan with a view to durability. The straw sandals worn out and replaced at each stage of a journey; the robe consisting of a few simple widths loosely stitched together for wearing, and unstitched again for washing; the fresh chopsticks served to each new guest at a hotel; the light *shōji* frames serving at once for windows and walls, and repapered twice a year; the mattings renewed every autumn - all these are but random examples of countless small things of daily life that illustrate the national contentment with impermanency.

What is the story of a common Japanese dwelling? Leaving my home in the morning, I observe, as I pass the corner of the next street crossing mine, some men setting up bamboo poles on a vacant lot there. Returning after five hours' absence, I find on the same lot the skeleton of a two-storey house. Next forenoon I see that the walls are nearly finished already - mud and wattles. By sun-down the roof has been completely tiled. On the following morning I observe that the mattings have been put down, and the inside plastering has been finished. In five days the house is completed. This, of course, is a cheap building; a fine one would take much longer to put up and finish. But Japanese cities are for the most part composed of such common buildings. They are as cheap as they are simple.

I cannot now remember where I first met with the observation that the curve of the Chinese roof might preserve the memory of the nomad tent. The idea haunted me long after I had ungratefully forgotten the book in which I found it; and when I first saw, in Izumo, the singular structure of the old Shinto temples, with queer cross-projections at their gable-ends and upon their roof-ridges, the suggestion of the forgotten essayist about the possible origin of much less ancient forms returned to me with great force. But there is much in Japan besides primitive architectural traditions to indicate a nomadic ancestry for the race. Always and everywhere there is a total absence of what we would call solidity; and the characteristics of impermanence seem to mark almost everything in the exterior life of the people, except, indeed, the immemorial costume of the peasant and the shape of the implements of his toil. Not to dwell upon the fact that even during the comparatively brief period of her written history Japan has had more than sixty capitals, of which the greater number have completely disappeared, it may be broadly stated that every Japanese city is rebuilt within the time of a generation. Some temples and a few colossal fortresses offer exceptions; but, as a general rule, the Japanese city changes its substance, if not its form, in the lifetime of a man. Fires, earthquakes, and many other causes partly account for this; the chief reason, however, is that houses are not built to last. The common people have no ancestral homes. The dearest spot to all is, not the place of birth, but the place of burial; and there is little that is permanent save the resting-places of the dead and the sites of the ancient shrines.

The land itself is a land of impermanence. Rivers shift their courses, coasts their outline, plains their level; volcanic peaks heighten or crumble; valleys are blocked by lava-floods or landslides; lakes appear and disappear. Even the matchless shape of Fuji, that snowy miracle which has been the inspiration of artists for centuries, is said to have been slightly changed since my advent to the country; and not a few other mountains have in the same short time taken totally new forms. Only the general lines of the land, the general aspects of its nature, the general character of the seasons, remain fixed. Even the very beauty of the landscapes is largely illusive - a beauty of shifting colours and moving mists. Only he to whom those landscapes are familiar can know how their mountain vapours make mockery of real changes which have been, and ghostly predictions of other changes yet to be, in the history of the archipelago.

The gods, indeed, remain - haunt their homes upon the hills, diffuse a soft religious awe through the twilight of their groves, perhaps because they are without form and substance. Their shrines seldom pass utterly into oblivion, like the dwellings of men. But every Shinto temple is necessarily rebuilt at more or less brief intervals; and the holiest - the shrine of Isé - in obedience to immemorial custom, must be demolished every twenty years, and its timbers cut into thousands of tiny charms, which are distributed to pilgrims.

From Aryan India, through China, came Buddhism, with its vast doctrine of impermanency. The builders of the first Buddhist temples in Japan - architects of another race - built well: witness the Chinese structures at Kamakura that have survived so many centuries, while of the great city which once surrounded them not a trace remains. But the psychical influence of Buddhism could in no land impel minds to the love of material stability. The teaching that the universe is an illusion; that life is but one momentary halt upon an infinite journey; that all attachment to persons, to places, or to things must be fraught with sorrow; that only through suppression of every desire - even the desire of Nirvana itself - can humanity reach the eternal peace, certainly harmonised with the older racial feeling. Though the people never much occupied themselves with the profounder philosophy of the foreign faith, its doctrine of impermanency must, in course of time, have profoundly influenced national character. It explained and consoled; it imparted new capacity to bear all things bravely; it strengthened that patience which is a trait of the race. Even in Japanese art - developed, if not actually created, under Buddhist influence - the doctrine of impermanency has left its traces. Buddhism taught that nature was a dream, an illusion, a phantasmagoria; but it also taught men how to seize the fleeting impressions of that dream, and how to interpret them in relation to the highest truth. And they learned well. In the flushed splendour of the blossom-bursts of spring, in the coming and the going of the cicadae, in the dying crimson of autumn foliage, in the ghostly beauty of snow, in the delusive motion of wave or cloud, they saw old parables of perpetual meaning. Even their calamities - fire, flood, earthquake, pestilence - interpreted to them unceasingly the doctrine of the eternal Vanishing.

All things which exist in Time must perish. The forests, the mountains - all things thus exist. In Time are born all things having desire.

The Sun and Moon, Sakra himself, with all the multitude of his attendants, will all, without exception, perish; there is not one that will endure.

In the beginning things were fixed; in the end again they separate: different combinations cause other substance; for in nature there is no uniform and constant principle.

All component things must grow old; impermanent are all component things. Even unto a grain of sesame seed there is no such thing as a compound which is permanent. All are transient; all have the inherent quality of dissolution.

All component things, without exception, are impermanent, unstable, despicable, sure to depart, disintegrating; all are temporary as a mirage, as a phantom, or as foam.... Even as all earthen vessels made by the potter end in being broken, so end the lives of men.

And a belief in matter itself is unmentionable and inexpressible - it is neither a thing nor no-thing: and this is known even by children and ignorant persons.

4

Now it is worthwhile to inquire if there be not some compensatory value attaching to this impermanency and this smallness in the national life.

Nothing is more characteristic of that life than its extreme fluidity. The Japanese population represents a medium whose particles are in perpetual circulation. The motion is in itself peculiar. It is larger and more eccentric than the motion of occidental populations, though feebler between points. It is also much more natural - so natural that it could not exist in Western civilisation. The relative mobility of a European population and the Japanese population might be expressed by a comparison between certain high velocities of vibration and certain low ones. But the high velocities would represent, in such a comparison, the consequence of artificial force applied; the slower vibrations would not. And this difference of kind would mean more than surface indications could announce. In once sense, Americans may be right in thinking themselves great travellers. In another, they are certainly wrong; the man of the people in America cannot compare, as a traveller, with the man of the people in Japan. And of course, in considering relative mobility of populations, one must consider chiefly the great masses, the workers - not merely the small class of wealth. In their own country, the Japanese are the greatest travellers of any civilised people. They are the greatest travellers because, even in a land composed mainly of mountain chains, they recognise no obstacles to travel. The Japanese who travels most is not the man who needs railways or steamers to carry him.

Now, with us, the common worker is incomparably less free than the common worker in Japan. He is less free because of the more complicated mechanism of Occidental societies, whose forces tend to agglomeration and solid integration. He is less free because the social and industrial machinery on which he must depend reshapes him to its own particular requirements, and always so as to evolve some special and artificial capacity at the cost of other inherent capacity. He is less free because he must live at a standard making it impossible for him to win financial independence by mere thrift. To achieve any such independence, he must possess exceptional character and exceptional faculties greater than those of thousands of exceptional competitors equally eager to escape from the same thraldom. In brief, then, he is less independent because the special character of his civilisation numbs his natural power to live without the help of machinery or large capital. To live thus artificially means to lose, sooner or later, the power of independent movement. Before a Western man can move he has many things to consider. Before a Japanese moves he has nothing to consider. He simply leaves the place he dislikes, and goes to the place he wishes, without any trouble. There is nothing to prevent him. Poverty is not an obstacle, but a stimulus. Impedimenta he has none, or only such as he can dispose of in a few minutes. Distances have no significance for him. Nature has given him perfect feet that can spring him over fifty miles a day without pain; a stomach whose chemistry can extract ample nourishmnent from food on which no European could live; and a constitution that scorns heat, cold, and damp alike, because still unimpaired by unhealthy clothing, by superfluous comforts, by the habit of seeking warmth from grates and stoves, and by the habit of wearing leather shoes.

It seems to me that the character of our footgear signifies more than is commonly supposed. The footgear represents in itself a check upon individual freedom. It signifies this even in costliness; but in form it signifies infinitely more. It has distorted the Western foot out of the original shape, and rendered it incapable of the work for which it was evolved. The physical results are not limited to the foot. Whatever acts as a check, directly or indirectly, upon the organs of locomotion must extend its effects to the whole physical constitution. Does the evil stop even there? Perhaps we submit to conventions the most absurd of any existing in any civilisation because we have too long submitted to the tyranny of shoemakers. There may be defects in our politics, in our social ethics, in our religious system, more or less related to the habit of wearing leather shoes. Submission to the cramping of the body must certainly aid in developing submission to the cramping of the mind.

The Japanese man of the people - the skilled labourer able to underbid without effort any Western artisan in the same line of industry - remains happily independent of both shoemakers and tailors. His feet are good to look at, his body is healthy, and his heart is free. If he desire to travel a thousand miles, he can get ready for his journey in five minutes. His whole outfit need not cost seventy-five cents; and all his baggage can be put into a handkerchief. On ten dollars he can travel simply on his ability to work, or he can travel as a pilgrim. You may reply that any savage can do the same thing. Yes, but any civilised man cannot; and the Japanese has been a highly civilised man for at least a thousand years. Hence his present capacity to threaten Western manufacturers.

We have been too much accustomed to associate this kind of independent mobility with the life of our own beggars and tramps, to have any just conception of its intrinsic meaning. We have thought of it also in connection with unpleasant things - uncleanliness and bad smells. But, as Professor Chamberlain has well said, 'a Japanese crowd is the sweetest in the world'. Your Japanese tramp takes his hot bath daily, if he has a fraction of a cent to pay for it, or his cold bath, if he has not. In his little bundle there are combs, toothpicks, razors, toothbrushes.

Ability to live without furniture, without impedimenta, with the least possible amount of neat clothing, shows more than the advantage held by this Japanese race in the struggle of life; it shows also the real character of some weaknesses in our own civilisation. It forces reflection upon the useless multiplicity of our daily wants. We must have meat and bread and butter; glass windows and fire; hats, white shirts, and woollen underwear; boots and shoes; trunks, bags, and boxes; bedsteads, mattresses, sheets, and blankets: all of which a Japanese can do without, and is really better off without. Think for a moment how important an article of Occidental attire is the single costly item of white shirts! Yet even the linen shirt, the so-called 'badge of a gentleman', is in itself a useless garment. It gives neither warmth nor comfort. It represents in our fashions the survival of something once a luxurious class distinction, but today meaningless and useless as the buttons sewn on the outside of coat-sleeves.

5

The absence of any huge signs of the really huge things that Japan has done bears witness to the very peculiar way in which her civilisation has been working. It cannot forever so work; but it has so worked thus far with amazing success. Japan is producing without capital, in our large sense of the word. She has become industrial without becoming essentially mechanical and artificial. The vast rice crop is raised upon millions of tiny, tiny farms; the silk crop, in millions of small poor homes; the tea crop, on countless little patches of soil. If you visit Kyoto to order something from one of the greatest porcelain makers in the world, one whose products are known better in London and in Paris than even in Japan, you will find the factory to be a wooden cottage in which no American farmer would live. The greatest maker of *cloisonné* vases, who may ask you two hundred dollars for something five inches high, produces his miracles behind a two-story frame dwelling containing perhaps six small rooms. The best girdles of silk made in Japan, and famous throughout the Empire, are woven in a house that cost scarcely five hundred dollars to build. The work is, of course, handwoven. But the factories weaving by machinery - and weaving so well as to ruin foreign industries of far vaster capacity - are hardly more imposing, with very few exceptions. Long, light, low one-storey or two-storey sheds they are, about as costly to erect as a row of wooden stables with us. Yet sheds like these turn out silks that sell all round the world. Sometimes only by inquiry, or by the humming of the machinery, can you distinguish a factory from an old *yashiki*, or an old-fashioned Japanese school building - unless indeed you can read the Chinese characters over the garden gate. Some big brick factories and breweries exist; but they are very few, and even when close to the foreign settlements they seem incongruities in the landscape.

Our own architectural monstrosities and our Babels of machinery have been brought into existence by vast integrations of industrial capital. But such integrations do not exist in the Far East; indeed, the capital to make them does not exist. And supposing that in the course of a few generations there should form in Japan corresponding combinations of money power, it is not easy to suppose correspondences in architectural construction. Even two-storey edifices of brick have given bad results in the leading commercial centre; and earthquakes seem to condemn Japan to perpetual simplicity in building. The very land revolts against the imposition of Western architecture and occasionally even opposes the new course of traffic by pushing railroad lines out of level and out of shape.

Not industry alone still remains thus unintegrated; government itself exhibits a like condition. Nothing is fixed except the Throne. Perpetual change is identical with state policy. Ministers, governors, superintendents, inspectors, all high civil and military officials, are shifted at irregular and surprisingly short intervals, and hosts of smaller officials scatter each time with the whirl. The province in which I passed the first twelve months of my residence in Japan has had four different governors in five years. During my stay at Kumamoto, and before the war had begun, the military command of that important post was three times changed. The government college had in three years three directors. In educational circles, especially, the rapidity of such changes has been phenomenal. There have been five different ministers of education in my own time, and more than five different educational policies. The twenty-six thousand public schools are so related in their management to the local assemblies that, even were no other influences at work, constant change would be inevitable because of the changes in the assemblies. Directors and teachers keep circling from post to post; there are men little more than thirty years old who have taught in almost every province of the country. That any educational system could have produced any great results under these conditions seems nothing short of miraculous.

We are accustomed to think that some degree of stability is necessary to all real progress, all great development. But Japan has given proof irrefutable that enormous development is possible without any stability at all. The explanation is in the race character - a race character in more ways than one the very opposite of our own. Uniformly mobile, and thus uniformly impressionable, the nation has moved unitedly in the direction of great ends; submitting the whole volume of its forty millions to be moulded by the ideas of its rulers, even as sand or as water is shaped by wind. And this submissiveness to reshaping belongs to the old conditions of its soul life - old conditions of rare unselfishness and perfect faith. The relative absence from the national character of egotistical individualism has been the saving of an empire; has enabled a great people to preserve its independence against prodigious odds. Wherefore Japan may well be grateful to her two great religions, the creators and the preservers of her moral power: to Shinto, which taught the individual to think of his Emperor and of his country before thinking either of his own family or of himself; and to Buddhism, which trained him to master regret, to endure pain, and to accept as eternal law the vanishing of things loved and the tyranny of things hated.

Today there is visible a tendency to hardening - a danger of changes leading to the integration of just such an officialism as that which has proved the curse and the weakness of China. The moral results of the new education have not been worthy of the material results. The charge of want of 'individuality', in the accepted sense of pure selfishness, will scarcely be made against the Japanese of the next century. Even the compositions of students already reflect the new conception of intellectual strength only as a weapon of offense, and the new sentiment of aggressive egotism. 'Impermanency', writes one, with a fading memory of Buddhism in his mind, 'is the nature of our life. We see often persons who were rich yesterday, and are poor today. This is the result of human competition, according to the law of evolution. We are exposed to that competition. We must fight each other, even if we are not inclined to do so. With what sword shall we fight? With the sword of knowledge, forged by education.'

Well, there are two forms of the cultivation of Self. One leads to the exceptional development of the qualities which are noble, and the other signifies something about which the less said the better. But it is not the former which the New Japan is now beginning to study. I confess to being one of those who believe that the human heart, even in the history of a race, may be worth infinitely more than the human intellect, and that it will sooner or later prove itself infinitely better able to answer all the cruel enigmas of the Sphinx of Life. I still believe that the old Japanese were nearer to the solution of those enigmas than are we, just because they recognised moral beauty as greater than intellectual beauty. And, by way of conclusion, I may venture to quote from an article on education by Ferdinand Brunetière:

'All our educational measures will prove vain, if there be no effort to force into the mind, and to deeply impress upon it, the sense of those fine words of Lamennais: *"Human society is based upon mutual giving, or upon the sacrifice of man for man, or of each man for all other men; and sacrifice is the very essence of all true society"*. It is this that we have been unlearning for nearly a century; and if we have to put ourselves to school afresh, it will be in order that we may learn it again. Without such knowledge there can be no society and no education - not, at least, if the object of education be to form man for society. Individualism is today the enemy of education, as it is also the enemy of social order. It has not been so always; but it has so become. It will not be so forever; but it is so now. And without striving to destroy it - which would mean to fall from one extreme into another - we must recognise that, no matter what we wish to do for the family, for society, for education, and for the country, it is against individualism that the work will have to be done.'

Footnotes:

1. In one limited sense, Western art has influenced Japanese literature and drama; but the character of the influence proves the racial differences to which I refer. European plays have been reshaped for the Japanese stage, and European novels rewritten for Japanese readers. But a literal version is rarely attempted; for the original incidents, thoughts, and emotions would be unintelligible to the average reader or play-goer. Plots are adapted; sentiments and incidents are totally transformed. 'The New Magdalen' becomes a Japanese girl who married an Eta. Victor Hugo's *Les Miserables* becomes a tale of the Japanese civil war; and Enjolras a Japanese student. There have been a few rare exceptions, including the marked success of a literal translation of the *Sorrows of Werther*.
2. Critics have tried to make fun of Sir Edwin Arnold's remark that a Japanese crowd smells like a geranium-flower. Yet the simile is exact! The perfume called *jako*, when sparingly used, might easily be taken for the odour of a musk-geranium. In almost any Japanese assembly including women a slight perfume of *jako* is discernible; for the robes worn have been laid in drawers containing a few grains of *jako*. Except for this delicate scent, a Japanese crowd is absolutely odourless.

Shinjū

1

Sometimes they simply put their arms round each other, and lie down together on the iron rails, just in front of an express train. (They cannot do it in Izumo, however, because there are no railroads there yet.) Sometimes they make a little banquet for themselves, write very strange letters to parents and friends, mix something bitter with their rice wine, and go to sleep for ever. Sometimes they select a more ancient and more honoured method: the lover first slays his beloved with a single sword stroke, and then pierces his own throat. Sometimes with the girl's long crape-silk under-girdle (*koshi-obi*) they bind themselves fast together, face to face, and so embracing leap into some deep lake or stream. Many are the modes by which they make their way to the Meido, when tortured by that world-old sorrow about which Schopenhauer wrote so marvellous a theory.

Their own theory is much simpler.

None love life more than the Japanese; none fear death less. Of a future world they have no dread; they regret to leave this one only because it seems to them a world of beauty and of happiness; but the mystery of the future, so long oppressive to Western minds, causes them little concern. As for the young lovers of whom I speak, they have a strange faith which effaces mysteries for them. They turn to the darkness with infinite trust. If they are too unhappy to endure existence, the fault is not another's, nor yet the world's; it is their own; it is *innen*, the result of errors in the previous life. If they can never hope to be united in this world, it is only because in some former birth they broke their promise to wed, or were otherwise cruel to each other. All this is not heterodox. But they believe likewise that by dying together they will find themselves at once united in another world, though Buddhism proclaims that self-destruction is a deadly sin. Now this idea of winning union through death is incalculably older than the faith of Shaka; but it has somehow borrowed in modern time from Buddhism a particular ecstatic colouring, a mystical glow. *Hasu no hana no ue ni oite matan*. On the lotus-blossoms of paradise they shall rest together. Buddhism teaches of transmigrations countless, prolonged through millions of millions of years, before the soul can acquire the Infinite Vision, the Infinite Memory, and melt into the bliss of Nehan, as a white cloud melts into the summer's blue. But these suffering ones think never of Nehan; love's union, their supremest wish, may be reached, they fancy, through the pang of a single death. The fancies of all indeed - as their poor letters show - are not the same. Some think themselves about to enter Amida's paradise of light; some see in their visional hope the *saki-no-yo* only, the future rebirth, when beloved shall meet beloved again, in the all-joyous freshness of another youth; while the idea of many, indeed of the majority, is vaguer far - only a shadowy drifting together through vapoury silences, as in the faint bliss of dreams.

They always pray to be buried together. Often this prayer is refused by the parents or the guardians, and the people deem this refusal a cruel thing, for 'tis believed that those who die for love of each other will find no rest, if denied the same tomb. But when the prayer is granted the ceremony of burial is beautiful and touching. From the two homes the two funeral processions issue to meet in the temple court, by light of lanterns. There, after the recitation of the *kyō*, and the accustomed impressive ceremonies, the chief priest utters an address to the souls of the dead. Compassionately he speaks of the error and the sin; of the youth of the victims, brief and comely as the flowers that blossom and fall in the first burst of spring. He speaks of the Illusion - *mayoi*- which so wrought upon them; he recites the warning of the Teacher. But sometimes he will even predict the future reunion of the lovers in some happier and higher life, re-echoing the popular heart-thought with a simple eloquence that makes his hearers weep. Then the two processions form into one, which takes its way to the cemetery where the grave has already been prepared. The two coffins are lowered together, so that their sides touch as they rest at the bottom of the excavation. Then the *yama-no-mono*[1] folk remove the planks which separate the pair - making the two coffins into one; above the reunited dead the earth is heaped; and a *haka*, bearing in chiselled letters the story of their fate, and perhaps a little poem, is placed above the mingling of their dust.

2

These suicides of lovers are termed *jōshi* or *shinjū* - (both words being written with the same Chinese characters) - signifying 'heart-death', 'passion-death', or 'love-death'. They most commonly occur, in the case of women, among the *jorō*[2] class; but occasionally also among young girls of a more respectable class. There is a fatalistic belief that if one *shinjū* occurs among the inmates of a *jorōya*, two more are sure to follow. Doubtless the belief itself is the cause that cases of *shinjū* do commonly occur in series of three.

The poor girls who voluntarily sell themselves to a life of shame for the sake of their families in time of uttermost distress do not, in Japan (except, perhaps, in those open ports where European vice and brutality have become demoralising influences), ever reach that depth of degradation to which their Western sisters descend. Many indeed retain, through all the period of their terrible servitude, a refinement of manner, a delicacy of sentiment, and a natural modesty that seem, under such conditions, as extraordinary as they are touching.

Only yesterday a case of *shinjū* startled this quiet city. The servant of a physician in the street called Nadamachi, entering the chamber of his master's son a little after sunrise, found the young man lying dead with a dead girl in his arms. The son had been disinherited. The girl was a *jorō*. Last night they were buried, but not together; for the father was not less angered than grieved that such a thing should have been.

Her name was Kane. She was remarkably pretty and very gentle; and from all accounts it would seem that her master had treated her with a kindness unusual in men of his infamous class. She had sold herself for the sake of her mother and a child-sister. The father was dead, and they had lost everything. She was then seventeen. She had been in the house scarcely a year when she met the youth. They fell seriously in love with each other at once. Nothing more terrible could have befallen them; for they could never hope to become man and wife. The young man, though still allowed the privileges of a son, had been disinherited in favour of an adopted brother of steadier habits. The unhappy pair spent all they had for the privilege of seeing each other: she sold even her dresses to pay for it. Then for the last time they met by stealth, late at night, in the physician's house, drank death, and lay down to sleep for ever.

I saw the funeral procession of the girl winding its way by the light of paper lanterns - the wan dead glow that is like a shimmer of phosphorescence - to the Street of the Temples, followed by a long train of women, white-hooded, white-robed, white-girdled, passing all soundlessly - a troop of ghosts.

So through blackness to the Meido the white Shapes flit - the eternal procession of Souls - in painted Buddhist dreams of the Underworld.

3

My friend who writes for the *San-in Shimbun*, which tomorrow will print the whole sad story, tells me that compassionate folk have already decked the new-made graves with flowers and with sprays of *shikimi*.[3] Then drawing from a long native envelope a long, light, thin roll of paper covered with beautiful Japanese writing, and unfolding it before me, he adds:

'She left this letter to the keeper of the house in which she lived: it has been given to us for publication. It is very prettily written. But I cannot translate it well; for it is written in woman's language. The language of letters written by women is not the same as that of letters written by men. Women use particular words and expressions. For instance, in men's language "I" is *watakushi*, or *ware*, or *yo*, or *boku*, according to rank or circumstance, but in the language of woman, it is *warawa*. And women's language is very soft and gentle; and I do not think it is possible to translate such softness and amiability of words into any other language. So I can only give you an imperfect idea of the letter.'

And he interprets, slowly, thus:

'I leave this letter:

'As you know, from last spring I began to love Tashirō-San; and he also fell in love with me. And now, alas! - the influence of our relation in some previous birth having come upon us - and the promise we made each other in that former life to become wife and husband having been broken - even today I must travel to the Meido.

'You not only treated me very kindly, though you found me so stupid and without influence,[4] but you likewise aided in many ways for my worthless sake my mother and sister. And now, since I have not been able to repay you even the one-myriadth part of that kindness and pity in which you enveloped me - pity great as the mountains and the sea,[5] - it would not be without just reason that you should hate me as a great criminal.

'But though I doubt not this which I am about to do will seem a wicked folly, I am forced to it by conditions and by my own heart.

Wherefore I still may pray you to pardon my past faults. And though I go to the Meido, never shall I forget your mercy to me - great as the mountains and the sea. From under the shadow of the grasses[6] I shall still try to recompense you - to send back my gratitude to you and to your house. Again, with all my heart I pray you: do not be angry with me.

'Many more things I would like to write. But now my heart is not a heart; and I must quickly go. And so I shall lay down my writing-brush.

'It is written so clumsily, this.

'Kane thrice prostrates herself before you.

    'From KANE

'To - - SAMA.'

'Well, it is a characteristic *shinjū* letter', my friend comments, after a moment's silence, replacing the frail white paper in its envelope. 'So I thought it would interest you. And now, although it is growing dark, I am going to the cemetery to see what has been done at the grave. Would you like to come with me?'

We take our way over the long white bridge, up the shadowy Street of the Temples, towards the ancient *hakaba* of Miokoji - and the darkness grows as we walk. A thin moon hangs just above the roofs of the great temples.

Suddenly a far voice, sonorous and sweet - a man's voice - breaks into song under the starred night: a song full of strange charm and tones like warblings - those Japanese tones of popular emotion which seem to have been learned from the songs of birds. Some happy workman returning home. So clear the thin frosty air that each syllable quivers to us; but I cannot understand the words:

Saité yuké toya, ano ya wo saité;
Yuké ba chikayoru nushi no soba.

'What is that'? I ask my friend.

He answers:

'A love-song. "*Go forward, straight forward that way, to the house that thou seest before thee; - the nearer thou goest thereto, the nearer to her[7] shalt thou be.*"'

Footnotes:

1. *Yama-no-mono* ('mountain-folk', so called from their settlement on the hills above Tokōji), a pariah-class whose special calling is the washing of the dead and the making of graves.
2. *Jorō*: a courtesan.
3. *Illicium religiosum.*
4. Literally: 'without shadow' or 'shadowless'.
5. *Umi-yama-no-on.*
6. *Kusaba-no-kage.*
7. Or 'him'. This is a free rendering. The word '*nushi*' simply refers to the owner of the house.

Of The Eternal Feminine

For metaphors of man we search the skies,
And find our allegory in all the air; -
We gaze on Nature with Narcissus-eyes,
Enamoured of our shadow everywhere.

WATSON

1

What every intelligent foreigner dwelling in Japan must sooner or later perceive is, that the more the Japanese learn of our aesthetics and of our emotional character generally, the less favourably do they seem to be impressed thereby. The European or American who tries to talk to them about Western art, or literature, or metaphysics will feel for their sympathy in vain. He will be listened to politely; but his utmost eloquence will scarcely elicit more than a few surprising comments, totally unlike what he hoped and expected to evoke. Many successive disappointments of this sort impel him to judge his Oriental auditors very much as he would judge Western auditors behaving in a similar way. Obvious indifference to what we imagine the highest expression possible of art and thought, we are led by our own occidental experiences to take for proof of mental incapacity. So we find one class of foreign observers calling the Japanese a race of children; while another, including a majority of those who have passed many years in the country, judge the nation essentially materialistic, despite the evidence of its religions, its literature, and its matchless art. I cannot persuade myself that either of these judgements is less fatuous than Goldsmith's observation to Johnson about the Literary Club: 'There can now be nothing new among us; we have travelled over one another's minds'. A cultured Japanese might well answer with Johnson's famous retort: 'Sir, you have not yet travelled over *my* mind, I promise you'! And all such sweeping criticisms seem to me due to a very imperfect recognition of the fact that Japanese thought and sentiment have been evolved out of ancestral habits, customs, ethics, beliefs, directly the opposite of our own in some cases, and in all cases strangely different. Acting on such phychological material, modern scientific education cannot but accentuate and develop race differences. Only half-education can tempt the Japanese to servile imitation of Western ways. The real mental and moral power of the race, its highest intellect, strongly resists Western influence; and those more competent than I to pronounce upon such matters assure me that this is especially observable in the case of superior men who have travelled or been educated in Europe. Indeed, the results of the new culture have served more than aught else to show the immense force of healthy conservatism in that race superficially characterised by Rein as a race of children. Even very imperfectly understood, the causes of this Japanese attitude to a certain class of Western ideas might well incite us to reconsider our own estimate of those ideas, rather than to tax the Oriental mind with incapacity. Now, of the causes in question, which are multitudinous, some can only be vaguely guessed at. But there is at least one - a very important one - which we may safely study, because a recognition of it is forced upon anyone who passes a few years in the Far East.

2

'Teacher, please tell us why there is so much about love and marrying in English novels; it seems to us very, very strange.'

This question was put to me while I was trying to explain to my literature class - young men from nineteen to twenty-three years of age - why they had failed to understand certain chapters of a standard novel, though quite well able to understand the logic of Jevons and the phychology of James. Under the circumstances, it was not an easy question to answer; in fact, I could not have replied to it in any satisfactory way had I not already lived for several years in Japan. As it was, though I endeavoured to be concise as well as lucid, my explanation occupied something more than two hours.

There are few of our society novels that a Japanese student can really comprehend; and the reason is, simply, that English society is something of which he is quite unable to form a correct idea. Indeed, not only English society, in a special sense, but even Western life, in a general sense, is a mystery to him. Any social system of which filial piety is not the moral cement; any social system in which children leave their parents in order to establish families of their own; any social system in which it is considered not only natural but right to love wife and child more than the authors of one's being; any social system in which marriage can be decided independently of the will of the parents, by the mutual inclination of the young people themselves, any social system in which the mother-in-law is not entitled to the obedient service of the daughter-in-law, appears to him of necessity a state of life scarcely better than that of the birds of the air and the beasts of the field, or at best a sort of moral chaos. And all this existence, as reflected in our popular fiction, presents him with provoking enigmas. Our ideas about love and our solicitude about marriage furnish some of these enigmas. To the young Japanese, marriage appears a simple, natural duty, for the due performance of which his parents will make all necessary arrangements at the proper time. That foreigners should have so much trouble about getting married is puzzling enough to him; but that distinguished authors should write novels and poems about such matters, and that those novels and poems should be vastly admired, puzzles him infinitely more - seems to him 'very, *very* strange'.

My young questioner said 'strange' for politeness' sake. His real thought would have been more accurately rendered by the word 'indecent'. But when I say that to the Japanese mind our typical novel appears indecent, highly indecent, the idea thereby suggested to my English readers will probably be misleading. The Japanese are not morbidly prudish. Our society novels do not strike them as indecent because the theme is love. The Japanese have a great deal of literature about love. No; our novels seem to them indecent for somewhat the same reason that the Scripture text, 'For this cause shall a man leave his father and mother, and shall cleave unto his wife', appears to them one of the most immoral sentences ever written. In other words, their criticism requires a sociological explanation. To explain fully why our novels are to their thinking indecent, I should have to describe the whole structure, customs, and ethics of the

Japanese family, totally different from anything in Western life; and to do this even in a superficial way would require a volume. I cannot attempt a complete explanation: I can only cite some facts of a suggestive character.

To begin with, then, I may broadly state that a great deal of our literature, besides its fiction, is revolting to the Japanese moral sense, not because it treats of the passion of love *per se*, but because it treats of that passion in relation to virtuous maidens, and therefore in relation to the family circle. Now, as a general rule, where passionate love is the theme in Japanese literature of the best class, it is not that sort of love which leads to the establishment of family relations. It is quite another sort of love - a sort of love about which the Oriental is not prudish at all - the *mayoi*, or infatuation of passion, inspired by merely physical attraction; and its heroines are not the daughters of refined families, but mostly *hetarae*, or professional dancing-girls. Neither does this Oriental variety of literature deal with its subject after the fashion of sensuous literature in the West - French literature, for example: it considers it from a different artistic stand-point, and describes rather a different order of emotional sensations.

A national literature is of necessity reflective; and we may presume that what it fails to portray can have little or no outward manifestation in the national life. Now, the reserve of Japanese literature regarding that love which is the great theme of our greatest novelists and poets is exactly paralleled by the reserve of Japanese society in regard to the same topic. The typical woman often figures in Japanese romance as a heroine; as a perfect mother; as a pious daughter, willing to sacrifice all for duty; as a loyal wife, who follows her husband into battle, fights by his side, saves his life at the cost of her own; never as a sentimental maiden, dying, or making others die, for love. Neither do we find her on literary exhibition as a dangerous beauty, a charmer of men; and in the real life of Japan she has never appeared in any such rôle. Society, as a mingling of the sexes, as an existence of which the supremely refined charm is the charm of woman, has never existed in the East. Even in Japan, society, in the special sense of the word, remains masculine. Nor is it easy to believe that the adoption of European fashions and customs within some restricted circles of the capital indicates the beginning of such a social change as might eventually remodel the national life according to Western ideas of society. For such a remodelling would involve the dissolution of the family, the disintegration of the whole social fabric, the destruction of the whole ethical system - the breaking up, in short, of the national life.

Taking the word 'woman' in its most refined meaning, and postulating a society in which woman seldom appears, a society in which she is never placed 'on display', a society in which wooing is utterly out of the question, and the faintest compliment to wife or daughter is an outrageous impertinence, the reader can at once reach some startling conclusions as to the impression made by our popular fiction upon members of that society. But, although partly correct, his conclusions must fall short of the truth in certain directions, unless he also possess some knowledge of the restraints of that society and of the ethical notions behind the restraints. For example, a refined Japanese never speaks to you about his wife (I am stating the general rule) and very seldom indeed about his children, however proud of them he may be. Rarely will he be heard to speak about any of the members of his family, about his domestic life, about any of his private affairs. But if he should happen to talk about members of his family, the persons mentioned will almost certainly be his parents. Of them he will speak with a reverence approaching religious feeling, yet in a manner quite different from that which would be natural to an Occidental, and never so as to imply any mental comparison between the merits of his own parents and those of other men's parents. But he will not talk about his wife even to the friends who were invited as guests to his wedding. And I think I may safely say that the poorest and most ignorant Japanese, however dire his need, would never dream of trying to obtain aid or to evoke pity by the mention of his wife - perhaps not even of his wife and children. But he would not hesitate to ask help for the sake of his parents or his grandparents. Love of wife and child, the strongest of all sentiments with the Occidental, is judged by the Oriental to be a selfish affection. He professes to be ruled by a higher sentiment - duty: duty, first, to his Emperor: next, to his parents. And since love can be classed only as an ego-altruistic feeling, the Japanese thinker is not wrong in his refusal to consider it the loftiest of motives, however refined or spiritualised it may be.

In the existence of the poorer classes of Japan there are no secrets; but among the upper classes, family life is much less open to observation than in any country of the West, not excepting Spain. It is a life of which foreigners see little, and know almost nothing, all the essays which have been written about Japanese women to the contrary notwithstanding.[1] Invited to the home of a Japanese friend, you may or may not see the family. It will depend upon circumstances. If you see any of them, it will probably be for a moment only, and in that event you will most likely see the wife. At the entrance you give your card to the servant, who retires to present it, and presently returns to usher you into the *zashiki*, or guest-room, always the largest and finest apartment in a Japanese dwelling, where your kneeling-cushion is ready for you, with a smoking-box before it. The servant brings you tea and cakes. In a little time the host himself enters, and after the indispensable salutations conversation begins. Should you be pressed to stay for dinner, and accept the invitation; it is probable that the wife will do you the honour, as her husband's friend, to wait upon you during an instant. You may or may not be formally introduced to her; but a glance at her dress and coiffure should be sufficient to inform you at once who she is, and you must greet her with the most profound respect. She will probably impress you (especially if your visit be to a *samurai* home) as a delicately refined and very serious person, by no means a woman of the much-smiling and much-bowing kind. She will say extremely little, but will salute you, and will serve you for a moment with a natural grace of which the mere spectacle is a revelation, and glide away again, to remain invisible until the instant of your departure, when she will reappear at the entrance to wish you good-bye. During other successive visits you may have similar charming glimpses of her; perhaps, also, some rarer glimpses of the aged father and mother; and if a much favoured visitor, the children may at last come to greet you, with wonderful politeness and sweetness. But the innermost intimate life of that family will never be revealed to you. All that you see to suggest it will be refined, courteous, exquisite, but of the relation of those souls to each other you will know nothing. Behind the beautiful screens which mask the further interior, all is silent, gentle mystery. There is no reason, to the Japanese mind, why it should be otherwise. Such family life is sacred; the home is a sanctuary, of which it were impious to draw aside the veil. Nor can I think this idea of the sacredness of home and of the family relation is anywise inferior to our highest conception of the home and the family in the West.

Should there be grown-up daughters in the family, however, the visitor is less likely to see the wife. More timid, but equally silent and reserved, the young girls will make the guest welcome. In obedience to orders, they may even gratify him by a performance upon some musical instrument, by exhibiting some of their own needlework or painting, or by showing to him some precious or curious objects among the family heirlooms. But all submissive sweetness and courtesy are inseparable from the high-bred reserve belonging to the finest native culture. And the guest must not allow himself to be less reserved. Unless possessing the privilege of great age, which would entitle him to paternal freedom of speech, he must never venture upon personal compliment, or indulge in anything resembling light flattery. What would be deemed gallantry in the West may be gross rudeness in the East. On no account can the visitor compliment a young girl about her looks, her grace, her toilette, much less dare address such a compliment to the wife. But, the reader may object, there are certainly occasions upon which a compliment of some character cannot be avoided. This is true, and on such an occasion politeness requires, as a preliminary, the humblest apology for making the compliment, which will then be accepted with a phrase more graceful than our 'Pray do not mention it'; that is, the rudeness of making a compliment at all.

But here we touch the vast subject of Japanese etiquette, about which I must confess myself still profoundly ignorant. I have ventured thus much only in order to suggest how lacking in refinement much of our Western society fiction must appear to the Oriental mind.

To speak of one's affection for wife or children, to bring into conversation anything closely related to domestic life, is totally incompatible with Japanese ideas of good breeding. Our open acknowledgement, or rather exhibition, of the domestic relation consequently appears to cultivated Japanese, if not absolutely barbarous, at least uxorious. And this sentiment may be found to explain not a little in Japanese life which has given foreigners a totally incorrect idea about the position of Japanese women. It is not the custom in Japan for the husband even to walk side by side with his wife in the street, much less to give her his arm, or to assist her in ascending or descending a flight of stairs. But this is not any proof upon his part of want of affection. It is only the result of a social sentiment totally different from our own; it is simply obedience to an etiquette founded upon the idea that public displays of the marital relation are improper. Why improper? Because they seem to Oriental judgement to indicate a confession of personal, and therefore selfish sentiment. For the

Oriental the law of life is duty. Affection must, in every time and place, be subordinated to duty. Any public exhibition of personal affection of a certain class is equivalent to a public confession of moral weakness. Does this mean that to love one's wife is a moral weakness? No; it is the duty of a man to love his wife; but it is moral weakness to love her more than his parents, or to show her, in public, more attention than he shows to his parents. Nay, it would be a proof of moral weakness to show her even the *same* degree of attention. During the lifetime of the parents her position in the household is simply that of an adopted daughter, and the most affectionate of husbands must not even for a moment allow himself to forget the etiquette of the family.

Here I must touch upon one feature of Western literature never to be reconciled with Japanese ideas and customs. Let the reader reflect for a moment how large a place the subject of kisses and caresses and embraces occupies in our poetry and in our prose fiction; and then let him consider the fact that in Japanese literature these have *no existence whatever*. For kisses and embraces are simply unknown in Japan as tokens of affection, if we except the solitary fact that Japanese mothers, like mothers all over the world, lip and hug their little ones betimes. After babyhood there is no more hugging or kissing. Such actions, except in the case of infants, are held to be highly immodest. Never do girls kiss one another; never do parents kiss or embrace their children who have become able to walk. And this rule holds good of all classes of society, from the highest nobility to the humblest peasantry. Neither have we the least indication throughout Japanese literature of any time in the history of the race when affection was more demonstrative than it is today. Perhaps the Western reader will find it hard even to imagine a literature in the whole course of which no mention is made of kisses, of embracing, even of pressing a loved hand; for hand-clasping is an action as totally foreign to Japanese impulse as kissing. Yet on these topics even the naïve songs of the country folk, even the old ballads of the people about unhappy lovers, are quite as silent as the exquisite verses of the court poets. Suppose we take for an example the ancient popular ballad of Shuntokumaru, which has given origin to various proverbs and household words familiar throughout western Japan. Here we have the story of two betrothed lovers, long separated by a cruel misfortune, wandering in search of each other all over the Empire, and at last suddenly meeting before Kiomidzu Temple by the favour of the gods. Would not any Aryan poet describe such a meeting as a rushing of the two into each other's arms, with kisses and cries of love? But how does the old Japanese ballad describe it? In brief, the twain only sit down together *and stroke each other a little*. Now, even this reserved form of caress is an extremely rare indulgence of emotion. You may see again and again fathers and sons, husbands and wives, mothers and daughters, meeting after years of absence, yet you will probably never see the least approach to a caress between them. They will kneel down and salute each other, and smile, and perhaps cry a little for joy; but they will neither rush into each other's arms, nor utter extraordinary phrases of affection. Indeed, such terms of affection as 'my dear', 'my darling', 'my sweet', 'my love', 'my life', do not exist in Japanese, nor any terms at all equivalent to our emotional idioms. Japanese affection is not uttered in words; it scarcely appears even in the tone of voice; it is chiefly shown in acts of exquisite courtesy and kindness. I might add that the opposite emotion is under equally perfect control; but to illustrate this remarkable fact would require a separate essay.

3

He who would study impartially the life and thought of the Orient must also study those of the Occident from the Oriental point of view. And the results of such a comparative study he will find to be in no small degree retroactive. According to his character and his faculty of perception, he will be more or less affected by those Oriental influences to which he submits himself. The conditions of Western life will gradually begin to assume for him new, undreamed-of meanings, and to lose not a few of their old familiar aspects. Much that he once deemed right and true he may begin to find abnormal and false. He may begin to doubt whether the moral ideals of the West are really the highest. He may feel more than inclined to dispute the estimate placed by Western custom upon Western civilisation. Whether his doubts be final is another matter: they will be at least rational enough and powerful enough to modify permanently some of his prior convictions - among others his conviction of the moral value of the Western worship of Woman as the Unattainable, the Incomprehensible, the Divine, the ideal of '*la femme que tu ne connaîtras pas*',[2] the ideal of the Eternal Feminine. For in this ancient East the Eternal Feminine does not exist at all. And after having become quite accustomed to live without it, one may naturally conclude that it is not absolutely essential to intellectual health, and may even dare to question the necessity for its perpetual existence upon the other side of the world.

4

To say that the Eternal Feminine does not exist in the Far East is to state but a part of the truth. That it could be introduced thereinto, in the remotest future, is not possible to imagine. Few, if any, of our ideas regarding it can even be rendered into the language of the country: a language in which nouns have no gender, adjectives no degrees of comparison, and verbs no persons; a language in which, says Professor Chamberlain, the absence of personification is 'a characteristic so deep-seated and so all-pervading as to interfere even with the use of neuter nouns in combination with transitive verbs'.[3] 'In fact', he adds, 'most metaphors and allegories are incapable of so much as explanation to Far-Eastern minds'; and he makes a striking citation from Wordsworth in illustration of his statement. Yet even poets much more lucid than Wordsworth are to the Japanese equally obscure. I remember the difficulty I once had in explaining to an advanced class this simple line from a well-known ballad of Tennyson -

'She is more beautiful than day.'

My students could understand the use of the adjective 'beautiful' to qualify 'day', and the use of the same adjective, separately, to qualify the word 'maid'. But that there could exist in any mortal mind the least idea of analogy between the beauty of day and the beauty of a young woman was quite beyond their understanding. In order to convey to them the poet's thought, it was necessary to analyse it psychologically - to prove a possible nervous analogy between two modes of pleasurable feeling excited by two different impressions.

Thus, the very nature of the language tells us how ancient and how deeply rooted in racial character are those tendencies by which we must endeavour to account - if there be any need of accounting at all - for the absence in the Far East of a dominant ideal corresponding to our own. They are causes incomparably older than the existing social structure, older than the idea of the family, older than ancestor worship, enormously older than that Confucian code which is the reflection rather than the explanation of many singular facts in Oriental life. But since beliefs and practices react upon character, and character again must react upon practices and beliefs, it has not been altogether irrational to seek in Confucianism for causes as well as for explanations. Far more irrational have been the charges of hasty critics against Shinto and against Buddhism as religious influences opposed to the natural rights of woman. The ancient faith of Shinto has been at least as gentle to woman as the ancient faith of the Hebrews. Its female divinities are not less numerous than its masculine divinities, nor are they presented to the imagination of worshippers in a form much less attractive than the dreams of Greek mythology. Of some, like So-tohori-no-Iratsumé, it is said that the light of their beautiful bodies passes through their garments; and the source of all life and light, the eternal Sun, is a goddess, fair Ama-terasu-oho-mi-kami. Virgins serve the ancient gods, and figure in all the pageants of the faith; and in a thousand shrines throughout the land the memory of woman as wife and mother is worshipped equally with the memory of man as hero and father. Neither can the later and alien faith of Buddhism be justly accused of relegating woman to a lower place in the spiritual world than monkish Christianity accorded her in the West. The Buddha, like the Christ, was born of a virgin; the most lovable divinities of Buddhism, Jizō excepted, are feminine, both in Japanese art and in Japanese popular fancy; and in the Buddhist as in the Roman Catholic hagiography, the lives of holy women hold honoured place. It is true that Buddhism, like early Christianity, used its utmost eloquence in preaching against the temptation of female loveliness; and it is true that in the teaching of its founder, as in the teaching of Paul, social and spiritual supremacy is accorded to the man. Yet, in our search for texts on this topic, we must not overlook the host of instances of favours shown by the Buddha to women of all classes, nor that remarkable legend of a later text, in which a dogma denying to woman the highest spiritual opportunities is sublimely rebuked.

In the eleventh chapter of the Sutra of the Lotus of the Good Law, it is written that mention was made before the Lord Buddha of a young girl who had in one instant arrived at supreme knowledge; who had in one moment acquired the merits of a thousand meditations, and the proofs of the essence of all laws. And the girl came and stood in the presence of the Lord.

But the Bodhissattva Pragnakuta doubted, saying, 'I have seen the Lord Sakyamuni in the time when he was striving for supreme enlightenment, and I know that he performed good works innumerable through countless aeons. In all the world there is not one spot so large as a grain of mustard-seed where he has not surrendered his body for the sake of living creatures. Only after all this did he arrive at enlightenment. Who then may believe this girl could in one moment have arrived at supreme knowledge?'

And the venerable priest Sariputra likewise doubted, saying, 'It may indeed happen, O Sister, that a woman fulfill the six perfect virtues; but as yet there is no example of her having attained to Buddhaship, because a woman cannot attain to the rank of a Bodhissattva.'

But the maiden called upon the Lord Buddha to be her witness. And instantly in the sight of the assembly her sex disappeared; and she manifested herself as a Bodhissattva, filling all directions of space with the radiance of the thirty-two signs. And the world shook in six different ways. And the priest Sariputra was silent.[4].

5

But to feel the real nature of what is surely one of the greatest obstacles to intellectual sympathy between the West and the Far East, we must fully appreciate the immense effect upon Occidental life of this ideal which has no existence in the Orient. We must remember what that ideal has been to Western civilisation - to all its pleasures and refinements and luxuries; to its sculpture, painting, decoration, architecture, literature, drama, music; to the development of countless industries. We must think of its effect upon manners and customs, and the language of taste, upon conduct and ethics, upon endeavour, upon philosophy and religion, upon almost every phase of public and private life - in short, upon national character. Nor should we forget that the many influences interfused in the shaping of it - Teutonic, Celtic, Scandinavian, classic, or medieval, the Greek apotheosis of human beauty, the Christian worship of the Mother of God, the exaltations of chivalry, the spirit of the Renaissance steeping and colouring all the pre-existing idealism in a new sensuousness - must have had their nourishment, if not their birth, in a race feeling ancient as Aryan speech, and as alien to the most eastern East.

Of all these various influences combined to form our ideal, the classic element remains perceptibly dominant. It is true that the Hellenic conception of human beauty, so surviving, has been wondrously informed with the conception of soul beauty never of the antique world nor of the Renaissance. Also it is true that the new philosophy of evolution, forcing recognition of the incalculable and awful cost of the Present to the Past, creating a totally new comprehension of duty to the Future, enormously enhancing our conception of character values, has aided more than all preceding influences together towards the highest possible spiritualisation of the ideal of woman. Yet, however further spiritualised it may become through future intellectual expansion, this ideal must in its very nature remain fundamentally artistic and sensuous.

We do not see Nature as the Oriental sees it, and as his art proves that he sees it. We see it less realistically, we know it less intimately, because, save through the lenses of the specialist, we contemplate it anthropomorphically. In one direction, indeed, our aesthetic sense has been cultivated to a degree incomparably finer than that of the Oriental; but that direction has been passional. We have learned something of the beauty of Nature through our ancient worship of the beauty of woman. Even from the beginning it is probable that the perception of human beauty has been the main source of all our aesthetic sensibility. Possibly we owe to it likewise our idea of proportion;[5] our exaggerated appreciation of regularity; our fondness for parallels, curves, and all geometrical symmetries. And in the long process of our aesthetic evolution, the ideal of woman has at last become for us an aesthetic abstraction. Through the illusion of that abstraction only do we perceive the charms of our world, even as forms might be perceived through some tropic atmosphere whose vapours are iridescent.

Nor is this all. Whatsoever has once been likened to woman by art or thought has been strangely informed and transformed by that momentary symbolism: wherefore, through all the centuries Western fancy has been making Nature more and more feminine. Whatsoever delights our imagination has feminised - the infinite tendernessof the sky, the mobility of waters, the rose of dawn, the vast caress of Day, Night and the lights of heaven - even the undulations of the eternal hills. And flowers, and the flush of fruit, and all things fragrant, fair, and gracious; the genial seasons with their voices; the laughter of streams, and whisper of leaves, and ripplings of song within the shadows; all sights, or sounds, or sensations that can touch our love of loveliness, of delicacy, of sweetness, of gentleness, make for us vague dreams of woman. Where our fancy lends masculinity to Nature, it is only in grimness and in force, as if to enhance by rugged and mighty contrasts the witchcraft of the Eternal Feminine. Nay, even the terrible itself, if fraught with terrible beauty - even Destruction, if only shaped with the grace of destroyers - becomes for us feminine. And not beauty alone, of sight or sound, but well-nigh all that is mystic, sublime, or holy, now makes appeal to us through some marvellously woven intricate plexus of passional sensibility. Even the subtlest forces of our universe speak to us of woman; new sciences have taught us new names for the thrill her presence wakens in the blood, for that ghostly shock which is first love, for the eternal riddle of her fascination. Thus, out of simple human passion, through influences and transformations innumerable, we have evolved a cosmic emotion, a feminine pantheism.

And now may not one venture to ask whether all the consequences of this passional influence in the aesthetic evolution of our Occident have been in the main beneficial? Underlying all those visible results of which we boast as art triumphs, may there not be lurking invisible results, some future revelation of which will cause more than a little shock to our self-esteem? Is it not quite possible that our aesthetic faculties have been developed even abnormally in one direction by the power of a single emotional idea which has left us nearly, if not totally blind to many wonderful aspects of Nature? Or rather, must not this be the inevitable effect of the extreme predominance of one particular emotion in the evolution of our aesthetic sensibility? And finally, one may surely be permitted to ask if the predominating influence itself has been the highest possible, and whether there is not a higher, known perhaps to the Oriental soul.

I may only suggest these questions, without hoping to answer them satisfactorily. But the longer I dwell in the East, the more I feel growing upon me the belief that there are exquisite artistic faculties and perceptions, developed in the Oriental, of which we can know scarcely more than we know of those unimaginable colours, invisible to the human eye, yet proven to exist by the spectroscope. I think that such a possibility is indicated by certain phases of Japanese art.

Here it becomes as difficult as dangerous to particularise. I dare hazard only some general observations. I think this marvellous art asserts that, out of the infinitely varied aspects of Nature, those which for us hold no suggestion whatever of sex character, those which cannot be looked at anthropomorphically, those which are neither masculine nor feminine, but neuter or nameless, are those most profoundly loved and comprehended by the Japanese. Nay, he sees in Nature much that for thousands of years has remained invisible to us; and we are now learning from him aspects of life and beauties of form to which we were utterly blind before. We have finally made the startling discovery that his art - notwithstanding all the dogmatic assertions of Western prejudice to the contrary, and notwithstanding the strangely weird impression of unreality which at first it produced - is never a mere creation of fantasy, but a veritable reflection of what has been and of what is: wherefore we have recognised that it is nothing less than a higher education in art simply to look at his studies of bird life, insect life, plant life, tree life. Compare, for example, our very finest drawings of insects with Japanese drawings of similar subjects. Compare Giacomelli's illustrations to Michelet's *L'Insecte* with the commonest Japanese figures of the same creatures decorating the stamped leather of a cheap tobacco pouch or the metal work of a cheap pipe. The whole minute exquisiteness of the European engraving has accomplished only an indifferent realism, while the Japanese artist, with a few dashes of his brush, has seized and reproduced, with an incomprehensible power of interpretation, not only every peculiarity of the creature's shape, but every special characteristic of its motion. Each figure flung from the Oriental painter's brush is a lesson, a revelation, to perceptions unbeclouded by prejudice, an opening of the eyes of those who can see, though it be only a spider in a wind shaken web, a dragon-fly riding a sunbeam, a pair of crabs running through sedge, the trembling of a fish's fins in a clear current, the lilt of a flying wasp, the pitch of a flying duck, a mantis in fighting position, or a *semi* toddling up a cedar branch to sing. All this art is alive, intensely alive, and our corresponding art looks absolutely dead beside it.

Take, again, the subject of flowers. An English or German flower painting, the result of months of trained labour, and valued at several hundred pounds, would certainly not compare as a nature study, in the higher sense, with a Japanese flower painting executed in twenty brush strokes, and worth perhaps five sen. The former would represent at best but an ineffectual and painful effort to imitate a massing of colours. The latter would prove a perfect memory of certain flower shapes instantaneously flung upon paper, without any model to aid, and showing, not the recollection of any individual blossoms, but the perfect realisation of a general law of form expression, perfectly mastered, with all its moods, tenses, and inflections. The French alone, among Western art critics, seem fully to understand these features of Japanese art; and among all Western artists it is the Parisian alone who approaches the Oriental in his methods. Without lifting his brush from the paper, the French artist may sometimes, with a single wavy line, create the almost speaking figure of a particular type of man or woman. But this high development of faculty is confined chiefly to humorous sketching; it is still either masculine or feminine. To understand what I mean by the ability of the Japanese artist, my reader must imagine just such a power of almost instantaneous creation as that which characterises certain French work, applied to almost every subject except individuality, to nearly all recognised general types, to all aspects of Japanese nature, to all forms of native landscape, to clouds and flowing water and mists, to all the life of woods and fields, to all the moods of seasons and the tones of horizons and the colours of the morning and the evening. Certainly, the deeper spirit of this magical art seldom reveals itself at first sight to unaccustomed eyes, since it appeals to so little in Western aesthetic experience. But by gentle degrees it will so enter into an appreciative and unprejudiced mind as to modify profoundly therein almost every pre-existing sentiment in relation to the beautiful. All of its meaning will indeed require many years to master, but something of its reshaping power will be felt in a much shorter time when the sight of an American illustrated magazine or of any illustrated European periodical has become almost unbearable.

Psychological differences of far deeper import are suggested by other facts, capable of exposition in words, but not capable of interpretation through Western standards of aesthetics or Western feeling of any sort. For instance, I have been watching two old men planting young trees in the garden of a neighbouring temple. They sometimes spend nearly an hour in planting a single sapling. Having fixed it in the ground, they retire to a distance to study the position of all its lines, and consult together about it. As a consequence, the sapling is taken up and replanted in a slightly different position. This is done no less than eight times before the little tree can be perfectly adjusted into the plan of the garden. Those two old men are composing a mysterious thought with their little trees, changing them, transferring them, removing or replacing them, even as a poet changes and shifts his words, to give to his verse the most delicate or the most forcible expression possible.

In every large Japanese cottage there are several alcoves, or *tokonoma*, one in each of the principal rooms. In these alcoves the art treasures of the family are exhibited.[6] Within each *toko* a *kakemono* is hung; and upon its slightly elevated floor (usually of polished wood) are placed flower vases and one or two artistic objects. Flowers are arranged in the *toko* vases according to ancient rules which Mr Conder's beautiful book will tell you a great deal about; and the *kakemono* and the art objects there displayed are changed at regular intervals, according to occasion and season. Now, in a certain alcove, I have at various times seen many different things of beauty: a Chinese statuette of ivory, an incense vase of bronze - representing a cloud-riding pair of dragons - the wood carving of a Buddhist pilgrim resting by the wayside and mopping his bald pate, masterpieces of lacquer ware and lovely Kyoto porcelains, and a large stone placed on a pedestal of heavy, costly wood, expressly made for it. I do not know whether you could see any beauty in that stone; it is neither hewn nor polished, nor does it possess the least imaginable intrinsic value. It is simply a grey water-worn stone from the bed of a stream. Yet it cost more than one of those Kyoto vases which sometimes replace it, and which you would be glad to pay a very high price for.

In the garden of the little house I now occupy in Kumamoto, there are about fifteen rocks, or large stones, of as many shapes and sizes. They also have no real intrinsic value, not even as possible building material. And yet the proprietor of the garden paid for them something more than seven hundred and fifty Japanese dollars, or considerably more than the pretty house itself could possibly have cost. And it would be quite wrong to suppose the cost of the stones due to the expense of their transportation from the bed of the Shirakawa. No; they are worth seven hundred and fifty dollars only because they are considered beautiful to a certain degree, and because there is a large local demand for beautiful stones. They are not even of the best class, or they would have cost a great deal more. Now, until you can perceive that a big rough stone may have more aesthetic suggestiveness than a costly steel engraving, that it is a thing of beauty and a joy forever, you cannot begin to understand how a Japanese sees Nature. 'But what', you may ask, 'can be beautiful in a common stone'? Many things; but I will mention only one - irregularity.

In my little Japanese house, the *fusuma*, or sliding screens of opaque paper between room and room, have designs at which I am never tired of looking. The designs vary in different parts of the dwelling; I will speak only of the *fusuma* dividing my study from a smaller apartment. The ground colour is a delicate cream-yellow; and the golden pattern is very simple - the mystic-jewel symbols of Buddhism scattered over the surface by pairs. But no two sets of pairs are placed at exactly the same distance from each other; and the symbols themselves are curiously diversified, never appearing twice in exactly the same position or relation. Sometimes one jewel is transparent, and its fellow opaque; sometimes both are opaque or both diaphanous; sometimes the transparent one is the larger of the two; sometimes the opaque is the larger; sometimes both are precisely the same size; sometimes they overlap, and sometimes do not touch; sometimes the opaque is on the left, sometimes on the right; sometimes the transparent jewel is above, sometimes below. Vainly does the eye roam over the whole surface in search of a repetition, or of anything resembling regularity, either in distribution, juxtaposition, grouping, dimensions, or contrasts. And throughout the whole dwelling nothing resembling regularity in the various decorative designs can be found. The ingenuity by which it is avoided is amazing - it rises to the dignity of genius. Now, all this is a common characteristic of Japanese decorative art; and after having lived a few years under its influences, the sight of a regular pattern upon a wall, a carpet, a curtain, a ceiling, upon any decorated surface, pains like a horrible vulgarism. Surely, it is because we have so long been accustomed to look at Nature anthropomorphically that we can still endure mechanical ugliness in our own decorative art, and that we remain insensible to charms of Nature which are clearly perceived even by the eyes of the Japanese child, wondering over its mother's shoulder at the green and blue wonder of the world.

'*He*', saith a Buddhist text, '*who discerns that nothingness is law - such a one hath wisdom*'.

Footnotes:

1. I do not, however, refer to those extraordinary persons who make their short residence in teahouses and establishments of a much worse kind, and then go home to write books about the women of Japan.
2. A phrase from Baudelaire.
3. See *Things Japanese*, second edition, pp. 255, 256; article 'Language'.
4. See the whole wonderful passage in Kern's translation of this magnificent Sutra, *Sacred Books of the East*, vol. xxi. chap. xi.
5. On the origin of the idea of bilateral symmetry, see Herbert Spencer's essay, 'The Sources of Architectural Types'.
6. The *tokonoma*, or *toko*, is said to have been first introduced into Japanese architecture about four hundred and fifty years ago, by the Buddhist priest Eisai, who had studied in China. Perhaps the alcove was originally devised and used for the exhibition of sacred objects; but today, among the cultivated, it would be deemed in very bad taste to display either images of the gods or sacred paintings in the *toko* of a guest-room. The *toko* is still, however a sacred place in a certain sense. No one should ever step upon it, or squat within it, or even place in it anything not pure, or anything offensive to taste. There is an elaborate code of etiquette in relation to it. The most honoured among guests is always placed nearest to it; and guests take their places, according to rank, nearer to or further from it.

JAPAN SPIRITUAL

The Household Shrine

1

In Japan there are two forms of the Religion of the Dead - that which belongs to Shinto, and that which belongs to Buddhism. The first is the primitive cult, commonly called ancestor-worship. But the term ancestor-worship seems to me much too confined for the religion which pays reverence not only to those ancient gods believed to be the fathers of the Japanese race, but likewise to a host of deified sovereigns, heroes, princes, and illustrious men. Within comparatively recent times, the great *daimyō* of Izumo, for example, were apotheosised; and the peasants of Shimane still pray before the shrines of the Matsudaira. Moreover Shinto, like the faiths of Hellas and of Rome, has its deities of the elements and special deities who preside over all the various affairs of life. Therefore ancestor-worship, though still a striking feature of Shinto, does not alone constitute the State Religion: neither does the term fully describe the Shinto cult of the dead - a cult which in Izumo retains its primitive character more than in other parts of Japan.

And here I may presume, though no sinologue, to say something about the State Religion of Japan - that ancient faith of Izumo - which, although even more deeply rooted in national life than Buddhism, is far less known to the Western world. Except in special works by such men of erudition as Chamberlain and Satow - works with which the occidental reader, unless himself a specialist, is not likely to become familiar outside of Japan - little has been written in English about Shinto which gives the least idea of what Shinto is. Of its ancient traditions and rites much of rarest interest may be learned from the works of the philologists just mentioned; but, as Mr Satow himself acknowledges, a definite answer to the question, 'What is the nature of Shinto'? is still difficult to give. How define the common element in the six kinds of Shinto which are known to exist, and some of which no foreign scholar has yet been able to examine for lack of time or of authorities or of opportunity? Even in its modern external forms, Shinto is sufficiently complex to tax the united powers of the historian, philologist, and anthropologist merely to trace out the multitudinous lines of its evolution, and to determine the sources of its various elements: primeval polytheisms and fetichisms, traditions of dubious origin, philosophical concepts from China, Korea, and elsewhere, all mingled with Buddhism, Taoism, and Confucianism. The so-called 'Revival of Pure Shinto' - an effort, aided by Government, to restore the cult to its archaic simplicity by divesting it of foreign characteristics, and especially of every sign or token of Buddhist origin - resulted only, so far as the avowed purpose was concerned, in the destruction of priceless art, and in leaving the enigma of origins as complicated as before. Shinto had been too profoundly modified in the course of fifteen centuries of change to be thus remodelled by a fiat. For the like reason scholarly efforts to define its relation to national ethics by mere historical and philological analysis must fail: as well seek to define the ultimate secret of Life by the elements of the body which it animates. Yet when the result of such efforts shall have been closely combined with a deep knowledge of Japanese thought and feeling - the thought and sentiment, not of a special class, but of the people at large - then indeed all that Shinto was and is may be fully comprehended. And this may be accomplished, I fancy, through the united labour of European and Japanese scholars.

Yet something of what Shinto signifies - in the simple poetry of its beliefs, in the home-training of the child, in the worship of filial piety before the tablets of the ancestors - may be learned during a residence of some years among the people, by one who lives their life and adopts their manners and customs. With such experience he can at least claim the right to express his own conception of Shinto.

2

Those far-seeing rulers of the Meiji era, who disestablished Buddhism to strengthen Shinto, doubtless knew they were giving new force not only to a faith in perfect harmony with their own state policy, but likewise to one possessing in itself a far more profound vitality than the alien creed, which although omnipotent as an art-influence, had never found deep root in the intellectual soil of Japan. Buddhism is already in decrepitude, though transplanted from China scarcely more than thirteen centuries before; while Shinto, though doubtless older by many a thousand years, seems rather to have gained than to have lost force through all the periods of change. Eclectic like the genius of the race, it had appropriated and assimilated all forms of foreign thought which could aid its material manifestation or fortify its ethics. Buddhism had attempted to absorb its gods, even as it had adopted previously the ancient deities of Brahmanism; but Shinto, while seeming to yield, was really only borrowing strength from its rival. And this marvellous vitality of Shinto is due to the fact that in the course of its long development out of unrecorded beginnings, it religion of the heart. Whatever be the origin of its rites and traditions, its ethical spirit has become identified with all the deepest and best emotions of the race. Hence, in Izumo especially, the attempt to create a Buddhist-Shintoism resulted only in the formation of a Shinto-Buddhism.

And the secret living force of Shinto today - that force which repels missionary efforts at proselytising - means something much more profound than tradition or worship or ceremonialism. Shinto may yet, without loss of real power, survive all these. Certainly the expansion of the popular mind through education, the influences of modern science, must compel modification or abandonment of many ancient Shinto conceptions; but the ethics of Shinto will surely endure. For Shinto signifies character in the higher sense - courage, courtesy, honour, and above all things loyalty. The spirit of Shinto is the spirit of filial piety, the zest of duty, the readiness to surrender life for a principle without a thought of wherefore. It is the docility of the child; it is the sweetness of the Japanese woman. It is conservatism likewise; the wholesome check upon the national tendency to cast away the worth of the entire past in rash eagerness to assimilate too much of the foreign present. It is religion - but religion transformed into hereditary moral impulse - religion transmuted into ethical instinct. It is the whole emotional life of the race - the Soul of Japan.

The child is born Shinto. Home teaching and school training only give expression to what is innate: they do not plant new seed; they do not quicken the ethical sense transmitted as a trait ancestral. Even as a Japanese infant inherits such ability to handle a writing-brush as never can be acquired by Western fingers, so does it inherit ethical sympathies totally different from our own. Ask a class of Japanese students - young students of fourteen to sixteen - to tell their dearest wishes; and if they have confidence in the questioner, perhaps nine out of ten will answer: 'To die for His Majesty Our Emperor'. And the wish soars from the heart pure as any wish for martyrdom ever born. How much this sense of loyalty may or may not have been weakened in such great centres as Tokyo by the new agnosticism and by the rapid growth of other nineteenth-century ideas among the student class, I do not know; but in the country it remains as natural to boyhood as joy. Unreasoning it also is - unlike those loyal sentiments with us, the results of maturer knowledge and settled conviction. Never does the Japanese youth ask himself why; the beauty of self-sacrifice alone is the all-sufficing motive. Such ecstatic loyalty is a part of the national life; it is in the blood, inherent as the impulse of the ant to perish for its little republic, unconscious as the loyalty of bees to their queen. It is Shinto.

That readiness to sacrifice one's own life for loyalty's sake, for the sake of a superior, for the sake of honour, which has distinguished the race in modern times, would seem also to have been a national characteristic from the earliest period of its independent existence. Long before the epoch of established feudalism, when honorable suicide became a matter of rigid etiquette, not for warriors only, but even for women and little children, the giving of one's life for one's prince, even when the sacrifice could avail nothing, was held a sacred duty. Among various instances became at a very ancient epoch, and below the surface still remains, a which might be cited from the ancient *Kojiki*, the following is not the least impressive:

'Prince Mayowa, at the age of only seven years, having killed his father's slayer, fled into the house of the Grandee (*Omi*) Tsubura. Then Prince Oho-hatsuse raised an army, and beseiged that house. And the arrows that were shot were for multitude like the ears of the reeds. And the Grandee Tsubura came forth himself, and having taken off the weapons with which he was girded, did obeisance eight times, and said: "The maiden-princess Kara, my daughter whom thou deignedst anon to woo, is at thy service. Again I will present to thee five granaries. Though a vile slave of a Grandee exerting his utmost strength in the fight can scarcely hope to conquer, yet must he die rather than desert a prince who, trusting in him, has entered into his house." Having thus spoken, he again took his weapons, and went in once more to fight. Then, their strength being exhausted, and their arrows finished, he said to the Prince: "My hands are wounded, and our arrows are finished. We cannot now fight: what shall be done?" The Prince replied saying: "There is nothing more to do. Do thou now slay me." So the Grandee Tsubura thrust the Prince to death with his sword, and forthwith killed himself by cutting off his own head.'

Thousands of equally strong examples could easily be quoted from later Japanese history, including many which occurred even within the memory of the living. Nor was it for persons alone that to die might become a sacred duty: in certain contingencies conscience held it scarcely less a duty to die for a purely personal conviction; and he who held any opinion which he believed of paramount importance would, when other means failed, write his views in a letter of farewell, and then take his own life, in order to call attention to his beliefs and to prove their sincerity. Such an instance occurred only last year in Tokyo,[1] when the young lieutenant of militia, Ōhara Takeyoshi, killed himself by *harakiri* in the cemetery of Saitokuji, leaving a letter stating as the reason for his act, his hope to force public recognition of the danger to Japanese independence from the growth of Russian power in the North Pacific. But a much more touching sacrifice, in May of the same year - a sacrifice conceived in the purest and most innocent spirit of loyalty - was that of the young girl, Yoko Hatakeyama, who, after the attempt to assassinate the Czarevitch, travelled from Tokyo to Kyoto and there killed herself before the gate of the Kenchō, merely as a vicarious atonement for the incident which had caused shame to Japan and grief to the Father of the people - His Sacred Majesty the Emperor.

3

As to its exterior forms, modern Shinto is indeed difficult to analyse; but through all the intricate texture of extraneous beliefs so thickly interwoven about it, indications of its earliest character are still easily discerned. In certain of its primitive rites, in its archaic prayers and texts and symbols, in the history of its shrines, and even in many of the artless ideas of its poorest worshippers, it is plainly revealed as the most ancient of all forms of worship - that which Herbert Spencer terms 'the root of all religions' - devotion to the dead. Indeed, it has been frequently so expounded by its own greatest scholars and theologians. Its divinities are ghosts; *all* the dead become deities. In the *Tama-no-mihashira* the great commentator, Hirata, says 'the spirits of the dead continue to exist in the unseen world which is everywhere about us, and they all become gods of varying character and degrees of influence. Some reside in temples built in their honour; others hover near their tombs; and they continue to render services to their prince, parents, wife and children, as when in the body.'[2] And they do more than this, for they control the lives and the doings of men, 'Every human action', says Hirata, 'is the work of a god'.[3] And Motowori, scarcely less famous an exponent of pure Shinto doctrine, writes: 'All the moral ideas which a man requires are implanted in his bosom by the gods, and are of the same nature with those instincts which impel him to eat when he is hungry or to drink when he is thirsty.'[4] With this doctrine of Intuition no decalogue is required, no fixed code of ethics; and the human conscience is declared to be the only necessary guide. Though every action be 'the work of a *kami*', yet each man has within him the power to discern the righteous impulse from the unrighteous, the influence of the good deity from that of the evil. No moral teacher is so infallible as one's own heart. 'To have learned that there is no way (*michi*)',[5] says Motowori, 'to be learned and practised, is really to have learned the Way of the Gods'.[6] And Hirata writes: 'If you desire to practise true virtue, learn to stand in awe of the Unseen; and that will prevent you from doing wrong. Make a vow to the Gods who rule over the Unseen, and cultivate the conscience (*ma-gokoro*) implanted in you; and then you will never wander from the way.' How this spiritual self-culture may best be obtained, the same great expounder has stated with almost equal brevity: 'Devotion to the memory of ancestors is the mainspring of all virtues. No one who discharges his duty to them will ever be disrespectful to the Gods or to his living parents. Such a man will be faithful to his prince, loyal to his friends, and kind and gentle with his wife and children.'[7]

How far are these antique beliefs removed from the ideas of the nineteenth century? Certainly not so far that we can afford to smile at them. The faith of the primitive man and the knowledge of the most profound psychologist may meet in strange harmony upon the threshold of the same ultimate truth, and the thought of a child may repeat the conclusions of a Spencer or a Schopenhauer. Are not our ancestors in very truth our *kami*? Is not every action indeed the work of the Dead who dwell within us? Have not our impulses and tendencies, our capacities and weaknesses, our heroisms and timidities, been created by those vanished myriads from whom we received the all-mysterious bequest of Life? Do we still think of that infinitely complex Something which is each one of us, and which we call *ego*, as 'I' or as 'They'? What is our pride or shame but the pride or shame of the Unseen in that which They have made? - and what our Conscience but the inherited sum of countless dead experiences with varying good and evil? Nor can we hastily reject the Shinto thought that all the dead become gods, while we respect the convictions of those strong souls of today who proclaim the divinity of man.

4

Shinto ancestor-worship, no doubt, like all ancestor-worship, was developed out of funeral rites, according to that general law of religious evolution traced so fully by Herbert Spencer. And there is reason to believe that the early forms of Shinto public worship may have been evolved out of a yet older family worship, much after the manner in which M. Fustel de Coulanges, in his wonderful book, *La Cité Antique*, has shown the religious public institutions among the Greeks and Romans to have been developed from the religion of the hearth. Indeed, the word *ujigami*, now used to signify a Shinto parish temple, and also its deity, means 'family god', and in its present form is a corruption or contraction of *uchi-no-kami*, meaning the 'god of the interior' or 'the god of the house'. Shinto expounders have, it is true, attempted to interpret the term otherwise; and Hirata, as quoted by Mr Ernest Satow, declared the name should be applied only to the *common ancestor*, or ancestors, or to one so entitled to the gratitude of a community as to merit equal honours. Such, undoubtedly, was the just use of the term in his time, and long before it; but the etymology of the word would certainly seem to indicate its origin in family worship, and to confirm modern scientific beliefs in regard to the evolution of religious institutions.

Now just as among the Greeks and Latins the family cult always continued to exist through all the development and expansion of the public religion, so the Shinto family worship has continued concomitantly with the communal worship at the countless *ujigami*, with popular worship at the famed Oho-yashiro of various provinces or districts, and with national worship at the great shrines of Ise and Kitzuki. Many objects connected with the family cult are certainly of alien or modern origin; but its simple rites and its unconscious poetry retain their archaic charm. And, to the student of Japanese life, by far the most interesting aspect of Shinto is offered in this home worship, which, like the home worship of the antique Occident, exists in a dual form.

Footnotes:

1. This was written early in 1892.
2. Quoted from Mr. Satow's masterly essay, 'The Revival of Pure Shinto', published in the *Transactions* of the Asiatic Society of Japan. By 'gods' are not necessarily meant beneficent *Kami*. Shinto has no devils; but it has its 'bad gods' as well as good deities.
3. Satow, 'The Revival of Pure Shinto'.
4. *Ibid*.
5. In the sense of *Moral Path* - an ethical system.
6. Satow, 'The Revival of Pure Shinto'. The whole force of Motowori's words will not be fully understood unless the reader knows that the term 'Shinto' is of comparatively modern origin in Japan, having been borrowed from the Chinese to distinguish the ancient faith from Buddhism; and that the old name for the primitive religion is Kami-no-michi, 'the Way of the Gods'.
7. Satow, 'The Revival of Pure Shinto'.

Two Strange Festivals

1

The outward signs of any Japanese *matsuri* are the most puzzling of enigmas to the stranger who sees them for the first time. They are many and varied; they are quite unlike anything in the way of holiday decoration ever seen in the Occident; they have each a meaning founded upon some belief or some tradition - a meaning known to every Japanese child; but that meaning is utterly impossible for any foreigner to guess. Yet whoever wishes to know something of Japanese popular life and feeling must learn the signification of at least the most common among festival symbols and tokens. Especially is such knowledge necessary to the student of Japanese art: without it, not only the delicate humour and charm of countless designs must escape him, but in many instances the designs themselves must remain incomprehensible to him. For hundreds of years the emblems of festivity have been utilised by the Japanese in graceful decorative ways: they figure in metalwork, on porcelain, on the red or black lacquer of the humblest household utensils, on little brass pipes, on the clasps of tobacco-pouches. It may even be said that the majority of common decorative design is emblematical. The very figures of which the meaning seems most obvious - those matchless studies[1] of animal or vegetable life with which the Western curio-buyer is most familiar - have usually some ethical signification which is not perceived at all. Or take the commonest design dashed with a brush upon the *fusuma* of a cheap hotel - a lobster, sprigs of pine, tortoises waddling in a curl of water, a pair of storks, a spray of bamboo. It is rarely that a foreign tourist thinks of asking why such designs are used instead of others - even when he has seen them repeated, with slight variation, at twenty different places along his route. They have become conventional simply because they are emblems of which the sense is known to all Japanese, however ignorant, but is never even remotely suspected by the stranger.

The subject is one about which a whole encyclopaedia might be written, but about which I know very little - much too little for a special essay. But I may venture, by way of illustration, to speak of the curious objects exhibited during two antique festivals still observed in all parts of Japan.

2

The first is the Festival of the New Year, which lasts for three days. In Matsue its celebration is particularly interesting, as the old city still preserves many *matsuri* customs which have either become, or are rapidly becoming, obsolete elsewhere. The streets are then profusely decorated, and all shops are closed. *Shimenawa* or *shimekazari*, the straw ropes which have been sacred symbols of Shinto from the mythical age, are festooned along the façades of the dwellings, and so interjoined that you see to right or left what seems but a single mile-long *shimenawa*, with its straw pendants and white fluttering paper cuttings (*gohei*), extending along either side of the street as far as the eye can reach. Japanese flags - bearing on a white ground the great crimson disk which is the emblem of the Land of the Rising Sun - flutter above the gateways; and the same national emblem glows upon countless paper lanterns strung in rows along the eaves or across the streets and temple avenues. And before every gate or doorway a *kadomatsu* ('gate pine-tree') has been erected. So that all the ways are lined with green, and full of bright colour.

The *kadomatsu* is more than its name implies. It is a young pine, or part of a pine, conjoined with plum branches and bamboo cuttings.[2] Pine, plum and bamboo are growths of emblematic significance. Anciently the pine alone was used; but from the era of O-ei, the bamboo was added; and within more recent times the plum-tree.

The pine has many meanings. But the fortunate one most generally accepted is that of endurance and successful energy in time of misfortune. As the pine keeps its green leaves when other trees lose their foliage, so the true man keeps his courage and his strength in adversity. The pine is also, as I have said elsewhere, a symbol of vigorous old age.

No European could possibly guess the riddle of the bamboo. It represents a sort of pun in symbolism. There are two Chinese characters both pronounced *setsu* - one signifying the *node* or joint of the bamboo, and the other virtue, fidelity, constancy. Therefore is the bamboo used as a felicitous sign. The name 'Setsu', be it observed, is often given to Japanese maidens, just as the names 'Faith', 'Fidelia' and 'Constance' are given to English girls.

The plum tree - of whose emblematic meaning I said something in a former paper about Japanese gardens - is not invariably used, however; sometimes *sakaki*, the sacred plant of Shinto, is substituted for it; and sometimes only pine and bamboo form the *kadomatsu*.

Every decoration used upon the New Year's festival has a meaning of a curious and unfamiliar kind; and the very commonest of all - the straw rope- possesses the most complicated symbolism. In the first place it is scarcely necessary to explain that its origin belongs to that most ancient legend of the Sun-Goddess being tempted to issue from the cavern into which she had retired, and being prevented from returning thereunto by a deity who stretched a rope of straw across the entrance - all of which is written in the *Kojiki*. Next observe that, although the *shimenawa* may be of any thickness, it must be twisted so that the direction of the twist is to the left; for in ancient Japanese philosophy the left is the 'pure' or fortunate side: owing perhaps to the old belief, common among the uneducated of Europe to this day, that the heart lies to the left. Thirdly, note that the pendent straws, which hang down from the rope at regular intervals, in tufts, like fringing, must be of different numbers according to the place of the tufts, beginning with the number three: so that the first tuft has three straws, the second five, the third seven, the fourth again three, the fifth five, and the sixth seven - and so on, the whole length of the rope. The origin of the pendant paper cuttings (*gohei*) which alternate with the straw tufts, is likewise to be sought in the legend of the Sun-Goddess; but the *gohei* also represent offerings of cloth anciently made to the gods according to a custom long obsolete.

But besides the *gohei*, there are many other things attached to the *shimenawa* of which you could not imagine the signification. Among these are fern-leaves, bitter oranges, *yuzuri* leaves, and little bundles of charcoal.

Why fern-leaves (*moromoki* or *urajirō*)? Because the fern-leaf is the symbol of the hope of exuberant posterity: even as it branches and rebranches so may the happy family increase and multiply through the generations.

Why bitter oranges (*daidai*)? Because there is a Chinese word *daidai* signifying 'from generation unto generation'. Wherefore the fruit called *daidai* has become a fruit of good omen.

But why charcoal (*sumi*)? It signifies 'prosperous *changelessness*'. Here the idea is decidedly curious. Even as the colour of charcoal cannot be changed, so may the fortunes of those we love remain forever unchanged in all that gives happiness! The signification of the *yuzuri* leaf I explained in a former paper.

Besides the great *shimenawa* in front of the house, *shimenawa* or *shimekazari*[3] are suspended above the *toko*, or alcoves, in each apartment; and over the back gate, or over the entrance to the gallery of the second story (if there be a second story), is hung a *wajime*, which is a very small *shimekazari* twisted into a sort of wreath, and decorated with fern-leaves, *gohei*, and *yuzuri* leaves.

But the great domestic display of the festival is the decoration of the *kamidana*, the shelf of the Gods. Before the household *miya* are placed great double rice cakes; and the shrine is beautified with flowers, a tiny *shimekazari*, and sprays of *sakaki*. There also are placed a string of cash; *kabu* (turnips); *daikon* (radishes); a tai-fish, which is the 'king of fishes', dried slices of salt cuttlefish; *jinbaso*, or 'the Seaweed of the Horse of the God';[4] - also the seaweed *kombu*, which is a symbol of pleasure and of joy, because its name is deemed to be a homonym for gladness; and *mochibana*, artificial blossoms formed of rice flour and straw.

The *sambō* is a curiously-shaped little table on which offerings are made to the Shinto gods; and almost every well-to-do household in Izumo has its own *sambō*; such a family *sambō* being smaller, however, than *sambō* used in the temples. At the advent of the New Year's Festival, bitter oranges, rice, and rice-flour cakes, native sardines (*iwashi*), *chikara-iwai* ('strength-rice-bread'), black peas, dried chestnuts, and a fine lobster, are all tastefully arranged upon the family *sambō*. Before each visitor the *sambō* is set; and the visitor, by saluting it with a prostration, expresses not only his heartfelt wish that all the good fortune symbolised by the objects upon the *sambō* may come to the family, but also his reverence for the household gods. The black peas (*mame*) signify bodily strength and health, because a word similarly pronounced, though written with a different ideograph, means 'robust'. But why a lobster? Here we have another curious conception. The lobster's body is bent double: the body of the man who lives to a very great old age is also bent. Thus the lobster stands for a symbol of extreme old age; and in artistic design signifies the wish that our friends may live so long that they will become bent like lobsters under the weight of years. And the dried chestnuts (*kachiguri*) are emblems of success, because the first character of their name in Japanese is the homonym of *kachi*, which means 'victory', 'conquest'.

There are at least a hundred other singular customs and emblems belonging to the New Year's Festival which would require a large volume to describe. I have mentioned only a few which immediately appeal to even casual observation.

3

The other festival I wish to refer to is that of the *Setsubun*, which, according the ancient Japanese calendar, corresponded with the beginning of the natural year - the period when winter first softens into spring. It is what we might term, according to Professor Chamberlain, 'a sort of movable feast'; and it is chiefly famous for the curious ceremony of the casting out of devils, *Oni-yarai*. On the eve of the *Setsubun*, a little after dark, the *yaku-otoshi*, or caster-out of devils, wanders through the streets from house to house, rattling his *shakujō*,[5] and uttering his strange professional cry: '*Oni wa soto! - fuku wa uchi*'! (Devils out! Good fortune in!) For a trifling fee he performs his little exorcism in any house to which he is called. This simply consists in the recitation of certain parts of a Buddhist *kyō*, or sutra, and the rattling of the *shakujō*. Afterwards dried peas (*shiro-mame*) are thrown about the house in four directions. For some mysterious reason, devils do not like dried peas - and flee therefrom. The peas thus scattered are afterwards swept up and carefully preserved until the first clap of spring thunder is heard, when it is the custom to cook and eat some of them. But just why, I cannot find out; neither can I discover the origin of the dislike of devils for dried peas. On the subject of this dislike, however, I confess my sympathy with devils.

After the devils have been properly cast out a small charm is placed above all the entrances of the dwelling to keep them from coming back again. This consists of a little stick about the length and thickness of a skewer, a single holly-leaf, and the head of a dried *iwashi* - a fish resembling a sardine. The stick is stuck through the middle of the holly leaf; and the fish's head is fastened into a split made in one end of the stick; the other end being slipped into some joint of the timber-work immediately above a door. But why the devils are afraid of the holly leaf and the fish's head, nobody seems to know. Among the people the origin of all these curious customs appears to be quite forgotten; and the families of the upper classes who still maintain such customs believe in the superstitions relating to the festival just as little as Englishmen today believe in the magical virtues of mistletoe or ivy.

This ancient and merry annual custom of casting out devils has been for generations a source of inspiration to Japanese artists. It is only after a fair acquaintance with popular customs and ideas that the foreigner can learn to appreciate the delicious humour of many art creations which he may wish, indeed, to buy just because they are so oddly attractive in themselves, but which must really remain enigmas to him, so far as their inner meaning is concerned, unless he knows Japanese life. The other day a friend gave me a little card-case of perfumed leather. One one side was stamped in relief the face of a devil, through the orifice of whose yawning mouth could be seen, painted upon the silk lining of the interior, the laughing, chubby face of Otafuku, joyful Goddess of Good Luck. In itself the thing was very curious and pretty; but the real merit of its design was this comical symbolism of good wishes for the New Year: *'Oni wa soto! - fuku wa uchi'*!

4

Since I have spoken of the custom of eating some of the *Setsubun* peas at the time of the first spring thunder, I may here take the opportunity to say a few words about superstitions in regard to thunder which have not yet ceased to prevail among the peasantry.

When a thunder-storm comes, the big brown mosquito curtains are suspended, and the women and children - perhaps the whole family - squat down under the curtains till the storm is over. From ancient days it has been believed that lightning cannot kill anybody under a mosquito curtain. The *Raijū*, or Thunder-Animal, cannot pass through a mosquito curtain. Only the other day, an old peasant who came to the house with vegetables to sell told us that he and his whole family, while crouching under their mosquito-netting during a thunder-storm, actually saw the lightning rushing up and down the pillar of the balcony opposite their apartment, furiously clawing the woodwork, but unable to enter because of the mosquito-netting. His house had been badly damaged by a flash; but he supposed the mischief to have been accomplished by the Claws of the Thunder-Animal.

The Thunder-Animal springs from tree to tree during a storm, they say; wherefore to stand under trees in time of thunder and lightning is very dangerous: the Thunder-Animal might step on one's head or shoulders. The Thunder-Animal is also alleged to be fond of eating the human navel; for which reason people should be careful to keep their navels well covered during storms, and to lie down upon their stomachs if possible. Incense is always burned during storms, because the Thunder-Animal hates the smell of incense. A tree stricken by lightning is thought to have been torn and scarred by the claws of the Thunder-Animal; and fragments of its bark and wood are carefully collected and preserved by dwellers in the vicinity; for the wood of a blasted tree is alleged to have the singular virtue of curing toothache.

There are many stories of the *Raijū* having been caught and caged. Once, it is said, the Thunder-Animal fell into a well, and got entangled in the ropes and buckets, and so was captured alive. And old Izumo folk say they remember that the Thunder-Animal was once exhibited in the court of the Temple of Tenjin in Matsue, enclosed in a cage of brass; and that people paid one sen each to look at it. It resembled a badger. When the weather was clear it would sleep contentedly in its cage. But when there was thunder in the air, it would become excited, and seem to obtain great strength, and its eyes would flash dazzlingly.

5

There is one very evil spirit, however, who is not in the least afraid of dried peas, and who cannot be so easily got rid of as the common devils; and that is Bimbogami.

But in Izumo people know a certain household charm whereby Bimbogami may sometimes be cast out.

Before any cooking is done in a Japanese kitchen, the little charcoal fire is first blown to a bright red heat with that most useful and simple household utensil called a *hifukidake* ('fire-blow-bamboo'), a bamboo tube usually about three feet long and about two inches in diameter. At one end - the end which is to be turned towards the fire - only a very small orifice is left; the woman who prepares the meal places the other end to her lips, and blows through the tube upon the kindled charcoal. Thus a quick fire may be obtained in a few minutes.

In course of time the *hifukidake* becomes scorched and cracked and useless. A new 'fire-blow-tube' is then made; and the old one is used as a charm against Bimbogami. One little copper coin (*rin*) is put into it, some magical formula is uttered, and then the old utensil, with the rin inside of it, is either simply thrown out through the front gate into the street, or else flung into some neighbouring stream. This - I know not why - is deemed equivalent to pitching Bimbogami out of doors, and rendering it impossible for him to return during a considerable period.
It may be asked how is the invisible presence of Bimbogami to be detected.

The little insect which makes that weird ticking noise at night called in England the Death-watch has a Japanese relative named by the people *Bimbo-mushi*, or the 'Poverty-Insect'. It is said to be the servant of Bimbogami, the God of Poverty; and its ticking in a house is believed to signal the presence of that most unwelcome deity.

6

One more future of the *Setsubun* festival is worthy of mention - the sale of the *hitogata* ('people-shapes'). These are little figures, made of white paper, representing men, women, and children. They are cut out with a few clever scissors strokes; and the difference of sex is indicated by variations in the shape of the sleeves and the little paper *obi*. They are sold in the Shinto temples. The purchaser buys one for every member of the family, the priest writing upon each the age and sex of the person for whom it is intended. These *hitogata* are then taken home and distributed; and each person slightly rubs his body or her body with the paper, and says a little Shinto prayer. Next day, the *hitogata* are returned to the *kannushi*, who, after having recited certain formulae over them, burns them with holy fire.[6] By this ceremony it is hoped that all physical misfortunes will be averted from the family during a year.

Footnotes:

1. As it has become, among a certain sect of Western Philistines and self-constituted art critics, the fashion to sneer at any writer who becomes enthusiastic about the *truth to nature* of Japanese art, I may cite here the words of England's most celebrated living *naturalist* on this very subject. Mr Wallace's authority will scarcely, I presume, be questioned, even by the Philistines referred to:

'Dr Mohnike possesses a large collection of coloured sketches of the plants of Japan made by a Japanese lady, *which are the most masterly things I have ever seen.* Every stem, twig, and leaf is produced by single touches of the brush, the character and perspective of very complicated plants being admirably given, and the articulations of stem and leaves shown in a *most scientific manner.*' (Malay Archipelago, chap. xx.)

Now this was written in 1857, before European methods of drawing had been introduced. The same art of painting leaves, etc. with single strokes of the brush is still common in Japan, even among the poorest class of decorators.

2. There is a Buddhist saying about the *kadomatsu:*

> Kadomatsu
> Meido no tabi no
> Ichi-ri-zuka.

The meaning is that each *kadomatsu* is a milestone on the journey to the Meido; or, in other words, that each New Year's festival signals only the completion of another stage of the ceaseless journey to death.

3. The difference between the *shimenawa* and *shimekazari* is that the latter is a strictly decorative straw rope, to which many curious emblems are attached.

4. It belongs to the sargassum family, and is full of air sacs. Various kinds of edible seaweed form a considerable proportion of Japanese diet.

5. This is a curiously shaped staff with which the divinity Jizō is commonly represented. It is still carried by Buddhist mendicants, and there are several sizes of it. That carried by the Yaku-otoshi is usually very short. There is a tradition that the *shakujō* was first invented as a means of giving warnings to insects or other little creatures in the path of the Buddhist pilgrim, so that they might not be trodden upon unawares.

6. I may make mention here of another matter, in no way relating to the *Setsubun*. There lingers in Izumo a wholesome - and I doubt not formerly a most valuable - superstition about the sacredness of writing. Paper upon which anything has been written, or even printed, must not be crumpled up, or trodden upon, or dirtied, or put to any base use. If it be necessary to destroy a document, the paper should be burned. I have been gently reproached in a little hotel at which I stopped for tearing up and crumpling some paper covered with my own writing.

Jizō

1

I have passed another day in wandering among the temples, both Shinto and Buddhist. I have seen many curious things; but I have not yet seen the face of the Buddha.

Repeatedly, after long wearisome climbing of stone steps, and passing under gates full of gargoyles - heads of elephants and heads of lions - and entering shoeless into scented twilight, into enchanted gardens of golden lotus-flowers of paper, and there waiting for my eyes to become habituated to the dimness, I have looked in vain for images. Only an opulent glimmering confusion of things half-seen - vague altar-splendours created by gilded bronzes twisted into riddles, by vessels of indescribable shape, by enigmatic texts of gold, by mysterious glittering pendent things - all framing only a shrine with doors fast closed.

What has most impressed me is the seeming joyousness of popular faith. I have seen nothing grim, austere, or self-repressive. I have not even noted anything approaching the solemn. The bright temple courts and even the temple steps are thronged with laughing children, playing curious games; and mothers, entering the sanctuary to pray, suffer their little ones to creep about the matting and crow. The people take their religion lightly and cheerfully: they drop their cash in the great alms-box, clap their hands, murmur a very brief prayer, then turn to laugh and talk and smoke their little pipes before the temple entrance. Into some shrines, I have noticed the worshippers do not enter at all; they merely stand before the doors and pray for a few seconds, and make their small offerings. Blessed are they who do not too much fear the gods which they have made!

2

Akira is bowing and smiling at the door. He slips off his sandals, enters in his white digitated stockings, and, with another smile and bow, sinks gently into the proffered chair. Akira is an interesting boy. With his smooth beardless face, and clear bronze skin, and blue-black hair trimmed into a shock that shadows his forehead to the eyes, he has almost the appearance, in his long wide-sleeved robe and snowy stockings, of a young Japanese girl.

I clap my hands for tea, hotel tea, which he calls 'Chinese tea'. I offer him a cigar, which he declines; but with my permission, he will smoke his pipe. Thereupon he draws from his girdle a Japanese pipe-case and tobacco-pouch combined; pulls out of the pipe-case a little brass pipe with a bowl scarcely large enough to hold a pea; pulls out of the pouch some tobacco so finely cut that it looks like hair, stuffs a tiny pellet of this preparation in the pipe, and begins to smoke. He draws the smoke into his lungs, and blows it out again through his nostrils. Three little whiffs, at intervals of about half a minute, and the pipe, emptied, is replaced in its case.

Meanwhile I have related to Akira the story of my disappointments.

'Oh, you can see him to-day', responds Akira, 'if you will take a walk with me to the Temple of Zotokuin. For this is the *Busshōe*, the festival of the Birthday of Buddha. But he is very small, only a few inches high. If you want to see a great Buddha, you must go to Kamakura. There is a Buddha in that place, sitting upon a lotus; and he is fifty feet high.'

So I go forth under the guidance of Akira. He says he may be able to show me 'some curious things'.

3

There is a sound of happy voices from the temple, and the steps are crowded with smiling mothers and laughing children. Entering, I find women and babies pressing about a lacquered table in front of the doorway. Upon it is a little tub-shaped vessel of sweet tea - *amacha*; and standing in the tea is a tiny figure of Buddha, one hand pointing upward and one downward. The women, having made the customary offering, take up some of the tea with a wooden ladle of curious shape, and pour it over the statue, and then, filling the ladle a second time, drink a little, and give a sip to their babies. This is the ceremony of washing the statue of Buddha.

Near the lacquered stand on which the vessel of sweet tea rests is another and lower stand supporting a temple bell shaped like a great bowl. A priest approaches with a padded mallet in his hand and strikes the bell. But the bell does not sound properly: he starts, looks into it, and stoops to lift out of it a smiling Japanese baby. The mother, laughing, runs to look at us with a frankness of mirth in which we join.

Akira leaves me a moment to speak with one of the temple attendants, and presently returns with a curious lacquered box, about a foot in length, and four inches wide on each of its four sides. There is only a small hole in one end of it; no appearance of a lid of any sort.

'Now', says Akira, 'if you wish to pay two sen, we shall learn our future lot according to the will of the gods'.

I pay the two sen, and Akira shakes the box. Out comes a narrow slip of bamboo, with Chinese characters written thereon.

'*Kitsu*'! cries Akira. 'Good fortune. The number is fifty-and-one'.

Again he shakes the box; a second bamboo slip issues from the slit.

'*Dai kitsu*! - great good fortune. The number is ninety-and-nine.'

Once more the box is shaken; once more the oracular bamboo protrudes.

'*Kyō*'! laughs Akira. 'Evil will befall us. The number is sixty-and-four'.

He returns the box to a priest, and receives three mysterious papers, numbered with numbers corresponding to the numbers of the bamboo slips: These little bamboo slips, or divining-sticks, are called *mikuji*.

This, as translated by Akira, is the substance of the text of the paper numbered fifty-and-one:

'He who draweth forth this *mikuji*, let him live according to the heavenly law and worship Kwannon. If his trouble be a sickness, it shall pass from him. If he have lost aught, it shall be found. If he have a suit at law, he shall gain. If he love a woman, he shall surely win her - though he should have to wait. And many happinesses will come to him.'

The *dai-kitsu* paper reads almost similarly, with the sole differences that, instead of Kwannon, the deities of wealth and prosperity - Daikoku, Bishamon, and Benten - are to be worshipped, and that the fortunate man will not have to wait at all for the woman loved. But the *kyō* paper reads thus:

'He who draweth forth this *mikuji*, it will be well for him to obey the heavenly law and to worship Kwannon the Merciful. If he have any sickness, even much more sick he shall become. If he have lost aught, it shall never be found. If he have a suit at law, he shall never gain it. If he love a woman, let him have no more expectation of winning her. Only by the most diligent piety can he hope to escape the most frightful calamities. And there shall be no felicity in his portion.'

'All the same, we are fortunate', declares Akira. 'Twice out of three times we have found luck. Now we will go to see another statue of Buddha'.

And he guides me, through many curious streets, to the southern verge of the city.

4

Before us rises a hill, with a broad flight of stone steps sloping to its summit, between foliage of cedars and maples. We climb; and I see above me the Lions of Buddha waiting, the male yawning menace, the female with mouth closed. Passing between them, we enter a large temple court, at whose farther end rises another wooded eminence.

And here is the temple, with roof of blue-painted copper tiles, and tilted eaves and gargoyles and dragons, all weather-stained to one neutral tone. The paper screens are open, but a melancholy rhythmic chant from within tells us that the noonday service is being held: the priests are chanting the syllables of Sanscrit texts transliterated into Chinese, intoning the Sutra called the Sutra of the Lotus of the Good Law. One of those who chant keeps time by tapping with a mallet, cotton-wrapped, some grotesque object shaped like a dolphin's head, all lacquered in scarlet and gold, which gives forth a dull, booming tone - a *mokugyo*.

To the right of the temple is a little shrine, filling the air with fragrance of incense-burning. I peer in through the blue smoke that curls up from half a dozen tiny rods planted in a small brazier full of ashes; and far back in the shadow I see a swarthy Buddha, tiara-coiffed, with head bowed and hands joined, just as I see the Japanese praying, erect in the sun, before the thresholds of temples. The figure is of wood, rudely wrought and rudely coloured: still the placid face has beauty of suggestion.

Crossing the court to the left of the building, I find another flight of steps before me, leading up a slope to something mysterious still higher, among enormous trees. I ascend these steps also, reach the top, guarded by two small symbolic lions, and suddenly find myself in cool shadow, and startled by a spectacle totally unfamiliar.

Dark - almost black - soil, and the shadowing of trees immemorially old, through whose vaulted foliage the sunlight leaks thinly down in rare flecks: a crepuscular light, tender and solemn, revealing the weirdest host of unfamiliar shapes - a vast congregation of grey, columnar, mossy things, stony, monumental, sculptured with Chinese ideographs. And about them, behind them, rising high above them, thickly set as rushes in a marsh-verge, tall slender wooden tablets, like laths, covered with similar fantastic lettering, pierce the green gloom by thousands, by tens of thousands.

And before I can note other details, I know that I am in a *hakaba*, a cemetery - a very ancient Buddhist cemetery.

These laths are called in the Japanese tongue *sotoba*.[1] All have notches cut upon their edges on both sides near the top - five notches; and all are painted with Chinese characters on both faces. One inscription is always the phrase '*To promote Buddhahood*', painted immediately below the dead man's name; the inscription upon the other surface is always a sentence in Sanscrit whose meaning has been forgotten even by those priests who perform the funeral rites. One such lath is planted behind the tomb as soon as the monument (*haka*) is set up; then another every seven days for forty-nine days; then one after the lapse of a hundred days; then one at the end of a year, then one after the passing of three years; and at successively longer periods others are erected during one hundred years.

And in almost every group I notice some quite new, of freshly planed unpainted white wood, standing beside others grey or even black with age; and there are many, still older, from whose surface all the characters have disappeared. Others are lying on the sombre clay. Hundreds stand so loose in the soil that the least breeze jostles and clatters them together.

Not less unfamiliar in their forms, but far more interesting, are the monuments of stone. One shape I know represents five of the Buddhist elements: a cube supporting a sphere which upholds a pyramid on which rests a shallow square cup with four crescent edges and tilted corners, and in the cup a pyriform body poised with the point upwards. These successively typify Earth, Water, Fire, Wind, Ether, the five substances wherefrom the body is shapen, and into which it is resolved by death; the absence of any emblem for the Sixth element, *Knowledge*, touches more than any imagery conceivable could do. And nevertheless, in the purpose of the symbolism, this omission was never planned with the same idea that it suggests to the Occidental mind.

Very numerous also among the monuments are low, square, flat-topped shafts, with a Japanese inscription in black or gold, or merely cut into the stone itself. Then there are upright slabs of various shapes and heights, mostly rounded at the top, usually bearing sculptures in relief. Finally, there are many curiously angled stones, or natural rocks, dressed on one side only, with designs etched upon the smoothed surface. There would appear to be some meaning even in the irregularity of the shape of these slabs; the rock always seems to have been broken out of its bed at five angles, and the manner in which it remains balanced perpendicularly upon its pedestal is a secret that the first hasty examination fails to reveal.

The pedestals themselves vary in construction; most have three orifices in the projecting surface in front of the monument supported by them, usually one large oval cavity, with two small round holes flanking it. These smaller holes serve for the burning of incense-rods; the larger cavity is filled with water. I do not know exactly why. Only my Japanese companion tells me 'it is an ancient custom in Japan thus to pour out water for the dead'. There are also bamboo cups on either side of the monument in which to place flowers.

Many of the sculptures represent Buddha in meditation, or in the attitude of exhorting; a few represent him asleep, with the placid, dreaming face of a child, a Japanese child; this means Nirvana. A common design upon many tombs also seems to be two lotus-blossoms with stalks intertwined.

In one place I see a stone with an English name upon it, and above that name a rudely chiselled cross. Verily the priests of Buddha have blessed tolerance; for this is a Christian tomb!

And all is chipped and mouldered and mossed: and the grey stones stand closely in hosts of ranks, only one or two inches apart, ranks of thousands upon thousands, always in the shadow of the great trees. Overhead innumerable birds sweeten the air with their trilling; and far below, down the steps behind us, I still hear the melancholy chant of the priests, faintly, like a humming of bees.

Akira leads the way in silence to where other steps descend into a darker and older part of the cemetery; and at the head of the steps, to the right, I see a group of colossal monuments, very tall, massive, mossed by time, with characters cut more than two inches deep into the grey rock of them. And behind them, in lieu of laths, are planted large *sotoba*, twelve to fourteen feet high, and thick as the beams of a temple roof. These are graves of priests.

5

Descending the shadowed steps, I find myself face to face with six little statues about three feet high, standing in a row upon the long pedestal. The first holds a Buddhist incense-box; the second, a lotus; the third, a pilgrim's staff (*tsue*); the fourth is telling the beads of a Buddhist rosary; the fifth stands in the attitude of prayer, with hands joined; the sixth bears in one hand the *shakujō* or mendicant priest's staff, having six rings attached to the top of it, and in the other hand the mystic jewel, *Nio-i hō-jiu*, by virtue whereof all desires may be accomplished. But the faces of the Six are the same: each figure differs from the other by the attitude only and emblematic attribute; and all are smiling the like faint smile. About the neck of each figure a white cotton bag is suspended; and all the bags are filled with pebbles; and pebbles have been piled high also about the feet of the statues, and upon their knees, and upon their shoulders; and even upon their aureoles of stone, little pebbles are balanced. Archaic, mysterious, but inexplicably touching, all these soft childish faces are.

Roku Jizō - 'The Six Jizō' - these images are called in the speech of the people; and such groups may be seen in many a Japanese cemetery. They are representations of the most beautiful and tender figure in Japanese popular faith, that charming divinity who cares for the souls of little children, and consoles them in the place of unrest, and saves them from the demons. 'But why are those little stones piled about the statues?' I ask.

Well, it is because some say the child-ghosts must build little towers of stones for penance in the *Sai-no-Kawara*, which is the place to which all children after death must go. And the *oni*, who are demons, come to throw down the little stone-piles as fast as the children build; and these demons frighten the children, and torment them. But the little souls run to Jizō, who hides them in his great sleeves, and comforts them, and makes the demons go away. And every stone one lays upon the knees or at the feet of Jizō, with a prayer from the heart, helps some child-soul in the *Sai-no-Kawara* to perform its long penance.[2]

'All little children', says the young Buddhist student who tells all this, with a smile as gentle as Jizō's own, 'must go to the *Sai-no-Kawara*

126

when they die. And there they play with Jizō. The *Sai-no-Kawara* is beneath us, below the ground.[3]

'And Jizō has long sleeves to his robe; and they pull him by the sleeves in their play; and they pile up little stones before him to amuse themselves. And those stones you see heaped about the statues are put there by people for the sake of the little ones, most often by mothers of dead children who pray to Jizō. But grown people do not go to the *Sai-no-Kawara* when they die.'[4]

And the young student, leaving the Roku-Jizō, leads the way to other strange surprises, guiding me among the tombs, showing me the sculptured divinities.

Some of them are quaintly touching; all are interesting; a few are positively beautiful.

The greater number have nimbi. Many are represented kneeling, with hands joined exactly like the figures of saints in old Christian art. Others, holding lotus-flowers, appear to dream the dreams that are meditations. One figure reposes on the coils of a great serpent. Another, coiffed with something resembling a tiara, has six hands, one pair joined in prayer, the rest, extended, holding out various objects; and this figure stands upon a prostrate demon, crouching face downwards. Yet another image, cut in low relief, has arms innumerable. The first pair of hands are joined, with the palms together; while from behind the line of the shoulders, as if shadowily emanating therefrom, multitudinous arms reach out in all directions, vapoury, spiritual, holding forth all kinds of objects as in answer to supplication, and symbolising, perhaps, the omnipotence of love. This is but one of the many forms of Kwannon, the goddess of mercy, the gentle divinity who refused the rest of Nirvana to save the souls of men, and who is most frequently pictured as a beautiful Japanese girl. But here she appears as Senjiu-Kwannon (Kwannon-of-the-Thousand-Hands). Close by stands a great slab bearing upon the upper portion of its chiselled surface an image in relief of Buddha meditating upon a lotus; and below are carven three weird little figures, one with hands upon its eyes, one with hands upon its ears, one with hands upon its mouth; these are Apes. 'What do they signify'? I inquire. My friend answers vaguely, mimicking each gesture of the three sculptured shapes:

'*I see no bad thing; I hear no bad thing; I speak no bad thing.*'
Gradually, by dint of reiterated explanations, I myself learn to recognise some of the gods at sight. The figure seated upon a lotus, holding a sword in its hand, and surrounded by bickering fire, is Fudō-Sama - Buddha as the Unmoved, the Immutable: the Sword signifies Intellect; the Fire, Power. Here is a meditating divinity, holding in one hand a coil of ropes: the divinity is Buddha; those are the ropes which bind the passions and desires. Here also is Buddha slumbering, with the gentlest, softest Japanese face, a child face, and eyes closed, and hand pillowing the cheek, in Nirvana. Here is a beautiful virgin-figure, standing upon a lily: Kwannon-Sama, the Japanese Madonna. Here is a solemn seated figure, holding in one hand a vase, and lifting the other with the gesture of a teacher: Yakushi-Sama, Buddha the All-Healer, Physician of Souls.

Also, I see figures of animals. The Deer of Buddhist birth-stories stands, all grace, in snowy stone, upon the summit of *tōrō*, or votive lamps. On one tomb I see, superbly chiselled, the image of a fish, or rather the idea of a fish, made beautifully grotesque for sculptural purposes, like the dolphin of Greek art. It crowns the top of a memorial column; the broad open jaws, showing serrated teeth, rest on the summit of the block bearing the dead man's name; the dorsal fin and elevated tail are elaborated into decorative impossibilities. '*Mokugyo*', says Akira. It is the same Buddhist emblem as that hollow wooden object, lacquered scarlet-and-gold, on which the priests beat with a padded mallet while chanting the Sutra. And, finally, in one place I perceive a pair of sitting animals, of some mythological species, supple of figure as greyhounds. '*Kitsune*', says Akira, 'foxes'. So they are, now that I look upon them with knowledge of their purpose; idealised foxes, foxes spiritualised, impossibly graceful foxes. They are chiselled in some grey stone. They have long, narrow, sinister, glittering eyes; they seem to snarl; they are weird, very weird creatures, the servants of the Rice-God, retainers of Inari-Sama, and properly belong, not to Buddhist iconography, but the imagery of Shinto.

Farther on, I find other figures of Jizō, single reliefs, sculptured upon tombs. But one of these is a work of art so charming that I feel a pain at being obliged to pass it by. More sweet, assuredly, than any imaged Christ, this dream in white stone of the playfellow of dead children, like a beautiful young boy, with gracious eyelids half closed, and face made heavenly by such a smile as only Buddhist art could have imagined, the smile of infinite lovingness of supremest gentleness. Indeed, so charming the ideal of Jizō is that in the speech of the people a beautiful face is always likened to his - *Jizō-kao*, as the face of Jizō.

6

And we come to the end of the cemetery, to the verge of the great grove.

Beyond the trees, what caressing sun, what spiritual loveliness in the tender day! A tropic sky always seemed to me to hang so low that one could almost bathe one's fingers in its lukewarm liquid blue by reaching upward from any dwelling-roof. But this sky, softer, fainter, arches so vastly as to suggest the heaven of a larger planet. And the very clouds are not clouds, but only dreams of clouds, so filmy they are; ghosts of clouds, diaphanous spectres, illusions!

All at once I become aware of a child standing before me, a very young girl who looks up wonderingly at my face; so light her approach that the joy of the birds and whispering of the leaves quite drowned the soft sound of her feet. Her ragged garb is Japanese; but her gaze, her loose fair hair, are not of Nippon only; the ghost of another race - perhaps my own - watches me through her flower-blue eyes. A strange playground surely is this for thee, my child; I wonder if all these shapes about thee do not seem very weird, very strange, to that little soul of thine. But no; 'tis only I who seem strange to thee; thou hast forgotten the Other Birth, and thy father's world.

Half-caste, and poor, and pretty, in this foreign port! Better thou wert with the dead about thee, child! better than the splendour of this soft blue light the unknown darkness for thee. There the gentle Jizō would care for thee, and hide thee in his great sleeves, and keep all evil from thee, and play shadowy play with thee; and this thy forsaken mother, who now comes to ask an alms for thy sake, dumbly pointing to thy strange beauty with her patient Japanese smile, would put little stones upon the knees of the dear god that thou mightest find rest.

7

'Oh, Akira! you must tell me something more about Jizō, and the ghosts of the children in the *Sai-no-Kawara*.'

'I cannot tell you much more', answers Akira, smiling at my interest in this charming divinity; 'but if you will come with me now to Kuboyama, I will show you, in one of the temples there, pictures of the *Sai-no-Kawara* and of Jizō, and the Judgment of Souls.'

Footnotes:

1. Derived from the Sanscrit *stupa*.
2. 'The real origin of the custom of piling stones before the images of Jizō and other divinities is not now known to the people. The custom is founded upon a passage in the famous Sutra, "The Lotus of the Good Law".

'Even the little boys who, in playing, erected here and there heaps of sand, with the intention of dedicating them as Stupas to the Ginas - they have all of them reached enlightenment.' - *Saddharma Pundarika*, c. II v. 81 (Kern's translation), 'Sacred Books of the East', vol. xxi.

3. The Original Jizō has been identified by Orientalists with the Sanscrit *Kshitegarbha*; as Professor Chamberlain observes, the resemblance in sound between the names Jizō and Jesus 'is quite fortuitous'. But in Japan Jizō has become totally transformed: he may justly be called the most Japanese of all Japanese divinities. According to the curious old Buddhist book, *Sai no Kawara Kuchi zu sami no den*, the whole *Sai-no-Kawara* legend originated in Japan, and was first written by the priest Kuya Shōnin, in the sixth year of the period called Ten-Kei, in the reign of the Emperor Shuyaku, who died in the year 946. To Kuya was revealed, in the village of Sai-in, near Kyoto, during a night passed by the dry bed of the neighbouring river, Sai-no-Kawa (said to be the modern Serikawa), the condition of child-souls in the Meido. [Such is the legend in the book; but Professor Chamberlain has shown that the name *Sai-no-Kawara*, as now written, signifies 'The Dry Bed of the River of Souls', and modern Japanese faith places that river in the Meido.] Whatever be the true history of the myth, it is certainly Japanese; and the conception of Jizō as the lover and playfellow of dead children belongs to Japan.

There are many other popular forms of Jizō, one of the most common being that Koyasu-Jizō to whom pregnant women pray. There are but few roads in Japan upon which statues of Jizō may not be seen; for he is also the patron of pilgrims.

Bon-Odori

1

Over the mountains to Izumo, the land of the *Kamiyo*,[1] the land of the Ancient Gods. A journey of four days by *kuruma*, with strong runners, from the Pacific to the Sea of Japan; for we have taken the longest and least frequented route.

Through valleys most of this long route lies, valleys always open to higher valleys, while the road ascends, valleys between mountains with rice-fields ascending their slopes by successions of diked terraces which look like enormous green flights of steps. Above them are shadowing sombre forests of cedar and pine; and above these wooded summits loom indigo shapes of farther hills over-topped by peaked silhouettes of vapoury grey. The air is lukewarm and windless; and distances are gauzed by delicate mists; and in this tenderest of blue skies, this Japanese sky which always seems to me loftier than any other sky which I ever saw, there are only, day after day, some few filmy, spectral, diaphanous white wandering things: like ghosts of clouds, riding on the wind.

But sometimes, as the road ascends, the rice-fields disappear a while: fields of barley and of indigo, and of rye and of cotton, fringe the route for a little space; and then it plunges into forest shadows. Above all else, the forests of cedar sometimes bordering the way are astonishments; never outside of the tropics did I see any growths comparable for density and perpendicularity with these. Every trunk is straight and bare as a pillar: the whole front presents the spectacle of an immeasurable massing of pallid columns towering up into a cloud of sombre foliage so dense that one can distinguish nothing overhead but branchings lost in shadow. And the profundities beyond the rare gaps in the palisade of blanched trunks are night-black, as in Doré's pictures of fir woods.

No more great towns; only thatched villages nestling in the folds of the hills, each with its Buddhist temple, lifting a tilted roof of blue-grey tiles above the congregation of thatched homesteads, and its *miya*, or Shinto shrine, with a *torii* before it like a great ideograph shaped in stone or wood. But Buddhism still dominates; every hilltop has its *tera*; and the statues of Buddhas or of Bodhisattvas appear by the roadside, as we travel on, with the regularity of milestones. Often a village *tera* is so large that the cottages of the rustic folk about it seem like little out-houses; and the traveller wonders how so costly an edifice of prayer can be supported by a community so humble. And everywhere the signs of the gentle faith appear: its ideographs and symbols are chiselled upon the faces of the rocks; its icons smile upon you from every shadowy recess by the way; even the very landscape betimes would seem to have been moulded by the soul of it, where hills rise softly as a prayer. And the summits of some are domed like the head of Shaka, and the dark bossy frondage that clothes them might seem the clustering of his curls.

But gradually, with the passing of the days, as we journey into the

130

loftier west, I see fewer and fewer *tera*. Such Buddhist temples as we pass appear small and poor; and the wayside images become rarer and rarer. But the symbols of Shinto are more numerous, and the structure of its *miya* larger and loftier. And the *torii* are visible everywhere, and tower higher, before the approaches to villages, before the entrances of courts guarded by strangely grotesque lions and foxes of stone, and before stairways of old mossed rock, upsloping between dense growths of ancient cedar and pine, to shrines that moulder in the twilight of holy groves.

At one little village I see, just beyond the *torii* leading to a great Shinto temple, a particularly odd small shrine, and feel impelled by curiosity to examine it. Leaning against its closed doors are many short gnarled sticks in a row, miniature clubs. Irreverently removing these, and opening the little doors, Akira bids me look within. I see only a mask - the mask of a goblin, a *Tengu*, grotesque beyond description, with an enormous nose, so grotesque that I feel remorse for having looked at it.

The sticks are votive offerings. By dedicating one to the shrine, it is believed that the *Tengu* may be induced to drive one's enemies away. Goblin-shaped though they appear in all Japanese paintings and carvings of them, the *Tengu-Sama* are divinities, lesser divinities, lords of the art of fencing and the use of all weapons.

And other changes gradually become manifest. Akira complains that he can no longer understand the language of the people. We are traversing regions of dialects. The houses are also architecturally different from those of the country-folk of the north-east; their high thatched roofs are curiously decorated with bundles of straw fastened to a pole of bamboo parallel with the roof-ridge, and elevated about a foot above it. The complexion of the peasantry is darker than in the north-east; and I see no more of those charming rosy faces one observes among the women of the Tokyo districts. And the peasants wear different hats, hats pointed like the straw roofs of those little wayside temples curiously enough called *an* (which means a straw hat).

The weather is more than warm, rendering clothing oppressive; and as we pass through the little villages along the road, I see much healthy, cleanly nudity: pretty naked children; brown men and boys with only a soft narrow white cloth about their loins, asleep on the matted floors, all the paper screens of the houses having been removed to admit the breeze. The men seem to be lightly and supply built; but I see no saliency of muscles; the lines of the figure are always smooth. Before almost every dwelling, indigo, spread out upon little mats of rice straw, may be seen drying in the sun.

The country-folk gaze wonderingly at the foreigner. At various places where we halt, old men approach to touch my clothes, apologising with humble bows and winning smiles for their very natural curiosity, and asking my interpreter all sorts of odd questions. Gentler and kindlier faces I never beheld; and they reflect the souls behind them; never yet have I heard a voice raised in anger, nor observed an unkindly act.

And each day, as we travel, the country becomes more beautiful - beautiful with that fantasticality of landscape only to be found in volcanic lands. But for the dark forests of cedar and pine, and this far faint dreamy sky, and the soft whiteness of the light, there are moments of our journey when I could fancy myself again in the West Indies, ascending some winding way over the mornes of Dominica or of Martinique. And, indeed, I find myself sometimes looking against the horizon glow for shapes of palms and ceibas. But the brighter green of the valleys and of the mountain-slopes beneath the woods is not the green of young cane, but of rice-fields - thousands upon thousands of tiny rice-fields no larger than cottage gardens, separated from each other by narrow serpentine dikes.

3

In the very heart of a mountain range, while rolling along the verge of a precipice above rice-fields, I catch sight of a little shrine in a cavity of the cliff overhanging the way, and halt to examine it. The sides and sloping roof of the shrine are formed by slabs of unhewn rock. Within smiles a rudely chiselled image of Batō-Kwannon - Kwannon-with-the-Horse's-Head - and before it bunches of wild flowers have been placed, and an earthen incense-cup, and scattered offerings of dry rice. Contrary to the idea suggested by the strange name, this form of Kwannon is not horse-headed; but the head of a horse is sculptured upon the tiara worn by the divinity. And the symbolism is fully explained by a large wooden *sotoba* planted beside the shrine, and bearing, among other inscriptions, the words, *Batō Kwan-ze-on Bosatsu, giu ba bodai han ye.* 'For Batō-Kwannon protects the horses and the cattle of the peasant; and he prays her not only that his dumb servants may be preserved from sickness, but also that their spirits may enter after death, into a happier state of existence.' Near the sotoba there has been erected a wooden framework about four feet square, filled with little tablets of pine set edge to edge so as to form one smooth surface; and on these are written, in rows of hundreds, the names of all who subscribed for the statue and its shrine. The number announced is ten thousand. But the whole cost could not have exceeded ten Japanese dollars (yen); wherefore I surmise that each subscriber gave not more than one rin - one tenth of one sen, or cent. For the *hyakushō* are unspeakably poor.[2]

In the midst of these mountain solitudes, the discovery of that little shrine creates a delightful sense of security. Surely nothing save goodness can be expected from a people gentle-hearted enough to pray for the souls of their horses and cows.[3]

As we proceed rapidly down a slope, my *kurumaya* swerves to one side with a suddenness that gives me a violent start, for the road overlooks a sheer depth of several hundred feet. It is merely to avoid hurting a harmless snake making its way across the path. The snake is so little afraid that on reaching the edge of the road it turns its head to look after us.

3

And now strange signs begin to appear in all these rice-fields: I see everywhere, sticking up above the ripening grain, objects like white-feathered arrows. Arrows of prayer! I take one up to examine it. The shaft is a thin bamboo, split down for about one-third of its length; into the slit of a piece of strong white paper with ideographs upon it - an *ofuda*, a Shinto charm - is inserted; and the separated ends of the cane are then rejoined and tied together just above it. The whole, at a little distance, has exactly the appearance of a long, light, well feathered arrow. That which I first examine bears the words, '*Yu-Asaki-jinja-kozen-son-chu-an-zen*' (From the God whose shrine is before the Village of Peace). Another reads, '*Miho-jinja-sho-gwan-jo-ju-go-kito-shugo*', signifying that the Deity of the temple Miho-jinja granteth fully every supplication made unto him. Everywhere, as we proceed, I see the white arrows of prayer glimmering above the green level of the grain; and always they become more numerous. Far as the eye can reach the fields are sprinkled with them, so that they make upon the verdant surface a white speckling as of flowers.

Sometimes, also, around a little rice-field, I see a sort of magical fence, formed by little bamboo rods supporting a long cord from which long straws hang down, like a fringe, and paper cuttings, which are symbols (*gohei*), are suspended at regular intervals. This is the *shimenawa*, sacred emblem of Shinto. Within the consecrated space enclosed by it no blight may enter - no scorching sun wither the young shoots. And where the white arrows glimmer the locust shall not prevail, nor shall hungry birds do evil.

But now I look in vain for the Buddhas. No more great *tera*, no Shaka, no Amida, no Dai-Nichi-Nyorai; even the Bosatsu have been left behind. Kwannon and her holy kin have disappeared; Kōshin, Lord of Roads, is indeed yet with us; but he has changed his name and become a Shinto deity; he is now Saruda-hiko-no-mikoto; and his presence is revealed only by the statues of the Three Mystic Apes which are his servants -

Mizaru, who sees no evil, covering his eyes with his hands,
Kikazaru, who hears no evil, covering his ears with his hands.
Iwazaru, who speaks no evil, covering his mouth with his hands.

Yet no! one Bosatsu survives in this atmosphere of magical Shinto: still by the roadside I see at long intervals the image of Jizō-Sama, the charming playfellow of dead children. But Jizō also is a little changed; even in his sextuple representation,[4] the Roku-Jizō, he appears not standing, but seated upon his lotus-flower, and I see no stones piled up before him, as in the eastern provinces.

4

At last, from the verge of an enormous ridge, the roadway suddenly slopes down into a vista of high peaked roofs of thatch and green-mossed eaves - into a village like a coloured print out of old Hiroshige's picture-books, a village with all its tints and colours precisely like the tints and colours of the landscape in which it lies. This is Kami-Ichi, in the land of Hōki.

We halt before a quiet, dingy little inn, whose host, a very aged man, comes forth to salute me; while a silent, gentle crowd of villagers, mostly children and women, gather about the *kuruma* to see the stranger, to wonder at him, even to touch his clothes with timid smiling curiosity. One glance at the face of the old innkeeper decides me to accept his invitation. I must remain here until tomorrow: my runners are too wearied to go farther tonight.

Weather-worn as the little inn seemed without, it is delightful within. Its polished stairway and balconies are speckless, reflecting like mirror-surfaces the bare feet of the maid-servants; its luminous rooms are fresh and sweet-smelling as when their soft mattings were first laid down. The carven pillars of the alcove (*toko*) in my chamber, leaves and flowers chiselled in some black rich wood, are wonders; and the *kakemono* or scroll-picture hanging there is an idyll, Hotei, God of Happiness, drifting in a bark down some shadowy stream into evening mysteries of vapoury purple. Far as this hamlet is from all art-centres, there is no object visible in the house which does not reveal the Japanese sense of beauty in form. The old gold-flowered lacquer-ware, the astonishing box in which sweetmeats (*kwashi*) are kept, the diaphanous porcelain wine-cups dashed with a single tiny gold figure of a leaping shrimp, the tea-cup holders which are curled lotus-leaves of bronze, even the iron kettle with its figurings of dragons and clouds, and the brazen *hibachi* whose handles are heads of Buddhist lions, delight the eye and surprise the fancy. Indeed wherever today in Japan one sees something totally uninteresting in porcelain or metal, something commonplace and ugly, one may be almost sure that detestable something has been shaped under foreign influence. But here I am in ancient Japan; probably no European eyes ever looked upon these things before.

A window shaped like a heart peeps out upon the garden, a wonderful little garden with a tiny pond and miniature bridges and dwarf trees, like the landscape of a tea-cup; also some shapely stones of course, and some graceful stone-lanterns, or *tōrō*, such as are placed in the courts of temples. And beyond these, through the warm dusk, I see lights, coloured lights, the lanterns of the *Bonku*, suspended before each home to welcome the coming of beloved ghosts; for by the antique calendar, according to which in this antique place the reckoning of time is still made, this is the first night of the Festival of the Dead.

As in all the other little country villages where I have been stopping, I find the people here kind to me with a kindness and a courtesy unimaginable, indescribable, unknown in any other country, and even in Japan itself only in the interior. Their simple politeness is not an art; their goodness is absolutely unconscious goodness; both come straight from the heart. And before I have been two hours among these people, their treatment of me, coupled with the sense of my utter inability to repay such kindness, causes a wicked wish to come into my mind. I wish these charming folk would do me some unexpected wrong, something surprisingly evil, something atrociously unkind, so that I should not be obliged to regret them, which I feel sure I must begin to do as soon as I go away.

While the aged landlord conducts me to the bath, where he insists upon washing me himself as if I were a child, the wife prepares for us a charming little repast of rice, eggs, vegetables, and sweetmeats. She is painfully in doubt about her ability to please me, even after I have eaten enough for two men, and apologises too much for not being able to offer me more.

'There is no fish', she says, 'for today is the first day of the *Bonku*, the Festival of the Dead; being the thirteenth day of the month. On the thirteenth, fourteenth, and fifteenth of the month nobody may eat fish. But on the morning of the sixteenth day, the fishermen go out to catch fish; and everybody who has both parents living may eat of it. But if one has lost one's father or mother then one must not eat fish, even upon the sixteenth day.'

While the good soul is thus explaining I become aware of a strange remote sound from without, a sound I recognise through memory of tropical dances, a measured clapping of hands. But this clapping is very soft and at long intervals. And at still longer intervals there comes to us a heavy muffled booming, the tap of a great drum, a temple drum.

'Oh! we must go to see it', cries Akira; 'it is the *Bon-odori*, the Dance of the Festival of the Dead. And you will see the *Bon-odori* danced here as it is never danced in cities - the *Bon-odori* of ancient days. For customs have not changed here; but in the cities all is changed.'

So I hasten out, wearing only, like the people about me, one of those light wide-sleeved summer robes - *yukata* which are furnished to male guests at all Japanese hotels; but the air is so warm that even thus lightly clad, I find myself slightly perspiring. And the night is divine - still, clear, vaster than nights of Europe, with a big white moon flinging down queer shadows of tilted eaves and horned gables and delightful silhouettes of robed Japanese. A little boy, the grandson of our host, leads the way with a crimson paper lantern; and the sonorous echoing of *geta*, the *koro-koro* of wooden sandals, fills all the street, for many are going whither we are going, to see the dance.

A little we proceed along the main street; then, traversing a narrow passage between two houses, we find ourselves in a great open space flooded by moonlight. This is the dancing-place; but the dance has ceased for a time. Looking about me, I perceive that we are in the court of an ancient Buddhist temple. The temple building itself remains intact, a low long peaked silhouette against the starlight; but it is void and dark and unhallowed now; it has been turned, they tell me, into a schoolhouse. The priests are gone; the great bell is gone; the Buddhas and the Bodhisattvas have vanished, all save one - a broken-handed Jizō of stone, smiling with eyelids closed, under the moon.

In the centre of the court is a framework of bamboo supporting a great drum; and about it benches have been arranged, benches from the schoolhouse, on which villagers are resting. There is a hum of voices, voices of people speaking very low, as if expecting something solemn; and cries of children betimes, and soft laughter of girls. And far behind the court, beyond a low hedge of sombre evergreen shrubs, I see soft white lights and a host of tall grey shapes throwing long shadows; and I know that the lights are the *white* lanterns of the dead (those hung in cemeteries only), and that the grey shapes are shapes of tombs.

Suddenly a girl rises from her seat, and taps the huge drum once. It is the signal for the Dance of Souls.

5

Out of the shadow of the temple a processional line of dancers files into the moonlight and as suddenly halts - all young women or girls, clad in their choicest attire; the tallest leads; her comrades follow in order of stature; little maids of ten or twelve years compose the end of the procession. Figures lightly poised as birds, figures that somehow recall the dreams of shapes circling about certain antique vases; those charming Japanese robes, close-clinging about the knees, might seem, but for the great fantastic drooping sleeves, and the curious broad girdles confining them, designed after the drawing of some Greek or Etruscan artist. And, at another tap of the drum, there begins a performance impossible to picture in words, something unimaginable, phantasmal - a dance, an astonishment.

All together glide the right foot forward one pace, without lifting the sandal from the ground, and extend both hands to the right, with a strange floating motion and a smiling, mysterious obeisance. Then the right foot is drawn back, with a repetition of the waving of hands and the mysterious bow. Then all advance the left foot and repeat the previous movements, half-turning to the left. Then all take two gliding paces forward, with a single simultaneous soft clap of the hands, and the first performance is reiterated, alternately to right and left; all the sandalled feet gliding together, all the supple hands waving together, all the pliant bodies bowing and swaying together. And so slowly, weirdly, the processional movement changes into a great round, circling about the moonlit court and around the voiceless crowd of spectators.[5]

And always the white hands sinuously wave together,as if weaving spells, alternately without and within the round, now with palms upward, now with palms downward; and all the elfish sleeves hover duskily together, with a shadowing as of wings; and all the feet poise together with such a rhythm of complex motion, that, in watching it, one feels a sensation of hypnotism - as while striving to watch a flowing and shimmering of water.

And this soporous allurement is intensified by a dead hush. No one speaks, not even a spectator, And, in the long intervals between the soft clapping of hands, one hears only the shrilling of the crickets in the trees, and the *shu-shu* of sandals, lightly stirring the dust. Unto what, I ask myself, may this be likened? Unto nothing; yet it suggests some fancy of somnambulism - dreamers, who dream themselves flying, dreaming upon their feet.

And there comes to me the thought that I am looking at something immemorially old, something belonging to the unrecorded beginnings of this Oriental life, perhaps to the crepuscular Kamiyo itself, to the magical Age of the Gods; a symbolism of motion whereof the meaning has been forgotten for innumerable years. Yet more and more unreal the spectacle appears, with its silent smilings, with its silent bowings, as if in obeisance to watchers invisible; and I find myself wondering whether, were I to utter but a whisper, all would not vanish for ever save the grey mouldering court and the desolate temple, and the broken statue of Jizō, smiling always the same mysterious smile I see upon the faces of the dancers.

Under the wheeling moon, in the midst of the round, I feel as one within the circle of a charm. And verily this is enchantment; I am bewitched, bewitched by the ghostly weaving of hands, by the rhythmic gliding of feet, above all by the flitting of the marvellous sleeves - apparitional, soundless, velvety as a flitting of great tropical bats. No; nothing I ever dreamed of could be likened to this. And with the consciousness of the ancient *hakaba* behind me, and the weird invitation of its lanterns, and the ghostly beliefs of the hour and the place, there creeps upon me a nameless, tingling sense of being haunted. But no! these gracious, silent, waving, weaving shapes are not of the Shadowy Folk, for whose coming the white fires were kindled a strain of song, full of sweet, clear quavering, like the call of a bird, gushes from some girlish mouth, and fifty soft voices join the chant:

Sorota soroimashita odorikoga sorota
Soroikite, kita hare yukata

'Uniform to view [*as ears of young rice ripening in the field*] all clad alike in summer festal robes, the company of dancers have assembled.'

Again only the shrilling of the crickets, the *shu-shu* of feet, the gentle clapping; and the wavering hovering measure proceeds in silence, with mesmeric lentor - with a strange grace, which, by its very naïveté, seems old as the encircling hills.

Those who sleep the sleep of centuries out there, under the grey stones where the white lanterns are, and their fathers, and the fathers of their fathers' fathers, and the unknown generations behind them, buried in cemeteries of which the place has been forgotten for a thousand years, doubtless looked upon a scene like this. Nay! the dust stirred by those young feet was human life, and so smiled and so sang under this self-same moon, 'with woven paces, and with waving hands'.

Suddenly, a deep male chant breaks the hush. Two giants have joined the round, and now lead it, two superb young mountain peasants nearly nude, towering head and shoulders above the whole of the assembly. Their kimono are rolled about their waists like girdles, leaving their bronzed limbs and torsos naked to the warm air; they wear nothing else save their immense straw hats, and white *tabi*, donned expressly for the festival. Never before among these people saw I such men, such thews; but their smiling beardless faces are comely and kindly as those of Japanese boys. They seem brothers, so like in frame, in movement, in the timbre of their voices, as they intone the same song:

No demo yama demo ko wa umiokeyo,
Sen ryō kura yori ko ga takara

'Whether brought forth upon the mountain or in the field, it matters nothing: more than a treasure of one thousand *ryō*, a baby precious is.'

And Jizō, the lover of children's ghosts, smiles across the silence.

Souls close to nature's Soul are these; artless and touching their thought, like the worship of that Kishibojin to whom wives pray. And

137

after the silence, the sweet thin voices of the women answer:

Oomu otoko ni sowa sanu oya wa,
Oyade gozaranu ko no kataki

'The parents who will not allow their girl to be united with her lover; they are not the parents, but the enemies of their child.'

And song follows song; and the round ever becomes larger; and the hours pass unfelt, unheard, while the moon wheels slowly down the blue steeps of the night.

A deep low boom rolls suddenly across the court, the rich tone of some temple bell telling the twelfth hour. Instantly the witchcraft ends, like the wonder of some dream broken by a sound; the chanting ceases; the round dissolves in an outburst of happy laughter, and chatting, and softly-vowelled callings of flower-names which are names of girls, and farewell cries of '*Sayōnara*'! as dancers and spectators alike betake themselves homeward, with a great *koro-koro* of *getas*.

And I, moving with the throng, in the bewildered manner of one suddenly roused from sleep, know myself ungrateful. These silvery-laughing folk who now toddle along beside me upon their noisy little clogs, stepping very fast to get a peep at my foreign face, these but a moment ago were visions of archaic grace, illusions of necromancy, delightful phantoms; and I feel a vague resentment against them for thus materialising into simple country-girls.

1

Lying down to rest, I ask myself the reason of the singular emotion inspired by that simple peasant-chorus. Utterly impossible to recall the air, with its fantastic intervals and fractional tones; as well attempt to fix in memory the purlings of a bird; but the indefinable charm of it lingers with me still.

Melodies of Europe awaken within us feelings we can utter, sensations familiar as mother-speech, inherited from all the generations behind us. But how explain the emotion evoked by a primitive chant totally unlike anything in Western melody - impossible even to write in those tones which are the ideographs of our music-tongue?

And the emotion itself - what is it? I know not; yet I feel it to be something infinitely more old than I, something not of only one place or time, but vibrant to all common joy or pain of being, under the universal sun. Then I wonder if the secret does not lie in some untaught spontaneous harmony of that chant with Nature's most ancient song, in some unconscious kinship to the music of solitudes - all trillings of summer life that blend to make the great sweet Cry of the Land.

Footnotes:

1. The period in which only deities existed.
2. *Hyakushō*, a peasant, husbandman. The two Chinese characters forming the word signify respectively, 'a hundred' (*hyaku*), and 'family name' (*sei*). One might be tempted to infer that the appellation is almost equivalent to our phrase, 'their name is legion'. And a Japanese friend assures me that the inference would not be far wrong. Anciently the peasants had no

family name; each was known by his personal appelation, coupled with the name of his lord, possessor or ruler. Thus a hundred peasants on one estate would all be known by the name of their master.

3. This custom of praying for the souls of animals is by no means general. But I have seen in the western provinces several burials of domestic animals at which such prayers were said. After the earth was filled in, some incense-rods were lighted above the grave in each instance, and the prayers were repeated in a whisper. A friend in the capital sends me the following curious information:

'At the Eko-in temple in Tokyo prayers are offered up every morning for the souls of certain animals whose *ihai* [mortuary tablets] are preserved in the building. A fee of thirty sen will procure burial in the temple-ground and a short service for any small domestic pet.'

Doubtless similar temples exist elsewhere. Certainly no one capable of affection for our dumb friends and servants can mock these gentle customs.

4. Why *six* Jizō instead of five or three or any other number, the reader may ask. I myself asked the question many times before receiving any satisfactory reply. Perhaps the following legend affords the most satisfactory explanation:

According to the Book *Taijo-Hoshi-mingyo-nenbutsu-den*, Jizō-Bosatsu was a woman ten thousand *ko* (*kalpas*) before this era, and became filled with desire to convert all living beings of the Six Worlds and the Four Births. And by virtue of the Supernatural Powers she multiplied herself and simultaneously appeared in all the Rokusshō or Six States of Sentient Existence at once, namely in the *Jigoku, Gaki, Chikushō, Shura, Ningen, Tenjō*, and converted the dwellers thereof. (A friend insists that in order to have done this Jizō must first have become a man).

Among the many names of Jizō, such as 'The Never Slumbering', 'The Dragon-Praiser', 'The Shining King', 'Diamond-of-Pity', I find the significant appelation of 'The Countless Bodied'.

5. Since this sketch was written, I have seen the *Bon-odori* in many different parts of Japan; but I have never witnessed exactly the same kind of dance. Indeed, I would judge from my experiences in Izumo, in Oki, in Tottori, in Hōki, in Bingo, and elsewhere, that the *Bon-odori* is not danced in the same way in any two provinces. Not only do the motions and gestures vary according to locality, but also the airs of the songs sung - and this even when the words are the same. In some places the measure is slow and solemn; in others it is rapid and merry, and characterised by a queer jerky swing, impossible to describe. But everywhere both the motion and the melody are curious and pleasing enough to fascinate the spectator for hours. Certainly these primitive dances are of far greater interest than the performances of geisha. Although Buddhism may have utilised them and influenced them, they are beyond doubt incomparably older than Buddhism.

JAPAN SUPERNATURAL

Kitsune

1

By every shady wayside and in every ancient grove, on almost every hilltop and in the outskirts of every village, you may see, while travelling through the Hondo country, some little Shinto shrine, before which, or at either side of which, are images of seated foxes in stone. Usually there is a pair of these, facing each other. But there may be a dozen, or a score, or several hundred, in which case most of the images are very small. And in more than one of the larger towns you may see in the court of some great miya, a countless host of stone foxes, of all dimensions, from toy-figures but a few inches high to the colossi whose pedestals tower above your head, all squatting around the temple in tiered ranks of thousands. Such shrines and temples, everybody knows, are dedicated to Inari, the God of Rice. After having travelled much in Japan, you will find that whenever you try to recall any country-place you have visited, there will appear in some nook or corner of that remembrance a pair of green-and-grey foxes of stone, with broken noses. In my own memories of Japanese travel, these shapes have become *de rigueur*, as picturesque detail.

In the neighbourhood of the capital and in Tokyo itself - sometimes in the cemeteries - very beautiful idealised figures of foxes may be seen, elegant as greyhounds. They have long green or grey eyes of crystal quartz or some other diaphanous substance; and they create a strong impression as mythological conceptions. But throughout the interior, fox-images are much less artistically fashioned. In Izumo, particularly, such stone-carving has a decidedly primitive appearance. There is an astonishing multiplicity and variety of fox-images in the Province of the Gods - images comical, quaint, grotesque, or monstrous, but, for the most part, very rudely

140

chiselled. I cannot, however, declare them less interesting on that account. The work of the Tokkaido sculptor copies the conventional artistic notion of light grace and ghostliness. The rustic foxes of Izumo have no grace: they are uncouth; but they betray in countless queer ways the personal fancies of their makers. They are of many moods - whimsical, apathetic, inquisitive, saturnine, jocose, ironical; they watch and snooze and squint and wink and sneer; they wait with lurking smiles; they listen with cocked ears most stealthily, keeping their mouths open or closed. There is an amusing individuality about them all, and an air of knowing mockery about most of them, even those whose noses have been broken off. Moreover, these ancient country foxes have certain natural beauties which their modern Tokyo kindred cannot show. Time has bestowed upon them divers speckled coats of beautiful soft colours while they have been sitting on their pedestals, listening to the ebbing and flowing of the centuries and snickering weirdly at mankind. Their backs are clad with finest green velvet of old mosses; their limbs are spotted and their tails are tipped with the dead gold or the dead silver of delicate fungi. And the places they most haunt are the loveliest - high shadowy groves where the *uguisu* sings in green twilight, above some voiceless shrine with its lamps and its lions of stone so mossed as to seem things born of the soil - like mushrooms.

I found it difficult to understand why, out of every thousand foxes, nine hundred should have broken noses. The main street of the city of Matsue might be paved from end to end with the tips of the noses of mutilated Izumo foxes. A friend answered my expression of wonder in this regard by the simple, but suggestive word, *kodomo*, which means 'The children'.

2

Inari, the name by which the Fox-God is generally known, signifies 'Load-of-Rice'. But the antique name of the deity is the August-Spirit-of-Food: he is the Uka-no-mi-tama-no-mikoto of the *Kojiki*. In much more recent times only has he borne the name that indicates his connection with the fox-cult, Miketsu-no-Kami, or the Three-Fox-God. Indeed, the conception of the fox as a supernatural being does not seem to have been introduced into Japan before the tenth or eleventh century; and although a shrine of the deity, with statues of foxes, may be found in the court of most of the large Shinto temples, it is worthy of note that in all the vast domains of the oldest Shinto shrine in Japan - Kitzuki - you cannot find the image of a fox. And it is only in modern art - the art of Toyokuni and others - that Inari is represented as a bearded man riding a white fox.[1]

Inari is not worshipped as the God of Rice only; indeed, there are many Inari, just as in antique Greece there were many deities called Hermes, Zeus, Athena, Poseidon - one in the knowledge of the learned, but essentially different in the imagination of the common people. Inari has been multiplied by reason of his different attributes. For instance, Matsue has a Kamiya-San-no-Inari-San, who is the God of Coughs and Bad Colds - afflictions extremely common and remarkably severe in the Land of Izumo. He has a temple in the Kamachi at which he is worshipped under the vulgar appellation of Kaze-no-Kami and the politer one of

Kamiya-San-no-Inari. And those who are cured of their coughs and colds after having prayed to him, bring to his temple offerings of *tofu*.

At Oba, likewise, there is a particular Inari, of great fame. Fastened to the wall of his shrine is a large box full of small clay foxes. The pilgrim who has a prayer to make puts one of these little foxes in his sleeve and carries it home. He must keep it, and pay it all due honour, until such time as his petition has been granted. Then he must take it back to the temple, and restore it to the box, and, if he be able, make some small gift to the shrine.

Inari is often worshipped as a healer; and still more frequently as a deity having power to give wealth. (Perhaps because all the wealth of Old Japan was reckoned in *koku* of rice). Therefore his foxes are sometimes represented holding keys in their mouths. And from being the deity who gives wealth, Inari has also become in some localities the special divinity of the *jorō* class. There is, for example, an Inari temple worth visiting in the neighbourhood of the Yoshiwara at Yokohama. It stands in the same court with a temple of Benten, and is more than usually large for a shrine of Inari. You approach it through a succession of *torii*, one behind the other: they are of different heights, diminishing in size as they are placed nearer to the temple, and planted more and more closely in proportion to their smallness. Before each *torii* sit a pair of weird foxes, one to the right and one to the left. The first pair are large as greyhounds; the second two are much smaller; and the sizes of the rest lessen as the dimensions of the *torii* lessen. At the foot of the wooden steps of the temple there is a pair of very graceful foxes of dark grey stone, wearing pieces of red cloth about their necks. Upon the steps themselves are white wooden foxes - one at each end of each step - each successive pair being smaller than the pair below; and at the threshold of the doorway are two very little foxes, not more than three inches high, sitting on sky-blue pedestals. These have the tips of their tails gilded. Then, if you look into the temple you will see on the left something like a long low table on which are placed thousands of tiny fox-images, even smaller than those in the doorway, having only plain white tails. There is no image of Inari; indeed, I have never seen an image of Inari as yet in any Inari temple. On the altar appear the usual emblems of Shinto; and before it, just opposite the doorway, stands a sort of lantern, having glass sides and a wooden bottom studded with nail-points on which to fix votive candles.[2]

And here, from time to time, if you will watch, you will probably see more than one handsome girl, with brightly painted lips and the beautiful antique attire that no maiden or wife may wear, come to the foot of the steps, toss a coin into the money-box at the door, and call out: '*O-rōsoku*'! which means 'an honourable candle'. Immediately, from an inner chamber, some old man will enter the shrine-room with a lighted candle, stick it upon a nail-point in the lantern, and then retire. Such candle-offerings are always accompanied by secret prayers for good-fortune. But this Inari is worshipped by many besides members of the *jorō* class.

The pieces of coloured cloth about the necks of the foxes are also votive offerings.

3

Fox-images in Izumo seem to be more numerous than in other provinces, and they are symbols there, so far as the mass of the peasantry is concerned, of something else besides the worship of the Rice-Diety. Indeed, the old conception of the Deity of Rice-fields has been overshadowed and almost effaced among the lowest classes by a weird cult totally foreign to the spirit of pure Shinto - the Fox-cult. The worship of the retainer has almost replaced the worship of the god. Originally the Fox was sacred to Inari only as the Tortoise is still sacred to Kompira; the Deer to the Great Deity of Kasuga; the Rat to Daikoku; the Tai-fish to Ebisu; the White Serpent to Benten; or the Centipede to Bishamon, God of Battles. But in the course of centuries the Fox usurped divinity. And the stone images of him are not the only outward evidences of his cult. At the rear of almost every Inari temple you will generally find in the wall of the shrine building, one or two feet above the ground, an aperture about eight inches in diameter and perfectly circular. It is often made so as to be closed at will by a sliding plank. This circular orifice is a Fox-hole, and if you find one open, and look within, you will probably see offerings of *tofu* or other food which foxes are supposed to be fond of. You will also, most likely, find grains of rice scattered on some little projection of woodwork below or near the hole, or placed on the edge of the hole itself; and you may see some peasant clap his hands before the hole, utter some little prayer, and swallow a grain or two of that rice in the belief that it will either cure or prevent sickness. Now the fox for whom such a hole is made is an invisible fox, a phantom fox, the fox respectfully referred to by the peasant as *O-Kitsune-San*. If he ever suffers himself to become visible, his colour is said to be snowy white.

According to some, there are various kinds of ghostly foxes. According to others, there are two sorts of foxes only, the Inari-fox (O-Kitsune-San) and the wild fox (*kitsune*). Some people again class foxes into Superior and Inferior Foxes, and allege the existence of four Superior Sorts - *Byakko, Kokko, Jenko,* and *Reiko* - all of which possess supernatural powers. Others again count only three kinds of foxes - the Field-fox, the Man-fox, and the Inari-fox. But many confound the Field-fox or wild fox with the Man-fox. One cannot possibly unravel the confusion of these beliefs, especially among the peasantry. The beliefs vary, moreover, in different districts. I have only been able, after a residence of fourteen months in Izumo, where the superstition is especially strong, and marked by certain unique features, to make the following very loose summary of them:

All foxes have supernatural power. There are good and bad foxes. The Inari-fox is good, and the bad foxes are afraid of the Inari-fox. The worst fox is the *ninko* or *hito-kitsune* (Man-fox): this is especially the fox of demoniacal possession. It is no larger than a weasel, and somewhat similar in shape, except for its tail, which is like the tail of any other fox. It is rarely seen, keeping itself invisible, except to those to whom it attaches itself. It likes to live in the houses of men, and to be nourished by them, and to the homes where it is well cared for it will bring prosperity. It will take care that the rice-fields shall never want for water, nor the cooking-pot for rice. But if offended, it will bring misfortune to the household, and ruin the crops. The wild fox (*nogitsune*) is also bad. It also sometimes takes possession of people; but it is especially a wizard, and prefers to deceive by enchantment. It has the power of assuming any shape and of making itself invisible; but the dog can always see it, so that it is extremely afraid of the dog. Moreover, while assuming another shape, if its shadow fall upon water, the water will only reflect the shadow of a fox. The peasantry kill it; but he who kills a fox incurs the risk of being bewitched by that fox's kindred, or even by the *ki*, or ghost of the fox. Still if one eat the flesh of a fox, he cannot be enchanted afterwards. The *nogitsune* also enters houses. Most families having foxes in their houses have only the small kind, or *ninko*; but occasionally both kinds will live together under the same roof. Some people say that if the *nogitsune* lives a hundred years it becomes all white, and then takes rank as an Inari-fox.

There are curious contradictions involved in these beliefs, and other contradictions will be found in the following pages of this sketch. To define the fox-superstition at all is difficult, not only on account of the confusion of ideas on the subject among the believers themselves, but also on account of the variety of elements out of which it has been shapen. Its origin is Chinese;[3] but in Japan it became oddly blended with the worship of a Shinto deity, and again modified and expanded by the Buddhist concepts of thaumaturgy and magic. So far as the common people are concerned, it is perhaps safe to say that they pay devotion to foxes chiefly because they fear them. The peasant still worships what he fears.

4

It is more than doubtful whether the popular notions about different classes of foxes, and about the distinction between the fox of Inari and the fox of possession, were ever much more clearly established than they are now, except in the books of old *literati*. Indeed, there exists a letter from Hideyoshi to the Fox-God which would seem to show that in the time of the great Taikō the Inari-fox and the demon fox were considered identical. This letter is still preserved at Nara, in the Buddhist temple called Todaiji:

KYOTO. *the seventeenth day*
of the Third Month.

TO INARI DAIMYŌJIN:

My Lord, I have the honour to inform you that one of the foxes under your jurisdiction has bewitched one of my servants, causing her and others a great deal of trouble. I have to request that you will make minute inquiries into the matter, and endeavour to find out the reason of your subject misbehaving in this way, and let me know the result.

If it turns out that the fox has no adequate reason to give for his behaviour, you are to arrest and punish him at once. If you hesitate to take action in this matter, I shall issue orders for the destruction of every fox in the land.

Any other particulars that you may wish to be informed of in reference to what has occurred, you can learn from the high-priest YOSHIDA.

Apologising for the imperfections of this letter, I have the honour to be

Your obedient servant,
HIDEYOSHI TAIKŌ.[4]

But there certainly were some distinctions established in localities, owing to the worship of Inari by the military caste. With the *samurai* of Izumo, the Rice-God, for obvious reasons, was a highly popular deity; and you can still find in the garden of almost every old *shizoku* residence in Matsue, a small shrine of Inari Daimyōjin, with little stone foxes seated before it. And in the imagination of the lower classes, all *samurai* families possessed foxes. But the *samurai* foxes inspired no fear. They were believed to be 'good foxes'; and the superstition of the *ninko* or *hito-kitsune* does not seem to have unpleasantly affected any samurai families of Matsue during the feudal era. It is only since the military caste has been abolished, and its name, simply as a body of gentry, changed to *shizoku*,[5] that some families have become victims of the superstition through intermarriage with the *chōnin*, or mercantile classes, among whom the belief has always been strong.

By the peasantry, the Matsudaira *daimyō* of Izumo were supposed to be the greatest fox-possessors. One of them was believed to use foxes as messengers to Tokyo (be it observed that a fox can travel, according to popular credence, from Yokohama to London in a few hours); and there is some Matsue story about a fox having been caught in a trap[6] near Tokyo, attached to whose neck was a letter written by the prince of Izumo only the same morning. The great temple of Inari in the castle grounds - O-Shiroyama-no-Inari-Sama - with its thousands upon thousands of foxes of stone, is considered by the country people a striking proof of the devotion of the Matsudaira, not to Inari, but to foxes.

At present, however, it is no longer possible to establish distinctions of genera in this ghostly zoology, where each species grows into every other. It is not even possible to disengage the *ki* or Soul of the Fox and the August-Spirit-of-Food from the confusion in which both have become hopelessly blended, under the name Inari, by the vague conception of their peasant-worshippers. The old Shinto mythology is indeed quite explicit about the August-Spirit-of-Food, and quite silent upon the subject of foxes. But the peasantry in Izumo, like the peasantry of Catholic Europe, make mythology for themselves. If asked whether they pray to Inari as to an evil or a good deity, they will tell you that Inari is good, and that Inari-foxes are good. They will tell you of white foxes and dark foxes - of foxes to be reverenced and foxes to be killed - of the good fox which cries '*kon-kon*', and the evil fox which cries '*kwai-kwai*'. But the peasant possessed by the fox cries out: '*I am Inari - Tamabushi-no-Inari*'! - or some other Inari.

5

Goblin foxes are peculiarly dreaded in Izumo for three evil habits attributed to them. The first is that of deceiving people by enchantment, either for revenge or pure mischief. The second is that of quartering themselves as retainers upon some family, and thereby making that family a terror to its neighbours. The third and worst is that of entering into people and taking diabolical possession of them and tormenting them into madness. This affliction is called *kitsune-tsuki*.

The favourite shape assumed by the goblin fox for the purpose of deluding mankind is that of a beautiful woman; much less frequently the form of a young man is taken in order to deceive some one of the other sex. Innumerable are the stories told or written about the wiles of fox-women. And a dangerous woman of that class whose art is to enslave men, and strip them of all they possess, is popularly named by a word of deadly insult - *kitsune*.

Many declare that the fox never really assumes human shape; but that he only deceives people into the belief that he does so by a sort of magnetic power, or by spreading about them a certain magical effluvium.

The fox does not always appear in the guise of a woman for evil purposes. There are several stories, and one really pretty play, about a fox who took the shape of a beautiful woman, and married a man, and bore him children - all out of gratitude for some favour received - the happiness of the family being only disturbed by some odd carnivorous propensities on the part of the offspring. Merely to achieve a diabolical purpose, the form of a woman is not always the best disguise. There are men quite insusceptible to feminine witchcraft. But the fox is never at a loss for a disguise; he can assume more forms than Proteus. Furthermore, he can make you see or hear or imagine whatever he wishes you to see, hear, or imagine. He can make you see out of Time and Space; he has not been destroyed by the introduction of Western ideas; for did he not, only a few years ago, cause phantom trains to run upon the Tokkaido railway, thereby greatly confounding, and terrifying the engineers of the company? But, like all goblins, he prefers to haunt solitary places. At night he is fond of making queer ghostly lights.[7] in semblance of lantern-fires, flit about dangerous places; and to protect yourself from this trick of his, it is necessary to learn that by joining your hands in a particular way, so as to leave a diamond-shaped aperture between the crossed fingers, you can extinguish the witch-fire at any distance simply by blowing through the aperture in the direction of the light and uttering a certain Buddhist formula.

But it is not only at night that the fox manifests his power for mischief: at high noon he may tempt you to go where you are sure to get killed, or frighten you into going by creating some apparition or making you imagine that you feel an earthquake. Consequently the old-fashioned peasant, on seeing anything extremely queer, is slow to credit the testimony of his own eyes. The most interesting and valuable witness of the stupendous eruption of Bandai-San in 1888 - which blew the huge volcano to pieces and devastated an area of twenty-seven square miles, levelling forests,

146

turning rivers from their courses, and burying numbers of villages with all their inhabitants - was an old peasant who had watched the whole cataclysm from a neighbouring peak as unconcernedly as if he had been looking at a drama. He saw a black column of ashes and steam rise to the height of twenty thousand feet and spread out at its summit in the shape of an umbrella, blotting out the sun. Then he felt a strange rain pouring upon him, hotter than the water of a bath. Then all became black; and he felt the mountain beneath him shaking to its roots, and heard a crash of thunders that seemed like the sound of the breaking of a world. But he remained quite still until everything was over. He had made up his mind not to be afraid, deeming that all he saw and heard was delusion wrought by the witchcraft of a fox.

6

Strange is the madness of those into whom demon foxes enter. Sometimes they run naked shouting through the streets. Sometimes they lie down and froth at the mouth, and yelp as a fox yelps. And on some part of the body of the possessed a moving lump appears under the skin, which seems to have a life of its own. Prick it with a needle, and it glides instantly to another place. By no grasp can it be so tightly compressed by a strong hand that it will not slip from under the fingers. Possessed folk are also said to speak and write languages of which they were totaly ignorant prior to possession. They eat only what foxes are believed to like - *tofu, aburagé,*[8] *azukimeshi,* etc. - and they eat a great deal, alleging that not they, but the possessing foxes, are hungry.

It not infrequently happens that the victims of fox-possession are cruelly treated by their relatives, being severely burned and beaten in the hope that the fox may be thus driven away. Then the *hōin,*[9] or *yamabushi* is sent for - the exorciser. The exorciser argues with the fox, who speaks through the mouth of the possessed. When the fox is reduced to silence by religious argument upon the wickedness of possessing people, he usually agrees to go away on condition of being supplied with plenty of *tofu* or other food; and the food promised must be brought immediately to that particular Inari temple of which the fox declares himself a retainer. For the possessing fox, by whomsoever sent, usually confesses himself the servant of a certain Inari, though sometimes even calling himself the god.

As soon as the possessed has been freed from the possessor, he falls down senseless, and remains for a long time prostrate. And it is said, also, that he who has once been possessed by a fox will never again be able to eat *tofu, aburagé, azukimeshi,* or any of those things which foxes like.

7

It is believed that the Man-fox (*hito-kitsune*) cannot be seen. But if he goes close to still water, his *shadow* can be seen in the water. Those 'having foxes' are therefore supposed to avoid the vicinity of rivers and ponds.

The invisible fox, as already stated, attaches himself to persons. Like a Japanese servant, he belongs to the household. But if a daughter of that household marry, the fox not only goes to that new family, following the bride, but also *colonises* his kind in all those families related by marriage or kinship with the husband's family. Now every fox is supposed to have a family of seventy-five - neither more, nor less than seventy-five - and all these must be fed. So that although such foxes, like ghosts, eat very little individually, it is expensive to have foxes. The fox-possessors (*kitsune-mochi*) must feed their foxes at regular hours; and the foxes always eat first - all the seventy-five. As soon as the family rice is cooked in the *kama* (a great iron cooking-pot), the *kitsune-mochi* taps loudly on the side of the vessel, and uncovers it. Then the foxes rise up through the floor. And although their eating is soundless to human ear and invisible to human eye, the rice slowly diminishes. Wherefore it is fearful for a poor man to have foxes.

But the cost of nourishing foxes is the least evil connected with the keeping of them. Foxes have no fixed code of ethics, and have proved themselves untrustworthy servants. They may initiate and long maintain the prosperity of some family; but should some grave misfortune fall upon that family in spite of the efforts of its seventy-five invisible retainers, then these will suddenly flee away, taking all the valuables of the household along with them. And all the fine gifts that foxes bring to their masters are things which have been stolen from somebody else. It is therefore extremely immoral to keep foxes. It is also dangerous for the public peace, inasmuch as a fox, being a goblin, and devoid of human susceptibilities, will not take certain precautions. He may steal the next-door neighbour's purse by night and lay it at his own master's threshold, so that if the next-door neighbour happens to get up first and see it there is sure to be a row.

Another evil habit of foxes is that of making public what they hear said in private, and taking it upon themselves to create undesirable scandal. For example, a fox attached to the family of Kobayashi-San, hears his master complain about his neighbour Nakayama-San, whom he secretly dislikes. Therewith the zealous retainer runs to the house of Nakayama-San, and enters into his body, and torments him grievously, saying: 'I am the retainer of Kobayashi-San to whom you did such-and-such a wrong; and until such time as he command me to depart, I shall continue to torment you.'

And last, but worst of all the risks of possessing foxes, is the danger that they may become wroth with some member of the family. Certainly a fox may be a good friend, and make rich the home in which he is domiciled. But as he is not human, and as his motives and feelings are not those of men, but of goblins, it is difficult to avoid incurring his displeasure. At the most unexpected moment he may take offence without any cause knowingly having been given, and there is no saying what the consequences may be. For the fox possesses Instinctive Infinite Vision - and the *Ten-Ni-Tsun*, or All-Hearing Ear - and the *Ta-Shin-Tsun*, which is the Knowledge of the Most Secret Thoughts of Others - and *Shiyuku-Mei-Tsun*, which is the Knowledge of the Past - and *Zhin-Kiyan-Tsun*, which means the Knowledge of the Universal Present - and also the Powers of

Transformation and of Transmutation.[10] So that even without including his special powers of bewitchment, he is by nature a being almost omnipotent for evil.

8

For all these reasons, and doubtless many more, people believed to have foxes are shunned. Intermarriage with a fox-possessing family is out of the question; and many a beautiful and accomplished girl in Izumo cannot secure a husband because of the popular belief that her family harbours foxes. As a rule, Izumo girls do not like to marry out of their own province; but the daughters of a *kitsune-mochi* must either marry into the family of another *kitsune-mochi*, or find a husband far away from the Province of the Gods. Rich fox-possessing families have not overmuch difficulty in disposing of their daughters by one of the means above indicated; but many a fine sweet girl of the poorer *kitsune-mochi* is condemned by superstition to remain unwedded. It is not because there are none to love her and desirous of marrying her - young men who have passed through public schools and who do not believe in foxes. It is because popular superstition cannot be yet safely defied in country districts except by the wealthy. The consequences of such defiance would have to be borne, not merely by the husband, but by his whole family, and by all other families related thereunto. Which are consequences to be thought about!

Among men believed to have foxes there are some who know how to turn the superstition to good account. The country-folk, as a general rule, are afraid of giving offence to a *kitsune-mochi*, lest he should send some of his invisible servants to take possession of them. Accordingly, certain *kitsune-mochi* have obtained great ascendancy over the communities in which they live. In the town of Yonago, for example, there is a certain prosperous *chōnin* whose will is almost law, and whose opinions are never opposed. He is practically the ruler of the place, and in a fair way of becoming a very wealthy man. All because he is thought to have foxes.

Wrestlers, as a class, boast of their immunity from fox-possession, and care neither for *kitsune-mochi* nor for their spectral friends. Very strong men are believed to be proof against all such goblinry. Foxes are said to be afraid of them, and instances are cited of a possessing fox declaring: 'I wished to enter into your brother, but he was too strong for me; so I have entered into you, as I am resolved to be revenged upon some one of your family.'

9

Now the belief in foxes does not affect persons only: it affects property. It affects the value of real estate in Izumo to the amount of hundreds of thousands.

The land of a family supposed to have foxes cannot be sold at a fair price. People are afraid to buy it; for it is believed the foxes may ruin the new proprietor. The difficulty of obtaining a purchaser is most great in the case of land terraced for rice-fields, in the mountain districts. The prime necessity of such agriculture is irrigation - irrigation by a hundred ingenious devices, always in the face of difficulties. There are seasons when water becomes terribly scarce, and when the peasants will even fight for water. It is feared that on lands haunted by foxes,the foxes may turn the water away from one field into another, or, for spite, make holes in the dikes and so destroy the crop.

There are not wanting shrewd men to take advantage of this queer belief. One gentleman of Matsue, a good agriculturist of the modern school, speculated in the fox-terror fifteen years ago, and purchased a vast tract of land in eastern Izumo which no one else would bid for. That land has sextupled in value, besides yielding generously under his system of cultivation; and by selling it now he could realise an immense fortune. His success, and the fact of his having been an official of the government, broke the spell: it is no longer believed that his farms are fox-haunted. But success alone could not have freed the soil from the curse of the superstition. The power of the farmer to banish the foxes was due to his official character. With the peasantry, the word 'Government' is talismanic.

Indeed, the richest and the most successful farmer of Izumo, worth more than a hundred thousand yen - Wakuri-San of Chinomiya in Kandegori - is almost universally believed by the peasantry to be a *kitsune-mochi*. They tell curious stories about him. Some say that when a very poor man he found in the woods one day a little white fox-cub, and took it home, and petted it, and gave it plenty of *tofu*, *azukimeshi*, and *aburagé* - three sorts of food which foxes love - and that from that day prosperity came to him. Others say that in his house there is a special *zashiki*, or guest-room for foxes; and that there, once in each month, a great banquet is given to hundreds of *hito-kitsune*. But Chinomiya-no-Wakuri, as they call him, can afford to laugh at all these tales. He is a refined man, highly respected in cultivated circles where superstition never enters.

10

When a *ninko* comes to your house at night and knocks, there is a peculiar muffled sound about the knocking by which you can tell that the visitor is a fox - if you have experienced ears. For a fox knocks at doors with its tail. If you open, then you will see a man, or perhaps a beautiful girl, who will talk to you only in fragments of words, but nevertheless in such a way that you can perfectly well understand. A fox cannot pronounce a whole word, but a part only - as '*Nish...Sa...*' for '*Nishida-San*': '*degoz...*' for '*degozarimasu*': or '*uch...de...*'? for '*uchi desuka*'? Then, if you are a friend of foxes, the visitor will present you with a little gift of some sort, and at once vanish away into the darkness. Whatever the gift may be, it will seem much larger that night than in the morning. Only a part of a fox-gift is real.

A Matsue *shizoku*, going home one night by way of the street called Horomachi, saw a fox running for its life pursued by dogs. He beat the dogs off with his umbrella, thus giving the fox a chance to escape. On the following evening he heard some one knock at his door, and on opening the *to* saw a very pretty girl standing there, who said to him: 'Last night

I should have died but for your august kindness. I know not how to thank you enough: this is only a pitiable little present.' And she laid a small bundle at his feet and went away. He opened the bundle and found two beautiful ducks and two pieces of silver money - those long, heavy, leaf-shaped pieces of money, each worth ten or twelve dollars - such as are now eagerly sought for by collectors of antique things. After a little while, one of the coins changed before his eyes into a piece of grass; the other was always good.

Sugitean-San, a physician of Matsue, was called one evening to attend a case of confinement at a house some distance from the city, on the hill called Shiragayama. He was guided by a servant carrying a paper lantern painted with an aristocratic crest.[11] He entered into a magnificent house, where he was received with superb samurai courtesy. The mother was safely delivered of a fine boy. The family treated the physician to an excellent dinner, entertained him elegantly, and sent him home, loaded with presents and money. Next day he went, according to Japanese etiquette, to return thanks to his hosts. He could not find the house: there was, in fact, nothing on Shiragayama except forest. Returning home, he examined again the gold which had been paid to him. All was good except one piece, which had changed into grass.

11

Curious advantages have been taken of the superstitions relating to the Fox-God.

In Matsue, several years ago, there was a *tofuya* which enjoyed an unusually large patronage. A *tofuya* is a shop where *tofu* is sold - a curd prepared from beans, and much resembling good custard in appearance. Of all eatable things, foxes are most fond of *tofu* and of *soba*, which is a preparation of buckwheat. There is even a legend that a fox, in the semblance of an elegantly attired man, once visited Nogi-no-Kuriharaya, a popular *sobaya* on the lake shore, and ate much *soba*. But after the guest was gone, the money he had paid changed into wooden shavings.

The proprietor of the *tofuya* had a different experience. A man in wretched attire used to come to his shop every evening to buy a *chō* of *tofu*, which he devoured on the spot with the haste of one long famished. Every evening for weeks he came, and never spoke; but the landlord saw one evening the tip of a bushy white tail protruding from beneath the stranger's rags. The sight aroused strange surmises and weird hopes. From that night he began to treat the mysterious visitor with obsequious kindness. But another month passed before the latter spoke. Then what he said was about as follows:

'Though I seem to you a man, I am not a man; and I took upon myself human form only for the purpose of visiting you. I come from Taka-machi, where my temple is, which you often visit. And being desirous to reward your piety and goodness of heart, I have come tonight to save you from a great danger. For by the power which I possess I know that tomorrow this street will burn, and all the houses in it shall be utterly destroyed except yours. To save it I am going to make a charm. But in order that

151

I may do this, you must open your go-down (*kura*) that I may enter, and allow no one to watch me; for should living eye look upon me there, the charm will not avail.'

The shopkeeper, with fervent words of gratitude, opened his storehouse, and reverently admitted the seeming Inari, and gave orders that none of his household or servants should keep watch. And these orders were so well obeyed that all the stores within the storehouse, and all the valuables of the family, were removed without hindrance during the night. Next day the *kura* was found to be empty. And there was no fire.

There is also a well-authenticated story about another wealthy shopkeeper of Matsue who easily became the prey of another pretended Inari. This Inari told him that whatever sum of money he should leave at a certain *miya* by night, he would find it doubled in the morning - as the reward of his lifelong piety. The shopkeeper carried several small sums to the *miya*, and found them doubled within twelve hours. Then he deposited larger sums, which were similarly multiplied; he even risked some hundreds of dollars, which were duplicated. Finally he took all his money out of the bank and placed it one evening within the shrine of the god - and never saw it again.

Footnotes:

1. The white fox is a favourite subject with Japanese artists. Some very beautiful kakemono representing white foxes were on display at the Tokyo exhibition of 1890. Phosphorescent foxes often appear in the old coloured prints, now so rare and precious, made by artists whose names have become world-famous. Occasionally foxes are represented wandering about at night, with lambent tongues of dim fire - *kitsune-bi* - above their heads. The end of the fox's tail, both in sculpture and drawing, is ordinarily decorated with the symbolic jewel (*tama*) of old Buddhist art. I have in my possession one kakemono representing a white fox with a luminous jewel in its tail. I purchased it at the Matsue temple of Inari, 'O-Shiroyama-no-Inari-Sama'. The art of the kakemono is clumsy; but the conception possesses curious interest.

2. The Japanese candle has a large hollow paper wick. It is usually placed upon an iron point which enters into the orifice of the wick at the flat end.

3. See Professor Chamberlain's *Things Japanese*, under the title 'Demoniacal Possession'.

4. Translated by Walter Dening.

5. The word *shizoku* is simply the Chinese for samurai. But the term now means little more than 'gentleman' in England.

6. The fox-messenger travels unseen. But if caught in a trap, or injured, his magic fails him, and he becomes visible.

7. The *Will-o'-the-Wisp* is called *Kitsune-bi*, or 'fox-fire'.

8. *Aburagé* is a name given to fried bean-curds or *tofu*. *Azukimeshi* is a preparation of red beans boiled with rice.

9. The *hōin* or *yamabushi* was a Buddhist exorciser, usually a priest. Strictly speaking, the *hōin* was a *yamabushi* of higher rank. The *yamabushi* used to practise divination as well as exorcism. They were forbidden to exercise these professions by the present government; and most of the little temples formerly occupied by them have disappeared or fallen into ruin. But among the peasantry Buddhist exorcisers are still called to attend cases of fox-possession, and while acting as exorcisers are still spoken of as *yamabushi*.

10. A most curious paper on the subject of *Ten-gan*, or Infinite Vision - being the translation of a Buddhist sermon by the priest, Sata Kaiseki - appeared in vol. vii of the *Transactions* of the Asiatic Society of Japan, from the pen of Mr J. M. James. It contains an interesting consideration of the supernatural powers of the Fox.

11. All the portable lanterns used to light the way upon dark nights bear a *mon* or crest of the owner.

The Legend Of Yurei-Daki

Near the village of Kurosaka, in the province of Hōki, there is a waterfall called Yurei-Daki, or The Cascade of Ghosts. Why it is so called I do not know. Near the foot of the fall there is a small Shinto shrine of the god of the locality, whom the people name Taki-Daimyōjin; and in front of the shrine is a little wooden money-box - *saisen-bako* - to receive the offerings of believers. And there is a story about that money-box.

One icy winter's evening, thirty-five years ago, the women and girls employed at a certain *asa-toriba*, or hemp-factory, in Kurosaka, gathered around the big brazier in the spinning-room after their day's work had been done. Then they amused themselves by telling ghost-stories. By the time that a dozen stories had been told, most of the gathering felt uncomfortable; and a girl cried out, just to heighten the pleasure of fear, 'Only think of going this night, all by one's self, to the Yurei-Daki!' The suggestion provoked a general scream, followed by nervous bursts of laughter.... 'I'll give all the hemp I spun to-day', mockingly said one of the party, 'to the person who goes!' 'So will I', exclaimed another. 'And I', said a third. 'All of us', affirmed a fourth.... Then from among the spinners stood up one Yasumoto O-Katsu, the wife of a carpenter; she had her only son, a boy of two years old, snugly wrapped up and asleep upon her back. 'Listen', said O-Katsu: 'if you will all really agree to make over to me all the hemp spun to-day, I will go to the Yurei-Daki'. Her proposal was received with cries of astonishment and of defiance. But after having been several times repeated, it was seriously taken. Each of the spinners in turn agreed to give up her share of the day's work to O-Katsu, providing that O-Katsu should go to the Yurei-Daki. 'But how are we to know if she really goes there?' a sharp voice asked. 'Why, let her bring back the money-box of the god', answered an old woman whom the spinners called Obaa-San, the Grandmother; 'that will be proof enough'. 'I'll bring it', cried O-Katsu. And out she darted into the street, with her sleeping boy upon her back.

The night was frosty, but clear. Down the empty street O-Katsu hurried; and she saw that all the house fronts were tightly closed, because of the piercing cold. Out of the village, and along the high road she ran - *pichā-pichā* - with the great silence of frozen rice-fields on either hand, and only the stars to light her. Half an hour she followed the open road; then she turned down a narrower way, winding under cliffs. Darker and rougher the path became as she proceeded; but she knew it well, and she soon heard the dull roar suddenly became a loud clamour, and before her she saw, looming against a mass of blackness, the long glimmering of the fall. Dimly she perceived the shrine - the money-box. She rushed forward, put out her hand....

'*Oi!*O-Katsu-San!'[1] suddenly called a warning voice above the crash of the water.

O-Katsu stood motionless, stupefied by terror.

'*Oi!* O-Katsu-San!' again pealed the voice - this time with more of menace in its tone.

153

But O-Katsu was really a bold woman. At once recovering from her stupefaction, she snatched up the money-box and ran. She neither heard nor saw anything more to alarm her until she reached the high road, where she stopped a moment to take breath. Then she ran on steadily - *pichā-pichā* - till she got to Kurosaka, and thumped at the door of the *asa-toriba*.

How the women and the girls cried out as she entered, panting, with the money-box of the god in her hand! Breathlessly they heard her story; sympathetically they screeched when she told them of the Voice that had called her name, twice, out of the haunted water.... What a woman! Brave O-Katsu! - well had she earned the hemp!.... 'But your boy must be cold, O-Katsu!' cried the Obaa-San, 'let us have him here by the fire!'

' He ought to be hungry,' exclaimed the mother; 'I must give him his milk presently.'... 'Poor O-Katsu!' said the Obaa-San, helping to remove the wraps in which the boy had been carried - 'why, you are all wet behind!' Then, with a husky scream, the helper vociferated, '*Ara! it is blood!*'

And out of the wrappings unfastened there fell to the floor a blood-soaked bundle of baby clothes that left exposed two very small brown feet, and two very small brown hands - nothing more.

The child's head had been torn off!....

Footnote:

1. The exclamation *Oi*! is used to call the attention of a person: it is the Japanese equivalent for such English exclamations as 'Halloa!' 'Ho, there!' etc.

The Story Of Mimi-Nashi-Hōïchi

More than seven hundred years ago, at Dan-o-ura, in the Straits of Shimonoseki, was fought the last battle of the long contest between the Heiké, or Taira clan, and the Genji, Minamoto clan. There the Heiké perished utterly, with their women and children, and their infant emperor likewise - now remembered as Antoku Tennō. And that sea and shore have been haunted for seven hundred years.... Elsewhere I told you about the strange crabs found there, called Heiké crabs, which have human faces on their backs, and are said to be the spirits of Heiké warriors.[1] But there are many strange things to be seen and heard along that coast. On dark nights thousands of ghostly fires hover about the beach, or flit above the waves - pale lights which the fishermen call *oni-bi*, or demon-fires; and, whenever the winds are up, a sound of great shouting comes from that sea, like a clamour of battle.

In former years the Heiké were much more restless than they now are. They would rise about ships passing in the night, and try to sink them; and at all times they would watch for swimmers, to pull them down. It was in order to appease those dead that the Buddhist temple, Amidaji, was built at Akamagaseki.² A cemetery also was made close by, near the beach; and within it were set up monuments inscribed with the names of the drowned emperor and of his great vassals; and Buddhist services were regularly performed there, on behalf of the spirits of them. After the temple had been built, and the tombs erected, the Heiké gave less trouble than before; but they continued to do queer things at intervals - proving that they had not found the perfect peace.

Some centuries ago there lived at Akamagaseki a blind man named Hōïchi, who was famed for his skill in recitation and in playing upon the *biwa*.³ From childhood he had been trained to recite and to play; and while yet a lad he had surpassed his teachers. As a professional *biwa-hōshi* he became famous chiefly by his recitations of the history of the Heiké and the Genji; and it is said that when he sang the song of the battle of Dan-no-ura 'even the goblins [*kijin*] could not refrain from tears'.

At the outset of his career, Hōïchi was very poor; but he found a good friend to help him. The priest of the Amidaji was fond of poetry and music; and he often invited Hōïchi to the temple, to play and recite. Afterwards, being much impressed by the wonderful skill of the lad, the priest proposed that Hōïchi should make the temple his home; and this offer was gratefully accepted. Hōïchi was given a room in the temple-building; and, in return for food and lodging, he was required only to gratify the priest with a musical performance on certain evenings, when otherwise disengaged.

One summer night the priest was called away, to perform a Buddhist service at the house of a dead parishioner; and he went there with his acolyte, leaving Hōïchi alone in the temple. It was a hot night; and the blind man sought to cool himself on the verandah before his sleeping-room. The verandah overlooked a small garden in the rear of the Amidaji. There Hōïchi waited for the priest's return, and tried to relieve his solitude by practising upon his *biwa*. Midnight passed; and the priest did not appear. But the atmosphere was still too warm for comfort within doors; and Hōïchi remained outside. At last he heard steps approaching from the back gate. Somebody crossed the garden, advanced to the verandah, and halted directly in front of him - but it was not the priest. A deep voice called the blind man's name - abruptly and unceremoniously, in the manner of a samurai summoning an inferior:

'Hōïchi!'

Hōïchi was too much startled, for the moment, to respond; and the voice called again, in a tone of harsh command -

'Hōïchi!'

'*Hai!*' answered the blind man, frightened by the menace in the voice - 'I am blind! - I cannot know who calls!'

'There is nothing to fear', the stranger exclaimed, speaking more gently. 'I am stopping near this temple, and have been sent to you with a message. My present lord, a person of exceedingly high rank, is now staying in Akamagaseki, with many noble attendants. He wished to view the scene of the battle of Dan-no-ura; and to-day he visited that place.

Having heard of your skill in reciting the story of the battle, he now desires to hear your performance: so you will take your *biwa* and come with me at once to the house where the august assembly is waiting.'

In those times, the order of a samurai was not to be lightly disobeyed. Hōïchi donned his sandals, took his *biwa*, and went away with the stranger, who guided him deftly, but obliged him to walk very fast. The hand that guided was iron; and the clank of the warrior's stride proved him fully armed - probably some palace-guard on duty. Hōïchi's first alarm was over: he began to imagine himself in good luck - for, remembering the retainer's assurance about a 'person of exceedingly high rank', he thought that the lord who wished to hear the recitation could not be less than a daimyō of the first class. Presently the samurai halted; and Hōïchi became aware that they had arrived at a large gateway - and he wondered, for he could not remember any large gate in that part of the town, except the main gate of the Amidaji. *'Kaimon'*[4] the samurai called - and there was a sound of unbarring; and the twain passed on. They traversed a space of garden, and halted again before some entrance; and the retainer cried in a loud voice, 'Within there! I have brought Hōïchi'. Then came sounds of feet hurrying, and screens sliding, and rain-doors opening, and voices of women in converse. By the language of the women Hōïchi knew them to be domestics in some noble household; but he could not imagine to what place he had been conducted. Little time was allowed him for conjecture. After he had been helped to mount several stone steps, upon the last of which he was told to leave his sandals, a woman's hand guided him along interminable reaches of polished planking, and round pillared angles too many to remember, and over widths amazing of matted floor - into the middle of some vast apartment. There he thought that many great people were assembled: the sound of the rustling of silk was like the sound of leaves in a forest. He heard also a great humming of voices - talking in undertones; and the speech was the speech of courts.

Hōïchi was told to put himself at ease, and he found a kneeling-cushion ready for him. After having taken his place upon it, and tuned his instrument, the voice of a woman - whom he divined to be the *Rōjo*, or matron in charge of the female service - addressed him, saying -

'It is now required that the history of the Heiké be recited, to the accompaniment of the *biwa*.'

Now the entire recital would have required a time of many nights: therefore Hōïchi ventured a question:

'As the whole of the story is not soon told, what portion is it augustly desired that I now recite?'

The woman's voice made answer:

'Recite the story of the battle at Dan-no-ura - for the pity of it is the most deep.'[5]

Then Hōïchi lifted up his voice, and chanted the chant of the fight on the bitter sea - wonderfully making his *biwa* to sound like the straining of oars and the rushing of ships, the whirr and the hissing of arrows, the shouting and trampling of men, the crashing of steel upon helmets, the plunging of slain in the flood. And to left and right of him, in the pauses of his playing, he could hear voices murmuring praise: 'How marvellous an artist'! - 'Never in our own province was playing heard like this'! - 'Not in all the empire is there another singer like Hōïchi'! Then fresh courage came to him, and he played and sang yet better than before; and a hush of wonder deepened about him. But when at last he came to tell the fate of the fair and helpless - the piteous perishing of the women and children - and the death-leap of Nii-no-Ama, with the imperial infant in her arms - then all the listeners uttered together one long, long shuddering cry of anguish; and thereafter they wept and wailed so loudly and so wildly that the blind man was frightened by the violence of the grief that he had made. For much time the sobbing and the wailing continued. But gradually the sounds of lamentation died away; and again, in the great stillness that followed, Hōïchi heard the voice of the woman whom he supposed to be the *Rōjo*.

She said:

'Although we had been assured that you were a very skilful player upon the *biwa*, and without an equal in recitative, we did not know that any one could be so skilful as you have proved yourself to-night. Our lord has been pleased to say that he intends to bestow upon you a fitting reward. But he desires that you shall perform before him once every night for the next six nights - after which time he will probably make his august return-journey. Tomorrow night, therefore, you are to come here at the same hour. The retainer who to-night conducted you will be sent for you.... There is another matter about which I have been ordered to inform you. It is required that you shall speak to no one of your visits here, during the time of our lord's august sojourn at Akamagaseki. As he is travelling incognito,[6] he commands that no mention of these things be made.... You are now free to go back to your temple.'

After Hōïchi had duly expressed his thanks, a woman's hand conducted him to the entrance of the house, where the same retainer, who had before guided him, was waiting to take him home. The retainer led him to the verandah at the rear of the temple, and there bade him farewell.

It was almost dawn when Hōïchi returned; but his absence from the temple had not been observed - as the priest, coming back at a very late hour, had supposed him asleep. During the day Hōïchi was able to take some rest; and he said nothing about his strange adventure. In the middle of the following night the samurai again came for him, and led him to the august assembly, where he gave another recitation with the same success that had attended his previous performance. But during this second visit his absence from the temple was accidentally discovered; and after his return in the morning he was summoned to the presence of the priest, who said to him, in a tone of kindly reproach:

'We have been very anxious about you, friend Hōïchi. To go out, blind and alone, at so late an hour, is dangerous. Why did you go without telling us? I could have ordered a servant to accompany you. And where have you been?'

Hōïchi answered, evasively -

'Pardon me, kind friend! I had to attend to some private business; and I could not arrange the matter at any other hour.'

The priest was surprised, rather than pained, by Hōïchi's reticence:

He felt it to be unnatural, and suspected something wrong. He feared that the blind lad had been bewitched or deluded by some evil spirits. He did not ask any more questions; but he privately instructed the men-servants of the temple to keep watch upon Hōïchi's movements, and to follow him in case that he should again leave the temple after dark.

On the very next night, Hōïchi was seen to leave the temple; and the servants immediately lighted their lanterns, and followed after him. But it was a rainy night, and very dark; and before the temple-folks could get to the roadway, Hōïchi had disappeared. Evidently he had walked very fast - a strange thing, considering his blindness; for the road was in a bad condition. The men hurried through the streets, making inquiries at every house which Hōïchi was accustomed to visit; but nobody could give them any news of him. At last, as they were returning to the temple by way of the shore, they were startled by the sound of a *biwa*, furiously played, in the cemetery of the Amidaji. Except for some ghostly fires - such as usually flitted there on dark nights - all was blackness in that direction. But the men at once hastened into the cemetery; and there, by the help of their lanterns, they discovered Hōïchi - sitting alone in the rain before the memorial tomb of Antoku Tennō, making his *biwa* resound, and loudly chanting the chant of the battle of Dan-no-ura. And behind him, and about him, and everywhere above the tombs, the fires of the dead were burning, like candles. Never before had so great a host of *oni-bi* appeared in the sight of mortal man....

'Hōïchi San! - Hōïchi San!' the servants cried - 'you are bewitched!... Hōïchi San!'

But the blind man did not seem to hear. Strenuously he made his *biwa* to rattle and ring and clang - more and more wildly he chanted the chant of the battle of Dan-no-ura. They caught hold of him - they shouted into his ear -

'Hōïchi San! - Hōïchi San! - come home with us at once!'

Reprovingly he spoke to them:

'To interrupt me in such a manner before this august assembly, will not be tolerated.'

Whereat, in spite of the weirdness of the thing, the servants could not help laughing. Sure that he had been bewitched, they now seized him, and pulled him up on his feet, and by main force hurried him back to the temple, where he was immediately relieved of his wet clothes, by order of the priest, and reclad, and made to eat and drink. Then the priest insisted upon a full explanation of his friend's astonishing behaviour.

Hōïchi long hesitated to speak. But at last, finding that his conduct had really alarmed and angered the good priest, he decided to abandon his reserve; and he related everything that had happened from the time of the first visit of the *samurai*.

The priest said:

'Hōïchi, my poor friend, you are now in great danger! How unfortunate that you did not tell me all this before! Your wonderful skill in music has indeed brought you into strange trouble. By this time you must be aware that you have not been visiting any house whatever, but have been passing your nights in the cemetery, among the tombs of the

Heiké; and it was before the memorial-tomb of Antoku Tennō that our people to-night found you, sitting in the rain. All that you have been imagining was illusion - except the calling of the dead. By once obeying them, you have put yourself in their power. If you obey them again, after what has already occurred, they will tear you in pieces. But they would have destroyed you, sooner or later, in any event.... Now I shall not be able to remain with you to-night: I am called away to perform another service. But, before I go, it will be necessary to protect your body by writing holy texts upon it.'

Before sundown the priest and his acolyte stripped Hōïchi: then, with their writing-brushes, they traced upon his breast and back, head and face and neck, limbs and hands and feet - even upon the soles of his feet, and upon all parts of his body - the text of the holy sutra called *Hannya-Shin-Kyō*.[7] When this had been done, the priest instructed Hōïchi, saying:

'To-night, as soon as I go away, you must seat yourself on the verandah, and wait. You will be called. But, whatever may happen, do not answer, and do not move. Say nothing, and sit still - as if meditating. If you stir, or make any noise, you will be torn asunder. Do not get frightened; and do not think of calling for help - because no help could save you. If you do exactly as I tell you, the danger will pass, and you will have nothing more to fear.'

After dark the priest and the acolyte went away; and Hōïchi seated himself on the verandah, according to the instructions given him. He laid his *biwa* on the planking beside him, and, assuming the attitude of meditation, remained quite still - taking care not to cough, or to breathe audibly. For hours he stayed thus.

Then, from the roadway, he heard the steps coming. They passed the gate, crossed the garden, approached the verandah, stopped - directly in front of him.

'Hōïchi!' the deep voice called. But the blind man held his breath, and sat motionless.

'Hōïchi!' grimly called the voice a second time. Then a third time - savagely:

'Hōïchi!'

Hōïchi remained as still as a stone, and the voice grumbled:

'No answer! - that won't do!.... Must see where the fellow is....'

There was a noise of heavy feet mounting upon the verandah. The feet approached deliberately, halted beside him. Then, for long minutes, during which Hōïchi felt his whole body shake to the beating of his heart, there was dead silence.

At last the gruff voice muttered close to him:

'Here is the *biwa*; but of the *biwa*-player I see - only two ears!.... So that explains why he did not answer: he had no mouth to answer with - there is nothing left of him but his ears.... Now to my lord those ears I will take - in proof that the august commands have been obeyed, so far as was possible...'

At that instant Hōïchi felt his ears gripped by fingers of iron, and torn off! Great as the pain was, he gave no cry. The heavy footfalls receded along the verandah - descended into the garden - passed out to the roadway

- ceased. From either side of his head, the blind man felt a thick warm trickling; but he dared not lift his hands....

Before sunrise the priest came back. He hastened at once to the verandah in the rear, stepped and slipped upon something clammy, and uttered a cry of horror; for he saw, by the light of his lantern, that the clamminess was blood. But he perceived Hōïchi sitting there, in the attitude of meditation - with the blood still oozing from his wounds.

'My poor Hōïchi!' cried the startled priest, - 'what is this?.... You have been hurt?'

At the sound of his friend's voice, the blind man felt safe. He burst out sobbing, and tearfully told his adventure of the night.

'Poor, poor Hōïchi!' the priest exclaimed - 'all my fault! - my very grievous fault!..... Everywhere upon your body the holy texts had been written - except upon your ears! I trusted my acolyte to do that part of the work; and it was very, very wrong of me not to have made sure that he had done it!.... Well, the matter cannot now be helped; - we can only try to heal your hurts as soon as possible.... Cheer up, friend! - the danger is now well over. You will never again be troubled by those visitors.'

With the aid of a good doctor, Hōïchi soon recovered from his injuries. The story of his strange adventure spread far and wide, and soon made him famous. Many noble persons went to Akamagaseki to hear him recite; and large presents of money were given to him - so that he became a wealthy man.... But from the time of his adventure, he was known only by the appellation of *Mimi-nashi-Hōïchi*: 'Hōïchi-the-Earless'.

Footnotes:

1. See my *Kōtto*, for a description of these curious crabs.

2. Or, Shimonoséki. The town is also known by the name of Bakkan.

3. The *biwa*, a kind of four-stringed lute, is chiefly used in musical recitative. Formerly the professional minstrels who recited the *Heiké-Monogatari*, and other tragical histories, were called *biwa-hōshi*, or 'lute-priests'. The origin of this appellation is not clear; but it is possible that it may have been suggested by the fact that 'lute-priests', as well as blind shampooers, had their heads shaven, like Buddhist priests. The *biwa* is played with a kind of plectrum, called *bachi*, usually made of horn.

4. A respectful term, signifying the opening of a gate. It was used by samurai when calling to the guards on duty at a lord's gate for admission.

5. Or the phrase might be rendered, 'for the pity of that part is the deepest'. The Japanese word for pity in the original text is *awaré*.

6. 'Travelling incognito' is at least the meaning of the original phrase - 'making a disguised august-journey' (*shinobi no go-ryokō*).

7. The Smaller Pragña-Pâramitâ-Hridaya-Sûtra is thus called in Japanese. Both the smaller and larger sutras called Pragña-Pâramitâ ('Transcendent Wisdom') have been translated by the late Professor Max Müller, and can be found in volume xlix of the *Sacred Books of the East* ('Buddhist Mahâyâna Sûtras'). - Apropos of the magical use of the text, as described in this story, it is worth remarking that the subject of the sutra is the Doctrine of the Emptiness of Forms - that is to say, of the unreal character of all phenomena or noumena.... 'Form is emptiness; and emptiness is form. Emptiness is not different from form; form is not different from emptiness. What is form - that is emptiness. What is emptiness - that is form.... Perception, name, concept, and knowledge, are also emptiness.... There is no eye, ear, nose, tongue, body, and mind.... But when the envelopment of consciousness has been annihilated, then he [*the seeker*] becomes free from all fear, and beyond the reach of change, enjoying final Nirvâna.'

Jikininki

Once, when Musō Kokushi, a priest of the Zen sect, was journeying alone through the province of Mino, he lost his way in a mountain-district where there was nobody to direct him. For a long time he wandered about helplessly; and he was beginning to despair of finding shelter for the night, when he perceived, on the top of a hill lighted by the last rays of the sun, one of those little hermitages, called *anjitsu*, which are built for solitary priests. It seemed to be in a ruinous condition; but he hastened to it eagerly, and found that it was inhabited by an aged priest, from whom he begged the favour of a night's lodging. This the old man harshly refused; but he directed Musō to a certain hamlet, in the valley adjoining, where lodging and food could be obtained.

Musō found his way to the hamlet, which consisted of less than a dozen farm-cottages; and he was kindly received at the dwelling of the headman. Forty or fifty persons were assembled in the principal apartment, at the moment of Musō's arrival; but he was shown into a small separate room, where he was promptly supplied with food and bedding. Being very tired, he lay down to rest at an early hour; but a little before midnight he was roused from sleep by a sound of loud weeping in the next apartment. Presently the sliding screens were gently pushed apart; and a young man, carrying a lighted lantern, entered the room, respectfully saluted him, and said:

'Reverend Sir, it is my painful duty to tell you that I am now the responsible head of this house. Yesterday I was only the eldest son. But when you came here, tired as you were, we did not wish that you should feel embarrassed in any way: therefore we did not tell you that father had died only a few hours before. The people whom you saw in the next room are the inhabitants of this village: they all assembled here to pay their last respects to the dead; and now they are going to another village, about three miles off - for, by our custom, no one of us may remain in this village during the night after a death has taken place. We make the proper offerings and prayers - then we go away, leaving the corpse alone. Strange things always happen in the house where a corpse has thus been left: so we think that it will be better for you to come away with us. We can find you good lodging in the other village. But perhaps, as you are a priest, you have no fear of demons or evil spirits; and, if you are not afraid of being left alone with the body, you will be very welcome to the use of this poor house. However, I must tell you that nobody, except a priest, would dare to remain here to-night.'

Musō made answer:

'For your kind intention and your generous hospitality, I am deeply grateful. But I am sorry that you did not tell me of your father's death when I came - for, though I was a little tired, I certainly was not so tired that I should have found any difficulty in doing my duty as a priest. Had you told me, I could have performed the service before your departure. As it is, I shall perform the service after you have gone away; and I shall

161

stay by the body until morning. I do not know what you mean by your words about the danger of staying here alone; but I am not afraid of ghosts or demons: therefore please to feel no anxiety on my account.'

The young man appeared to be rejoiced by these assurances, and expressedhis gratitude in fitting words. Then the other members of the family, and the folk assembled in the adjoining room, having been told of the priest's kind promises, came to thank him - after which the master of the house said:

'Now, reverend Sir, much as we regret to leave you alone, we must bid you farewell. By the rule of our village, none of us can stay here after midnight. We beg, kind Sir, that you will take every care of your honourable body, while we are unable to attend upon you. And if you happen to hear or see anything strange during our absence, please tell us of the matter when we return in the morning.'

All then left the house, except the priest, who went to the room where the dead body was lying. The usual offerings had been set before the corpse; and a small Buddhist lamp - *tōmyō* - was burning. The priest recited the service, and performed the funeral ceremonies - after which he entered into meditation. So meditating he remained through several silent hours; and there was no sound in the deserted village. But, when the hush of the night was at its deepest, there noiselessly entered a Shape, vague and vast; and in the same moment Musō found himself without power to move or speak. He saw that Shape lift the corpse, as with hands, and devour it, more quickly than a cat devours a rat - beginning at the head, and eating everything: the hair and the bones and even the shroud. And the monstrous Thing, having thus consumed the body, turned to the offerings, and ate them also. Then it went away, as mysteriously as it had come.

When the villagers returned next morning, they found the priest awaiting them at the door of the headman's dwelling. All in turn saluted him; and when they had entered, and looked about the room, no one expressed any surprise at the disappearance of the dead body and the offerings. But the master of the house said to Musō:

'Reverend Sir, you have probably seen unpleasant things during the night: all of us were anxious about you. But now we are very happy to find you alive and unharmed. Gladly we would have stayed with you, if it had been possible. But the law of our village, as I told you last evening, obliges us to quit our houses after a death has taken place, and to leave the corpse alone. Whenever this law has been broken, heretofore, some great misfortune has followed. Whenever it is obeyed, we find that the corpse and the offerings disappear during our absence. Perhaps you have seen the cause.'

Then Musō told of the dim and awful Shape that had entered the death-chamber to devour the body and the offerings. No person seemed to be surprised by his narration; and the master of the house observed:

'What you have told us, reverend Sir, agrees with what has been said about this matter from ancient times.'

Musō then inquired:

'Does not the priest on the hill sometimes perform the funeral-service for your dead?'

'What priest'? the young man asked.

'The priest who yesterday evening directed me to this village', answered Musō. 'I called at his *anjitsu* on the hill yonder. He refused me lodging, but told me the way here.'

The listeners looked at each other, as in astonishment; and, after a moment of silence, the master of the house said:

'Reverend Sir, there is no priest and there is no *anjitsu* on the hill. For the time of many generations there has not been any resident-priest in the neighbourhood.'

Musō said nothing more on the subject; for it was evident that his kind hosts supposed him to have been deluded by some goblin. But after having bidden them farewell, and obtained all necessary information as to his road, he determined to look again for the hermitage on the hill, and so to ascertain whether he had really been deceived. He found the *anjitsu* without any difficulty; and, this time its aged occupant invited him to enter. When he had done so, the hermit humbly bowed down before him, exclaiming: 'Ah! I am ashamed! - I am very much ashamed! - I am exceedingly ashamed!'

'You need not be ashamed for having refused me shelter', said Musō. 'You directed me to the village yonder, where I was very kindly treated; and I thank you for that favour.'

'I can give no man shelter', the recluse made answer - 'and it is not for the refusal that I am ashamed. I am ashamed only that you should have seen me in my real shape - for it was I who devoured the corpse and the offerings last night before your eyes.... Know, reverend Sir, that I am a *jikininki*[1] - an eater of human flesh. Have pity upon me, and suffer me to confess the secret fault by which I became reduced to this condition.

'A long, long time ago, I was a priest in this desolate region. There was no other priest for many leagues around. So, in that time, the bodies of the mountain-folk who died used to be brought here - sometimes from great distances - in order that I might repeat over them the holy service. But I repeated the service and performed the rites only as a matter of business; I thought only of the food and the clothes that my sacred profession enabled me to gain. And because of this selfish impiety I was reborn, immediately after my death, into the state of a *jikininki*. Since then I have been obliged to feed upon the corpses of the people who die in this district: every one of them I must devour in the way that you saw last night.... Now, reverend Sir, let me beseech you to perform a Ségaki-service[2] for me: help me by your prayers, I entreat you, so that I may be soon able to escape from this horrible state of existence.'...

No sooner had the hermit uttered this petition than he disappeared; and the hermitage also disappeared at the same instant. And Musō Kokushi found himself kneeling alone in the high grass, beside an ancient and moss-grown tomb, of the form called *go-rin-ishi*,[3] which seemed to be the tomb of a priest.

Footnotes:

1. Literally, a man-eating goblin. The Japanese narrator gives also the Sanscrit term, 'Râkshasa'; but this word is quite as vague as *jikininki*, since there are many kinds of Râkshasas. Apparently the word *jikininki* signifies here one of the *Baramon-Rasetsu-Gaki* - forming the twenty-sixth class of pretas enumerated in the old Buddhist books.
2. A *Ségaki*-service is a special Buddhist service performed on behalf of beings supposed to have entered into the condition of *gaki* (pretas), or hungry spirits. For a brief account of such a service, see my *Japanese Miscellany*.
3. Literally, 'five-circle [or "five-zone"] stone'. A funeral monument consisting of five parts superimposed - each of a different form - symbolising the five mystic elements: Ether, Air, Fire, Water, Earth.

Mujina

On the Akasaka Road, in Tokyo, there is a slope called Kii-no-kuni-zaka, which means the Slope of the Province of Kii. I do not know why it is called the Slope of the Province of Kii. On one side of this slope you see an ancient moat, deep and very wide, with high green banks rising up to some place of gardens; and on the other side of the road extend the long and lofty walls of an imperial palace. Before the era of street-lamps and *jinrickshas*, this neighbourhood was very lonesome after dark; and belated pedestrians would go miles out of their way rather than mount the Kii-no-kuni-zaka, alone, after sunset.

All because of a *mujina* that used to walk there.

The last man who saw the *mujina* was an old merchant of the Kyōbashi quarter, who died about thirty years ago. This is the story, as he told it:

One night, at a late hour, he was hurrying up the Kii-no-kuni-zaka, when he perceived a woman crouching by the moat, all alone, and weeping bitterly. Fearing that she intended to drown herself, he stopped to offer her any assistance or consolation in his power. She appeared to be a slight and graceful person, handsomely dressed; and her hair was arranged like that of a young girl of good family. 'O-jochū',[1] he exclaimed, approaching her - 'O-jochū, do not cry like that!.... Tell me what the trouble is; and if there be any way to help you, I shall be glad to help you.' (He really meant what he said; for he was a very kind man). But she continued to weep, hiding her face from him with one of her long sleeves. 'O-jochū', he said again, as gently as he could, 'please, please listen to me!.... This is no place for a young lady at night! Do not cry, I implore you! - only tell me how I may be of some help to you!' Slowly she rose up, but turned her back to him, and continued to moan and sob behind her sleeve. He laid his hand lightly upon her shoulder, and pleaded: 'O-jochū! - O-jochū! - O-jochū!'... Then that O-jochū turned round, and dropped her sleeve, and stroked her face with her hand - and the man saw that she had no eyes or nose or mouth - and he screamed and ran away.

Up Kii-no-kuni-zaka he ran and ran; and all was black and empty before him. On and on he ran, never daring to look back; and at last he saw a lantern, so far away that it looked like the gleam of a firefly; and he made for it. It proved to be only the lantern of an itinerant *soba*-seller,[2] who had set down his stand by the roadside; but any light and any human companionship was good after that experience; and he flung himself down at the feet of the *soba*-seller, crying out, 'Ah! - aa!! - aa!!!...'

'*Kore! kore!*' roughly exclaimed the *soba*-man. 'Here! what is the matter with you? Anybody hurt you?'

'No - nobody hurt me', panted the other - 'only.... *Aa! - aa!...*'

' - Only scared you?' queried the pedlar, unsympathetically. 'Robbers?'

'Not robbers - not robbers', gasped the terrified man.... 'I saw.... I saw a woman - by the moat - and she showed me.... *Aa*! I cannot tell you what she showed me!....'

'*He*! Was it anything like *this* that she showed you?' cried the *soba*-man, stroking his own face - which therewith became like unto an Egg.... And, simultaneously, the light went out.

Footnotes:

1. O-jochū ('honourable damsel') - a polite form of address used in speaking to a young lady whom one does not know.
2. *Soba* is a preparation of buckwheat, somewhat resembling vermicelli.

Rokuro-Kubi

Nearly five hundred years ago there was a *samurai*, named Isogai Heidazaemon Taketsura, in the service of the Lord Kikuji, of Kyushu. This Isogai had inherited, from many warlike ancestors, a natural aptitude for military exercises, and extraordinary strength. While yet a boy he had surpassed his teachers in the art of swordsmanship, in archery, and in the use of the spear, and had displayed all the capacities of a daring and skilful soldier. Afterwards, in the time of the Eikyō[1] war, he so distinguished himself that high honours were bestowed upon him. But when the house of Kikuji came to ruin, Isogai found himself without a master. He might then easily have obtained service under another *daimyō*; but as he had never sought distinction for his own sake alone, and as his heart remained true to his former lord, he preferred to give up the world. So he cut off his hair, and became a travelling priest, taking the Buddhist name of Kwairyō.

But always, under the *koromo*[2] of the priest, Kwairyō kept warm within him the heart of the *samurai*. As in other years he had laughed at peril, so now also he scorned danger; and in all weathers and all seasons he journeyed to preach the good Law in places where no other priest would have dared to go. For that age was an age of violence and disorder; and upon the highways there was no security for the solitary traveller, even if he happened to be a priest.

In the course of his first long journey, Kwairyō had occasion to visit the province of Kai. One evening, as he was travelling through the mountains of that province, darkness overtook him in a very lonesome district, leagues away from any village. So he resigned himself to pass the night under the stars; and having found a suitable grassy spot, by the roadside, he lay down there, and prepared to sleep. He had always welcomed discomfort; and even a bare rock was for him a good bed, when nothing better could be found, and the root of a pine-tree an excellent pillow. His body was iron; and he never troubled himself about dews or rain or frost or snow.

Scarcely had he lain down when a man came along the road, carrying an axe and a great bundle of chopped wood. This wood-cutter halted on seeing Kwairyō lying down, and, after a moment of silent observation, said to him in a tone of great surprise:

'What kind of a man can you be, good Sir, that you dare to lie down alone in such a place as this?... There are haunters about here - many of them. Are you not afraid of Hairy Things?'

'My friend', cheerfully answered Kwairyō, 'I am only a wandering priest - a "Cloud-and-Water-Guest", as folks call it: *Un-sui-no-ryokaku*. And I am not in the least afraid of Hairy Things, if you mean goblin-foxes, or goblin-badgers, or any creatures of that kind. As for lonesome places, I like them: they are suitable for meditation. I am accustomed to sleeping in the open air: and I have learned never to be anxious about my life.'

'You must be indeed a brave man, Sir Priest', the peasant responded, 'to lie down here! This place has a bad name - a very bad name. But, as the proverb has it, *Kunshi ayayuki ni chikayorazu* ["The superior man does not needlessly expose himself to peril"]; and I must assure you, Sir, that it is very dangerous to sleep here. Therefore, although my house is only a wretched thatched hut, let me beg of you to come home with me at once. In the way of food, I have nothing to offer you; but there is a roof at least, and you can sleep under it without risk.'

He spoke earnestly; and Kwairyō, liking the kindly tone of the man, accepted this modest offer. The woodcutter guided him along a narrow path, leading up from the main road through mountain-forest. It was a rough and dangerous path, sometimes skirting precipices, sometimes offering nothing but a network of slippery roots for the foot to rest upon, sometimes winding over or between masses of jagged rock. But at last Kwairyō found himself upon a cleared space at the top of a hill, with a full moon shining overhead; and he saw before him a small thatched cottage, cheerfully lighted from within. The woodcutter led him to a shed at the back of the house, whither water had been conducted, through bamboo-pipes, from some neighbouring stream; and the two men washed their feet. Beyond the shed was a vegetable garden, and a grove of cedars and bamboos; and beyond the trees appeared the glimmer of a cascade, pouring from some loftier height, and swaying in the moonshine like a long white robe.

As Kwairyō entered the cottage with his guide, he perceived four persons - men and women - warming their hands at a little fire kindled in the *ro*[3] of the principal apartment. They bowed low to the priest, and greeted him in the most respectful manner. Kwairyō wondered that persons so poor, and dwelling in such solitude, should be aware of the polite forms of greeting. 'These are good people', he thought to himself; 'and they must have been taught by some one well acquainted with the rules of propriety.' Then turning to his host - the *aruji*, or house-master, as the others called him - Kwairyō said:

'From the kindness of your speech, and from the very polite welcome given me by your household, I imagine that you have not always been a woodcutter. Perhaps you formerly belonged to one of the upper classes?'

Smiling, the woodcutter answered:

'Sir, you are not mistaken. Though now living as you find me, I was once a person of some distinction. My story is the story of a ruined life - ruined by my own fault. I used to be in the service of a *daimyō*; and my rank in that service was not inconsiderable. But I loved women and wine too well; and under the influence of passion I acted wickedly. My selfishness brought about the ruin of our house, and caused the death of many persons. Retribution followed me; and I long remained a fugitive in the land. Now I often pray that I may be able to make some atonement for the evil which I did, and to re-establish the ancestral home. But I fear that I shall never find any way of so doing. Nevertheless, I try to overcome the *karma* of my errors by sincere repentance, and by helping, as far as I can, those who are unfortunate.'

Kwairyō was pleased by this announcement of good resolve; and he said to the *aruji*:

'My friend, I have had occasion to observe that men, prone to folly in their youth, may in after years become very earnest in right living. In the holy sutras it is written that those strongest in wrong-doing can become, by power of good resolve, the strongest in right-doing. I do not doubt that you have a good heart; and I hope that better fortune will come to you. Tonight I shall recite the sutras for your sake, and pray that you may obtain the force to overcome the karma of any past errors.'

With these assurances, Kwairyō bade the *aruji* good-night; and his host showed him to a very small side-room, where a bed had been made ready. Then all went to sleep except the priest, who began to read the sutras by the light of a paper lantern. Until a late hour he continued to read and pray: then he opened a window in his little sleeping-room, to take a last look at the landscape before lying down. The night was beautiful: there was no cloud in the sky; there was no wind; and the strong moonlight threw down sharp black shadows of foliage, and glittered on the dews of the garden. Shrillings of crickets and bell-insects made a musical tumult; and the sound of the neighbouring cascade deepened with the night. Kwairyō felt thirsty as he listened to the noise of the water; and, remembering the bamboo aqueduct at the rear of the house, he thought that he could go there and get a drink without disturbing the sleeping household. Very gently he pushed apart the sliding-screens that separated his room from the main apartment; and he saw, by the light of the lantern, five recumbent bodies - without heads!

For one instant he stood bewildered, imagining a crime. But in another moment he perceived that there was no blood, and that the headless necks did not look as if they had been cut. Then he thought to himself: 'Either this is an illusion made by goblins, or I have been lured into the dwelling of a Rokuro-kubi.... In the book *Sōshinki* it is written that if one finds the body of a Rokuro-kubi without its head, and remove the body to another place, the head will never be able to join itself again to the neck. And the book further says that when the head comes back and finds that its body has been moved, it will strike itself upon the floor three times, bounding like a ball, and will pant as in great fear, and presently die. Now, if these be Rokuro-kubi, they mean me no good; so I shall be justified in following the instructions of the book.'...

He seized the body of the aruji by the feet, pulled it to the window, and pushed it out. Then he went to the back-door, which he found barred; and he surmised that the heads had made their exit through the smoke-hole in the roof, which had been left open. Gently unbarring the door, he made his way to the garden, and proceeded with all possible caution to the grove beyond it. He heard voices talking in the grove; and he went in the direction of the voices - stealing from shadow to shadow, until he reached a good hiding-place. Then, from behind a trunk, he caught sight of the heads - all five of them - flitting about, and chatting as they flitted. They were eating worms and insects which they found on the ground or among the trees. Presently the head of the aruji stopped eating and said:

'Ah, that travelling priest who came tonight! - how fat all his body is! When we shall have eaten him, our bellies will be well filled.... I was foolish to talk to him as I did - it only set him to reciting the sutras on behalf of my soul! To go near him while he is reciting would be difficult; and we cannot touch him so long as he is praying. But as it is now nearly morning, perhaps he has gone to sleep.... Some one of you go to the house and see what the fellow is doing.'

Another head - the head of a young woman - immediately rose up and flitted to the house, lightly as a bat. After a few minutes it came back, and cried out huskily, in a tone of great alarm:

'That travelling priest is not in the house - he is gone! But that is not the worst of the matter. He has taken the body of our *aruji*; and I do not know where he has put it.'

At this announcement the head of the *aruji* - distinctly visible in the moonlight - assumed a frightful aspect: its eyes opened monstrously; its hair stood up bristling; and its teeth gnashed. Then a cry burst from its lips; and - weeping tears of rage - it exclaimed:

'Since my body has been moved, to rejoin it is not possible! Then I must die!... And all through the work of that priest! Before I die I will get at that priest! - I will tear him! - I will devour him!... *And there he is* - behind that tree! - hiding behind that tree! See him! - the fat coward!'...

In the same moment the head of the *aruji*, followed by the other four heads, sprang at Kwairyō. But the strong priest had already armed himself

168

by plucking up a young tree; and with that tree he struck the heads as they came, knocking them from him with tremendous blows. Four of them fled away. But the head of the *aruji*, though battered again and again, desperately continued to bound at the priest, and at last caught him by the left sleeve of his robe. Kwairyō, however, as quickly gripped the head by its topknot, and repeatedly struck it. It did not release its hold; but it uttered a long moan, and thereafter ceased to struggle. It was dead. But its teeth still held the sleeve; and, for all his great strength, Kwairyō could not force open the jaws.

With the head still hanging to his sleeve he went back to the house, and there caught sight of the other four Rokuro-kubi squatting together, with their bruised and bleeding heads reunited to their bodies. But when they perceived him at the back-door all screamed, 'The priest! the priest'! - and fled through the other doorway out into the woods.

Eastward the sky was brightening; day was about to dawn; and Kwairyō knew that the power of the goblins was limited to the hours of darkness. He looked at the head clinging to his sleeve - its face all fouled with blood and foam and clay; and he laughed aloud as he thought to himself: 'What a *miyagé*[4] - the head of a goblin'! After which he gathered together his few belongings, and leisurely descended the mountain to continue his journey.

Right on he journeyed, until he came to Suwa in Shinano; and into the main street of Suwa he solemnly strode, with the head dangling at his elbow. Then women fainted, and children screamed and ran away; and there was a great crowding and clamouring until the *torité* (as the police in those days were called) seized the priest, and took him to jail. For they supposed the head to be the head of a murdered man who, in the moment of being killed, had caught the murderer's sleeve in his teeth. As for Kwairyō, he only smiled and said nothing when they questioned him. So, after having passed a night in prison, he was brought before the magistrates of the district. Then he was ordered to explain how he, a priest, had been found with the head of a man fastened to his sleeve, and why he had dared thus shamelessly to parade his crime in the sight of the people.

Kwairyō laughed long and loudly at these questions; and then he said:

'Sirs, I did not fasten the head to my sleeve: it fastened itself there - much against my will. And I have not committed any crime. For this is not the head of a man; it is the head of a goblin; and, if I caused the death of the goblin, I did not do so by any shedding of blood, but simply by taking the precautions necessary to assure my own safety.'... And he proceeded to relate the whole of the adventure - bursting into another hearty laugh as he told of his encounter with the five heads.

But the magistrates did not laugh. They judged him to be a hardened criminal, and his story an insult to their intelligence. Therefore, without further questioning, they decided to order his immediate execution - all of them except one, a very old man. This aged officer had made no remark during the trial; but, after having heard the opinion of his colleagues, he rose up, and said:

'Let us first examine the head carefully; for this, I think, has not yet been done. If the priest has spoken truth, the head itself should bear witness for him.... Bring the head here!'

So the head, still holding in its teeth the *koromo* that had been stripped from Kwairyō's shoulders, was put before the judges. The old man turned it round and round, carefully examined it, and discovered, on the nape of its neck, several strange red characters. He called the attention of his colleagues to these, and also bade them observe that the edges of the neck nowhere presented the appearance of having been cut by any weapon. On the contrary, the line of severance was smooth as the line at which a falling leaf detaches itself from the stem.... Then said the elder:

'I am quite sure that the priest told us nothing but the truth. This is the head of a Rokuro-kubi. In the book *Nan-hō-i-butsu-shi* it is written that certain red characters can always be found upon the nape of the neck of a real Rokuro-kubi. There are the characters; you can see for yourselves that they have not been painted. Moreover, it is well known that such goblins have been dwelling in the mountains of the province of Kai from very ancient time.... But you, Sir', he exclaimed, turning to Kwairyō, 'what sort of sturdy priest may you be? Certainly you have given proof of a courage that few priests possess; and you have the air of a soldier rather than of a priest. Perhaps you once belonged to the samurai-class?'

'You have guessed rightly, Sir', Kwairyō responded. 'Before becoming a priest, I long followed the profession of arms; and in those days I never feared man or devil. My name then was Isogai Heidazaemon Taketsura, of Kyushu: there may be some among you who remember it.'

At the utterance of that name, a murmur of admiration filled the court-room; for there were many present who remembered it. And Kwairyō immediately found himself among friends instead of judges - friends anxious to prove their admiration by fraternal kindness. With honour they escorted him to the residence of the *daimyō*, who welcomed him, and feasted him, and made him a handsome present before allowing him to depart. When Kwairyō left Suwa, he was as happy as any priest is permitted to be in this transitory world. As for the head, he took it with him, jocosely insisting that he intended it for a *miyagé*.

And now it only remains to tell what became of the head.

A day or two after leaving Suwa, Kwairyō met with a robber, who stopped him in a lonesome place, and bade him strip. Kwairyō at once removed his *koromo*, and offered it to the robber, who then first perceived what was hanging to the sleeve. Though brave, the highwayman was startled: he dropped the garment, and sprang back. Then he cried out: 'You! - what kind of a priest are you? Why, you are a worse man than I am! It is true that I have killed people; but I never walked about with anybody's head fastened to my sleeve.... Well, Sir priest, I suppose we are of the same calling; and I must say that I admire you!... Now that head would be of use to me: I could frighten people with it. Will you sell it? You can have my robe in exchange for your *koromo*; and I will give you five ryō for the head.'

Kwairyō answered:

'I shall let you have the head and the robe if you insist; but I must tell you that this is not the head of a man. It is a goblin's head. So, if you buy it, and have any trouble in consequence, please do remember that you were not deceived by me.'

'What a nice priest you are!' exclaimed the robber. 'You kill men, and jest about it!... But I am really in earnest. Here is my robe and here is my money - and let me have the head.... What is the use of joking?'

'Take the thing', said Kwairyō. 'I was not joking. The only joke - if there be any joke at all - is that you are fool enough to pay good money for a goblin's head.' And Kwairyō, loudly laughing, went upon his way.

Thus the robber got the head and the *koromo*; and for some time he played goblin-priest upon the highways. But, reaching the neighbourhood of Suwa, he there learned the real history of the head; and he then became afraid that the spirit of the Rokuro-kubi might give him trouble. So he made up his mind to take back the head to the place from which it had come, and to bury it with its body. He found his way to the lonely cottage in the mountains of Kai; but nobody was there, and he could not discover the body. Therefore he buried the head by itself, in the grove behind the cottage; and he had a tombstone set up over the grave; and he caused a Segaki-service to be performed on behalf of the spirit of the Rokuro-kubi. And that tombstone - known as the Tombstone of the Rokuro-kubi - may be seen (at least so the Japanese story-teller declares) even unto this day.

Footnotes:

1. The period of Eikyo lasted from 1429 to 1441.
2. The upper robe of a Buddhist priest is thus called.
3. A sort of little fireplace, contrived in the floor of a room, is thus described. The *ro* is usually a square shallow cavity, lined with metal and half-filled with ashes, in which charcoal is lighted.
4. A present made to friends or to the household on returning from a journey is thus called. Ordinarily, of course, the *miyagé* consists of something produced in the locality to which the journey has been made: this is the point of Kwairyō's jest.

Yuki-Onna

In a village of Musashi Province, there lived two woodcutters: Mosaku and Minokichi. At the time of which I am speaking, Mosaku was an old man; and Minokichi, his apprentice, was a lad of eighteen years. Every day they went together to a forest situated about five miles from their village. On the way to that forest there is a wide river to cross; and there is a ferry-boat. Several times a bridge was built where the ferry is; but the bridge was each time carried away by a flood. No common bridge can resist the current there when the river rises.

Mosaku and Minokichi were on their way home, one very cold evening, when a great snowstorm overtook them. They reached the ferry;

and they found that the boatman had gone away, leaving his boat on the other side of the river. It was no day for swimming; and the woodcutters took shelter in the ferryman's hut - thinking themselves lucky to find any shelter at all. There was no brazier in the hut, nor any place in which to make a fire: it was only a two-mat[1] hut, with a single door, but no window. Mosaku and Minokichi fastened the door, and lay down to rest, with their straw rain-coats over them. At first they did not feel very cold; and they thought that the storm would soon be over.

The old man almost immediately fell asleep; but the boy, Minokichi, lay awake a long time, listening to the awful wind, and the continual slashing of the snow against the door. The river was roaring; and the hut swayed and creaked like a junk at sea. It was a terrible storm; and the air was every moment becoming colder; and Minokichi shivered under his raincoat. But at last, in spite of the cold, he too fell asleep.

He was awakened by a showering of snow in his face. The door of the hut had been forced open; and, by the snowlight (*yukiakari*), he saw a woman in the room - a woman all in white. She was bending above Mosaku and blowing her breath upon him; and her breath was like a bright white smoke. Almost in the same moment she turned to Minokichi, and stooped over him. He tried to cry out, but found that he could not utter any sound. The white woman bent down over him, lower and lower, until her face almost touched him; and he saw that she was very beautiful - though her eyes made him afraid. For a little time she continued to look at him - then she smiled, and she whispered: 'I intended to treat you like the other man. But I cannot help feeling some pity for you - because you are so young.... You are a pretty boy, Minokichi; and I will not hurt you now. But, if you ever tell anybody - even your own mother - about what you have seen this night, I shall know it; and then I will kill you.... Remember what I say!'

With these words, she turned from him, and passed through the doorway. Then he found himself able to move; and he sprang up, and looked out. But the woman was nowhere to be seen; and the snow was driving furiously into the hut. Minokichi closed the door, and secured it by fixing several billets of wood against it. He wondered if the wind had blown it open - he thought that he might have been only dreaming, and might have mistaken the gleam of the snow-light in the doorway for the figure of a white woman: but he could not be sure. He called to Mosaku, and was frightened because the old man did not answer. He put out his hand in the dark, and touched Mosaku's face, and found that it was ice! Mosaku was stark and dead....

By dawn the storm was over; and when the ferryman returned to his station, a little after sunrise, he found Minokichi lying senseless beside the frozen body of Mosaku. Minokichi was promptly cared for, and soon came to himself; but he remained a long time ill from the effects of the cold of that terrible night. He had been greatly frightened also by the old man's death; but he said nothing about the vision of the woman in white. As soon as he got well again, he returned to his calling - going alone every morning to the forest, and coming back at nightfall with his bundles of wood, which his mother helped him to sell.

One evening, in the winter of the following year, as he was on his way home, he overtook a girl who happened to be travelling by the same road. She was a tall, slim girl, very good-looking; and she answered Minokichi's greeting in a voice as pleasant to the ear as the voice of a song-bird. Then he walked beside her; and they began to talk. The girl said that her name was O-Yuki;[2] that she had lately lost both of her parents; and that she was going to Yedo, where she happened to have some poor relations, who might help her to find a situation as servant. Minokichi soon felt charmed by this strange girl; and the more that he looked at her, the handsomer she appeared to be. He asked her whether she was yet betrothed; and she answered, laughingly, that she was free. Then, in her turn, she asked Minokichi whether he was married, or pledged to marry; and he told her that although he had only a widowed mother to support, the question of an 'honourable daughter-in-law' had not yet been considered, as he was very young.... After these confidences, they walked on for a long while without speaking; but, as the proverb declares, *Ki ga aréba, mé mo kuchi hodo ni mono wo iu*: 'When the wish is there, the eyes can say as much as the mouth'. By the time they reached the village, they had become very much pleased with each other; and then Minokichi asked O-Yuki to rest awhile at his house. After some shy hesitation, she went there with him; and his mother made her welcome, and prepared a warm meal for her. O-Yuki behaved so nicely that Minokichi's mother took a sudden fancy to her, and persuaded her to delay her journey to Yedo. And the natural end of the matter was that Yuki never went to Yedo at all. She remained in the house, as an 'honourable daughter-in-law'.

O-Yuki proved a very good daughter-in-law. When Minokichi's mother came to die - some five years later - her last words were words of affection and praise for the wife of her son. And O-Yuki bore Minokichi ten children, boys and girls - handsome children all of them, and very fair of skin.

The country-folk thought O-Yuki a wonderful person, by nature different from themselves. Most of the peasant-women age early; but O-Yuki, even after having become the mother of ten children, looked as young and fresh as on the day when she had first come to the village.

One night, after the children had gone to sleep, O-Yuki was sewing by the light of a paper lamp; and Minokichi, watching her said:

'To see you sewing there, with the light on your face, makes me think of a strange thing that happened when I was a lad of eighteen. I then saw somebody as beautiful and white as you are now - indeed, she was very like you.'...

Without lifting her eyes from her work, O-Yuki responded:

'Tell me about her.... Where did you see her?'

Then Minokichi told her about the terrible night in the ferryman's hut - and about the White Woman that had stooped above him, smiling and whispering - and about the silent death of old Mosaku. And he said:

'Asleep or awake, that was the only time that I saw a being as beautiful as you. Of course, she was not a human being; and I was afraid of her - very much afraid - but she was so white!.... Indeed, I have never been sure whether it was a dream that I saw, or the Woman of the Snow.'...

173

O-Yuki flung down her sewing, and arose, and bowed above Minokichi where he sat and shrieked into his face:

'It was I-I-I! Yuki it was! And I told you then that I would kill you if you ever said one word about it!... But for those children asleep there, I would kill you this moment! And now you had better take very, very good care of them; for if ever they have reason to complain of you, I will treat you as you deserve!'...

Even as she screamed, her voice became thin, like a crying of wind - then she melted into a bright white mist that spired to the roofbeams, and shuddered away through the smokehole.... Never again was she seen.

Footnotes:

1. That is to say, with a floor-surface of about six feet square.
2. This name, signifying 'Snow', is not uncommon. On the subject of Japanese female names, see my paper in the volume entitled *Shadowings*.

Gaki

- 'Venerable Nagasena, are there such things as demons in the world?'
- 'Yes, O King.'
- 'Do they ever leave that condition of existence?'
- 'Yes, they do.'
- 'But, if so, why is it that the remains of those demons are never found?' ...
- 'Their remains are found, O King ... The remains of bad demons can be found in the form of worms and beetles and ants and snakes and scorpions and centipedes.'...
- *The Questions of King Milinda*

1

There are moments in life when truths but dimly known before - beliefs first vaguely reached through multiple processes of reasoning - suddenly assume the vivid character of emotional convictions. Such an experience came to me the other day, on the Suruga coast. While resting under the pines that fringed the beach, something in the vital warmth and luminous peace of the hour - some quivering rapture of wind and light - very strangely bestirred an old belief of mine: the belief that all being is One. One I felt myself to be with the thrilling of breeze and the racing of wave, with every flutter of shadow and flicker of sun, with the azure of sky and sea, with the great green hush of the land. In some new and wonderful way I found myself assured that there never could have been a beginning, that there never could be an end. Nevertheless, the ideas of the moment were not new: the novelty of the experience was altogether in the peculiar intensity with which they presented themselves; making me feel that the flashing dragon-flies, and the long grey sand-crickets, and the shrilling *semi* overhead, and the little red crabs astir under the roots of the pines, were all of them brothers and sisters. I seemed to understand, as never before, how the mystery that is called the Soul of me must have quickened in every form of past existence, and must as certainly continue to behold the sun, for other millions of summers, through eyes of other countless shapes of future being. And I tried to think the long slow thoughts of the long grey crickets, and the thoughts of the darting, shimmering dragon-flies, and the thoughts of the basking, trilling cicadae, and the thoughts of the wicked little crabs that lifted up their claws from between the roots of the pines.

Presently I discovered myself wondering whether the consequence of such thoughts could have anything to do with the recombination of my soul-dust in future spheres of existence. For thousands of years the East has been teaching that what we think or do in this life really decides - through some inevitable formation of atom-tendencies, or polarities - the future place of our substance, and the future state of our sentiency. And the belief is worth thinking about - though no amount of thinking can enable us either to confirm or to disprove it. Very possibly, like other Buddhist doctrines, it may adumbrate some cosmic truth; but its literal assertions I doubt, because I must doubt the power ascribed to thought. By the whole infinite past I have been moulded, within and without: how should the impulse of a moment reshape me against the weight of the eternities?... Buddhism indeed answers how, and that astounding answer is irrefutable - but I doubt....

Anyhow, acts and thoughts, according to Buddhist doctrine, are creative. Visible matter is made by acts and thoughts - even the universe of stars, and all that has form and name, and all the conditions of existence. What we think or do is never for the moment only, but for measureless time: it signifies some force directed to the shaping of worlds, to the making of future bliss or pain. Remembering this, we may raise ourselves to the zones of the Gods. Ignoring it, we may deprive ourselves even of the right to be reborn among men, and may doom ourselves, though innocent of the crimes that cause rebirth in hell, to re-enter existence in the form of animals, or of insects, or of goblins - *gaki*.[1]

So it depends upon ourselves whether we are to become insects or goblins hereafter; and in the Buddhist system the difference between insects and goblins is not so well defined as might be supposed. The belief in a mysterious relation between ghosts and insects, or rather between spirits and insects, is a very ancient belief in ᵗhe East, where it now assumes innumerable forms - some unspeakably horrible, others full of weird beauty. *The White Moth* of Mr Quiller-Couch would not impress a Japanese reader as novel; for the night-moth or the butterfly figures in many a Japanese poem and legend as the soul of a lost wife. The night-cricket's thin lament is perhaps the sorrowing of a voice once human; the strange red marks upon the heads of cicadae are characters of spirit-names; dragon-flies and grasshoppers are the horses of the dead. All these are to be pitied with the pity that is kin to love. But the noxious and dangerous insects represent the results of another quality of *karma* - that which produces goblins and demons. Grisly names have been given to some of these insects - as, for example, *Jigokumushi*, or 'Hell-insect', to the ant-lion; and *Kappa-mushi*, to a gigantic water-beetle which seizes frogs and fish, and devours them alive, thus realising, in a microcosmic way, the hideous myth of the *Kappa*, or River-goblin. Flies, on the other hand, are especially identified with the world of hungry ghosts. How often, in the season of flies, have I heard some persecuted toiler exclaim, '*Kyō no hai wa, gaki no yo da ne*'? (The flies today, how like *gaki* they are!)

2

In the old Japanese, or, more correctly speaking, Chinese Buddhist literature relating to the *gaki*, the Sanscrit names of the *gaki* are given in a majority of cases; but some classes of *gaki* described have only Chinese names. As the Indian belief reached Japan by way of China and Korea, it is likely to have received a peculiar colouring in the course of its journey. But, in a general way, the Japanese classification of *gaki* corresponds closely to the Indian classification of the *pretas*.

The place of *gaki* in the Buddhist system is but one degree removed from the region of the hells, or *Jigokudō* - the lowest of all the States of Existence. Above the *Jigokudō* is the *Gakidō*, or World of Hungry Spirits; above the *Gakidō* is the *Chikushōdō*, or World of Animals; and above this, again, is the *Shuradō*, a region of perpetual fighting and slaughter. Higher than these is placed the *Ningendō*, or World of Mankind.

Now a person released from hell, by exhaustion of the *karma* that sent him there, is seldom reborn at once into the zone of human existence, but must patiently work his way upward thither, through all the intermediate states of being. Many of the *gaki* have been in hell.

But there are *gaki* also who have not been in hell. Certain kinds of degrees of sin may cause a person to be reborn as a gaki immediately after having died in this world. Only the greatest degree of sin condemns the sinner directly to hell. The second degree degrades him to the *Gakidō*. The third causes him to be reborn as an animal.

Japanese Buddhism recognises thirty-six principal classes of gaki. 'Roughly counting', says the *Shōhō-nen-jō-kyō*, 'we find thirty-six classes of *gaki*; but should we attempt to distinguish all the different varieties, we should find them to be innumerable.' The thirty-six classes form two great divisions, or orders. One comprises all 'Gaki-World-dwellers' (*Gaki-Sekai-Jū*); that is to say, all Hungry Spirits who remain in the *Gakidō* proper, and are, therefore, never seen by mankind. The other division is called *Nin-chū-Jū*, or 'Dwellers among men'; these *gaki* remain always in this world, and are sometimes seen.

There is yet another classification of *gaki*, according to the character of their penitential torment. All *gaki* suffer hunger and thirst; but there are three degrees of this suffering. The *Muzai-gaki* represent the first degree: they must hunger and thirst uninterruptedly, without obtaining any nourishment whatever. The *Shōzai-gaki* suffer only in the second degree: they are able to feed occasionally upon impure substances. The *Usai-gaki* are more fortunate: they can eat such remains of food as are thrown away by men, and also the offerings of food set before the images of the gods, or before the tablets of the ancestors. The last two classes of *gaki* are especially interesting, because they are supposed to meddle with human affairs.

Before modern science introduced exact knowledge of the nature and cause of certain diseases, Buddhists explained the symptoms of such diseases by the hypothesis of *gaki*. Certain kinds of intermittent fever, for example, were said to be caused by a *gaki* entering the human body for the sake of nourishment and warmth. At first the patient would shiver with cold, because the *gaki* was cold. Then as the *gaki* gradually became warm, the chill would pass, to be succeeded by a burning heat. At last the satiated haunter would go away, and the fever disappear; but upon another day, and usually at an hour corresponding to that of the first attack, a second fit of ague would announce the return of the *gaki*. Other zymotic disorders could be equally well explained as due to the action of *gaki*.

In the *Shōbō-nen-jō-kyō* a majority of the thirty-six kinds of *gaki* are associated with putrescence, disease, and death. Others are plainly identified with insects. No particular kind of *gaki* is identified by name with any particular kind of insect; but the descriptions suggest conditions of insect-life; and such suggestions are reinforced by a knowledge of popular superstitions. Perhaps the descriptions are vague in the case of such spirits as the *Jiki-ketsu-gaki*, or Blood-suckers; the *Jiki-niku-gaki*, or Flesh-eaters; the *Jiki-doku-gaki*, or Poison-eaters; the *Jiki-fu-gaki*, or Wind-eaters; the *Jiki-ke-gaki*, or Smell-eaters; the *Jiki-kwa-gaki*, or Fire-eaters (perhaps they fly into lamps?); the *Shikkō-gaki*, who devour corpses and cause pestilence; the *Shinen-gaki*, who appear by night as wandering fires; *Shin-ko-gaki*, or Needle-mouthed; and the *Kwaku-shin-gaki*, or Cauldron-bodied - each a living furnace, filled with flame that keeps the fluids of its body humming like a boiling pot. But the suggestion of the following excerpts[2] will not be found at all obscure:

'*Jiki-man-gaki*. - These *gaki* can live only by eating the wigs of false hair with which the statues of certain divinities are decorated.... Such will be the future condition of persons who steal objects of value from Buddhist temples.

'*Fujō-ko-hyaku-gaki*. - These *gaki* can eat only street filth and refuse. Such a condition is the consequence of having given putrid or unwholesome food to priests or nuns, or pilgrims in need of alms.

'*Cho-ken-jū-jiki-netsu-gaki*. - These are the eaters of the refuse of funeral-pyres and of the clay of graves.... They are the spirits of men who despoiled Buddhist temples for the sake of gain.

'*Ju-chū-gaki*. - These spirits are born within the wood of trees, and are tormented by the growing of the grain.... Their condition is the result of having cut down shade-trees for the purpose of selling the timber. Persons who cut down the trees in Buddhist cemeteries or temple-grounds are especially likely to become *ju-chū-gaki*.'[3]

Moths, flies, beetles, grubs, worms, and other unpleasant creatures seem thus to be indicated. But some kinds of *gaki* cannot be identified with insects - for example, the species called *Jiki-hō-gaki* or 'Doctrine-eaters'. These can exist only by hearing the preaching of the Law of the

177

Buddha in some temple. While they hear such preaching, their torment is assuaged; but at all other times they suffer agonies unspeakable. To this condition are liable after death all Buddhist priests or nuns who proclaim the law for the mere purpose of making money.... Also there are *gaki* who appear sometimes in beautiful human shapes. Such are the *Yoku-shiki-gaki*, spirits of lewdness, corresponding in some sort to the *incubi* and *succubi* of our own Middle Ages. They can change their sex at will, and can make their bodies as large or as small as they please. It is impossible to exclude them from any dwelling, except by the use of holy charms and spells, since they are able to pass through an orifice even smaller than the eye of a needle. To seduce young men, they assume beautiful feminine shapes - often appearing at wine parties as waitresses or dancing girls. To seduce women they take the form of handsome lads. This state of *Yoku-shiki-gaki* is a consequence of lust in some previous human existence; but the supernatural powers belonging to their condition are results of meritorious Karma which the evil Karma could not wholly counterbalance.

Even concerning the *Yoku-shiki-gaki*, however, it is plainly stated that they may take the form of insects. Though wont to appear in human shape, they can assume the shape of any animal or other creature, and 'fly freely in all directions of space' - or keep their bodies 'so small that mankind cannot see them'.... All insects are not necessarily *gaki*; but most *gaki* can assume the form of insects when it serves their purpose.

3

Grotesque as these beliefs now seem to us, it was not unnatural that ancient Eastern fancy should associate insects with ghosts and devils. In our visible world there are no other creatures so wonderful and so mysterious: and the true history of certain insects actually realises the dreams of mythology. To the minds of primitive men, the mere facts of insect-metamorphosis must have seemed uncanny; and what but goblinry or magic could account for the monstrous existence of beings so similar to dead leaves, or to flowers, or to joints of grass, that the keenest human sight could detect their presence only when they began to walk or to fly? Even for the entomologist of today, insects remain the most incomprehensible of creatures. We have learned from him that they must be acknowledged 'the most successful of organised beings' in the battle for existence; that the delicacy and the complexity of their structures surpass anything ever imagined or marvellous before the age of the microscope; that their senses so far exceed our own in refinement as to prove us deaf and blind by comparison. Nevertheless the insect world remains a world of hopeless enigmas. Who can explain for us the mystery of the eyes of a myriad facets, or the secret of the ocular brains connected with them? Do those astounding eyes perceive the ultimate structure of matter? does their vision pierce opacity, after the manner of the Röntgen rays? (Or how interpret the deadly aim of that ichneumon-fly which plunges its ovipositor through solid wood to reach the grub embedded in the grain?) What, again, of those marvellous ears in breasts and thighs and knees and feet - ears that hear sounds beyond the limit of human audition? and what of the musical structures evolved to produce such fairy melody? What of the ghostly feet that walk upon flowing water? What of the chemistry that kindles the firefly's lamp, making the cold and beautiful light that all our electric science cannot imitate? And those newly discovered, incomparably delicate organs for which we have yet no name, because our wisest cannot decide the nature of them - do they really, as some would suggest, keep the insect-mind informed of things unknown to human sense - visibilities of magnetism, odours of light, tastes of sound?... Even the little that we have been able to learn about insects fills us with the wonder that is akin to fear. The lips that are hands, and the horns that are eyes, and the tongues that are drills; the multiple devilish mouths that move in four ways at once; the living scissors and saws and boring-pumps and brace-bits; the exquisite elfish weapons which no human skill can copy, even in the finest watch-spring steel - what superstition of old ever dreamed of sights like these? Indeed, all that nightmare ever conceived of faceless horror, and all that ecstasy ever imagined of phantasmal pulchritude, can appear but vapid and void by comparison with the stupefying facts of entomology. But there is something spectral, something alarming, in the very beauty of insects....

4

Whether *gaki* do or do not exist, there is at least some shadowing of truth in the Eastern belief that the dead become insects. Undoubtedly our human dust must help, over and over again for millions of ages, to build up numberless weird shapes of life. But as to that question of my revery under the pine trees - whether present acts and thoughts can have anything to do with the future distribution and requickening of that dust; whether human conduct can of itself predetermine that shapes into which human atoms will be recast - no reply is possible. I doubt - but I do not know. Neither does anybody else.

Supposing, however, that the order of the universe were really as Buddhists believe, and that I knew myself foredoomed, by reason of stupidities in this existence, to live hereafter the life of an insect, I am not sure that the prospect would frighten me. There are insects of which it is difficult to think with equanimity; but the state of an independent, highly organised, respectable insect could not be so very bad. I should even look forward, with some pleasurable curiosity, to any chance of viewing the world through the marvellous compound eyes of a beetle, an ephemera, or a dragon-fly. As an ephemera, indeed, I might enjoy the possession of three different kinds of eyes, and the power to see colours now totally unimaginable. Estimated in degrees of human time, my life would be short - a single summer day would include the best part of it; but to ephemeral consciousness a few minutes would appear a season; and my one day of winged existence - barring possible mishaps - would be one unwearied joy of dancing in golden air. And I could feel in my winged state neither hunger nor thirst - having no real mouth or stomach: I should be, in very truth, a Wind-eater.... Nor should I fear to enter upon the much less ethereal condition of a dragon-fly. I should then have to bear carnivorous hunger, and to hunt a great deal; but even dragon-flies, after the fierce joy of the chase, can indulge themselves in solitary meditation. Besides, what wings would then be mine! - and what eyes!... I could pleasurably anticipate even the certainty of becoming an *Amembō*,[4] and so being able to run and to slide upon water - though children might catch me, and bite off my long fine legs. But I think that I should better enjoy the existence of a *semi* - a large and lazy cicada, basking on wind-rocked trees, sipping only dew, and singing from dawn till dusk. Of course there would be perils to encounter - danger from hawks and crows and sparrows - danger from insects of prey - danger from bamboos tipped with birdlime by naughty little boys. But in every condition of life there must be risks; and in spite of the risks, I imagine that Anacreon uttered little more than the truth, in his praise of the cicada: '*O thou earth-born - song-loving, free from pain, having flesh without blood - thou art nearly equal to the Gods*'!... In fact I have not been able to convince myself that it is really an inestimable privilege to be reborn a human being. And if the thinking of this thought, and the act of writing it down, must inevitably affect my next rebirth, then let me hope that the state to which I am destined will not be worse than that of a cicada or of a dragon-fly; climbing the cryptomerias to clash my tiny cymbals in the sun, or haunting, with soundless flicker of amethyst and gold, some holy silence of lotus-pools.

Footnotes:

1. The word *gaki* is the Japanese Buddhist rendering of the Sanscrit term 'preta', signifying a spirit in that circle or state of torment called the World of Hungry Ghosts.
2. Abridged from the *Shōbō-nen-jō-Kyō*. A full translation of the extraordinary chapter relating to the gaki would try the reader's nerves rather severely.
3. The following story of a tree-spirit is typical:
    In the garden of a *samurai* named Satsuma Shichizaemon, who lived in the village of Echigawa in the province of Ōmi, there was a very old *énoki*. (The *énoki*, or 'Celtis chinensis', is commonly thought to be a goblin-tree.) From ancient times the ancestors of the family had been careful never to cut a branch of this tree or to remove any of its leaves. But Shichizaemon, who was very self willed, one day announced that he intended to have the tree cut down. During the following night a monstrous being appeared to the mother of Shichizaemon, in a dream, and told her that if the *énoki* were cut down, every member of the household should die. But when this warning was communicated to Shichizaemon, he only laughed; and he then sent a man to cut down the tree. No sooner had it been cut down than Shichizaemon became violently insane. For several days he remained furiously mad, crying out at intervals, 'The tree! the tree! the tree'! He said that the tree put out its branches, like hands, to tear him. In this condition he died. Soon afterwards his wife went mad, crying out that the tree was killing her; and she died screaming with fear. One after another, all the people in that house, not excepting the servants, went mad and died. The dwelling long remained unoccupied thereafter, no one daring even to enter the garden. At last it was remembered that before these things happened a daughter of the Satsuma family had become a Buddhist nun, and that she was still living, under the name of Jikun, in a temple at Yamashirō. This nun was sent for; and by request of the villagers she took up her residence in the house, where she continued to live until the time of her death - daily reciting a special service on behalf of the spirit that had dwelt in the tree. From the time that she began to live in the house the tree-spirit ceased to give trouble. This story is related on the authority of the priest Shungyō, who said that he heard it from the lips of the nun herself.
4. A water-insect, much resembling what we call a 'skater'. In some parts of the country it is said that the boy who wants to become a good swimmer must eat the legs of an *amembō*.

JAPAN'S LESSER BEINGS?

Frogs

'With hands resting upon the floor, reverentially you repeat your poem, O frog!'

Ancient Poem

1

Few of the simpler sense-impressions of travel remain more intimately and vividly associated with the memory of a strange land than sounds - sounds of the open country. Only the traveller knows how Nature's voices - voices of forest and river and plain - vary according to zone; and it is nearly always some local peculiarity of their tone or character that appeals to feeling and penetrates into memory, giving us the sensation of the foreign and the faraway. In Japan this sensation is especially aroused by the music of insects - hemiptera uttering a sound-language wonderfully different from that of their Western congeners. To a lesser degree the exotic accent is noticeable also in the chanting of Japanese frogs - though the sound impresses itself upon remembrance rather by reason of its ubiquity. Rice being cultivated all over the country - not only upon mountain-slopes and hill-tops, but even within the limits of the cities - there are flushed levels everywhere, and everywhere frogs. No one who has travelled in Japan will forget the clamour of the rice-fields.

Hushed only during the later autumn and brief winter, with the first wakening of spring waken all the voices of the marsh-lands, the infinite bubbling chorus that might be taken for the speech of the quickening soil itself. And the universal mystery of life seems to thrill with a peculiar melancholy in that vast utterance - heard through forgotten thousands of years by forgotten generations of toilers, but doubtless older by myriad

181

ages than the race of man.

Now this song of solitude has been for centuries a favourite theme with Japanese poets; but the Western reader may be surprised to learn that it has appealed to them rather as a pleasant sound than as a nature-manifestation.

Innumerable poems have been written about the singing of frogs; but a large proportion of them would prove unintelligible if understood as referring to common frogs. When the general chorus of the rice-field finds praise in Japanese verse, the poet expresses his pleasure only in the great volume of sound produced by the blending of millions of little croakings - a blending which really has a pleasant effect, well compared to the lulling sound of the falling of rain. But when the poet pronounces an individual frog-call melodious, he is not speaking of the common frog of the rice-fields. Although most kinds of Japanese frogs are croakers, there is one remarkable exception (not to mention tree-frogs) - the *kajika*, or true singing-frog of Japan. To say that it croaks would be an injustice to its note, which is sweet as the chirrup of a song-bird. It used to be called *kawazu*; but as this ancient appellation latterly became confounded in common parlance with *kaeru*, the general name for ordinary frogs, it is now called only *kajika*. The *kajika* is kept as a domestic pet, and is sold in Tokyo by several insect-merchants. It is housed in a peculiar cage, the lower part of which is a basin containing sand and pebbles, fresh water and small plants; the upper part being a framework of fine wire-gauze. Sometimes the basin is fitted up as a *ko-niwa* or model landscape-garden. In these times the *kajika* is considered as one of the singers of spring and summer; but formerly it was classed with the melodists of autumn; and people used to make autumn-trips to the country for the mere pleasure of hearing it sing. And just as various places used to be famous for the music of particular varieties of night-crickets, so there were places celebrated only as haunts of the *kajika*. The following were especially noted:

Tamagawa and Ōsawa-no-Ike - a river and a lake in the province of Yamashiro.

Miwagawa, Asukagawa, Sawogawa, Furu-no-Yamada, and Yoshinogawa - all in the province of Yamato.

Koya-no-Ike in Settsu.

Ukinu-no-Ike in Iwami.

Ikawa-no-Numa in Kozuke.

Now it is the melodious cry of the *kajika*, or *kawazu*, which is so often praised in far-Eastern verse; and, like the music of insects, it is mentioned in the oldest extant collections of Japanese poems. In the preface to the famous anthology called *Kokinshū*, compiled by Imperial Decree during the fifth year of the period of Engi (AD 905), the poet Ki-no-Tsurayuki, chief editor of the work, makes these interesting observations:

'The poetry of Japan has its roots in the human heart, and thence has grown into a multiform utterance. Man in this world, having a thousand millions of things to undertake and to complete, has been moved to express his thoughts and his feelings concerning all that he sees and hears. When we hear the *uguisu*[1] singing among flowers, and the voice of the *kawazu* which inhibits the waters, what mortal [*lit.: "who among the living that lives*"] does not compose poems?'

The *kawazu* thus referred to by Tsurayuki is of course the same creature as the modern *kajika*: no common frog could have been mentioned as a songster in the same breath with that wonderful bird, the *uguisu*. And no common frog could have inspired any classical poet with so pretty a fancy as this:

> *Té wo tsuité,*
> *Uta moshi-aguru,*
> *Kawazu kana!*

'With hands resting on the ground, reverentially you repeat your poem, O frog!' The charm of this little verse can best be understood by those familiar with the far-Eastern etiquette of posture while addressing a superior - kneeling, with the body respectfully inclined, and hands resting upon the floor, with the fingers pointing outwards.[2]

It is scarcely possible to determine the antiquity of the custom of writing poems about frogs; but in the *Manyoshū*, dating back to the middle of the eighth century, there is a poem which suggests that even at that time the river Asuka had long been famous for the singing of its frogs:

> *Ima mo ka mo*
> *Asuka no kawa no*
> *Yū sarazu*
> *Kawazu naku sé no*
> *Kiyoku aruran.*

'Still clear in our day remains the stream of Asuka, where the kawazu nightly sing.' We find also in the same anthology the following curious reference to the singing of frogs:

> *Omoboyezu*
> *Kimaseru kimi wo,*
> *Sasagawa no*
> *Kawazu kikasezu*
> *Kayeshi tsuru kamo!*

'Unexpectedly I received the august visit of my lord.... Alas, that he should have returned without hearing the frogs of the river Sawa!' And in the *Rokujōshū*, another ancient compilation, are preserved these pleasing verses on the same theme:

> *Tamagawa no*
> *Hito wo mo yogizu*
> *Naku kawazu,*
> *Kono yū kikéba*
> *Oshiku ya wa aranu?*

'Hearing tonight the frogs of the Jewel River [or Tamagawa], that sing without fear of man, how can I help loving the passing moment.'

2

Thus it appears that for more than eleven hundred years the Japanese have been making poems about frogs; and it is at least possible that verses on this subject, which have been preserved in the *Manyōshū*, were composed even earlier than the eighth century. From the oldest classical period to the present day, the theme has never ceased to be a favourite one with poets of all ranks. A fact noteworthy in this relation is that the first poem written in the measure called *hokku*, by the famous Bashō, was about frogs. The triumph of this extremely brief form of verse (three lines of 5, 7, and 5 syllables respectively) is to create one complete sensation-picture; and Bashō's original accomplishes the feat - difficult, if not impossible, to repeat in English:

Furu iké ya,
Kawazu tobikomu,
Midzu no oto.

('Old pond - frogs jumping in - sound of water'.) An immense number of poems about frogs were subsequently written in this measure. Even at the present time professional men of letters amuse themselves by making short poems on frogs. Distinguished among these is a young poet known to the Japanese literary world by the pseudonym of 'Roséki', who lives in Osaka and keeps in the pond of his garden hundreds of singing frogs. At fixed intervals he invites all his poet-friends to a feast, with the proviso that each must compose, during the entertainment, one poem about the inhabitants of the pond. A collection of the verses thus obtained was privately printed in the spring of 1897, with funny pictures of frogs decorating the covers and illustrating the text.

But unfortunately it is not possible through English translation to give any fair idea of the range and character of the literature of frogs. The reason is that the greater number of compositions about frogs depend chiefly for their literary value upon the untranslatable - upon local allusions, for example, incomprehensible outside of Japan; upon puns; and upon the use of words with double or even triple meanings. Scarcely two or three in every one hundred poems can bear translation. So I can attempt little more than a few general observations.

That love-poems should form a considerable proportion of this curious literature will not seem strange to the reader when he is reminded that the lovers' trysting-hour is also the hour when the frog-chorus is in full cry, and that, in Japan at least, the memory of the sound would be associated with the memory of a secret meeting in almost any solitary place. The frog referred to in such poems is not usually the *kajika*. But frogs are introduced into love-poetry in countless clever ways. I can give two examples of modern popular compositions of this kind. The first contains an allusion to the famous proverb - *I no naka no kawazu daikai wo shirazu*: 'The frog in the well knows not the great sea.' A person quite innocent of the ways of the world is compared to a frog in a well; and we may suppose the speaker of the following lines to be some sweet-hearted country-girl, answering an ungenerous remark with very pretty tact:

Laugh me to scorn if you please; call me your 'frog-in-the-well':
Flowers fall into my well; and its water mirrors the moon!

The second poem is supposed to be the utterance of a woman having good reason to be jealous:

Dull as a stagnant pond you deemed the mind of your mistress;
But the stagnant pond can speak: you shall hear the cry of the frog!

Outside of love-poems there are hundreds of verses about the common frogs of ponds or rice-fields. Some refer chiefly to the volume of the sound that the frogs make:

Hearing the frogs of the rice-fields, methinks that the water sings.
As we flush the rice-fields of spring, the frog-song flows with the water.
From rice-field to rice-field they call: unceasing the challenge and answer.
Ever as deepens the night, louder the chorus of pond-frogs.

So many the voices of frogs that I cannot but wonder if the pond be not wider at night than by day!

Even the rowing boats can scarce proceed, so thick the clamour of the frogs of Hōrie!

The exaggeration of the last verse is of course intentional, and in the original not uneffective. In some parts of the world - in the marshes of Florida and of southern Louisiana, for example - the clamour of the frogs at certain seasons resembles the roaring of a furious sea; and whoever has heard it can appreciate the fancy of sound as obstacle.

Other poems compare or associate the sound made by frogs with the sound of rain:

The song of the earliest frogs, fainter than falling of rain.

What I took for the falling of rain is only the singing of frogs.

Now I shall dream, lulled by the patter of rain and the song of the frogs.

Other poems, again, are intended only as tiny pictures - thumb-nail sketches - such as this *hokku,*

Path between rice-fields; frogs jumping away to right and left.

- or this, which is a thousand years old:

Where the flowers of the yamabuki are imaged in the still marsh-water, the voice of the kawazu is heard;

- or the following pretty fancy:

Now sings the frog, and the voice of the frog is perfumed: for into the shining stream the cherry-petals fall.

The last two pieces refer, of course, to the true singing frog.

Many short poems are addressed directly to the frog itself - whether *kaeru* or *kajika*. There are poems of melancholy, of affection, of humour, of religion, and even of philosophy among these. Sometimes the frog is likened to a spirit resting on a lotus-leaf; sometimes, to a priest repeating sutras for the sake of the dying flowers; sometimes to a pining lover; sometimes to a host receiving travellers; sometimes to a blasphemer, 'always beginning' to say something against the gods, but always afraid to finish it. Most of the following examples are taken from the recent book of frog-poems published by Rosēki; each paragraph of my prose rendering, it should be remembered, represents a distinct poem:

Now all the guests being gone, why still thus respectfully sitting, O frog?

So resting your hands on the ground, do you welcome the Rain, O frog?

You disturb in the ancient well the light of the stars, O frog!

Sleepy the sound of the rain; but your voice makes me dream, O frog!

Always beginning to say something against the great Heaven, O frog!

You have learned that the world is void: you never look at it as you float, O frog!

Having lived in clear-rushing mountain-streams, never can your voice become stagnant, O frog!

The last pleasing conceit shows the esteem in which the superior vocal powers of the *kajika* are held.

3

I thought it strange that out of hundreds of frog-poems collected for me I could not discover a single mention of the coldness and clamminess of the frog. Except a few jesting lines about the queer attitudes sometimes assumed by the creature, the only reference to its uninviting qualities that I could find was the mild remark,

Seen in the daytime, how uninteresting you are, O frog!

While wondering at this reticence concerning the chilly, slimy, flaccid nature of frogs, it all at once occurred to me that in other thousands of

Japanese poems which I had read there was a total absence of allusions to tactual sensations. Sensations of colours, sounds, and odours were rendered with exquisite and surprising delicacy; but sensations of taste were seldom mentioned, and sensations of touch were absolutely ignored. I asked myself whether the reason for this reticence or indifference should be sought in the particular temperament or mental habit of the race; but I have not yet been able to decide the question. Remembering that the race has been living for ages upon food which seems tasteless to the Western palate, and that impulses to such action as hand-clasping, embracing, kissing, or other physical display of affectionate feeling, are really foreign to far-Eastern character, one is tempted to the theory that gustatory and tactual sensations, pleasurable and otherwise, have been less highly evolved with the Japanese than with us. But there is much evidence against such a theory; and the triumphs of Japanese handicraft assure us of an almost incomparable delicacy of touch developed in special directions. Whatever be the physiological meaning of the phenomenon, its moral meaning is of most importance. So far as I have been able to judge, Japanese poetry usually ignores the inferior qualities of sensation, while making the subtlest of appeals to those superior qualities which we call aesthetic. Even if representing nothing else, this fact represents the healthiest and happiest attitude towards Nature. Do not we Occidentals shrink from many purely natural impressions by reason of repulsion developed through a morbid tactual sensibility? The question is at least worth considering. Ignoring or mastering such repulsion - accepting naked Nature as she is, always lovable when understood - the Japanese discover beauty where we blindly imagine ugliness or formlessness or loathsomeness - beauty in insects, beauty in stones, beauty in frogs. Is the fact without significance that they alone have been able to make artistic use of the form of the centipede?...You should see my Kyoto tobacco-pouch, with centipedes of gold running over its figured leather like ripplings of fire!

Footnotes:

1. *Cettia cantans* - The Japanese nightingale.
2. Such, at least, is the posture prescribed by the old etiquette for *men*. But the rules were very complicated, and varied somewhat according to rank as well as to sex. Women usually turn the fingers inward instead of outward when assuming this posture.

Heiké-Gani

In various countries of which the peoples appear strange to us, by reason of beliefs, ideas, customs and arts having nothing in common with our own, there can be found something in the nature of the land - something in its flora or fauna - characterised by a corresponding strangeness. Probably the relative queerness of the exotic nature in such regions helped more or less to develop the apparent oddity of the exotic mind. National differences of thought or feeling should not be less evolutionally interpretable than the forms of vegetables or of insects; and, in the mental evolution of a people, the influence of environment upon imagination must be counted as a factor.

These reflections were induced by a box of crabs sent me from the province of Chōshū - crabs possessing the very same quality of grotesqueness which we are accustomed to think of as being peculiarly Japanese. On the backs of these creatures there are bossings and depressions that curiously simulate the shape of a human face - a distorted face - a face modelled in relief as a Japanese craftsman might have modelled it in some moment of artistic whim.

Two varieties of such crabs - nicely dried and polished - are constantly exposed for sale in the shops of Akamagaseki (better known to foreigners by the name of Shimonoseki). They are caught along the neighbouring stretch of coast called Dan-no-Ura, where the great clan of the Heiké, or Taira, were exterminated in a naval battle, seven centuries ago, by the rival clan of Genji, or Minamoto. Readers of Japanese history will remember the story of the Imperial Nun, Nii-no-Ama, who in the hour of that awful tragedy composed a poem, and then leaped into the sea, with the child-emperor Antoku in her arms.

Now the grotesque crabs of this coast are called Heiké-gani, or 'Heiké-crabs', because of a legend that the spirits of the drowned and slaughtered warriors of the Heiké clan assumed such shapes; and it is said that the fury or the agony of the death-struggle can still be discerned in the faces upon the backs of the crabs. But to feel the romance of this legend you should be familiar with old pictures of the fight of Dan-no-Ura - old coloured prints of the armoured combatants, with their grim battle-masks of iron and their great fierce eyes.

The smaller variety of crab is known simply as a 'Heiké-crab' - Heiké-gani. Each Heiké-gani is supposed to be animated by the spirit of a common Heiké warrior only, an ordinary samurai. But the larger kind of crab is also termed Taishō-gani ('Chieftain-crab'), or Tatsugashira ('Dragon-helmet'); and all Taishō-gani or Tatsugashira are thought to be animated by ghosts of those great Heiké captains who bore upon their helmets monsters unknown to Western heraldry, and glittering horns, and dragons of gold.

I got a Japanese friend to draw for me the two pictures of Heiké-gani herewith reproduced; and I can vouch for their accuracy. But I told him that I could not see anything resembling a helmet, either in his drawing

187

of the Tatsugashira, nor in the original figure upon the back of the crab.

'Can you see it?'

'Why, yes - somewhat like this', he answered, making the following sketch:

'Well, I can make out part of the head-gear', I said; 'but that outline of yours is not according to facts - and that face is vapid as the face of the Moon. Look at the nightmare on the back of the real crab!'...

Fireflies

1

I want to talk about Japanese fireflies, but not entomologically. If you are interested, as you ought to be, in the scientific side of the subject, you should seek enlightenment from a Japanese professor of biology, now lecturing at the Imperial University of Tokyo. He signs himself 'Mr S. Watase' (the 'S' standing for the personal name Shozaburo); and he has been a teacher as well as a student of science in America, where a number of his lectures have been published[1] - lectures upon animal phosphorescence, animal electricity, the light-producing organs of insects and fishes, and other wonderful topics of biology. He can tell you all that is known concerning the morphology of fireflies, the physiology of fireflies, the photometry of fireflies, the chemistry of their luminous substance, the spectroscopic analysis of their light, and the significance of that light in terms of ether-vibration. By experiment he can show you that, under normal conditions of temperature and environment, the number of light-pulsations produced by one species of Japanese firefly averages twenty-six per minute; and that the rate suddenly rises to sixty-three per minute, if the insect be frightened by seizure. Also he can prove to you that another and smaller kind of firefly, when taken in the hand, will increase the number of its light-pulsings to upward of two hundred per minute. He suggests that the light may be of some protective value to the insect, like the 'warning colours' of sundry nauseous caterpillars and butterflies - because the firefly has a very bitter taste, and birds appear to find it unpalatable. (Frogs, he has observed, do not mind the bad taste: they fill their cold bellies with fireflies till the light shines through them, much as the light of a candle-flame will glow through a porcelain jar.) But whether of protective value or not, the tiny dynamo would seem to be used in a variety of ways - as a photo-telegraph, for example. As other insects converse by sound or by touch, the firefly utters its emotion in luminous pulsings: its speech is a language of light.... I am only giving you some hints about the character of the professor's lectures, which are never merely technical. And for the best part of this non-scientific essay of mine -

especially that concerning the capture and the sale of fireflies in Japan - I am indebted to some delightful lectures which he delivered last year to Japanese audiences in Tokyo.

2

As written today, the Japanese name of the firefly (*hotaru*) is ideographically composed with the sign for fire, doubled, above the sign for insect. The real origin of the word is nevertheless doubtful; and various etymologies have been suggested. Some scholars think that the appellation anciently signified 'the First-born of Fire'; while others believe that it was first composed with syllables meaning 'star' and 'drop'. The more poetical of the proposed derivations, I am sorry to say, are considered the least probable. But whatever may have been the primal meaning of the word *hotaru*, there can be no doubt as to the romantic quality of certain folk-names still given to the insect.

Two species of firefly have a wide distribution in Japan; and these have been popularly named *Genji-hotaru* and *Heiké-hotaru*: that is to say, 'the Minamoto-Firefly' and 'the Taira-Firefly'. A legend avers that these fireflies are the ghosts of the old Minamoto and Taira warriors; that, even in their insect shapes, they remember the awful clan-struggle of the twelfth century; and that once every year, on the night of the twentieth day of the fourth month,[2] they fight a great battle on the Uji River. Therefore, on that night all caged fireflies should be set free, in order that they may be able to take part in the contest.

The *Genji-hotaru* is the largest of Japanese fireflies - the largest species, at least, in Japan proper, not including the Loochoo Islands. It is found in almost every part of the country from Kyushu to Ōshū. The *Heiké-hotaru* ranges further north, being especially common in Yezo; but it is found also in the central and southern provinces. It is smaller than the Genji, and emits a feebler light. The fireflies commonly sold by insect-dealers in Tokyo, Osaka, Kyoto, and other cities, are of the larger species. Japanese observers have described the light of both insects as 'tea-coloured' (*cha-iro*) - the tint of the ordinary Japanese infusion, when the leaf is of good quality, being a clear greenish yellow. But the light of a fine Genji-firefly is so brilliant that only a keen eye can detect the greenish colour: at first sight the flash appears yellow as the flame of a wood-fire, and its vivid brightness has not been overpraised in the following *hokku*:

Kagaribi mo

Hotaru mo hikaru -

Genji kana!

'Whether it be a glimmering of festal-fires[3] [far away], or a glimmering of fireflies, [one can hardly tell] - ah, it is the Genji!'

Although the appellations *Genji-hotaru* and *Heiké-hotaru* are still in general use, both insects are known by other folk-names. In different provinces the Genji is called *Ō-hotaru*, or 'Great Firefly'; *Ushi-hotaru*, or 'Ox-Firefly'; *Kuma-hotaru*, or 'Bear-Firefly'; and *Uji-hotaru*, or 'Firefly of Uji' - not to mention such picturesque appellations as *Komoso-hotaru* and *Yamabuki-hotaru*, which could not be appreciated by the average Western reader. The *Heiké-hotaru* is also called *Hime-hotaru*, or 'Princess-Firefly'; *Nennei-hotaru*, or 'Baby-firefly'; and *Yurei-hotaru*, or 'Ghost-Firefly'. But these are only examples chosen at random: in almost every part of Japan there is a special folk-name for the insect.

3

There are many places in Japan which are famous for fireflies - places which people visit in summer merely to enjoy the sight of the fireflies. Anciently the most celebrated of all such places was a little valley near Ishiyama, by the lake of Omi. It is still called Hotaru-Dani, or the Valley of Fireflies. Before the Period of Genroku (1688-1703), the swarming of the fireflies in this valley, during the sultry season, was accounted one of the natural marvels of the country. The fireflies of the Hotaru-Dani are still celebrated for their size; but that wonderful swarming of them, which old writers described, is no longer to be seen there. At present the most famous place for fireflies is in the neighbourhood of Uji, in Yamashiro. Uji, a pretty little town in the centre of the celebrated tea-district, is situated on the Ujigawa, and is scarcely less famed for its fireflies than for its teas. Every summer special trains run from Kyoto and Osaka to Uji, bringing thousands of visitors to see the fireflies. But it is on the river, at a point several miles from the town, that the great spectacle is to be witnessed - the *Hotaru-Kassen*, or Firefly Battle. The stream there winds between hills covered with vegetation; and myriads of fireflies dart from either bank, to meet and cling above the water. At moments they so swarm together as to form what appears to the eye like a luminous cloud, or like a great ball of sparks. The cloud soon scatters, or the ball drops and breaks upon the surface of the current, and the fallen fireflies drift glittering away; but another swarm quickly collects in the same locality. People wait all night in boats upon the river to watch the phenomenon. After the *Hotaru-Kassen* is done, the Ujikawa, covered with the still sparkling bodies of the drifting insects, is said to appear like the Milky Way, or, as the Japanese more poetically call it, the River of Heaven. Perhaps it was after witnessing such a spectacle that the great female poet, Chiyo of Kaga, composed these verses:

> *Kawa bakari,*
> *Yami wa nagarete - ?*
> *Hotaru kana!*

- Which may be thus freely rendered:
    'It is the river only? - or is the darkness itself drifting?... Oh, the fireflies!'...[4]

4

Many persons in Japan earn their living during the summer months by catching and selling fireflies: indeed, the extent of this business entitles it to be regarded as a special industry. The chief centre of this industry is the region about Ishiyama, in Goshū, by the Lake of Ōmi, a number of houses there supplying fireflies to many parts of the country, and especially to the great cities of Osaka and Kyoto. From sixty to seventy firefly-catchers are employed by each of the principal houses during the busy season. Some training is required for the occupation. A tyro might find it no easy matter to catch a hundred fireflies in a single night; but an expert has been known to catch three thousand. The methods of capture, although of the simplest possible kind, are very interesting to see.

Immediately after sunset, the firefly-hunter goes forth, with a long bamboo pole upon his shoulder, and a long bag of brown mosquito-netting wound, like a girdle, about his waist. When he reaches a wooded place frequented by fireflies - usually some spot where willows are planted on the bank of a river or lake - he halts and watches the trees. As soon as the trees begin to twinkle satisfactorily, he gets his net ready, approaches the most luminous tree, and with his long pole strikes the branches. The fireflies, dislodged by the shock, do not immediately take flight, as more active insects would do under like circumstances, but drop helplessly to the ground, beetle-wise, where their light - always more brilliant in moments of fear or pain - renders them conspicuous. If suffered to remain upon the ground for a few moments, they will fly away. But the catcher, picking them up with astonishing quickness, using both hands at once, deftly tosses them *into his mouth* - because he cannot lose the time required to put them, one by one, into the bag. Only when his mouth can hold no more, does he drop the fireflies, unharmed, into the netting.

Thus the firefly-catcher works until about two o'clock in the morning - the old Japanese hour of ghosts - at which time the insects begin to leave the trees and seek the dewy soil. There they are said to bury their tails, so as to remain viewless. But now the hunter changes his tactics. Taking a bamboo broom he brushes the surface of the turf, lightly and quickly. Whenever touched or alarmed by the broom, the fireflies display their lanterns, and are immediately nipped and bagged. A little before dawn, the hunters return to town.

At the firefly-shops the captured insects are sorted as soon as possible, according to the brilliancy of their light, the more luminous being the higher-priced. Then they are put into gauze-covered boxes or cages, with a certain quantity of moistened grass in each cage. From one hundred to two hundred fireflies are placed in a single cage, according to grade. To these cages are attached small wooden tablets inscribed with the names of customers - such as hotel proprietors, restaurant-keepers, wholesale and retail insect-merchants, and private persons who have ordered large quantities of fireflies for some particular festivity. The boxes are despatched to their destinations by nimble messengers, for goods of this class cannot be safely intrusted to express companies.

Great numbers of fireflies are ordered for display at evening parties in the summer season. A large Japanese guest-room usually overlooks a garden; and during a banquet or other evening entertainment, given in the sultry season, it is customary to set fireflies at liberty in the garden after sunset, that the visitors may enjoy the sight of the sparkling. Restaurant-keepers purchase largely. In the famous Dōtombori of Osaka, there is a house where myriads of fireflies are kept in a large space enclosed by mosquito-netting; and customers of this house are permitted to enter the enclosure and capture a certain number of fireflies to take home with them.

The wholesale price of living fireflies ranges from three sen per hundred up to thirteen sen per hundred, according to season and quality. Retail dealers sell them in cages; and in Tokyo the price of a cage of fireflies ranges from three sen up to several dollars. The cheapest kind of cage, containing only three or four fireflies, is scarcely more than two inches square; but the costly cages - veritable marvels of bamboo work, beautifully decorated - are as large as cages for song-birds. Firefly cages of charming or fantastic shapes - model houses, junks, temple-lanterns, etc. - can be bought at prices ranging from thirty sen up to one dollar.

Dead or alive, fireflies are worth money. They are delicate insects, and they live but a short time in confinement. Great numbers die in the insect-shops; and one celebrated insect-house is said to dispose every season of no less than five *shō* - that is to say, about one peck - of dead fireflies, which are sold to manufacturing establishments in Osaka. Formerly fireflies were used much more than at present in the manufacture of poultices and pills, and in the preparation of drugs peculiar to the practice of Chinese medicine. Even today some curious extracts are obtained from them; and one of these, called *Hotaru-no-abura*, or Firefly-grease, is still used by wood-workers for the purpose of imparting rigidity to objects made of bent bamboo.

A very curious chapter on firefly-medicine might be written by somebody learned in the old-fashioned literature. The queerest part of the subject is Chinese, and belongs much more to demonology than to therapeutics. Firefly-ointments used to be made which had power, it was alleged, to preserve a house from the attacks of robbers, to counteract the effect of any poison, and to drive away 'the hundred devils'. And pills were made with firefly-substance which were believed to confer invulnerability; one kind of such pills being called *Kanshōgan*, or 'Commander-in-Chief Pills', and another, *Buigan*, or 'Military-Power Pills'.

5

Firefly-catching, as a business, is comparatively modern; but firefly-hunting, as a diversion, is a very old custom. Anciently it was an aristocratic amusement; and great nobles used to give firefly-hunting parties - *hotaru-gari*. In this busy era of Meiji the hotaru-gari is rather an amusement for children than for grown-up folks; but the latter occasionally find time to join in the sport. All over Japan, the children have their firefly-hunts every summer: moonless nights being usually chosen for such expeditions. Girls follow the chase with paper fans; boys, with long light poles, to the ends of which wisps of fresh bamboo-grass are tied. When struck down by a fan or a wisp, the insects are easily secured, as many are slow to take wing after having once been checked in actual flight. While hunting, the children sing little songs, supposed to attract the shining prey. These songs differ according to locality; and the number of them is wonderful. But there are very few possessing that sort of interest which justifies quotation. Two examples will probably suffice:

(*Province of Chōshū*)

Hotaru, koi! koi!
Koi-tomosé!
Nippon ichi no
Jōsan ga
Chōchin tomoshite,
Koi to ina!

Come, firefly, come! Come with your light burning! The nicest girl in Japan wants to know if you will not light your lantern and come!

(*Dialect of Shimonoseki*)

Hōchin, kio!
Hōchin, koi!
Seki no machi no bon-san ga,
Chōchin tomoshite,
Koi!
Koi!

Firefly, come! firefly, come! All the boys of Seki [want you to come] with your lantern lighted! Come! Come!

Of course, in order to hunt fireflies successfully, it is necessary to know something about their habits; and on this subject Japanese children are probably better informed than a majority of my readers, for whom the following notes may possess a novel interest:

Fireflies frequent the neighbourhbood of water, and like to circle above it; but some kinds are repelled by impure or stagnant water, and are only to be found in the vicinity of clear streams or lakes. The Genji-firefly shuns swamps, ditches, or foul canals; while the Heikē-firefly seems to be satisfied with any water. All fireflies seek by preference grassy banks shaded by trees; but they dislike certain trees and are attracted by others. They avoid pine trees, for instance; and they will not light upon rose-bushes. But upon willow trees - especially weeping willows - they gather in great swarms. Occasionally, on a summer night, you may see a drooping willow so covered and illuminated with fireflies that all its branches appear 'to be budding fire'. During a bright moonlight night fireflies keep as much as possible in shadow; but when pursued they fly at once into the moonshine, where their shimmering is less easily perceived. Lamplight, or any strong artificial light, drives them away; but small bright lights attract them. They can be lured, for example, by the sparkling of a small piece of lighted charcoal, or by the glow of a little Japanese pipe, kindled in the dark. But the lamping of a single lively firefly, confined in a bottle, or cup, of clear glass, is the best of all lures.

As a rule the children hunt only in parties, for obvious reasons. In former years it would have been deemed foolhardy to go alone in pursuit of fireflies, because there existed certain uncanny beliefs concerning them. And in some of the country districts these beliefs still prevail. What appear to be fireflies may be malevolent spirits, or goblin-flies, or fox-lights, kindled to delude the wayfarer. Even real fireflies are not always to be trusted - the weirdness of their kinships might be inferred from their love of willow trees. Other trees have their particular spirits, good or evil, hamadryads or goblins; but the willow is particularly the tree of the dead - the favourite of human ghosts. Any firefly may be a ghost - who can tell? Besides, there is an old belief that the soul of a person still alive may sometimes assume the shape of a firefly. And here is a little story that was told me in Izumo:

One cold winter's night a young *shizoku* of Matsue, while on his way home from a wedding-party, was surprised to perceive a firefly-light hovering above the canal in front of his dwelling. Wondering that such an insect should be flying abroad in the season of snow, he stopped to look at it; and the light suddenly shot towards him. He struck at it with a stick; but it darted away, and flew into the garden of a residence adjoining his own. his own.

Next morning he made a visit to that house intending to relate the adventure to his neighbours and friends. But before he found a chance to speak of it, the eldest daughter of the family, happening to enter the guest-room without knowing of the young man's visit, uttered a cry of surprise, and exclaimed, 'Oh! how you startled me! No one told me that you had called; and just as I came in I was thinking about you. Last night I had so strange a dream! I was flying in my dream - flying above the canal in front of our house. It seemed very pleasant to fly over the water; and while I was flying there I saw you coming along the bank. Then I went to you to tell you that I had learned how to fly; but you struck at me, and frightened me so that I still feel afraid when I think if it.'... After hearing, this, the visitor thought it best not to relate his own experience for the time being, lest the coincidence should alarm the girl, to whom he was betrothed.

Footnotes:

1. Professor Watase is a graduate of John Hopkins. Since this essay was written, his popular Japanese lectures upon the firefly have been reissued in a single pretty volume. The coloured frontispiece - showing fireflies at night upon a willow-branch - is alone worth the price of the book.
2. By the old calendar. According to the new calendar, the date of the Firefly Battle would be considerably later: last year (1901) it fell upon the tenth day of the sixth month.
3. The term *kagari-bi*, often translated by 'bonfire', here especially refers to the little wood-fires which are kindled, on certain festival occasions, in front of every threshold in the principal street of a country town, or village. During the festival of the Bon such little fires are lighted in many parts of the country to welcome the returning ghosts.
4. That is to say, 'Do I see only fireflies drifting with the current? or is the Night itself drifting, with its swarming of stars?'

JAPAN SOCIAL

Strangeness and Charm

The majority of the first impressions of Japan recorded by travellers are pleasurable impressions. Indeed, there must be something lacking, or something very harsh, in the nature to which Japan can make no emotional appeal. The appeal itself is the clue to a problem; and that problem is the character of a race and of its civilisation.

My own first impressions of Japan - Japan as seen in the white sunshine of a perfect spring day - had doubtless much in common with the average of such experiences. I remember especially the wonder and the delight of the vision. The wonder and the delight have never passed away: they are often revived for me even now, by some chance happening, after fourteen years of sojourn. But the reason of these feelings was difficult to learn - or at least to guess; for I cannot yet claim to know much about Japan.... Long ago the best and dearest Japanese friend I ever had said to me, a little before his death: 'When you find, in four or five years more, that you cannot understand the Japanese at all, then you will begin to know something about them.' After having realised the truth of my friend's prediction - after having discovered that I cannot understand the Japanese at all - I feel better qualified to attempt this essay.

As first perceived, the outward strangeness of things in Japan produces (in certain minds, at least) a queer thrill impossible to describe - a feeling of weirdness which comes to us only with the perception of the totally unfamiliar. You find yourself moving through queer small streets full of odd small people, wearing robes and sandals of extraordinary shapes; and you can scarcely distinguish the sexes at sight. The houses are constructed and furnished in ways alien to all your experience; and you are astonished to find that you cannot conceive the use or meaning of numberless things on display in the shops. Food-stuffs of unimaginable derivation; utensils of enigmatic forms; emblems incomprehensible of some mysterious belief;

strange masks or toys that commemorate legends of gods or demons; odd figures, too, of the gods themselves, with monstrous ears and smiling faces - all these you may perceive as you wander about; though you must also notice telegraph poles and typewriters, electric lamps and sewing machines. Everywhere on signs and hangings, and on the backs of people passing by, you will observe wonderful Chinese characters; and the wizardry of all these texts makes the dominant tone of the spectacle.

Further acquaintance with this fantastic world will in nowise diminish the sense of strangeness evoked by the first vision of it. You will soon observe that even the physical actions of the people are unfamiliar - that their work is done in ways the opposite of Western ways. Tools are of surprising shapes, and are handled after surprising methods: the blacksmith squats at his anvil, wielding a hammer such as no Western smith could use without long practice; the carpenter pulls, instead of pushing, his extraordinary plane and saw. Always the left is the right side, and the right side the wrong; the keys must be turned, to open or close a lock, in what we are accustomed to think the wrong direction. Mr Percival Lowell has truthfully observed that the Japanese speak backwards, read backwards, write backwards - and that this is 'only the *abc* of their contrariety'. For the habit of writing backwards there are obvious evolutional reasons: and the requirements of Japanese calligraphy sufficiently explain why the artist pushes his brush or pencil instead of pulling it. But why, instead of putting the thread through the eye of the needle, should the Japanese maiden slip the eye of the needle over the point of the thread? Perhaps the most remarkable, out of a hundred possible examples of antipodal action, is furnished by the Japanese art of fencing. The swordsman, delivering his blow with both hands, does not pull the blade towards him in the moment of striking, but pushes it from him. He uses it, indeed, as other Asiatics do, not on the principle of the wedge, but of the saw; yet there is a pushing motion where we should expect a pulling motion in the stroke.... These and other forms of unfamiliar action are strange enough to suggest the notion of a humanity even physically as little related to us as might be the population of another planet - the notion of some anatomical unlikeness. No such unlikeness, however, appears to exist; and all this oppositeness probably implies, not so much the outcome of a human experience entirely independent of Aryan experience, as the outcome of an experience evolutionally younger than our own.

Yet that experience has been one of no mean order. Its manifestations do not merely startle: they also delight. The delicate perfection of workmanship, the light strength and grace of objects, the power manifest to obtain the best results with the least material, the achieving of mechanical ends by the simplest possible means, the comprehension of irregularity as aesthetic value, the shapeliness and perfect taste of everything, the sense displayed of harmony in tints or colours - all this must convince you at once that our Occident has much to learn from this remote civilisation, not only in matters of art and taste, but in matters likewise of economy and utility. It is no barbarian fancy that appeals to you in those amazing porcelains, those astonishing embroideries, those wonders of lacquer and ivory and bronze, which educate imagination in unfamiliar ways. No:

these are the products of a civilisation which became, within its own limits, so exquisite that none but an artist is capable of judging its manufactures - a civilisation that can be termed imperfect only by those who would also term imperfect the Greek civilisation of three thousand years ago.

But the underlying strangeness of this world - the psychological strangeness - is much more startling than the visible and superficial. You begin to suspect the range of it after having discovered that no adult Occidental can perfectly master the language. East and West the fundamental parts of human nature - the emotional bases of it - are much the same: the mental difference between a Japanese and a European child is mainly potential. But with growth the difference rapidly develops and widens, till it becomes, in adult life, inexpressible. The whole of the Japanese mental superstructure evolves into forms having nothing in common with Western psychological development: the expression of thought becomes regulated, and the expression of emotion inhibited in ways that bewilder and astound. The ideas of this people are not our ideas; their sentiments are not our sentiments; their ethical life represents for us regions of thought and emotion yet unexplored, or perhaps long forgotten. Any one of their ordinary phrases, translated into Western speech, makes hopeless nonsense; and the literal rendering into Japanese of the simplest English sentence would scarcely be comprehended by any Japanese who had never studied a European tongue. Could you learn all the words in a Japanese dictionary, your acquisition would not help you in the least to make yourself understood in speaking, unless you had learned also to think like a Japanese - that is to say, to think backwards, to think upside-down and inside-out, to think in directions totally foreign to Aryan habit. Experience in the acquisition of European languages can help you to learn Japanese about as much as it could help you to acquire the language spoken by the inhabitants of Mars. To be able to use the Japanese tongue as a Japanese uses it, one would need to be born again, and to have one's mind completely reconstructed, from the foundation upwards. It is possible that a person of European parentage, born in Japan, and accustomed from infancy to use the vernacular, might retain in after-life that *instinctive* knowledge which could alone enable him to adapt his mental relations to the relations of any Japanese environment. There is actually an Englishman named Black, born in Japan, whose proficiency in the language is proved by the fact that he is able to earn a fair income as a professional story-teller (*hanashika*). But this is an extraordinary case.... As for the literary language, I need only observe that to make acquaintance with it requires very much more than a knowledge of several thousand Chinese characters. It is safe to say that no Occidental can undertake to render at sight any literary text laid before him - indeed the number of native scholars able to do so is very small - and although the learning displayed in this direction by various Europeans may justly compel our admiration, the work of none could have been given to the world without Japanese help.

But as the outward strangeness of Japan proves to be full of beauty, so the inward strangeness appears to have its charm - an ethical charm reflected in the common life of the people. The attractive aspects of that life do not indeed imply, to the ordinary observer, a psychological differentiation measurable by scores of centuries: only a scientific mind, like that of Mr Percival Lowell, immediately perceives the problem presented. The less gifted stranger, if naturally sympathetic, is merely pleased and puzzled, and tries to explain, by his own experience of happy life on the other side of the world, the social conditions that charm him. Let us suppose that he has the good fortune of being able to live for six months or a year in some old-fashioned town of the interior. From the beginning of this sojourn he can scarcely fail to be impressed by the apparent kindliness and joyousness of the existence about him. In the relations of the people to each other, as well as in all their relations to himself, he will find a constant amenity, a tact, a good-nature such as he will elsewhere have met with only in the friendship of exclusive circles. Everybody greets everybody with happy looks and pleasant words; faces are always smiling; the commonest incidents of everyday life are transfigured by a courtesy at once so artless and so faultless that it appears to spring directly from the heart, without any teaching.

Under all circumstances a certain outward cheerfulness never fails: no matter what troubles may come - storm or fire, flood or earthquake - the laughter of greeting voices, the bright smile and graceful bow, the kindly inquiry and the wish to please, continue to make existence beautiful. Religion brings no gloom into this sunshine: before the Buddhas and the gods folk smile as they pray: the temple-courts are playgrounds for the children: and within the enclosure of the great public shrines - which are places of festivity rather than of solemnity - dancing-platforms are erected. Family existence would seem to be everywhere characterised by gentleness; there is no visible quarrelling, no loud harshness, no tears and reproaches. Cruelty, even to animals, appears to be unknown: one sees farmers, coming to town, trudging patiently beside their horses or oxen, aiding their dumb companions to bear the burden, and using no whips or goads. Drivers or pullers of carts will turn out of their way, under the most provoking circumstances, rather than overrun a lazy dog or a stupid chicken.... For no inconsiderable time one may live in the midst of appearances like these, and perceive nothing to spoil the pleasure of the experience.

Of course the conditions of which I speak are now passing away; but they are still to be found in the remoter districts. I have lived in districts where no case of theft had occurred for hundreds of years - where the newly-built prisons of Meiji remained empty and useless - where the people left their doors unfastened by night as well as by day. These facts are familiar to every Japanese. In such a district, you might recognise that the kindness shown to you, as a stranger, is the consequence of official command; but how explain the goodness of the people to each other? When you discover no harshness, no rudeness, no dishonesty, no breaking of laws, and learn that this social condition has been the same for centuries, you are tempted to believe that you have entered into the domain of a morally superior humanity. All this soft urbanity, impeccable honesty, ingenuous kindliness of speech and act, you might naturally interpret as conduct directed by perfect goodness of heart. And the simplicity that delights you is no simplicity of barbarism. Here every one has been taught; every one knows how to write and speak beautifully, how to compose poetry, how to behave politely; there is everywhere cleanliness and good taste; interiors are bright and pure; the daily use of the hot bath is universal. How refuse to be charmed by a civilisation in which every relation appears to be governed by altruism, every action directed by duty, and every object shaped by art?

You cannot help being delighted by such conditions, or feeling indignant at hearing them denounced as 'heathen'. And according to the degree of altruism within yourself, these good folk will be able, without any apparent effort, to make you happy. The mere sensation of the *milieu* is a placid happiness: it is like the sensation of a dream in which people greet us exactly as we like to be greeted, and say to us all that we like to hear, and do for us all that we wish to have done - people moving soundlessly through spaces of perfect repose, all bathed in vapoury light. Yes - for no little time these fairy-folk can give you all the soft bliss of sleep. But sooner or later, if you dwell long with them, your contentment will prove to have much in common with the happiness of dreams. You will never forget the dream - never; but it will lift at last, like those vapours of spring which lend preternatural loveliness to a Japanese landscape in the forenoon of radiant days. Really you are happy because you have entered bodily into Fairyland - into a world that is not, and never could be your own. You have been transported out of your own century - over spaces enormous of perished time - into an era forgotten, into a vanished age - back to something ancient as Egypt or Nineveh. That is the secret of the strangeness and beauty of things - the secret of the thrill they give - the secret of the elfish charm of the people and their ways. Fortunate mortal! the tide of Time has turned for you! But remember that here all is enchantment - that you have fallen under the spell of the dead - that the lights and the colours and the voices must fade away at last into emptiness and silence.

*   *   *

Some of us, at least, have often wished that it were possible to live for a season in the beautiful vanished world of Greek culture. Inspired by our first acquaintance with the charm of Greek art and thought, this wish comes to us even before we are capable of imagining the true conditions of the antique civilisation. If the wish could be realised, we should certainly find it impossible to accommodate ourselves to those conditions - not so much because of the difficulty of learning the environment, as because of the much greater difficulty of feeling just as people used to feel some thirty centuries ago. In spite of all that has been done for Greek studies since the Renaissance, we are still unable to understand many aspects of the old Greek life: no modern mind can really feel, for example, those sentiments and emotions to which the great tragedy of Oedipus made appeal. Nevertheless we are much in advance of our forefathers of the eighteenth century, as regards the knowledge of Greek civilisation. In the time of the French Revolution, it was thought possible to re-establish in France the conditions of a Greek republic, and to educate children according to the system of Sparta. Today, we are well aware that no mind developed by modern civilisation could find happiness under any of those socialistic despotisms which existed in all the cities of the ancient world before the Roman conquest. We could no more mingle with the old Greek life, if it were resurrected for us - no more become a part of it - than we could change our mental identities. But how much would we not give for the delight of beholding it - for the joy of attending one festival in Corinth, or of witnessing the Pan-Hellenic games?...

And yet, to witness the revival of some perished Greek civilisation - to walk about the very Crotona of Pythagoras - to wander through the Syracuse of Theocritus - were not any more of a privilege than is the opportunity actually afforded us to study Japanese life. Indeed, from the evolutional point of view, it were less of a privilege - since Japan offers us the living spectacle of conditions older, and psychologically much farther away from us, than those of any Greek period with which art and literature have made us closely acquainted.

The reader scarcely needs to be reminded that a civilisation less evolved than our own, and intellectually remote from us, is not on that account to be regarded as necessarily inferior in all respects. Hellenic civilisation at its best represented an early stage of sociological evolution; yet the arts which it developed still furnish our supreme and unapproachable ideals of beauty. So, too, this much more archaic civilisation of Old Japan attained an average of aesthetic and moral culture well worthy of our wonder and praise. Only a shallow mind - a very shallow mind - will pronounce the best of that culture inferior. But Japanese civilisation is peculiar to a degree for which there is perhaps no Western parallel, since it offers us the spectacle of many successive layers of alien culture superimposed above the simple indigenous basis, and forming a very bewilderment of complexity.

Most of this alien culture is Chinese, and bears but an indirect relation to the real subject of these studies. The peculiar and surprising fact is that, in spite of all superimposition, the original character of the people and of their society should still remain recognisable. The wonder of Japan is not to be sought in the countless borrowings with which she has clothed herself - much as a princess of the olden time would don twelve ceremonial robes, of diverse colours and qualities, folded one upon the other so as to show their many-tinted edges at throat and sleeves and skirt - no, the real wonder is the Wearer. For the interest of the costume is much less in its beauty of form and tint than in its significance as idea - as representing something of the mind that devised or adopted it. And the supreme interest of the old Japanese civilisation lies in what it expresses of the race-character - that character which yet remains essentially unchanged by all the changes of Meiji.

'Suggests' were perhaps a better word than 'expresses', for this race-character is rather to be divined than recognised. Our comprehension of it might be helped by some definite knowledge of origins; but such knowledge we do not yet possess. Ethnologists are agreed that the Japanese race has been formed by a mingling of peoples, and that the dominant element is Mongolian; but this dominant element is represented in two very different types - one slender and almost feminine of aspect; the other, squat and powerful. Chinese and Korean elements are known to exist in the populations of certain districts; and there appears to have been a large infusion of Aino blood. Whether there be any Malay or Polynesian element also has not been decided. Thus much only can be safely affirmed - that the race, like all good races, is a mixed one; and that the peoples who originally united to form it have been so blended together as to develop, under long social discipline, a tolerably uniform type of character. This character, though immediately recognisable in some of its aspects, presents us with many enigmas that are very difficult to explain.

Nevertheless, to understand it better has become a matter of importance. Japan has entered into the world's competitive struggle; and the worth of any people in that struggle depends upon character quite as much as upon force. We can learn something about Japanese character if we are able to ascertain the nature of the conditions which shaped it - the great general facts of the moral experience of the race. And these facts we should find expressed or suggested in the history of those social institutions derived from and developed by religion.

The Religion of Loyalty

'Militant societies', says the author of the *Principles of Sociology*, 'must have a patriotism which regards the triumph of their society as the supreme end of action; they must possess the loyalty whence flows obedience to authority - and, that they may be obedient, they must have abundant faith.' The history of the Japanese people strongly exemplifies these truths. Among no other people has loyalty ever assumed more impressive and extraordinary forms; and among no other people has obedience ever been nourished by a more abundant faith - that faith derived from the cult of the ancestors.

The reader will understand how filial piety - the domestic religion of obedience - widens in range with social evolution, and eventually differentiates both into that political obedience required by the community, and that military obedience exacted by the war-lord - obedience implying not only submission, but affectionate submission - not merely the sense of obligation, but the sentiment of duty. In its origin such dutiful obedience is essentially religious; and, as expressed in loyalty it retains the religious character - becomes the constant manifestation of a religion of self-sacrifice. Loyalty is developed early in the history of a militant people; and we find touching examples of it in the earliest Japanese chronicles. We find also terrible ones - stories of self-immolation.

*   *   *

To his divinely descended lord, the retainer owed everything - in fact, not less than in theory: goods, household, liberty, and life. Any or all of these he was expected to yield up without a murmur, on demand, for the sake of the lord. And duty to the lord, like the duty to the family ancestor, did not cease with death. As the ghosts of parents were to be supplied with food by their living children, so the spirit of the lord was to be worshipfully served by those who, during his lifetime, owed him direct obedience. It could not be permitted that the spirit of the ruler should enter unattended into the world of shadows: some, at least, of those who served him living were bound to follow him in death. Thus in early societies arose the custom of human sacrifices - sacrifices at first obligatory, afterwards voluntary. In Japan as stated in a former chapter, they remained an indispensable feature of great funerals, up to the first century, when images of baked clay were first substituted for the official victims. I have already mentioned how, after this abolition of obligatory *junshi*, or following of one's Lord in death, the practice of voluntary *junshi* continued up to the sixteenth century, when it actually became a military fashion. At the death of a *daimyō* it was then common for fifteen or twenty of his retainers to disembowel themselves. Iyeyasu determined to put an end to this custom of suicide, which is thus considered in the 76th article of his celebrated *Legacy*:

'Although it is undoubtedly the ancient custom for a vassal to follow his Lord in death, there is not the slightest reason in the practice. Confucius has ridiculed the making of *Yō* [effigies buried with the dead]. These practices are strictly forbidden, more especially to primary retainers, but to secondary retainers likewise, even of the lowest rank. He is the reverse of a faithful servant who disregards this prohibition. His posterity shall be impoverished by the confiscation of his property, as a warning for those who disobey the laws.'

Iyeyasu's command ended the practice of *junshi* among his own vassals; but it continued, or revived again, after his death. In 1664 the shogunate issued an edict proclaiming that the family of any person performing *junshi* should be punished; and the shogunate was in earnest. When this edict was disobeyed by one Uyemon no Hyoge, who disembowelled himself at the death of his lord, Okudaira Tadamasa, the government promptly confiscated the lands of the family of the suicide, executed two of his sons, and sent the rest of the household into exile. Though cases of *junshi* have occurred even within this present era of Meiji, the determined attitude of the Tokugawa government so far checked the practice that even the most fervid loyalty latterly made its sacrifices through religion, as a rule. Instead of performing *harakiri*, the retainer shaved his head at the death of his lord, and became a Buddhist monk.

★   ★   ★

The custom of *junshi* represents but one aspect of Japanese loyalty: there were other customs equally, if not even more, significant - for example, the custom of military suicide, not as *junshi*, but as a self-inflicted penalty exacted by the traditions of *samurai* discipline. Against *harakiri*, as punitive suicide, there was no legislative enactment, for obvious reasons. It would seem that this form of self-destruction was not known to the Japanese in early ages; it may have been introduced from China, with other military customs. The ancient Japanese usually performed suicide by strangulation, as the *Nihoni* bears witness. It was the military class that established the *harakiri* as a custom and privilege. Previously, the chiefs of a routed army, or the defenders of a castle taken by storm, would thus end themselves to avoid falling into the enemy's hands - a custom which continued into the present era.

About the close of the fifteenth century, the military custom of permitting any *samurai* to perform *harakiri*, instead of subjecting him to the shame of execution, appears to have been generally established. Afterwards it became the recognised duty of a *samurai* to kill himself at the word of command. All *samurai* were subject to this disciplinary law, even lords of provinces; and in *samurai* families, children of both sexes were trained how to perform suicide whenever personal honour or the will of a liege-lord, might require it.... Women, I should observe, did not perform *harakiri*, but *jigai* - that is to say, piercing the throat with a dagger so as to sever the arteries by a single thrust-and-cut movement....

The particulars of the *harakiri* ceremony have become so well known through Mitford's translation of Japanese texts on the subject, that I need not touch upon them. The important fact to remember is that honour and loyalty required the *samurai* man or woman to be ready at any moment to perform self-destruction by the sword. As for the warrior, any breach of trust (voluntary or involuntary), failure to execute a difficult mission, a clumsy mistake, and even a look of displeasure from one's liege, were sufficient reasons for *harakiri*, or, as the aristocrats preferred to call it, by the Chinese term, *seppuku*. Among the highest class of retainers, it was also a duty to make protest against misconduct on the part of their lord by performing *seppuku*, when all other means of bringing him to reason had failed - which heroic custom has been made the subject of several popular dramas founded upon fact. In the case of married women of the *samurai* class - directly responsible to their husbands, not to the lord - *jigai* was resorted to most often as a means of preserving honour in time of war, though it was sometimes performed merely as a sacrifice of loyalty to the spirit of the husband, after his untimely death.[1] In the case of girls it was not uncommon for other reasons - *samurai* maidens often entering into the service of noble households, where the cruelty of intrigue might easily bring about a suicide, or where loyalty to the wife of the lord might exact it. For the *samurai* maiden in service was bound by loyalty to her mistress not less closely than the warrior to the lord; and the heroines of Japanese feudalism were many.

In the early ages it appears to have been the custom for the wives of officials condemned to death to kill themselves - the ancient chronicles are full of examples. But this custom is perhaps to be partly accounted for by the ancient law, which held the household of the offender equally responsible with him for the offence, independently of the facts in the case. However, it was certainly also common enough for a bereaved wife to perform suicide, not through despair, but through the wish to follow her husband into the other world, and there to wait upon him as in life. Instances of female suicide, representing the old ideal of duty to a dead husband, have occurred in recent times. Such suicides are usually performed according to the feudal rules - the woman robing herself in white for the occasion. At the time of the late war with China there occurred in Tokyo one remarkable suicide of this kind; the victim being the wife of Lieutenant Asada, who had fallen in battle. She was only twenty-one. On hearing of her husband's death, she at once began to make preparations for her own - writing letters of farewell to her relatives, putting her affairs in order, and carefully cleaning the house, according to old-time rule. Thereafter she donned her deathrobe; laid mattings down opposite to the alcove in the guest-room; placed her husband's portrait in the alcove, and set offerings before it. When everything had been arranged, she seated herself before the portrait, took up her dagger, and with a single skilful thrust divided the arteries of her throat.

Besides the duty of suicide for the sake of preserving honour, there was also, for the *samurai* woman, the duty of suicide as a moral protest. I have already said that among the highest class of retainers it was thought a moral duty to perform *harakiri* as a remonstrance against shameless conduct on the part of one's lord, when all other means of persuasion had been tried in vain. Among *samurai* women - taught to consider their husbands as their lords, in the feudal meaning of the term - it was held a moral obligation to perform *jigai*, by way of protest against disgraceful behaviour upon the part of a husband who would not listen to advice or reproof. The ideal of wifely duty which impelled such sacrifice still survives; and more than one recent example might be cited of a generous life thus laid down in rebuke of some moral wrong. Perhaps the most touching instance occurred in 1892, at the time of the district elections in Nagono prefecture. A rich voter named Ishijima, after having publicly pledged himself to aid in the election of a certain candidate, transferred his support to the rival candidate. On learning of this breach of promise, the wife of Ishijima, robed herself in white, and performed *jigai* after the old *samurai* manner. The grave of this brave woman is still decorated with flowers by the people of the district; and incense is burned before her tomb.

* * *

To kill oneself at command - a duty which no loyal *samurai* would have dreamed of calling in question - appears to us much less difficult than another duty, also fully accepted: the sacrifice of children, wife, and household for the sake of the lord. Much of Japanese popular tragedy is devoted to incidents of such sacrifice made by retainers or dependents of *daimyō* - men or women who gave their children to death in order to save the children of their masters.[2] Nor have we any reason to suppose that the facts have been exaggerated in these dramatic compositions, most of which are based upon feudal history. The incidents, of course, have been rearranged and expanded to meet theatrical requirements; but the general pictures thus given of the ancient society are probably even less grim than the vanished reality. The people still love these tragedies; and the foreign critic of their dramatic literature is wont to point out only the blood-spots, and to comment upon them as evidence of a public taste for gory spectacles - as proof of some innate ferocity in the race. Rather, I think, is this love of the old tragedy proof of what foreign critics try always to ignore as much as possible - the deeply religious character of the people. These plays continue to give delight - not because of their horror, but because of their moral teaching - because of their exposition of the duty of sacrifice and courage, the religion of loyalty. They represent the martyrdoms of feudal society for its noblest ideals.

All down through that society, in varying forms, the same spirit of loyalty had its manifestations. As the *samurai* to his liege-lord, so the apprentice was bound to the patron, and the clerk to the merchant. Everywhere there was trust, because everywhere there existed the like sentiment of mutual duty between servant and master. Each industry and occupation had its religion of loyalty - requiring, on the one side, absolute obedience and sacrifice at need; and on the other, kindliness and aid. And the rule of the dead was over all.

*   *   *

Not less ancient than the duty of dying for parent or lord was the social obligation to avenge the killing of either. Even before the beginnings of settled society, this duty is recognised. The oldest chronicles of Japan teem with instances of obligatory vengeance. Confucian ethics more than affirmed the obligation - forbidding a man to live 'under the same heaven' with the slayer of his lord, or parent, or brother; and fixing all the degrees of kinship, or other relationship, within which the duty of vengeance was to be considered imperative. Confucian ethics, it will be remembered, became at an early date the ethics of the Japanese ruling classes, and so remained down to recent times. The whole Confucian system, as I have remarked elsewhere, was founded upon ancestor-worship, and represented scarcely more than an amplification and elaboration of filial piety: it was therefore in complete accord with Japanese moral experience. As the military power developed in Japan, the Chinese code of vengeance became universally accepted; and it was sustained by law as well as by custom in later ages. Iyeyasu himself maintained it - exacting only that preliminary notice of an intended vendetta should be given in writing to the district criminal court. The text of his article on the subject is interesting:

'In respect to avenging injury done to master or father, it is acknowledged by the Wise and Virtuous [*Confucius*] that you and the injurer cannot live together under the canopy of heaven. A person harbouring such vengeance shall give notice in writing to the criminal court; and although no check or hindrance may be offered to the carrying out of his design within the period allowed for that purpose, it is forbidden that the chastisement of an enemy be attended with riot. Fellows who neglect to give notice of their intended revenge are like wolves of pretext:[3] their punishment or pardon should depend upon the circumstances of the case.'

Kindred, as well as parents; teachers, as well as lords, were to be revenged. A considerable proportion of popular romance and drama is devoted to the subject of vengeance taken by women; and, as a matter of fact, women, and even children, sometimes became avengers when there were no men of a wronged family left to perform the duty. Apprentices avenged their masters; and even sworn friends were bound to avenge each other.

Why the duty of vengeance was not confined to the circle of natural kinship is explicable, of course, by the peculiar organisation of society. We have seen that the patriarchal family was a religious corporation; and that the family-bond was not the bond of natural affection, but the bond of the cult. We have also seen that the relation of the household to the community, and of the community to the clan, and of the clan to the tribe, was equally a religious relation. As a necessary consequence, the earlier customs of vengeance were regulated by the bond of the family, communal, or tribal cult, as well as by the bond of blood; and with the introduction of Chinese ethics, and the development of militant conditions, the idea of revenge as duty took a wider range. The son or the brother by adoption was in respect of obligation the same as the son or brother by blood; and the teacher stood to his pupil in the relation of father to child. To strike one's natural parent was a crime punishable by death: to strike one's teacher was, before the law, an equal offence. This notion of the teacher's claim to filial reverence was of Chinese importation: an extension of the duty of filial piety to 'the father of the mind'. There were other such extensions; and the origin of all, Chinese or Japanese, may be traced alike to ancestor-worship.

Now, what has never been properly insisted upon, in any of the books treating of ancient Japanese customs, is the originally religious significance of the *kataki-uchi*. That a religious origin can be found for all customs of vendetta established in early societies is, of course, well known; but a peculiar interest attaches to the Japanese vendetta in view of the fact that it conserved its religious character unchanged down to the present era. The *kataki-uchi* was essentially an act of propitiation, as is proved by the rite with which it terminated - the placing of the enemy's head upon the tomb of the person avenged, as an offering of atonement. And one of the most impressive features of this rite, as formerly practised, was the delivery of an address to the ghost of the person avenged. Sometimes the address was only spoken; sometimes it was also written, and the manuscript left upon the tomb.

There is probably none of my readers unacquainted with Mitford's ever-delightful *Tales of Old Japan*, and his translation of the true story of the 'Forty-Seven Ronins'. But I doubt whether many persons have noticed the significance of the washing of Kira Kotsuke-no-Suke's severed head, or the significance of the address inscribed to their dead lord by the brave men who had so long waited and watched for the chance to avenge him. This address, of which I quote Mitford's translation, was laid upon the tomb of the Lord Asano. It is still preserved at the temple called Sengakuji:

'*The fifteenth year of Genroku [1703], the twelfth month, the fifteenth day.* - We have come this day to do homage here: forty-seven men in all, from Oishi Kuranosuke down to the foot-soldier Terasaka Kichiyemon - all cheerfully about to lay down our lives on your behalf. We reverently announce this to the honoured spirit of our dead master. On the fourteenth day of the third month of last year, our honoured master was pleased to attack Kira Kotsuke-no-Suke, for what reason we know not. Our honoured master put an end to his own life; but Kira Kotsuke-no-Suke lived. Although we fear that after the decree issued by the Government, this plot of ours will be displeasing to our honoured master, still we, who have eaten of your food, could not without blushing repeat the verse, "*Thou shalt not live under the same heaven, nor tread the same earth with the enemy of thy father or lord*", nor could we have dared to leave hell [Hades] and present ourselves before you in Paradise, unless we had carried out the vengeance which you began. Every day that we waited seemed as three autumns to us. Verily we have trodden the snow for one day, nay, for two days, and have tasted food but once. The old and decrepit, the sick and the ailing, have come forth gladly to lay down their lives. Men might laugh at us, as at grasshoppers trusting in the strength of their arms, and thus shame our honoured lord; but we could not halt in our deed of vengeance. Having taken counsel together last night, we have escorted my Lord Kosuke-no-Suke hither to your tomb. This dirk, by which our honoured lord set great store last year, and entrusted to our care, we now bring back. If your noble spirit be now present before this tomb, we pray you, as a sign to take the dirk, and, striking the head of your enemy with it a second time, to dispel your hatred forever. This is the respectful statement of forty-seven men.'

It will be observed that the Lord Asano is addressed as if he were present and visible. The head of the enemy has been carefully washed, according to the rule concerning the presentation of heads to a living superior. It is laid upon the tomb together with the nine-inch sword, or dagger, originally used by the Lord Asano in performing *harakiri* at Government command, and afterwards used by Oishi Kuranosuke in cutting off the head of Kira Kotsuke-no-Suke - and the spirit of the Lord Asano is requested to take up the weapon and to strike the head, so that the pain of ghostly anger may be dissipated forever. Then, having been themselves all sentenced to perform *harakiri*, the forty-seven retainers join their lord in death, and are buried in front of his tomb. Before their graves the smoke of incense, offered by admiring visitors, has been ascending daily for two hundred years.[4]

One must have lived in Japan, and have been able to feel the true spirit of the old Japanese life, in order to comprehend the whole of this romance of loyalty; but I think that whoever carefully reads Mr Mitford's version of it, and his translation of the authentic documents relating to it, will confess himself moved. The address especially touches - because of the affection and the faith to which it testifies, and the sense of duty beyond this life. However much revenge must be condemned by our modern ethics, there is a noble side to many of the old Japanese stories of loyal vengeance; and these stories affect us by the expression of what has nothing to do with vulgar revenge - by their exposition of gratitude, self-denial, courage in facing death, and faith in the unseen. And this means, of course, that we are, consciously or unconsciously, impressed by their religious quality. Mere individual revenge - the postponed retaliation for some personal injury - repels our moral feeling: we have learned to regard the emotion inspiring such revenge as simply brutal - something shared by man with lower forms of animal life. But in the story of a homicide exacted by the sentiment of duty or gratitude to a dead master, there may be circumstances which can make appeal to our higher moral sympathies - to our sense of the force and beauty of unselfishness, unswerving fidelity, unchanging affection. And the story of the Forty-seven Ronin is one of this class....

*   *   *

Yet it must be borne in mind that the Japanese religion of loyalty, which found its supreme manifestation in those three terrible customs of *junshi*, harakiri, and *kataki-uchi*, was narrow in its range. It was limited by the very constitution of society. Though the nation was ruled, through all its groups, by notions of duty everywhere similar in character, the circle of that duty, for each individual, did not extend beyond the clan-group to which he belonged. For his own lord the retainer was always ready to die; but he did not feel equally bound to sacrifice himself for the military government, unless he happened to belong to the special military following of the shogun. His fatherland, his country, his world, extended only to the boundary of his chief's domain. Outside of that domain he could be only a wanderer - a *rōnin*, or 'wave-man', as the masterless samurai was termed. Under such conditions that larger loyalty which identifies itself with love of king and country - which is patriotism in the modern, not in the narrower antique sense - could not fully evolve. Some common peril, some danger to the whole race - such as the attempted Tartar conquest of Japan - might temporarily arouse the true sentiment of patriotism; but otherwise that sentiment had little opportunity for development. The Ise cult represented, indeed, the religion of the nation, as distinguished from the clan or tribal worship; but each man had been taught to believe that his first duty was to his lord. One cannot efficiently serve two masters; and feudal government practically suppressed any tendencies in that direction. The lordship so completely owned the individual, body and soul, that the idea of any duty to the nation, outside of the duty to the chief, had neither time nor chance to define itself in the mind of the vassal. To the ordinary samurai, for example, an imperial order would not have been law: he recognised no law above the law of his *daimyō*. As for the *daimyō*, he might either disobey or obey an imperial command according to circumstances: his direct superior was the shogun; and he was obliged to make for himself a politic distinction between the Heavenly Sovereign as deity, and the Heavenly Sovereign as a human personality.

Before the ultimate centralisation of the military power, there were many instances of lords sacrificing themselves for their emperor; but there were even more cases of open rebellion by lords against the imperial will. Under the Tokugawa rule, the question of obeying or resisting an imperial command would have depended upon the attitude of the shogun; and no *daimyō* would have risked such obedience to the court at Kyoto as might have signified disobedience to the court at Yedo. Not at least until the shogunate had fallen into decay. In Iyemitsu's time the *daimyō* were strictly forbidden to approach the imperial palace on their way to Yedo - even in response to an imperial command; and they were also forbidden to make any direct appeal to the Mikado. The policy of the shogunate was to prevent all direct communication between the Kyoto court and the *daimyō*. This policy paralysed intrigue for two hundred years; but it prevented the development of patriotism.

And for that very reason, when Japan at last found herself face to face with the unexpected peril of Western aggression, the abolition of the daimiates was felt to be a matter of paramount importance. The supreme danger required that the social units should be fused into one coherent mass, capable of uniform action - that the clan and tribal groupings should be permanently dissolved - that all authority should immediately be centred in the representative of the national religion - that the duty of obedience to the Heavenly Sovereign should replace, at once and forever, the feudal duty of obedience to the territorial lord. The religion of loyalty, evolved by a thousand years of war, could not be cast away: properly utilised, it would prove a national heritage of incalculable worth - a moral power capable of miracles if directed by one wise will to a single wise end. Destroyed by reconstruction it could not be; but it could be diverted and transformed. Diverted, therefore, to nobler ends - expanded to larger needs - it became the new national sentiment of trust and duty: the modern sense of patriotism. What wonders it has wrought, within the space of thirty years, the world is now obliged to confess: what more it may be able to accomplish remains to be seen. One thing at least is certain - that the future of Japan must depend upon the maintenance of this new religion of loyalty, evolved, through the old, from the ancient religion of the dead.

Footnotes:

1. The Japanese moralist Yekken wrote: 'A woman has no feudal lord: she must reverence and obey her husband'.
2. See, for a good example, the translation of the drama *Terakoya*, published, with admirable illustrations, by T. Hasegawa (Tokyo).
3. Or 'hypocritical wolves' - that is to say, brutal murderers seeking to excuse their crime on the pretext of justifiable vengeance. (The translation is by Lowder).
4. It has long been the custom also for visitors to leave their cards upon the tombs of the Forty-seven Ronin. When I last visited Sengakuji, the ground about the tombs was white with visiting-cards.

From The Diary of an English Teacher

1

MATSUE, SEPTEMBER 2, 1890.I am under contract to serve as English teacher in the Jinjō Chūgakkō, or Ordinary Middle School, and also in the Shihan-Gakkō, or Normal School, of Matsue, Izumo, for the term of one year.

The Jinjō Chūgakkō is an immense two-storey wooden building in European style, painted a dark grey-blue. It has accommodations for nearly three hundred day scholars. It is situated in one corner of a great square of ground, bounded on two sides by canals, and on the other two by very quiet streets. This site is very near the ancient castle.

The Normal School is a much larger building occupying the opposite angle of the square. It is also much handsomer, is painted snowy white, and has a little cupola upon its summit. There are only about one hundred and fifty students in the Shihan-Gakkō, but they are boarders.

Between these two schools are other educational buildings, which I shall learn more about later.

It is my first day at the schools. Nishida Sentaro, the Japanese teacher of English, has taken me through the buildings, introduced me to the

Directors, and to all my future colleagues, given me all necessary instructions about hours and about text-books, and furnished my desk with all things necessary. Before teaching begins, however, I must be introduced to the Governor of the Province, Koteda Yasusada, with whom my contract has been made, through the medium of his secretary. So Nishida leads the way to the Kenchō, or Prefectural office, situated in another foreign-looking edifice across the street.

We enter it, ascend a wide stairway, and enter a spacious room carpeted in European fashion - a room with bay windows and cushioned chairs. One person is seated at a small round table, and about him are standing half a dozen others: all are in full Japanese costume, ceremonial costume - splendid silken *hakama*, or Chinese trousers, silken robes, silken *haori* or overdress, marked with their *mon* or family crests: rich and dignified attire which makes me ashamed of my commonplace Western garb. These are officials of the Kenchō, and teachers: the person seated is the Governor. He rises to greet me, gives me the hand-grasp of a giant: and as I look into his eyes, I feel I shall love that man to the day of my death. A face fresh and frank as a boy's, expressing much placid force and large-hearted kindness - all the calm of a Buddha. Beside him, the other officials look very small: indeed the first impression of him is that of a man of another race. While I am wondering whether the old Japanese heroes were cast in a similar mould, he signs to me to take a seat, and questions my guide in a mellow basso. There is a charm in the fluent depth of the voice pleasantly confirming the idea suggested by the face. An attendant brings tea.

'The Governor asks', interprets Nishida, 'if you know the old history of Izumo.'

I reply that I have read the *Kojiki*, translated by Profesor Chamberlain, and have therefore some knowledge of the story of Japan's most ancient province. Some converse in Japanese follows. Nishida tells the Governor that I came to Japan to study the ancient religion and customs, and that I am particularly interested in Shinto and the traditions of Izumo. The Governor suggests that I make visits to the celebrated shrines of Kitzuki, Yaegaki, and Kumano, and then asks:

'Does he know the tradition of the origin of the clapping of hands before a Shinto shrine?'

I reply in the negative; and the Governor says the tradition is given in a commentary upon the *Kojiki*.

'It is in the thirty-second section of the fourteenth volume, where it is written that Ya-he-Koto-Shiro-nushi-no-Kami clapped his hands.'

I thank the Governor for his kind suggestions and his citation. After a brief silence I am graciously dismissed with another genuine hand grasp; and we return to the school.

2

I have been teaching for three hours in the Middle School, and teaching Japanese boys turns out to be a much more agreeable task than I had imagined. Each class has been so well prepared for me beforehand by

Nishida that my utter ignorance of Japanese makes no difficulty in regard to teaching: moreover, although the lads cannot understand my words always when I speak, they can understand whatever I write upon the blackboard with chalk. Most of them have already been studying English from childhood, with Japanese teachers. All are wonderfully docile and patient. According to old custom, when the teacher enters, the whole class rises and bows to him. He returns the bow, and calls the roll.

Nishida is only too kind. He helps me in every way he possibly can, and is constantly regretting that he cannot help me more. There are, of course, some difficulties to overcome. For instance, it will take me a very, very long time to learn the names of the boys, most of which names I cannot even pronounce, with the class-roll before me. And although the names of the different classes have been painted upon the doors of their respective rooms in English letters, for the benefit of the foreign teacher, it will take me some weeks at least to become quite familiar with them. For the time being Nishida always guides me to the rooms. He also shows me the way, through long corridors, to the Normal School, and introduces me to the teacher Nakayama who is to act there as my guide.

I have been engaged to teach only four times a week at the Normal School; but I am furnished there also with a handsome desk in the teachers' apartment, and am made to feel at home almost immediately. Nakayama shows me everything of interest in the building before introducing me to my future pupils. The introduction is pleasant and novel as a school experience. I am conducted along a corridor, and ushered into a large luminous white-washed room full of young men in dark blue military uniform. Each sits at a very small desk, supported by a single leg, with three feet. At the end of the room is a platform with a high desk and a chair for the teacher. As I take my place at the desk, a voice rings out in English: '*Stand up*'! And all rise with a springy movement as if moved by machinery. '*Bow down*'! the same voice again commands - the voice of a young student wearing a captain's stripes upon his sleeve; and all salute me. I bow in return; we take our seats; and the lesson begins.

All teachers at the Normal School are saluted in the same military fashion before each class-hour - only the command is given in Japanese. For my sake only, it is given in English.

3

SEPTEMBER 22, 1890. The Normal School is a State institution. Students are admitted upon examination and production of testimony as to good character; but the number is, of course, limited. The young men pay no fees, no boarding money, nothing even for books, college-outfits, or wearing apparel. They are lodged, clothed, fed, and educated by the State; but they are required in return, after their graduation, to serve the State as teachers for the space of five years. Admission, however, by no means assures graduation. There are three or four examinations each year; and the students who fail to obtain a certain high average of examination marks must leave the school, however exemplary their conduct or earnest their study. No leniency can be shown where the educational needs of the State are concerned, and these call for natural ability and a high standard of its proof.

The discipline is military and severe. Indeed, it is so thorough that the graduate of a Normal School is exempted by military law from more than a year's service in the army: he leaves college a trained soldier. Deportment is also a requisite: special marks are given for it; and however gawky a freshman may prove at the time of his admission, he cannot remain so. A spirit of manliness is cultivated, which excludes roughness but develops self-reliance and self-control. The student is required, when speaking, to look his teacher in the face, and to utter his words not only distinctly, but sonorously. Demeanour in class is partly enforced by the class-room fittings themselves. The tiny tables are too narrow to allow of being used as supports for the elbows; the seats have no backs against which to lean, and the student must hold himself rigidly erect as he studies. He must also keep himself faultlessly neat and clean. Whenever and wherever he encounters one of his teachers he must halt, bring his feet together, draw himself erect, and give the military salute. And this is done with a swift grace difficult to describe.

The demeanour of a class during study hours is if anything too faultless. Never a whisper is heard, never is a head raised from the book without permission. But when the teacher addresses a student by name, the youth rises instantly, and replies in a tone of such vigour as would seem to unaccustomed ears almost startling by contrast with the stillness and self-repression of the others.

The female department of the Normal School, where about fifty young women are being trained as teachers, is a separate two-storey quadrangle of buildings, large, airy, and so situated, together with its gardens, as to be totally isolated from all other buildings and invisible from the street. The girls are not only taught European science by the most advanced methods, but are trained as well in Japanese arts - the arts of embroidery, of decoration, of painting, and of arranging flowers. European drawing is also taught, and beautifully taught, not only here, but in all the schools. It is taught, however, in combination with Japanese methods; and the results of this blending may certainly be expected to have some charming influence upon future art-production. The average capacity of the Japanese student in drawing is, I think, at least fifty per cent higher than that of European students. The soul of the race is essentially artistic; and the extremely difficult art of learning to write the Chinese characters, in which all are trained from early childhood, has already disciplined the hand and the eye to a marvellous degree - a degree undreamed of in the Occident - long before the drawing-master begins his lessons of perspective.

Attached to the great Normal School, and connected by a corridor with the Jinjō Chūgakkō likewise, is a large elementary school for little boys and girls: its teachers are male and female students of the graduating classes, who are thus practically trained for their profession before entering the service of the State. Nothing could be more interesting as an educational spectacle to any sympathetic foreigner than some of this elementary teaching. In the first room which I visit a class of very little girls and boys

- some as quaintly pretty as their own dolls - are bending at their desks over sheets of coal-black paper which you would think they were trying to make still blacker by energetic use of writing-brushes and what we call Indian-ink. They are really learning to write Chinese and Japanese characters, stroke by stroke. Until one stroke has been well learned, they are not suffered to attempt another - much less a combination. Long before the first lesson is thoroughly mastered, the white paper has become all evenly black under the multitude of tyro brush-strokes. But the same sheet is still used; for the wet ink makes a yet blacker mark upon the dry, so that it can easily be seen.

In a room adjoining, I see another child-class learning to use scissors - Japanese scissors, which, being formed in one piece, shaped something like the letter U, are much less easy to manage than ours. The little folk are being taught to cut out patterns, and shapes of special objects or symbols to be studied. Flower-forms are the most ordinary patterns; sometimes certain ideographs are given as subjects.

And in another room a third small class is learning to sing; the teacher writing the music notes (*do, re, mi*) with chalk upon a blackboard, and accompanying the song with an accordion. The little ones have learned the Japanese national anthem (*Kimi ga yo wa*) and two native songs set to Scottish airs - one of which calls back to me, even in this remote corner of the Orient, many a charming memory: *Auld Lang Syne*.

No uniform is worn in this elementary school: all are in Japanese dress - the boys in dark blue kimono, the little girls in robes of all tints, radiant as butterflies. But in addition to their robes, the girls wear *hakama*,[1] and these are of a vivid, warm sky-blue.

Between the hours of teaching, ten minutes are allowed for play or rest. The little boys play at Demon-Shadows or at blindman's-buff or at some other funny game: they laugh, leap, shout, race, and wrestle, but, unlike European children, never quarrel or fight.[2] As for the little girls, they get by themselves, and either play at hand-ball, or form into circles to play at some round game, accompanied by song. Indescribably soft and sweet the chorus of those little voices in the round.

> *Kango-kango shō-ya,*
> *Naka yoni shō-ya,*
> *Don-don to kunde*
> *Jizō-San no midzu wo*
> *Matsuba no midzu irete,*
> *Makkuri kaeso.*[3]

I notice that the young men, as well as the young women, who teach these little folk, are extremely tender to their charges. A child whose kimono is out of order, or dirtied by play, is taken aside and brushed and arranged as carefully as by an elder brother.

Besides being trained for their future profession by teaching the children of the elementary school, the girl students of the Shihan-Gakkō are also trained to teach in the neighbouring kindergarten. A delightful kindergarten it is, with big cheerful sunny rooms, where stocks of the most ingenious educational toys are piled upon shelves for daily use.

4

OCTOBER 1, 1890. Nevertheless I am destined to see little of the Normal School. Strictly speaking, I do not belong to its staff: my services being only lent by the Middle School, to which I give most of my time. I see the Normal School students in their class-rooms only, for they are not allowed to go out to visit their teachers' homes in the town. So I can never hope to become as familiar with them as with the students of the Chūgakkō, who are beginning to call me 'Teacher' instead of 'Sir', and to treat me as a sort of elder brother. (I objected to the word 'master', for in Japan the teacher has no need of being masterful.) And I feel less at home in the large, bright, comfortable apartments of the Normal School teachers than in our dingy, chill teachers' room at the Chūgakkō, where my desk is next to that of Nishida.

On the walls there are maps, crowded with Japanese ideographs; a few large charts representing zoological facts in the light of evolutional science; and an immense frame filled with little black lacquered wooden tablets, so neatly fitted together that the entire surface is uniform as that of a blackboard. On these are written, or rather painted, in white, names of teachers, subjects, classes, and order of teaching hours; and by the ingenious tablet arrangement any change of hours can be represented by simply changing the places of the tablets. As all this is written in Chinese and Japanese characters, it remains to me a mystery, except in so far as the general plan and purpose are concerned. I have learned only to recognise the letters of my own name, and the simpler form of numerals.

On every teacher's desk there is a small *hibachi* of glazed blue-and-white ware, containing a few lumps of glowing charcoal in a bed of ashes. During the brief intervals between classes each teacher smokes his tiny Japanese pipe of brass, iron, or silver. The *hibachi* and a cup of hot tea are our consolations for the fatigues of the class-room.

Nishida and one or two other teachers know a good deal of English, and we chat together sometimes between classes. But more often no one speaks. All are tired after the teaching hour, and prefer to smoke in silence. At such times the only sounds within the room are the ticking of the clock, and the sharp clang of the little pipes being rapped upon the edges of the *hibachi* to empty out the ashes.

5

OCTOBER 15, 1890. Today I witnessed the annual athletic contests (*undō-kwai*) of all the schools in Shimane Ken. These games were celebrated in the broad castle grounds of Ninomaru. Yesterday a circular race-track had been staked off, hurdles erected for leaping, thousands of wooden seats prepared for invited or privileged spectators, and a grand lodge built for the Governor, all before sunset. The place looked like a vast circus, with its tiers of plank seats rising one above the other, and the Governor's lodge magnificent with wreaths and flags. School children from all the villages and towns within twenty-five miles had arrived in surprising multitude. Nearly six thousand boys and girls were entered to take part in the contests.

Their parents and relatives and teachers made an imposing assembly upon the benches and within the gates. And on the ramparts overlooking the huge enclosure a much larger crowd had gathered, representing perhaps one-third of the population of the city.

The signal to begin or to end a contest was a pistol-shot. Four different kinds of games were performed in different parts of the grounds at the same time, as there was room enough for an army; and prizes were awarded to the winners of each contest by the hand of the Governor himself.

There were races between the best runners in each class of the different schools; and the best runner of all proved to be Sakane, of our own fifth class, who came in first by nearly forty yards without seeming even to make an effort. He is our champion athlete, and as good as he is strong, so that it made me very happy to see him with his arms full of prize books. He won also a fencing contest decided by the breaking of a little earthenware saucer tied to the left arm of each combatant. And he also won a leaping match between our older boys.

But many hundreds of other winners there were too, and many hundreds of prizes were given away. There were races in which the runners were tied together in pairs, the left leg of one to the right leg of the other. There were equally funny races, the winning of which depended on the runner's ability not only to run, but to crawl, to climb, to vault, and to jump alternately. There were races also for the little girls - pretty as butterflies they seemed in their sky-blue *hakama* and many coloured robes - races in which the contestants had each to pick up as they ran three balls of three different colours out of a number scattered over the turf. Besides this, the little girls had what is called a flag-race, and a contest with battledores and shuttlecocks.

Then came the tug-of-war. A magnificent tug-of-war, too - one hundred students at one end of a rope, and another hundred at the other. But the most wonderful spectacles of the day were the dumb-bell exercises. Six thousand boys and girls, massed in ranks about five hundred deep; six thousand pairs of arms rising and falling exactly together; six thousand pairs of sandalled feet advancing or retreating together, at the signal of the masters of gymnastics, directing all from the tops of various little wooden towers; six thousand voices chanting at once the 'one, two, three', of the dumb-bell drill: '*Ichi, ni - san, shi - go, roku - shichi, hachi*'.

Last came the curious game called 'Taking the Castle'. Two models of Japanese towers, about fifteen feet high, made with paper stretched over a framework of bamboo, were set up, one at each end of the field. Inside the castles an inflammable liquid had been placed in open vessels, so that if the vessels were overturned the whole fabric would take fire. The boys, divided into two parties, bombarded the castles with wooden balls, which passed easily through the paper walls; and in a short time both models were making a glorious blaze. Of course the party whose castle was the first to blaze lost the game.

The games began at eight o'clock in the morning, and at five in the evening came to an end. Then at a signal fully ten thousand voices pealed out the superb national anthem, '*Kimi ga yo*', and concluded it with three cheers for their Imperial Majesties, the Emperor and Empress of Japan.

The Japanese do not shout or roar as we do when we cheer. They chant. Each long cry is like the opening tone of an immense musical chorus: *A-a-a-a-a-a-a-a*!

6

It is no small surprise to observe how botany, geology, and other sciences are daily taught even in this remotest part of old Japan. Plant physiology and the nature of vegetable tissues are studied under excellent microscopes, and in their relations to chemistry; and at regular intervals the instructor leads his classes into the country to illustrate the lessons of the term by examples taken from the flora of their native place. Agriculture, taught by a graduate of the famous Agricultural School of Sapporo, is practically illustrated upon farms purchased and maintained by the schools for purely educational ends. Each series of lessons in geology is supplemented by visits to the mountains about the lake, or to the tremendous cliffs of the coast, where the students are taught to familiarise themselves with forms of stratification and the visible history of rocks. The basin of the lake, and the country about Matsue, is physiographically studied, after the plans of instruction laid down in Huxley's excellent manual. Natural History, too, is taught according to the latest and best methods, and with the help of the microscope. The results of such teaching are sometimes surprising. I know of one student, a lad of only sixteen, who voluntarily collected and classified more than two hundred varieties of marine plants for a Tokyo professor. Another, a youth of seventeen, wrote down for me in my notebook, without a work of reference at hand, and, as I afterwards discovered, almost without an omission or error, a scientific list of all the butterflies to be found in the neighbourhbood of the city.

7

Through the Minister of Public Instruction, His Imperial Majesty has sent to all the great public schools of the Empire a letter bearing date of the thirteenth day of the tenth month of the twenty-third year of Meiji. And the students and teachers of the various schools assemble to hear the reading of the Imperial Words on Education.

At eight o'clock we of the Middle School are all waiting in our own assembly hall for the coming of the Governor, who will read the Emperor's letter in the various schools.

We wait but a little while. Then the Governor comes with all the officers of the Kenchō and the chief men of the city. We rise to salute him: then the national anthem is sung.

Then the Governor, ascending the platform, produces the Imperial Missive - a scroll of Chinese manuscript sheathed in silk. He withdraws it slowly from its woven envelope, lifts it reverentially to his forehead, unrolls it, lifts it again to his forehead, and after a moment's dignified pause begins in that clear deep voice of his to read the melodious syllables after the ancient way, which is like a chant:

'CHO-KU-GU. Chin omommiru ni waga kōso kosō kani wo.'...
'We consider that the Founder of Our Empire and the ancestors of Our Imperial House placed the foundation of the country on a grand and permanent basis, and established their authority on the principles of profound humanity and benevolence.

'That Our subjects have throughout ages deserved well of the state by their loyalty and piety and by their harmonious cooperation is in accordance with the essential character of Our nation; and on these very same principles Our education has been founded.

'You, Our subjects, be therefore filial to your parents; be affectionate to your brothers; be harmonious as husbands and wives; and be faithful to your friends; conduct yourselves with propriety and carefulness; extend generosity and benevolence towards your neighbours; attend to your studies and follow your pursuits; cultivate your intellects and elevate your morals; advance public benefits and promote social interests; be always found in the good observance of the laws and constitution of the land; display your personal courage and public spirit for the sake of the country whenever required; and thus support the Imperial prerogative, which is coexistent with the Heavens and the Earth.

'Such conduct on your part will not only strengthen the character of Our good and loyal subjects, but conduce also to the maintenance of the fame of your worthy forefathers.

'This is the instruction bequeathed by Our ancestors and to be followed by Our subjects; for it is the truth which has guided and guides them in their own affairs and in their dealings towards aliens.

'We hope, therefore, We and Our subjects will regard these sacred precepts with one and the same heart in order to attain the same ends.'[4]

Then the Governor and the Headmaster speak a few words - dwelling upon the full significance of His Imperial Majesty's august commands, and exhorting all to remember and to obey them to the uttermost.

After which the students have a holiday, to enable them the better to recollect what they have heard.

8

All teaching in the modern Japanese system of education is conducted with the utmost kindness and gentleness. The teacher is a teacher only: he is not, in the English sense of mastery, a master. He stands to his pupils in the relation of an elder brother. He never tries to impose his will upon them: he never scolds, he seldom criticises, he scarcely ever punishes. No Japanese teacher ever strikes a pupil: such an act would cost him his post at once. He never loses his temper: to do so would disgrace him in the eyes of his boys and in the judgement of his colleagues. Practically speaking, there is no punishment in Japanese schools. Sometimes very mischievous lads are kept in the schoolhouse during recreation time; yet even this light penalty is not inflicted directly by the teacher, but by the director of the school on complaint of the teacher. The purpose in such cases is not to inflict pain by deprivation of enjoyment, but to give public illustration of a fault; and in the great majority of instances, consciousness of the fault thus brought home to a lad before his comrades is quite enough to prevent its repetition. No such cruel punition as that of forcing a dull pupil to learn an additional task, or of sentencing him to strain his eyes copying four or five hundred lines, is ever dreamed of. Nor would such forms of punishment, in the present state of things, be long tolerated by the pupils themselves. The general policy of the educational authorities everywhere throughout the empire is to get rid of students who cannot be perfectly well managed without punishment; and expulsions, nevertheless, are rare.

I often see a pretty spectacle on my way home from the school, when I take the short cut through the castle grounds. A class of about thirty little boys, in kimono and sandals, bareheaded, being taught to march and to sing by a handsome young teacher, also in Japanese dress. While they sing, they are drawn up in line; and keep time with their little bare feet. The teacher has a pleasant high clear tenor; he stands at one end of the rank and sings a single line of the song. Then all the children sing it after him. Then he sings a second line, and they repeat it. If any mistakes are made, they have to sing the verse again.

It is the Song of Kusunoki Masashigé, noblest of Japanese heroes and patriots.

9

I have said that severity on the part of teachers would scarcely be tolerated by the students themselves - a fact which may sound strange to English or American ears. Tom Brown's school does not exist in Japan; the ordinary public school much more resembles the ideal Italian institution so charmingly painted for us in the *Cuore* of De Amicis. Japanese students furthermore claim and enjoy an independence contrary to all Occidental ideas of disciplinary necessity. In the Occident the master expels the pupil. In Japan it happens quite as often that the pupil expels the master. Each public school is an earnest, spirited little republic, to which director and teachers stand only in the relation of president and cabinet. They are indeed appointed by the prefectural government upon recommendation by the Educational Bureau at the capital; but in actual practice they maintain their positions by virtue of their capacity and personal character as estimated by their students, and are likely to be deposed by a revolutionary movement whenever found wanting. It has been alleged that the students frequently abuse their power. But this allegation has been made by European residents, strongly prejudiced in favour of masterful English ways of discipline. (I recollect that an English Yokohama paper, in this connection, advocated the introduction of the birch.) My own observations have convinced me, as larger experience has convinced some others, that in most instances of pupils rebelling against a teacher, reason is upon their side. They will rarely insult a teacher whom they dislike, or cause any disturbance in his class: they will simply refuse to attend school until he be removed. Personal feeling may often be a secondary, but it is seldom, so far as I have been able to learn, the primary cause for such a demand. A teacher whose manners are unsympathetic, or even positively disagreeable, will be nevertheless obeyed and revered while his students remain persuaded of his capacity as a teacher, and his sense of justice; and they are as keen to discern ability as they are to detect partiality. And, on the other hand, an amiable disposition alone will never atone with them either for want of knowledge or for want of skill to impart it. I knew one case, in a neighbouring public school, of a demand by the students for the removal of their professor of chemistry. In making their complaint, they frankly declared: 'We like him. He is kind to all of us; he does the best he can. But he does not know enough to teach us as we wish to be taught. He cannot answer our questions. He cannot explain the experiments which he shows us. Our former teacher could do all these things. We must have another teacher.' Investigation proved that the lads were quite right. The young teacher had graduated at the university; he had come well recommended; but he had no thorough knowledge of the science which he undertook to impart, and no experience as a teacher. The instructor's success in Japan is not guaranteed by a degree, but by his *practical* knowledge and his capacity to communicate it simply and thoroughly.

10

NOVEMBER 3, 1890. Today is the birthday of His Majesty the Emperor. It is a public holiday throughout Japan; and there will be no teaching this morning. But at eight o'clock all the students and instructors enter the great assembly hall of the Jinjō Chūgakkō to honour the anniversary of His Majesty's august birth.

On the platform of the assembly hall a table, covered with dark silk, has been placed; and upon this table the portraits of Their Imperial Majesties, the Emperor and the Empress of Japan, stand side by side upright, framed in gold. The alcove above the platform has been decorated with flags and wreaths.

Presently, the Governor enters, looking like a French general in his gold-embroidered uniform of office, and followed by the Mayor of the city, the Chief Military Officer, the Chief of Police, and all the officials of the provincial government. These take their places in silence to left and right of the platform. Then the school organ suddenly rolls out the slow, solemn, beautiful national anthem; and all present chant those ancient syllables, made sacred by the reverential love of a century of generations:

> Ki-mi ga-a yo-o wa
> Chi-yo ni-i-i ya-chi-yo ni sa-za-re
> I-shi no
> I-wa o to na-ri-te
> Ko-ke no
> Mu-u su-u ma-a-a-de.[5]

The anthem ceases. The Governor advances with a slow dignified step from the right side of the apartment to the centre of the open space before the platform and the portraits of Their Majesties, turns his face to them, and bows profoundly. Then he takes three steps forward towards the platform, and halts, and bows again. Then he takes three more steps forward, and bows still more profoundly. Then he retires, walking backwards six steps, and bows once more. Then he returns to his place.

After this the teachers, by parties of six, perform the same beautiful ceremony. When all have saluted the portrait of His Imperial Majesty, the Governor ascends the platform and makes a few eloquent remarks to the students about their duty to their Emperor, to their country, and to their teachers. Then the anthem is sung again; and all disperse to amuse themselves for the rest of the day.

11

MARCH 1, 1891. The majority of the students of the Jinjō Chūgakkō are day-scholars only (*externes*, as we would say in France): they go to school in the morning, take their noon meal at home, and return at one o'clock to attend the brief afternoon classes. All the city students live with their own families; but there are many boys from remote country districts who have no city relatives, and for such the school furnishes boarding houses, where a wholesome moral discipline is maintained by special masters. They are free, however, if they have sufficient means, to choose another boarding-house (provided it be a respectable one), or to find quarters in some good family; but few adopt either course.

I doubt whether in any other country the cost of education - education of the most excellent and advanced kind - is so little as in Japan. The Izumo student is able to live at a figure so far below the Occidental idea of necessary expenditure that the mere statement of it can scarcely fail to surprise the reader. A sum equal in American money to about twenty dollars supplies him with board and lodging *for one year*. The whole of his expenses, including school fees, are about seven dollars a month. For his room and three ample meals a day he pays every four weeks only one yen eighty-five sen - not much more than a dollar-and-a-half in American currency. If very, very poor, he will not be obliged to wear a uniform; but nearly all students of the higher classes do wear uniforms, as the cost of a complete uniform, including cap and shoes of leather, is only about three-and-a-half yen for the cheaper quality. Those who do not wear leather shoes, however, are required, while in the school, to exchange their noisy wooden *geta* for *zori* or light straw sandals.

12

But the mental education so admirably imparted in an ordinary middle school is not, after all, so cheaply acquired by the student as might be imagined from the cost of living and the low rate of school fees. For Nature exacts a heavier school fee, and rigidly collects her debt - in human life.

To understand why, one should remember that the modern knowledge which the modern Izumo student must acquire upon a diet of boiled rice and bean-curd was discovered, developed, and synthesised by minds strengthened upon a costly diet of flesh. National underfeeding offers the

220

most cruel problem which the educators of Japan must solve in order that she may become fully able to assimilate the civilisation we have thrust upon her. As Herbert Spencer has pointed out, the degree of human energy, physical or intellectual, must depend upon the nutritiveness of food; and history shows that the well-fed races have been the energetic and the dominant. Perhaps mind will rule in the future of nations; but mind is a mode of force, and must be fed - through the stomach. The thoughts that have shaken the world were never framed upon bread and water: they were created by beefsteak and mutton-chops, by ham and eggs, by pork and puddings, and were stimulated by generous wines, strong ales, and strong coffee. And science also teaches us that the growing child or youth requires an even more nutritious diet than the adult, and that the student especially needs strong nourishment to repair the physical waste involved by brain-exertion.

And what is the waste entailed upon the Japanese schoolboy's system by study? It is certainly greater than that which the system of the European or American student must suffer at the same period of life. Seven years of study are required to give the Japanese youth merely the necessary knowledge of his own triple system of ideographs - or, in less accurate but plainer speech, the enormous alphabet of his native literature. That literature, also, he must study, and the art of two forms of his language - the written and the spoken: likewise, of course, he must learn native history and native morals. Besides these Oriental studies, his course includes foreign history, geography, arithmetic, astronomy, physics, geometry, natural history, agriculture, chemistry, drawing, and mathematics. Worst of all, he must learn English - a language of which the difficulty to the Japanese cannot be even faintly imagined by any one unfamiliar with the construction of the native tongue - a language so different from his own that the very simplest Japanese phrase cannot be intelligibly rendered into English by a literal translation of the words or even the form of the thought. And he must learn all this upon a diet no English boy could live on; and always thinly clad in his poor cotton dress without even a fire in his schoolroom during the terrible winter, only a hibachi containing a few lumps of glowing charcoal in a bed of ashes.[6] Is it to be wondered at that even those Japanese students who pass successfully through all the educational courses the Empire can open to them can only in rare instances show results of their long training as large as those manifested by students of the West? Better conditions are coming; but at present, under the new strain, young bodies and young minds too often give way. And those who break down are not the dullards, but the pride of schools, the captains of classes.

13

Yet, so far as the finances of the school allow, everything possible is done to make the students both healthy and happy - to furnish them with ample opportunities both for physical exercise and for mental enjoyment. Though the course of study is severe, the hours are not long: and one of the daily five is devoted to military drill, made more interesting to the lads by the use of real rifles and bayonets, furnished by government. There is a fine gymnastic ground near the school, furnished with trapezes, parallel bars, vaulting horses, etc.; and there are two masters of gymnastics attached to the Middle School alone. There are row-boats, in which the boys can take their pleasure on the beautiful lake whenever the weather permits.

There is an excellent fencing-school conducted by the Governor himself, who, although so heavy a man, is reckoned one of the best fencers of his own generation. The style taught is the old one, requiring the use of both hands to wield the sword; thrusting is little attempted, it is nearly all heavy slashing. The foils are made of long splinters of bamboo tied together so as to form something resembling elongated fasces: masks and wadded coats protect the head and body, for the blows given are heavy. This sort of fencing requires considerable agility, and gives more active exercise than our severer Western styles. Yet another form of healthy exercise consists of long journeys on foot to famous places. Special holidays are allowed for these. The students march out of town in military order, accompanied by some of their favourite teachers, and perhaps a servant to cook for them. Thus they may travel for a hundred, or even a hundred and fifty miles and back; but if the journey is to be a very long one, only the strong lads are allowed to go. They walk in *waraji*, the true straw sandal, closely tied to the naked foot, which it leaves perfectly supple and free, without blistering or producing corns. They sleep at night in Buddhist temples; and their cooking is done in the open fields, like that of soldiers in camp.

For those little inclined to such sturdy exercise there is a school library which is growing every year. There is also a monthly school magazine, edited and published by the boys. And there is a Students' Society, at whose regular meetings debates are held upon all conceivable subjects of interest to students.

14

APRIL 4, 1891. The students of the third, fourth, and fifth year classes write for me once a week brief English compositions upon easy themes which I select for them. As a rule the themes are Japanese. Considering the immense difficulty of the English language to Japanese students, the ability of some of my boys to express their thoughts in it is astonishing. Their compositions have also another interest for me as revelations, not of individual character, but of national sentiment, or of aggregate sentiment of some sort or other. What seems to me most surprising in the compositions of the average Japanese student is that they have no personal *cachet* at all. Even the handwriting of twenty English compositions will be found to have a curious family resemblance; and striking exceptions are too few to affect the rule. Here is one of the best compositions on my table, by a student at the head of his class. Only a few idiomatic errors have been corrected:

'THE MOON'

'The Moon appears melancholy to those who are sad, and joyous to those who are happy. The Moon makes memories of home come to those who travel, and creates homesickness. So when the Emperor Godaigo, having been banished to Oki by the traitor Hojō, beheld the moonlight upon the seashore, he cried out, "*The Moon is heartless*"!

'The sight of the Moon *makes an immeasurable feeling in our hearts* when we look up at it through the clear air of a beauteous night.

'Our hearts ought to be pure and calm like the light of the Moon.

'Poets often compare the Moon to a Japanese [metal] mirror (*kagami*); and indeed its shape is the same when it is full.

'The refined man amuses himself with the Moon. He seeks some house looking upon water, to watch the Moon, and to make verses about it.

'The best places from which to see the Moon are Tsuki-gashi, and the mountain Obasute.

'The light of the Moon shines alike upon foul and pure, upon high and low. That beautiful Lamp is neither yours nor mine, but everybody's.

'When we look at the Moon we should remember that its waxing and its waning are the signs of the truth that the culmination of all things is likewise the beginning of their decline.'

Any person totally unfamiliar with Japanese educational methods might presume that the foregoing composition shows some original power of thought and imagination. But this is not the case. I found the same thoughts and comparisons in thirty other compositions upon the same subject. Indeed, the compositions of any number of middle-school students upon the same subject are certain to be very much alike in idea and sentiment - though they are none the less charming for that. As a rule the Japanese student shows little originality in the line of imagination. His imagination was made for him long centuries ago - partly in China, partly in his native land. From his childhood he is trained to see and to feel Nature exactly in the manner of those wondrous artists who, with a few swift brush-strokes, fling down upon a sheet of paper the colour-sensation of a chilly dawn, a fervid noon, an autumn evening. Through all his boyhood he is taught to commit to memory the most beautiful thoughts and comparisons to be found in his ancient native literature. Every boy has thus learned that the vision of Fuji against the blue resembles a white half-opened fan, hanging inverted in the sky. Every boy knows that cherry-trees in full blossom look as if the most delicate of flushed summer clouds were caught in their branches. Every boy knows the comparison between the falling of certain leaves on snow and the casting down of texts upon a sheet of white paper with a brush. Every boy and girl knows the verses comparing the print of cat's-feet on snow to plum-flowers,[7] and that comparing the impression of *bokkuri* on snow to the Japanese character for the number 'two'.[8] These were thoughts of old, old poets; and it would be very hard to invent prettier ones. Artistic power in composition is chiefly shown by the correct memorising and clever combination of these old thoughts.

And the students have been equally well trained to discover a moral in almost everything, animate or inanimate. I have tried them with a hundred subjects - Japanese subjects - for composition; I have never found them to fail in discovering a moral, when the theme was a native one. If I suggested 'Fireflies', they at once approved the topic, and wrote for me the story of that Chinese student who, being too poor to pay for a lamp, imprisoned many fireflies in a paper lantern, and thus was able to obtain light enough to study after dark, and to become eventually a great scholar. If I said 'Frogs', they wrote for me the legend of Ono-no-Tofu, who was persuaded to become a learned celebrity by witnessing the tireless perseverance of a frog trying to leap up to a willow-branch. I subjoin a few specimens of the moral ideas which I thus evoked. I have corrected some common mistakes in the originals, but have suffered a few singularities to stand:

'THE BOTAN'

'The *botan* [Japanese peony] is large and beautiful to see; but it has a disagreeable smell. This should make us remember that what is only outwardly beautiful in human society should not attract us. *To be attracted by beauty only may lead us into fearful and fatal misfortune.* The best place to see the *botan* is the island of Daikonshima in the lake Nakaumi. There in the season of its flowering all the island is red with its blossoms.'

'THE DRAGON'

'When the Dragon tries to ride the clouds and come into heaven there happens immediately a furious storm. When the Dragon dwells on the ground it is supposed to take the form of a stone or other object; but when it wants to rise it calls a cloud. Its body is composed of parts of many animals. It has the eyes of a tiger and the horns of a deer and the body of a crocodile and the claws of an eagle and two trunks like the trunk of an elephant. It has a moral *We should try to be like the dragon, and find out and adopt all the good qualities of others*.'

At the close of this essay on the dragon is a note to the teacher, saying: 'I believe not there is any Dragon. But there are many stories and curious pictures about Dragon.'

'MOSQUITOES'

'On summer nights we hear the sound of faint voices: and little things come and sting our bodies very violently. We call them *ka* - in English "mosquitoes". I think the sting is useful for us, because if we begin to sleep, the *ka* shall come and sting us, uttering a small voice - *then we shall be bringed back to study by the sting*.'

The following, by a lad of sixteen, is submitted only as a characteristic expression of half-formed ideas about a less familiar subject.

'EUROPEAN AND JAPANESE CUSTOMS'

'Europeans wear very narrow clothes and they wear shoes always in the house. Japanese wear clothes which are very *lenient* and they do not *shoe* except when they walk *out-of-the-door*.

'What we think very strange is that in Europe every wife loves her husband more than her parents. In Nippon there is no wife who more loves not her parents than her husband.

'And Europeans walk out in the road with their wives, which we utterly refuse to, except on the festival of Hachiman.

'The Japanese woman is treated by man as a servant, while the European woman is respected as a master. I think these customs are both bad.

'We think it is very much trouble to treat European ladies; and we do not know why ladies are so much respected by Europeans.'

Conversation in the class-room about foreign subjects is often equally amusing and suggestive:

'Teacher, I have been told that if a European and his father and his wife were all to fall into the sea together, and that he only could swim, he would try to save his wife first. Would he really?'

'Probably', I reply.

'But why?'

'One reason is that Europeans consider it a man's duty to help the weaker first - especially women and children.'

'And does a European love his wife more than his father and mother?'

'Not always - but generally, perhaps, he does.'

'Why, Teacher, according to our ideas that is very immoral.'

...'Teacher, how do European women carry their babies?'

'In their arms.'

'Very tiring! And how far can a woman walk carrying a baby in her arms?'

'A strong woman can walk many miles with a child in her arms.'

'But she cannot use her hands while she is carrying a baby that way, can she?'

'Not very well.'

'Then it is a very bad way to carry babies', etc.

15

MAY 1, 1891. My favourite students often visit me of afternoons. They first send me their cards, to announce their presence. On being told to come in they leave their footgear on the doorstep, enter my little study, prostrate themselves; and we all squat down together on the floor, which is in all Japanese houses like a soft mattress. The servant brings *zabuton* or small cushions to kneel upon, and cakes, and tea.

To sit as the Japanese do requires practice; and some Europeans can never acquire the habit. To acquire it, indeed, one must become accustomed to wearing Japanese costume. But once the habit of thus sitting has been formed, one finds it the most natural and easy of positions, and assumes it by preference for eating, reading, smoking, or chatting. It is not to be recommended, perhaps, for writing with a European pen - as the motion in our Occidental style of writing is from the supported wrist; but it is the best posture for writing with the Japanese fude, in using which the whole arm is unsupported, and the motion from the elbow. After having become habituated to Japanese habits for more than a year, I must confess that I find it now somewhat irksome to use a chair.

When we have all greeted each other, and taken our places upon the kneeling cushions, a little polite silence ensues, which I am the first to break. Some of the lads speak a good deal of English. They understand me well when I pronounce every word slowly and distinctly, using simple phrases, and avoiding idioms. When a word with which they are not familiar must be used, we refer to a good English-Japanese dictionary, which gives each vernacular meaning both in the kana and in the Chinese characters.

Usually my young visitors stay a long time, and their stay is rarely tiresome. Their conversation and their thoughts are of the simplest and frankest. They do not come to learn: they know that to ask their teacher to teach out of school would be unjust. They speak chiefly of things which they think have some particular interest for me. Sometimes they scarcely speak at all, but appear to sink into a sort of happy reverie. What they come really for is the quiet pleasure of sympathy. Not an intellectual sympathy, but the sympathy of pure good-will: the simple pleasure of being quite comfortable with a friend. They peep at my books and pictures; and sometimes they bring books and pictures to show me, delightfully queer things - family heirlooms which I regret much that I cannot buy. They also like to look at my garden, and enjoy all that is in it even more than I. Often they bring me gifts of flowers. Never by any possible chance are they troublesome, impolite, curious, or even talkative. Courtesy in its utmost possible exquisiteness - an exquisiteness of which even the French have no conception - seems natural to the Izumo boy as the colour of his hair or the tint of his skin. Nor is he less kind than courteous. To contrive pleasurable surprises for me is one of the particular delights of my boys; and they either bring or cause to be brought to the house all sorts of strange things.

Of all the strange or beautiful things which I am thus privileged to examine, none gives me so much pleasure as a certain wonderful *kakemono* of Amida Nyorai. It is rather a large picture, and has been borrowed from a priest that I may see it. The Buddha stands in the attitude of exhortation, with one hand uplifted. Behind his head a huge moon makes an aureole; and across the face of that moon stream winding lines of thinnest cloud. Beneath his feet like a rolling of smoke, curl heavier and darker clouds. Merely as a work of colour and design, the thing is a marvel. But the real wonder of it is not in colour or design at all. Minute examination reveals the astonishing fact that every shadow and clouding is formed by a fairy text of Chinese characters so minute that only a keen eye can discern them; and this text is the entire text of two famed sutras - the Kwammuryō-ju-kyō and the Amida-kyō - 'text no larger than the limbs of fleas'. And all the strong dark lines of the figure, such as the seams of the Buddha's robe, are formed by the characters of the holy invocation of the Shin-shū sect, repeated thousands of times: '*Namu Amida Butsu*'! Infinite patience, tireless silent labour of loving faith, in some dim temple, long ago.

Another day one of my boys persuades his father to let him bring to my house a wonderful statue of Kōshi (Confucius), made, I am told, in China, towards the close of the period of the Ming dynasty. I am also assured it is the first time the statue has ever been removed from the family residence to be shown to anyone. Previously, whoever desired to pay it reverence had to visit the house. It is truly a beautiful bronze. The figure of a smiling, bearded old man, with fingers uplifted and lips apart as if discoursing. He wears quaint Chinese shoes, and his flowing robes are adorned with the figure of the mystic phoenix. The microscopic finish of detail seems indeed to reveal the wonderful cunning of a Chinese hand: each tooth, each hair, looks as though it had been made the subject of a special study.

Another student conducts me to the home of one of his relatives, that I may see a cat made of wood, said to have been chiselled by the famed Hidari Jingorō - a cat crouching and watching, and so life-like that real cats have been known to put up their backs and spit at it.

16

Nevertheless I have a private conviction that some old artists even now living in Matsue could make a still more wonderful cat. Among these is the venerable Arakawa Junosuke, who wrought many rare things for the *daimyō* of Izumo in the Tempō era, and whose acquaintance I have been enabled to make through my school-friends. One evening he brings to my house something very odd to show me, concealed in his sleeve. It is a doll: just a small carven and painted head without a body - the body being represented by a tiny robe only, attached to the neck. Yet as Arakawa Junosuke manipulates it, it seems to become alive. The back of its head is like the back of a very old man's head; but its face is the face of an amused child, and there is scarcely any forehead nor any evidence of a thinking disposition. And whatever way the head is turned, it looks so funny that one cannot help laughing at it. It represents a *kirakubo* - what we might call in English 'a jolly old boy' - one who is naturally too hearty and too innocent to feel trouble of any sort. It is not an original, but a model of a very famous original, whose history is recorded in a faded scroll which Arakawa takes out of his other sleeve, and which a friend translates for me. This little history throws a curious light upon the simple-hearted ways of Japanese life and thought in other centuries:

> *Yo no naka wo*
> *Kiraku ni kurase*
> *Nani goto mo*
> *Omoeba omou*
> *Omowaneba koso.*[9]

'On the death of the Emperor this doll became the property of Prince Konoye, in whose family it is said to be still preserved.

'About one hundred and seven years ago, the then Ex-Empress, whose posthumous name is Sei-Kwa-Mon-Yin, borrowed the doll from Prince Konoye, and ordered a copy of it to be made. This copy she kept always beside her, and was very fond of it.

'After the death of the good Empress this doll was given to a lady of the court, whose family name is not recorded. Afterwards this lady, for reasons which are not known, cut off her hair and became a Buddhist nun, taking the name of Shingyō-in.

'And one who knew the Nun Shingyō-in - a man whose name was Kondo-ju-haku-in-Hokyō, had the honour of receiving the doll as a gift.

'Now I, who write this document, at one time fell sick; and my sickness was caused by despondency. And my friend Kondo-ju-haku-in-Hokyō, coming to see me, said: "I have in my house something which will make you well." And he went home and, presently returning, brought to me this doll, and lent it to me, putting it by my pillow that I might see it and laugh at it.

'Afterwards, I myself, having called upon the Nun Shingyō-in, whom I now also have the honour to know, wrote down the history of the doll, and made a poem thereupon.' (Dated about ninety years ago: no signature.)

17

JUNE 1, 1891. I find among the students a healthy tone of scepticism in regard to certain forms of popular belief. Scientific education is rapidly destroying credulity in old superstitions yet current among the unlettered, and especially among the peasantry - as, for instance, faith in *mamori* and *ofuda*. The outward forms of Buddhism - its images, its relics, its commoner practices - affect the average student very little. He is not, as a foreigner may be, interested in iconography, or religious folk-lore, or the comparative study of religions; and in nine cases out of ten he is rather ashamed of the signs and tokens of popular faith all around him. But the deeper religious sense, which underlies all symbolism, remains with him; and the Monistic Idea in Buddhism is being strengthened and expanded, rather than weakened, by the new education. What is true of the effort of the public schools upon the lower Buddhism is equally true of its effect upon the lower Shinto. Shinto the students all sincerely are, or very nearly all; yet not as fervent worshippers of certain *kami*, but as rigid observers of what the higher Shinto signifies - loyalty, filial piety, obedience to parents, teachers, and superiors, and respect to ancestors. For Shinto means more than faith.

When, for the first time, I stood before the shrine of the Great Deity of Kitzuki, as the first Occidental to whom that privilege had been accorded, not without a sense of awe there came to me the thought: 'This is the Shrine of the Father of a Race; this is the symbolic centre of a nation's reverence for its past.' And I, too, paid reverence to the memory of the progenitor of this people.

As I then felt, so feels the intelligent student of the Meiji era whom education has lifted above the common plane of popular creeds. And Shinto also means for him - whether he reasons upon the question or not - all the ethics of the family, and all that spirit of loyalty which has become so innate that, at the call of duty, life itself ceases to have value save as an instrument for duty's accomplishment. As yet, this Orient little needs to reason about the origin of its loftier ethics. Imagine the musical sense in our own race so developed that a child could play a complicated instrument so soon as the little fingers gained sufficient force and flexibility to strike the notes. By some such comparison only can one obtain a just idea of what inherent religion and instinctive duty signify in Izumo.

Of the rude and aggressive form of scepticism so common in the

Occident, which is the natural reaction after sudden emancipation from superstitious belief, I find no trace among my students. But such sentiment may be found elsewhere, especially in Tokyo, among the university students, one of whom, upon hearing the tones of a magnificent temple bell, exclaimed to a friend of mine: *'Is it not a shame that in this nineteenth century we must still hear such a sound?'*

For the benefit of curious travellers, however, I may here take occasion to observe that to talk Buddhism to Japanese gentlemen of the new school is in just as bad taste as to talk Christianity at home to men of that class whom knowledge has placed above creeds and forms. There are, of course, Japanese scholars willing to aid researches of foreign scholars in religion or in folk-lore; but these specialists do not undertake to gratify idle curiosity of the 'globe-trotting' description. I may also say that the foreigner desirous to learn the religious ideas or superstitions of the common people must obtain them from the people themselves, not from the educated classes.

18

Among all my favourite students - two or three from each class - I cannot decide whom I like the best. Each has a particular merit of his own. But I think the names and faces of those of whom I am about to speak will longest remain vivid in my remembrance - Ishihara, Otani-Masanobu, Adzukizawa, Yokogi, Shida.

Ishihara is a *samurai*, a very influential lad in his class because of his uncommon force of character. Compared with others, he has a somewhat brusque, independent manner, pleasing, however, by its honest manliness. He says everything he thinks, and precisely in the tone that he thinks it, even to the degree of being a little embarrassing sometimes. He does not hesitate, for example, to find fault with a teacher's method of explanation, and to insist upon a more lucid one. He has criticised me more than once; but I never found that he was wrong. We like each other very much. He often brings me flowers.

One day that he had brought two beautiful sprays of plum-blossoms, he said to me:

'I saw you bow before our Emperor's picture at the ceremony on the birthday of His Majesty. You are not like a former English teacher we had.'

'How.'

'He said we were savages.'

'Why?'

'He said there is nothing respectable except God - *his* God - and that only vulgar and ignorant people respect anything else.'

'Where did he come from?'

'He was a Christian clergyman, and said he was an English subject.'

'But if he was an English subject, he was bound to respect Her Majesty the Queen. He could not even enter the office of a British consul without removing his hat.'

'I don't know what he did in the country he came from. But that was what he said. Now we think we should love and honour our Emperor.

We think it is a duty. We think it is a joy. We think it is happiness to be able to give our lives for our Emperor.[10] But he said we were only savages - ignorant savages. What do you think of that?'

'I think, my dear lad, that he himself was a savage - a vulgar, ignorant, savage bigot. I think it is your highest social duty to honour your Emperor, to obey his laws, and to be ready to give your blood whenever he may require it of you for the sake of Japan. I think it is your duty to respect the gods of your fathers, the religion of your country - even if you yourself cannot believe all that others believe. And I think, also, that it is your duty, for your Emperor's sake and for your country's sake, to resent any such wicked and vulgar language as that you have told me of, no matter by whom uttered.'

Masanobu visits me seldom and always comes alone. A slender, handsome lad, with rather feminine features, reserved and perfectly self-possessed in manner, refined. He is somewhat serious, does not often smile; and I never heard him laugh. He has risen to the head of his class, and appears to remain there without any extraordinary effort. Much of his leisure time he devotes to botany - collecting and classifying plants. He is a musician, like all the male members of his family. He plays a variety of instruments never seen or heard of in the West, including flutes of marble, flutes of ivory, flutes of bamboo of wonderful shapes and tones, and that shrill Chinese instrument called *shō* - a sort of mouth-organ consisting of seventeen tubes of different lengths fixed in a silver frame. He first explained to me the uses in temple music of the *taiko* and *shōko*, which are drums; of the flutes called *fei* or *teki*; of the flageolet termed *hichiriki*; and of the *kakko*, which is a little drum shaped like a spool with very narrow waist. On great Buddhist festivals, Masanobu and his father and his brothers are the musicians in the temple services, and they play the strange music called *Ōjō* and *Batto* - music which at first no Western ear can feel pleasure in, but which, when often heard, becomes comprehensible, and is found to possess a weird charm of its own. When Masanobu comes to the house, it is usually in order to invite me to attend some Buddhist or Shinto festival (*matsuri*) which he knows will interest me.

Adzukizawa bears so little resemblance to Masanobu that one might suppose the two belonged to totally different races. Adzukizawa is large, raw-boned, heavy-looking, with a face singularly like that of a North American Indian. His people are not rich; he can afford few pleasures which cost money, except one - buying books. Even to be able to do this he works in his leisure hours to earn money. He is a perfect bookworm, a natural-born researcher, a collector of curious documents, a haunter of all the queer second-hand stores in Teramachi and other streets where old manuscripts or prints are on sale as waste paper. He is an omnivorous reader, and a perpetual borrower of volumes, which he always returns in perfect condition after having copied what he deemed of most value to him. But his special delight is philosophy and the history of philosophers in all countries. He has read various epitomes of the history of philosophy in the Occident, and everything of modern philosophy which has been translated into Japanese, including Spencer's *First Principles* . I have been able to introduce him to Lewes and John Fiske, both of which he appreciates - although the strain of studying philosophy in English is no small one. Happily he is so strong that no amount of study is likely to injure his health, and his nerves are tough as wire. He is quite an ascetic withal. As it is the Japanese custom to set cakes and tea before visitors, I always have both in readiness, and an especially fine quality of *kwashi* made at Kitzuki, of which the students are very fond. Adzukizawa alone refuses to taste cakes or confectionery of any kind, saying: 'As I am the youngest brother, I must begin to earn my own living soon. I shall have to endure much hardship. And if I allow myself to like dainties now, I shall only suffer more later on.' Adzukizawa has seen much of human life and character. He is naturally observant; and he has managed in some extraordinary way to learn the history of everybody in Matsue. He has brought me old tattered prints to prove that the opinions now held by our director are diametrically opposed to the opinions he advocated fourteen years ago in a public address. I asked the director about it. He laughed and said, 'Of course that is Adzukizawa! But he is right: I was very young then.' And I wonder if Adzukizawa was ever young.

Yokogi, Adzukizawa's dearest friend, is a very rare visitor; for he is always studying at home. He is always first in his class - the third year class - while Adzukizawa is fourth. Adzukizawa's account of the beginning of their acquaintance is this: 'I watched him when he came and saw that he spoke very little, walked very quickly, and looked straight into everybody's eyes. So I knew he had a particular character. I like to know people with a particular character.' Adzukizawa was perfectly right: under a very gentle exterior, Yokogi has an extremely strong character. He is the son of a carpenter: and his parents could not afford to send him to the Middle School. But he had shown such exceptional qualities while in the Elementary School that a wealthy man became interested in him, and offered to pay for his education.[11] He is now the pride of the school. He has a remarkably placid face, with peculiarly long eyes, and a delicious smile. In class he is always asking intelligent questions - questions so original that I am sometimes extremely puzzled how to answer them; and he never ceases to ask until the explanation is quite satisfactory to himself. He never cares about the opinion of his comrades if he thinks he is right. On one occasion when the whole class refused to attend the lectures of a new teacher of physics, Yokogi alone refused to act with them, arguing that although the teacher was not all that could be desired, there was no immediate possibility of his removal, and no just reason for making unhappy a man who, though unskilled, was sincerely doing his best. Adzukizawa finally stood by him. These two alone attended the lectures until the remainder of the students, two weeks later, found that Yokogi's views were rational. On another occasion when some vulgar proselytism was attempted by a Christian missionary, Yokogi went boldly to the proselytiser's house, argued with him on the morality of his effort, and reduced him to silence. Some of his comrades praised his cleverness in the argument. 'I am not clever', he made answer: 'it does not require cleverness to argue against what is morally wrong; it requires only the knowledge that one is morally right.' At least such is about the translation of what he said as told me by Adzukizawa.

Shida, another visitor, is a very delicate, sensitive boy, whose soul is full of art. He is very skilful at drawing and painting; and he has a wonderful set of picture-books by the old Japanese masters. The last time he came he brought some prints to show me - rare ones - fairy maidens and ghosts. As I looked at his beautiful pale face and weirdly frail fingers, I could not help fearing for him - fearing that he might soon become a little ghost.

I have not seen him now for more than two months. He has been very, very ill; and his lungs are so weak that the doctor has forbidden him to converse. But Adzukizawa has been to visit him, and brings me this translation of a Japanese letter which the sick boy wrote and pasted upon the wall above his bed:

'Thou, my Lord-Soul, dost govern me. Thou knowest that I cannot now govern myself. Deign, I pray thee, to let me be cured speedily. Do not suffer me to speak much. Make me to obey in all things the command of the physician.

'This ninth day of the eleventh month of the twenty-fourth year of Meiji.

'From the sick body of Shida to his Soul.'

19

SEPTEMBER 4, 1891. The long summer vacation is over; a new school year begins.

There have been many changes. Some of the boys I taught are dead. Others have graduated and gone away from Matsue forever. Some teachers, too, have left the school, and their places have been filled; and there is a new Director.

And the dear good Governor has gone - been transferred to cold Niigata in the north-west. It was a promotion. But he had ruled Izumo for seven years, and everybody loved him, especially, perhaps the students, who looked upon him as a father. All the population of the city crowded to the river to bid him farewell. The streets through which he passed on his way to take the steamer, the bridge, the wharves, even the roofs were thronged with multitudes eager to see his face for the last time. Thousands were weeping. And as the steamer glided from the wharf such a cry arose - '*A-a-a-a-a-a-a-a-a-a-a*'! It was intended for a cheer, but it seemed to me the cry of a whole city sorrowing, and so plaintive that I hope never to hear such a cry again.

The names and faces of the younger classes are all strange to me. Doubtless this was why the sensation of my first day's teaching in the school came back to me with extraordinary vividness when I entered the class-room of First Division A this morning.

Strangely pleasant is the first sensation of a Japanese class, as you look over the ranges of young faces before you. There is nothing in them familiar to inexperienced Western eyes; yet there is an indescribable pleasant something common to all. Those traits have nothing incisive, nothing forcible: compared with Occidental faces they seem but 'half-sketched', so soft their outlines are - indicating neither aggressiveness nor shyness, neither eccentricity nor sympathy, neither curiosity nor indifference. Some, although faces of youths well grown, have a childish freshness and frankness indescribable; some are as uninteresting as others are attractive; a few are beautifully feminine. But all are equally characterised by a singular placidity, expressing neither love nor hate nor anything save perfect repose and gentleness, like the dreamy placidity of Buddhist images. At a later day you will no longer recognise this aspect of passionless composure: with growing acquaintance each face will become more and more individualised for you by characteristics before imperceptible. But the recollection of that first impression will remain with you; and the time will come when you will find, by many varied experiences, how strangely it foreshadowed something in Japanese character to be fully learned only after years of familiarity. You will recognise in the memory of that first impression one glimpse of the race-soul, with its impersonal lovableness and its impersonal weaknesses - one glimpse of the nature of a life in which the Occidental, dwelling alone, feels a psychic comfort comparable only to the nervous relief of suddenly emerging from some stifling atmospheric pressure into thin, clear, free living air.

20

Was it not the eccentric Fourier who wrote about the horrible faces of 'the *civilisés*'? Whoever it was, would have found seeming confirmation of his physiognomical theory could he have known the effect produced by the first sight of European faces in the most eastern East. What we are taught at home to consider handsome, interesting, or characteristic in physiognomy does not produce the same impression in China or Japan. Shades of facial expression familiar to us as letters of our own alphabet are not perceived at all in Western features by these Orientals at first acquaintance. What they discern at once is the race-characteristic, not the individuality. The evolutional meaning of the deep-set Western eye, protruding brow, accipitrine nose, ponderous jaw - symbols of aggressive force and habit - was revealed to the gentler race by the same sort of intuition through which a tame animal immediately comprehends the dangerous nature of the first predatory enemy which it sees. To Europeans the smooth-featured, slender, low-statured Japanese seemed like boys; and 'boy' is the term by which the native attendant of a Yokohama merchant is still called. To Japanese the first red-haired, rowdy, drunken European sailors seemed fiends, *shōjō*, demons of the sea; and by the Chinese the Occidentals are still called 'foreign devils'. The great stature and massive strength and fierce gait of foreigners in Japan enhanced the strange impression created by their faces. Children cried for fear on seeing them pass through the streets. And in remoter districts, Japanese children are still apt to cry at the first sight of a European or American face.

A lady of Matsue related in my presence this curious souvenir of her childhood: 'When I was a very little girl', she said, 'our *daimyō* hired a foreigner to teach the military art. My father and a great many *samurai* went to receive the foreigner; and all the people lined the streets to see, for no foreigner had ever come to Izumo before; and we all went to look.

The foreigner came by ship: there were no steamboats here then. He was very tall, and walked quickly with long steps; and the children began to cry at the sight of him, because his face was not like the faces of the people of Nihon. My little brother cried out loud, and hid his face in mother's robe; and mother reproved him and said: "This foreigner is a very good man who has come here to serve our prince; and it is very disrespectful to cry at seeing him." But he still cried. I was not afraid; and I looked up at the foreigner's face as he came and smiled. He had a great beard; and I thought his face was good though it seemed to me a very strange face and stern. Then he stopped and smiled too, and put something in my hand, and touched my head and face very softly with his great fingers, and said something I could not understand, and went away. After he had gone I looked at what he put into my hand and found that it was a pretty little glass to look through. If you put a fly under that glass it looks quite big. At that time I thought the glass was a very wonderful thing. I have it still.' She took from a drawer in the room and placed before me a tiny, dainty pocket-microscope.

The hero of this little incident was a French military officer. His services were necessarily dispensed with on the abolition of the feudal system. Memories of him still linger in Matsue; and old people remember a popular snatch about him - a sort of rapidly-vociferated rigmarole, supposed to be an imitation of his foreign speech.

> *Tōjin no negoto niwa kinkarakuri*
> *medagashō,*
> *Saiboji ga shimpeishite harishite keisan,*
> *Hanryō na* 'Sacr-r-r-r-r-é-na-nom-da-
> Jiu!'

21

NOVEMBER 2, 1891. Shida will never come to school again. He sleeps under the shadow of the cedars, in the old cemetery of Tōkōji. Yokogi, at the memorial service, read a beautiful address (*saibun*) to the soul of his dead comrade.

But Yokogi himself is down. And I am very much afraid for him. He is suffering from some affection of the brain, brought on, the doctor says, by studying a great deal too hard. Even if he gets well, he will always have to be careful. Some of us hope much; for the boy is vigorously built and so young. Strong Sakane burst a blood-vessel last month and is now well. So we trust that Yokogi may rally. Adzukizawa daily brings news of his friend.

But the rally never comes. Some mysterious spring in the mechanism of the young life has been broken. The mind lives only in brief intervals between long hours of unconsciousness. Parents watch, and friends, for these living moments to whisper caressing things, or to ask: 'Is there anything thou dost wish'? And one night the answer comes:

'Yes: I want to go to the school; I want to see the school.'

Then they wonder if the fine brain has not wholly given way, while they make answer:

'It is midnight past, and there is no moon. And the night is cold.'

'No; I can see by the stars - I want to see the school again.'

They make kindliest protests in vain: the dying boy only repeats, with the plaintive persistence of a last wish -

'I want to see the school again; I want to see it now.'

So there is a murmured consultation in the neighbouring room; and *tansu* (drawers) are unlocked, warm garments prepared. Then Fusaichi, the strong servant, enters with lantern lighted, and cries out in his kind rough voice:

'Master Tomi will go to the school upon my back: 'tis but a little way; he shall see the school again.'

Carefully they wrap up the lad in wadded robes; then he puts his arms about Fusaichi's shoulders like a child; and the strong servant bears him lightly through the wintry street; and the father hurries beside Fusaichi, bearing the lantern. And it is not far to the school, over the little bridge.

The huge dark gray building looks almost black in the night; but Yokogi can see. He looks at the windows of his own class-room; at the roofed side-door where each morning for four happy years he used to exchange his *getas* for soundless sandals of straw; at the lodge of the slumbering *kodzukai*;[12] at the silhouette of the bell hanging black in its little turret against the stars.

Then he murmurs:

'I can remember all now. I had forgotten - so sick I was. I remember everything again. Oh, Fusaichi, you are very good. I am so glad to have seen the school again.'

And they hasten back through the long void streets.

22

NOVEMBER 26, 1891. Yokogi will be buried tomorrow evening beside his comrade Shida.

When a poor person is about to die, friends and neighbours come to the house and do all they can to help the family. Some bear the tidings to distant relatives; others prepare all necessary things; others, when the death has been announced, summon the Buddhist priests.[13]

It is said that the priests know always of a parishioner's death at night, before any messenger is sent to them; for the soul of the dead knocks heavily, once, upon the door of the family temple. Then the priests arise and robe themselves, and when the messenger comes make answer: 'We know: we are ready.'

Meanwhile the body is carried out before the family *butsudan*, and laid upon the floor. No pillow is placed under the head. A naked sword is laid across the limbs to keep evil spirits away. The doors of the *butsudan* are opened; and tapers are lighted before the tablets of the ancestors; and incense is burned. All friends send gifts of incense. Wherefore a gift of incense, however rare and precious, given upon any other occasion, is held to be unlucky.

But the Shinto household shrine must be hidden from view with white paper; and the Shinto *ofuda* fastened upon the house door must be covered up during all the period of mourning.[14] And in all that time no member of the family may approach a Shinto temple, or pray to the *kami*, or even pass beneath a *torii*.

A screen (*biōbu*) is extended between the body and the principal entrance of the death chamber; and the *kaimyō*, inscribed upon a strip of white paper, is fastened upon the screen. If the dead be young the screen must be turned upside-down; but this is not done in the case of old people.

Friends pray beside the corpse. There a little box is placed, containing one thousand peas, to be used for counting during the recital of those one thousand pious invocations, which, it is believed, will improve the condition of the soul on its unfamiliar journey.

The priests come and recite the sutras; and then the body is prepared for burial. It is washed in warm water, and robed all in white. But the kimono of the dead is lapped over to the left side. Wherefore it is considered unlucky at any other time to fasten one's kimono thus, even by accident.

When the body has been put into that strange square coffin which looks something like a wooden palanquin, each relative puts also into the coffin some of his or her hair or nail parings, symbolising their blood. And six *rin* are also placed in the coffin, for the six Jizō who stand at the heads of the ways of the Six Shadowy Worlds.

The funeral procession forms at the family residence. A priest leads it, ringing a little bell; a boy bears the *ihai* of the newly dead. The van of the procession is wholly composed of men - relatives and friends. Some carry *hata*, white symbolic bannerets; some bear flowers; all carry paper lanterns - for in Izumo the adult dead are buried after dark: only children are buried by day. Next comes the *kwan* or coffin, borne palanquin-wise upon the shoulders of men of that pariah caste whose office it is to dig graves and assist at funerals. Lastly come the women mourners.

They are all white-hooded and white-robed from head to feet, like phantoms.[15] Nothing more ghostly than this sheeted train of an Izumo funeral procession, illuminated only by the glow of paper lanterns, can be imagined. It is a weirdness that, once seen, will often return in dreams.

At the temple the *kwan* is laid upon the pavement before the entrance; and another service is performed, with plaintive music and recitation of sutras. Then the procession forms again, winds once round the temple court, and takes its way to the cemetery. But the body is not buried until twenty-four hours later, lest the supposed dead should awake in the grave.

Corpses are seldom burned in Izumo. In this, as in other matters, the predominance of Shinto sentiment is manifest.

23

For the last time I see his face again, as he lies upon his bed of death, white-robed from neck to feet, white-girdled for his shadowy journey - but smiling with closed eyes in almost the same queer gentle way he was wont to smile at class on learning the explanation of some seeming riddle in our difficult English tongue. Only, methinks, the smile is sweeter now, as with sudden larger knowledge of more mysterious things. So smiles, through dusk of incense in the great temple of Tōkōji, the golden face of Buddha.

24

DECEMBER 23, 1891.The great bell of Tōkōji is booming for the memorial service - for the *tsuito-kwai* of Yokogi - slowly and regularly as a minute-gun. Peal on peal of its rich bronze thunder shakes over the lake, surges over the roofs of the town, and breaks in deep sobs of sound against the green circle of the hills.

It is a touching service, this *tsuito-kwai*, with quaint ceremonies which, although long since adopted into Japanese Buddhism, are of Chinese origin and are beautiful. It is also a costly ceremony; and the parents of Yokogi are very poor. But all the expenses have been paid by voluntary subscription of students and teachers. Priests from every great temple of the Zen sect in Izumo have assembled at Tōkōji. All the teachers of the city and all the students have entered the *hondo* of the huge temple, and taken their places to the right and to the left of the high altar, kneeling on the matted floor, and leaving, on the long broad steps without, a thousand shoes and sandals.

Before the main entrance, and facing the high shrine, a new *butsudan* has been placed, within whose open doors the *ihai* of the dead boy glimmers in lacquer and gilding. And upon a small stand before the *butsudan* have been placed an incense-vessel with bundles of senko-rods and offerings of fruits, confections, rice, and flowers. Tall and beautiful flower vases on each side of the *butsudan* are filled with blossoming sprays, exquisitely arranged. Before the *honzon* tapers burn in massive candelabra whose stems of polished brass are writhing monsters - the Dragon Ascending and the Dragon Descending; and incense curls up from vessels shaped like the sacred deer, like the symbolic tortoise, like the meditative stork of Buddhist legend. And beyond these, in the twilight of the vast alcove, the Buddha smiles the smile of Perfect Rest.

Between the *butsudan* and the *honzon* a little table has been placed; and on either side of it the priests kneel in ranks, facing each other: rows of polished heads, and splendours of vermilion silks and vestments gold-embroidered.

The great bell ceases to peal; the Segaki prayer, which is the prayer uttered when offerings of food are made to the spirits of the dead, is recited; and a sudden sonorous measured tapping, accompanied by a plaintive chant, begins the musical service. The tapping is the tapping of the *mokugyo* - a huge wooden fish-head, lacquered and gilded, like the

237

head of a dolphin grotesquely idealised - marking the time; and the chant is the chant of the Chapter of Kwannon in the Hokkekyō, with its magnificent invocation:

'O Thou whose eyes are clear, whose eyes are kind, whose eyes are full of pity and of sweetness - O Thou Lovely One, with thy beautiful face, with thy beautiful eyes -

'O Thou Pure One, whose luminosity is without spot, whose knowledge is without shadow - O Thou forever shining like that Sun whose glory no power may repel - Thou Sun-like in the course of Thy mercy, pourest Light upon the world!'

And while the voices of the leaders chant clear and high in vibrant unison, the multitude of the priestly choir recite in profoundest undertone the mighty verses; and the sound of their recitation is like the muttering of surf.

The *mokugyo* ceases its dull echoing, the impressive chant ends, and the leading officiants, one by one, high priests of famed temples, approach the ihai. Each bows low, ignites an incense-rod, and sets it upright in the little vase of bronze. Each at a time recites a holy verse of which the initial sound is the sound of a letter in the *kaimyō* of the dead boy; and these verses, uttered in the order of the characters upon the *ihai*, form the sacred Acrostic whose name is The Words of Perfume.

Then the priests retire to their places; and after a little silence begins the reading of the *saibun* - the reading of the addresses to the soul of the dead. The students speak first, one from each class, chosen by election. The elected rises, approaches the little table before the high altar, bows to the *honzon*, draws from his bosom a paper and reads it in those melodious, chanting, and plaintive tones which belong to the reading of Chinese texts. So each one tells the affection of the living to the dead, in words of loving grief and loving hope. And last among the students a gentle girl rises - a pupil of the Normal School - to speak in tones soft as a bird's. As each *saibun* is finished, the reader lays the written paper upon the table before the *honzon*, and bows, and retires.

It is now the turn of the teachers; and an old man takes his place at the little table - old Katayama, the teacher of Chinese, famed as a poet, adored as an instructor. And because the students all love him as a father, there is a strange intensity of silence as he begins - *Kō-Shimane-Ken-Jinjō-Chūgakkō-yo-nen-sei.*

'Here upon the twenty-third day of the twelfth month of the twenty-fourth year of Meiji, I, Katayama Shōkei, teacher of the Jinjō Chūgakkō of Shimane Ken, attending in great sorrow the holy service of the dead [*tsui-fuku*], do speak unto the soul of Yokogi Tomisaburo, my pupil.

'Having been, as thou knowest, for twice five years, at different periods, a teacher of the school, I have indeed met with not a few most excellent students. But very, very rarely in any school may the teacher find one such as thou - so patient and so earnest, so diligent and so careful in all things - so distinguished among thy comrades by the blameless conduct, observing every precept, never breaking a rule.

'Of old in the land of Kihoku, famed for its horses, whenever a horse of rarest breed could not be obtained, men were wont to say: "*There is no horse*". Still there are many fine lads among our students - many *ryume*, fine young steeds; but we have lost the best.

'To die at the age of seventeen - the best period of life for study -

even when of the Ten Steps thou hadst already ascended six! Sad is the thought; but sadder still to know that thy last illness was caused only by thine own tireless zeal of study. Even yet more sad our conviction that with those rare gifts, and with that rare character of thine, thou wouldst surely, in that career to which thou wast destined, have achieved good and great things, honouring the names of thine ancestors, couldst thou have lived to manhood.

'I see thee lifting thy hand to ask some question; then, bending above thy little desk to make note of all thy poor old teacher was able to tell thee. Again I see thee in the ranks, thy rifle upon thy shoulder, so bravely erect during the military exercises. Even now thy face is before me, with its smile, as plainly as if thou wert present in the body; thy voice I think I hear distinctly as though thou hadst but this instant finished speaking; yet I know that, except in memory, these never will be seen and heard again. O Heaven, why didst thou take away that dawning life from the world, and leave such a one as I - old Shōkei, feeble, decrepit, and of no more use?

'To thee my relation was indeed only that of teacher to pupil. Yet what is my distress! I have a son of twenty-four years; he is now far from me, in Yokohama. I know he is only a worthless youth;[16] yet never for so much as the space of one hour does the thought of him leave his old father's heart. Then how must the father and mother, the brothers and the sisters of this gentle and gifted youth feel now that he is gone! Only to think of it forces the tears from my eyes: I cannot speak - so full my heart is.

'*Aa! aa*! - thou hast gone from us; thou hast gone from us! Yet though thou hast died, thy earnestness, thy goodness, will long be honoured and told of as examples to the students of our school.

'Here, therefore, do we, thy teachers and they schoolmates, hold this service in behalf of thy spirit - with prayer and offerings. Deign thou, O gentle Soul, to honour our love by the acceptance of our humble gifts.'

Then a sound of sobbing is suddenly whelmed by the resonant booming of the great fish's head, as the high-pitched voices of the leaders of the chant begin the grand Nehan-gyō, the Sutra of Nirvana, the song of passage triumphant over the Sea of Death and Birth; and deep below those high tones and the hollow echoing of the *mokugyo*, the surging bass of the century of voices reciting the sonorous words, sounds like the breaking of a sea:

'*Shō-gyō mu-jō, je-sho meppō. - Transient are all. They, being born, must die. And being born, are dead. And being dead, are glad to be at rest.*'

Footnotes:

1. There is a legend that the Sun-Goddess invented the first *hakama*, by tying together the skirts of her robe.
2. Since the above was written I have had two years' experience as a teacher in various large Japanese schools; and I have never had personal knowledge of any serious quarrel between students, and have never even heard of a fight among my pupils. And I have taught some eight hundred boys and young men.
3. 'Let us play the game called *kango-kango*. Plenteously the water of Jizō-San quickly draw,

and pour on the pine-leaves, and turn back again.' Many of the games of Japanese children, like many of their toys, have a Buddhist origin, or at least a Buddhist significance.

4. I take the above translation from a Tokyo educational journal, entitled *The Museum*. The original document, however, was impressive to a degree that perhaps no translation could give. The Chinese words by which the Emperor refers to himself and his will are far more impressive than our Western 'We' or 'Our'; and the words relating to duties, virtues, wisdom, and other matters are words that evoke in a Japanese mind ideas which only those who know Japanese life perfectly can appreciate, and which, though variant from our own, are neither less beautiful nor less sacred.

5. *Kimi ga yo wa chiyo ni yachiyo ni sazare ishi no iwa o to narite oke no musu made.* Freely translated: 'May Our Gracious Sovereign reign a thousand years - reign ten thousand thousand years - reign till the little stone grows into a mighty rock, thick-velveted with ancient moss!'

6. Stoves, however, are being introduced. In the higher government schools, and in the Normal Schools, the students who are boarders obtain a better diet than most poor boys can get at home. Their rooms are also well warmed.

7. *Hachi yuki ya*
   Neko no ashi ato
   Ume no hana.

8. *Ni no ji fumi dasu*
   Bokkuri kana.

9. This little poem signifies that whoever in this world thinks much, must have care, and that not to think about things is to pass one's life in untroubled felicity.

10. Having asked in various classes for written answers to the question. 'What is your dearest wish?' I found about twenty per cent of the replies expressed, with little variation of words, the simple desire to die 'for His Sacred Majesty, Our Beloved Emperor'. But a considerable proportion of the remainder contained the same aspiration, less directly stated in the wish to emulate the glory of Nelson, or to make Japan first among nations by heroism and sacrifice. While this splendid spirit lives in the hearts of her youth, Japan should have little to fear for the future.

11. Beautiful generosities of this kind are not uncommon in Japan.

12. The college porter.

13. Except in those comparatively rare instances where the family is exclusively Shinto in its faith, or, although belonging to both faiths, prefers to bury its dead according to Shinto rites. In Matsue, as a rule, high officials only have Shinto funerals.

14. Unless the dead be buried according to the Shinto rite. In Matsue the mourning period is usually fifty days. On the fifty-first day after the decease, all members of the family go to Enjōji-nada (the lake-shore at the foot of the hill on which the great temple of Enjōji stands) to perform the ceremony of purification. At Enjōji-nada, on the beach, stands a lofty stone statue of Jizō. Before it the mourners pray; then wash their mouths and hands with the water of the lake. Afterwards they go to a friend's house for breakfast, the purification being always performed at daybreak, if possible. During the mourning period, no member of the family can eat at a friend's house. But if the burial has been according to the Shinto rite, all these ceremonial observances may be dispensed with.

15. But at samurai funerals in the olden time the women were robed in black.

16. Said only in courteous self-depreciation. In the same way a son, writing to his parent, would never, according to Japanese ideas of true courtesy and duty, sign himself '*Your affectionate son*', but '*Your ungrateful*', or '*unloving son*'.

With Kyushu Students

1

The students of the Government College, or Higher Middle School, can scarcely be called boys; their ages ranging from the average of eighteen, for the lowest class, to that of twenty-five for the highest. Perhaps the course is too long. The best pupil can hardly hope to reach the Imperial University before his twenty-third year, and will require for his entrance thereinto a mastery of written Chinese as well as a good practical knowledge of either English or German, or of English and French.[1] Thus he is obliged to learn three languages besides all that relates to the elegant literature of his own; and the weight of his task cannot be understood without knowledge of the fact that his study of Chinese alone is equal to the labour of acquiring six European tongues.

The impression produced upon me by the Kumamoto students was very different from that received on my first acquaintance with my Izumo pupils. This was not only because the former had left well behind them the delightfully amiable period of Japanese boyhood, and had developed into earnest, taciturn men, but also because they represented to a marked degree what is called Kyushu character. Kyushu still remains, as of yore, the most conservative part of Japan, and Kumamoto, its chief city, the centre of conservative feeling. This conservatism is, however, both rational and practical. Kyushu was not slow in adopting rail-roads, improved methods of agriculture, applications of science to certain industries; but it remains, of all districts of the Empire, the least inclined to imitation of Western manners and customs. The ancient *samurai* spirit still lives on; and that spirit in Kyushu was for centuries one that exacted severe simplicity in habits of life. Sumptuary laws against extravagance in dress and other forms of luxury used to be rigidly enforced; and though the laws themselves have been obsolete for a generation, their influence continues to appear in the very simple attire and the plain, direct manners of the people. Kumamoto folk are also said to be characterised by their adherence to traditions of conduct which have been almost forgotten elsewhere, and by a certain independent frankness in speech and action, difficult for any foreigner to define, but immediately apparent to an educated Japanese. And here, too, under the shadow of Kiyomasa's mighty fortress - now occupied by an immense garrison - national sentiment is declared to be stronger than in the very capital itself - the spirit of loyalty and the love of country. Kumamoto is proud of all these things, and boasts of her traditions. Indeed, she has nothing else to boast of.

A vast, straggling, dull, unsightly town is Kumamoto: there are no quaint, pretty streets, no great temples, no wonderful gardens. Burnt to the ground in the civil war of the tenth Meiji, the place still gives you the impression of a wilderness of flimsy shelters erected in haste almost before the soil had ceased to smoke. There are no remarkable places to visit (not, at least, within city limits), no sights, few amusements. For this very reason the college is thought to be well located: there are neither temptations nor distractions for its inmates. But for another reason, also, rich men far away in the capital try to send their sons to Kumamoto. It is considered desirable that a young man should be imbued with what is called 'the Kyushu spirit', and should acquire what might be termed the Kyushu 'tone'. The students of Kumamoto are said to be the most peculiar students in the Empire by reason of this 'tone'. I have never been able to learn enough about it to define it well; but it is evidently something akin to the deportment of the old Kyushu *samurai*. Certainly the students sent from Tokyo or Kyoto to Kyushu have to adapt themselves to a very different *milieu*.

The Kumamoto, and also the Kagoshima youths - whenever not obliged to don military uniform for drill-hours and other special occasions - still cling to a costume somewhat resembling that of the ancient *bushi*, and therefore celebrated in sword-songs - the short robe and *hakama* reaching a little below the knee, and sandals. The material of the dress is cheap, coarse, and sober in colour; cleft stockings (*tabi*) are seldom worn, except in very cold weather, or during long marches, to keep the sandal-thongs from cutting into the flesh. Without being rough, the manners are not soft; and the lads seem to cultivate a certain outward hardness of character. They can preserve an imperturbable exterior under quite extraordinary circumstances, but under this self-control there is a fiery consciousness of strength which will show itself in a menacing form on rare occasions. They deserve to be termed rugged men, too, in their own oriental way. Some I know, who, though born to comparative wealth, find no pleasure so keen as that of trying how much physical hardship they can endure. The greater number would certainly give up their lives without hesitation rather than their high principles. And a rumour of national danger would instantly transform the whole four hundred into a body of iron soldiery. But their outward demeanour is usually impassive to a degree that is difficult even to understand.

For a long time I used to wonder in vain what feelings, sentiments, ideas might be hidden beneath all that unsmiling placidity. The native teachers, *de facto* government officials, did not appear to be on intimate terms with any of their pupils: there was no trace of that affectionate familiarity I had seen in Izumo; the relation between instructors and instructed seemed to begin and end with the bugle-calls by which classes were assembled and dismissed. In this I afterwards found myself partly mistaken; still such relations as actually existed were for the most part formal rather than natural, and quite unlike those old-fashioned, loving sympathies of which the memory had always remained with me since my departure from the Province of the Gods.

But later on, at frequent intervals, there came to me suggestions of an inner life much more attractive than this outward seeming - hints of emotional individuality. A few I obtained in casual conversations, but the most remarkable in written themes. Subjects given for composition occasionally coaxed out some totally unexpected blossoming of thoughts and feelings. A very pleasing fact was the total absence of any false shyness, or indeed shyness of any sort: the young men were not ashamed to write exactly what they felt or hoped. They would write about their homes, about their reverential love of their parents, about happy experiences of their childhood, about their friendships, about their adventures during the holidays; and this often in a way I thought beautiful, because of its artless, absolute sincerity. After a number of such surprises, I learned to regret keenly that I had not from the outset kept notes upon all the remarkable compositions received. Once a week I used to read aloud and correct in class a selection from the best handed in, correcting the remainder at home. The very best I could not always presume to read aloud and criticise for the general benefit, because treating of matters too sacred to be methodically commented upon, as the following examples may show.

I had given as a subject for English composition this question: 'What do men remember longest'? One student answered that we remember our happiest moments longer than we remember all other experiences, because it is in the nature of every rational being to try to forget what is disagreeable or painful as soon as possible. I received many still more ingenious answers, some of which gave proof of a really keen psychological study of the question. But I liked best of all the simple reply of one who thought that painful events are longest remembered. He wrote exactly what follows: I found it needless to alter a single word:
'What do men remember longest? I think men remember longest that which they hear or see under painful circumstances.

'When I was only four years old, my dear, dear mother died. It was a winter's day. The wind was blowing hard in the trees, and round the roof of our house. There were no leaves on the branches of the trees. Quails were whistling in the distance, making melancholy sounds. I recall something I did. As my mother was lying in bed, a little before she died, I gave her a sweet orange. She smiled and took it, and tasted it. It was the last time she smiled.... From the moment when she ceased to breathe to this hour more than sixteen years have elapsed. But to me the time is as a moment. Now also it is winter. The winds that blew when my mother died blow just as then; the quails utter the same cries; all things are the same. But my mother has gone away, and will never come back again.'

The following, also, was written in reply to the same question:
'The greatest sorrow in my life was my father's death. I was seven years old. I can remember that he had been ill all day, and that my toys had been put aside, and that I tried to be very quiet. I had not seen him that morning, and the day seemed very long. At last I stole into my father's room, and put my lips close to his cheek, and whispered *"Father! Father"*! - and his cheek was very cold. He did not speak. My uncle came and carried me out of the room, but said nothing. Then I feared my father would die, because his cheek felt cold just as my little sister's had been when she died. In the evening a great many neighbours and other people came to the house, and caressed me, so that I was happy for a time. But they carried my father away during the night, and I never saw him after.'

2

From the foregoing one might suppose a simple style characteristic of English compositions in Japanese higher schools. Yet the reverse is the fact. There is a general tendency to prefer big words to little ones, and long complicated sentences to plain short periods. For this there are some reasons which would need a philological essay by Professor Chamberlain to explain. But the tendency itself - constantly strengthened by the absurd text-books in use - can be partly understood from the fact that the very simplest forms of English expression are the most obscure to a Japanese, because they are idiomatic. The student finds them riddles, since the root-ideas behind them are so different from his own that, to explain those ideas, it is first necessary to know something of Japanese psychology; and in avoiding simple idioms he follows instinctively the direction of least resistance.

I tried to cultivate an opposite tendency by various devices. Sometimes I would write familiar stories for the class, all in simple sentences, and in words of one syllable. Sometimes I would suggest themes to write upon, of which the nature almost compelled simple treatment. Of course I was not very successful in my purpose, but one theme chosen in relation to it - 'My First Day at School' - evoked a large number of compositions that interested me in quite another way, as revelations of sincerity of feeling and of character. I offer a few selections, slightly abridged and corrected. Their naïveté is not their least charm - especially if one reflects they are not the recollections of boys. The following seemed to me one of the best:

'I could not go to school until I was eight years old. I had often begged my father to let me go, for all my playmates were already at school; but he would not, thinking I was not strong enough. So I remained at home, and played with my brother.

'My brother accompanied me to school the first day. He spoke to the teacher, and commanded me to sit on a bench, then he also left me. I felt sad as I sat there in silence: there was no brother to play with now - only many strange boys. A bell rang twice; and a teacher entered our classroom, and told us to take out our slates. Then he wrote a Japanese character on the blackboard, and told us to copy it. That day he taught us how to write two Japanese words, and told us some story about a good boy. When I returned home I ran to my mother, and knelt down by her side to tell her what the teacher had taught me. Oh! how great my pleasure then was! I cannot even tell how I felt - much less write it. I can only say that I then thought the teacher was a more learned man than father, or any one else whom I knew - the most awful, and yet the most kindly person in the world.'

The following also shows the teacher in a very pleasing light:

'My brother and sister took me to school the first day. I thought I could sit beside them in the school, as I used to do at home: but the teacher ordered me to go to a classroom which was very far away from that of my brother and sister. I insisted upon remaining with my brother and sister; and when the teacher said that could not be, I cried and made a great noise. Then they allowed my brother to leave his own class, and accompany me to mine. But after a while I found playmates in my own class; and class; and then I was not afraid to be without my brother.'

This also is quite pretty and true:

'A teacher (I think, the headmaster) called me to him, and told me that I must become a great scholar. Then he bade some man take me into a classroom where there were forty or fifty scholars. I felt afraid and pleased at the same time, at the thought of having so many playfellows. They looked at me shyly, and I at them. I was at first afraid to speak to them. Little boys are innocent like that. But after a while, in some way or other, we began to play together; and they seemed to be pleased to have me play with them.'

The above three compositions were by young men who had their first schooling under the existing educational system, which prohibits harshness on the part of masters. But it would seem that the teachers of the previous era were less tender. Here are three compositions by older students who appear to have had quite a different experience:

1. 'Before Meiji, there were no such public schools in Japan as there are now. But in every province there was a sort of student society composed of the sons of *samurai*. Unless a man were a *samurai*, his son could not enter such a society. It was under the control of the Lord of the province, who appointed a director to rule the students. The principal study of the *samurai* was that of the Chinese language and literature. Most of the Statesmen of the present government were once students in such *samurai* schools. Common citizens and country people had to send their sons and daughters to primary schools called *terakoya*, where all the teaching was usually done by one teacher. It consisted of a little more than reading, writing, calculating, and some moral instruction. We could learn to write an ordinary letter, or a very easy essay. At eight years old, I was sent to a *terakoya*, as I was not the son of a *samurai*. At first I did not want to go; and every morning my grandfather had to strike me with his stick to make me go. The discipline at that school was very severe. If a boy did not obey, he was beaten with a bamboo - being held down to receive his punishment. After a year, many public schools were opened: and I entered a public school.'

2. 'A great gate, a pompous building, a very large dismal room with benches in rows - these I remember. The teachers looked very severe; I did not like their faces. I sat on a bench in the room and felt hateful. The teachers seemed unkind; none of the boys knew me, or spoke to me. A teacher stood up by the black-board, and began to call the names. He had a whip in his hand. He called my name. I could not answer, and burst out crying. So I was sent home. That was my first day at school.'

3. 'When I was seven years old I was obliged to enter a school in my native village. My father gave me two or three writing-brushes and some paper; I was very glad to get them, and promised to study as earnestly as I could. But how unpleasant the first day at school was! When I went to the school none of the students knew me, and I found myself without a friend. I entered a class-room. A teacher, with a whip in his hand, called my name in a *large* voice. I was very much surprised at it, and so frightened that I could not help crying. The boys laughed very loudly at me; but the teacher scolded them, and whipped one of them, and then said to me, "Don't be

245

afraid of my voice: what is your name"? I told him my name snuffling. I thought then that school was a very disagreeable place, where we could neither weep nor laugh. I wanted only to go back home at once; and though I felt it was out of my power to go, I could scarcely bear to stay until the lessons were over. When I returned home at last, I told my father what I had felt at school, and said: I do not like to go to school at all.'

Needless to say the next memory is of Meiji. It gives, as a composition, evidence of what we should call in the West, character. The suggestion of self-reliance at six years old is delicious: so is the recollection of the little sister taking off her white *tabi* to deck her child-brother on his first school-day:

'I was six years old. My mother awoke me early. My sister gave me ner own stockings (*tabi*) to wear, and I felt very happy. Father ordered a servant to attend me to the school; but I refused to be accompanied: I wanted to feel that I could go all by myself. So I went alone; and, as the school was not far from the house, I soon found myself in front of the gate. There I stood still a little while, because I knew none of the children I saw going in. Boys and girls were passing into the schoolyard, accompanied by servants or relatives; and inside I saw others playing games which filled me with envy. But all at once a little boy among the players saw me, and with a laugh came running to me. Then I was very happy. I walked to and fro with him, hand in hand. At last a teacher called all of us into a school-room, and made a speech which I could not understand. After that we were free for the day because it was the first day. I returned home with my friend. My parents were waiting for me, with fruits and cakes; and my friend and I ate them together.'

Another writes:

'When I first went to school I was six years old. I remember only that my grandfather carried my books and slate for me, and that the teacher and the boys were very, very, very kind and good to me - so that I thought school was a paradise in this world, and did not want to return home.'

I think this little bit of natural remorse is also worth the writing down:

'I was eight years old when I first went to school. I was a bad boy. I remember on the way home from school I had a quarrel with one of my playmates - younger than I. He threw a very little stone at me which hit me. I took a branch of a tree lying in a road, and struck him across the face with all my might. Then I ran away, leaving him crying in the middle of the road. My heart told me what I had done. After reaching my home, I thought I still heard him crying. My little playmate is not any more in this world now. Can anyone know my feelings?'

All this capacity of young men to turn back with perfect naturalness of feeling to scenes of their childhood appears to me essentially Oriental. In the Occident men seldom begin to recall their childhood vividly before the approach of the autumn season of life. But childhood in Japan is certainly happier than in other lands, and therefore perhaps is regretted earlier in adult life. The following extract from a student's record of his holiday experience touchingly expresses such regret:

'During the spring vacation, I went home to visit my parents. Just before the end of the holidays, when it was nearly time for me to return to the college, I heard that the students of the middle school of my native town were also going to Kumamoto on an excursion, and I resolved to go with them.

'They marched in military order with their rifles. I had no rifle, so I took my place in the rear of the column. We marched all day, keeping time to military songs which we sung all together.

'In the evening we reached Soyeda. The teachers and students of the Soyeda school, and the chief men of the village, welcomed us. Then we were separated into detachments, each of which was quartered in a different hotel. I entered a hotel, with the last detachment, to rest for the night.

'But I could not sleep for a long time. Five years before, on a similar "military excursion", I had rested in that very hotel, as a student of the same middle school. I remembered the fatigue and the pleasure; and I compared my feelings of the moment with the recollection of my feelings then as a boy. I could not help a weak wish to be young again like my companions. They were fast asleep, tired with their long march; and I sat up and looked at their faces. How pretty their faces seemed in that young sleep!'

3

The preceding selections give no more indication of the general character of the students' compositions than might be furnished by any choice made to illustrate a particular feeling. Examples of ideas and sentiments from themes of a graver kind would show variety of thought and not a little originality in method, but would require much space. A few notes, however, copied out of my class-register, will be found suggestive, if not exactly curious.

At the summer examinations of 1893 I submitted to the graduating classes for a composition theme, the question, 'What is eternal in literature'? I expected original answers, as the subject had never been discussed by us, and was certainly new to the pupils, so far as their knowledge of Western thought was concerned. Nearly all the papers proved interesting. I select twenty replies as examples. Most of them immediately preceded a long discussion, but a few were embodied in the text of the essay:

1. 'Truth and Eternity are identical: these make the Full Circle - in Chinese, Yen-Man.'

2. 'All that in human life and conduct which is according to the laws of the Universe.'

3. 'The lives of patriots, and the teachings of those who have given pure maxims to the world.'

4. 'Filial Piety, and the doctrine of its teachers. Vainly the books of Confucius were burned during the Shin dynasty; they are translated today into all the languages of the civilised world.'

5. 'Ethics, and scientific truth.'

6. 'Both evil and good are eternal, said a Chinese sage. We should read only that which is good.'

7. 'The great thoughts and ideas of our ancestors.'

8. 'For a thousand million centuries truth is truth.'
9. 'Those ideas of right and wrong upon which all schools of ethics agree.'
10. 'Books which rightly explain the phenomena of the Universe.'
11. 'Conscience alone is unchangeable. Wherefore books about ethics based upon conscience are eternal.'
12. 'Reasons for noble action: these remain unchanged by time.'
13. 'Books written upon the best moral means of giving the greatest possible happiness to the greatest possible number of people - that is, to mankind.'
14. 'The Gokyō (the Five great Chinese Classics).'
15. 'The holy books of China, and of the Buddhists.'
16. 'All that which teaches the Right and Pure Way of human conduct.'
17. 'The Story of Kusunoki Masashige, who vowed to be reborn seven times to fight against the enemies of his Sovereign.'
18. 'Moral sentiment, without which the world would be only an enormous clod of earth, and all books waste-paper.'
19. 'The *Tao-te-King*.'
20. Same as 19, but with this comment: 'He who reads that which is eternal, *his soul shall hover eternally in the Universe*.'

4

Some particularly Oriental sentiments were occasionally drawn out through discussions. The discussions were based upon stories which I would relate to a class by word of mouth, and invite written or spoken comment about. The results of such a discussion are hereafter set forth. At the time it took place, I had already told the students of the higher classes a considerable number of stories. I had told them many of the Greek myths; among which that of Oedipus and the Sphinx seemed especially to please them, because of the hidden moral, and that of Orpheus, like all our musical legends, to have no interest for them. I had also told them a variety of our most famous modern stories. The marvellous tale of 'Rappacini's Daughter' proved greatly to their liking; and the spirit of Hawthorne might have found no little ghostly pleasure in their interpretation of it. 'Monos and Daimonos' found favour: and Poe's wonderful fragment, 'Silence', was appreciated after a fashion that surprised me. On the other hand, the story of 'Frankenstein' impressed them very little. None took it seriously. For Western minds the tale must always hold a peculiar horror, because of the shock it gives to feelings evolved under the influence of Hebraic ideas concerning the origin of life, the tremendous character of divine prohibitions, and the awful punishments destined for those who would tear the veil from Nature's secrets, or mock, even unconsciously, the work of a jealous Creator. But to the Oriental mind, unshadowed by such grim faith - feeling no distance between gods and men - conceiving life as a multiform whole ruled by one uniform law that shapes the consequence of every act into a reward or a punishment - the ghastliness of the story makes no appeal. Most of the written criticisms showed me that it was generally regarded as a comic or semi-comic parable. After all this, I was rather puzzled one morning by the request for a 'very strong moral story of the Western kind'.

I suddenly resolved - though knowing I was about to venture on dangerous ground - to try the full effect of a certain Arthurian legend which I felt sure somebody would criticise with a vim. The moral is rather more than 'very strong'; and for that reason I was curious to hear the result.

So I related to them the story of Sir Bors, which is in the sixteenth book of Sir Thomas Malory's 'Morte d'Arthur' - 'how Sir Bors met his brother Sir Lionel taken and beaten with thorns - and how Sir Bors left his brother to rescue the damsel - and how it was told them that Lionel was dead.' But I did not try to explain to them the knightly idealism imaged in the beautiful old tale, as I wished to hear them comment, in their own Oriental way, upon the bare facts of the narrative.

Which they did as follows:

'The action of Malory's knight', exclaimed Iwai, 'was contrary even to the principles of Christianity - if it be true that the Christian religion declares all men brothers. Such conduct might be right if there were no society in the world. But while any society exists which is formed of families, family love must be the strength of that society; and the action of that knight was against family love, and therefore against society. The principle he followed was opposed not only to all society, but was contrary to all religion, and contrary to the morals of all countries.'

'The story is certainly immoral', said Orito. 'What it relates is opposed to all our ideas of love and loyalty, and even seems to us contrary to nature. Loyalty is not a mere duty. It must be from the heart, or it is not loyalty. It must be an inborn feeling. And it is in the nature of every Japanese.'

'It is a horrible story', said Andō. 'Philanthropy itself is only an expansion of fraternal love. The man who could abandon his own brother to death merely to save a strange woman was a wicked man. Perhaps he was influenced by passion.'

'No', I said: 'You forget I told you that there was no selfishness in his action - that it must be interpreted as a heroism.'

'I think the explanation of the story must be religious', said Yasukochi. 'It seems strange to us; but that may be because we do not understand Western ideas very well. Of course to abandon one's own brother in order to save a strange woman is contrary to all our knowledge of right. But if that knight was a man of pure heart, he must have imagined himself obliged to do it because of some promise or some duty. Even then it must have seemed to him a very painful and disgraceful thing to do, and he could not have done it without feeling that he was acting against the teaching of his own heart.'

'There you are right', I answered. 'But you should also know that the sentiment obeyed by Sir Bors is one which still influences the conduct of brave and noble men in the societies of the West - even of men who cannot be called religious at all in the common sense of that word.'

'Still, we think it a very bad sentiment', said Iwai; 'and we would rather hear another story about another form of society.'

Then it occurred to me to tell them the immortal story of Alkestis. I thought for the moment that the character of Herakles in that divine drama would have a particular charm for them. But the comments proved I was mistaken. No one even referred to Herakles. Indeed I ought to have remembered that our ideals of heroism, strength of purpose, contempt of death, do not readily appeal to Japanese youth. And this for the reason that no Japanese gentleman regards such qualities as exceptional. He considers heroism a matter of course - something belonging to manhood and inseparable from it. He would say that a woman may be afraid without shame, but never a man. Then as a mere idealisation of physical force, Herakles could interest Orientals very little: their own mythology teems with impersonations of strength; and, besides, dexterity, sleight, quickness, are much more admired by a true Japanese than strength. No Japanese boy would sincerely wish to be like the giant Benkei; but Yoshitsune, the slender, supple conqueror and master of Benkei, remains an ideal of perfect knighthood dear to the hearts of all Japanese youth.

Kamekawa said:

'The story of Alkestis, or at least the story of Admetus, is a story of cowardice, disloyalty, immorality. The conduct of Admetus was abominable. His wife was indeed noble and virtuous - too good a wife for so shameless a man. I do not believe that the father of Admetus would not have been willing to die for his son if his son had been worthy. I think he would gladly have died for his son had he not been disgusted by the cowardice of Admetus. And how disloyal the subjects of Admetus were! The moment they heard of their king's danger they should have rushed to the palace, and humbly begged that they might be allowed to die in his stead. However cowardly or cruel he might have been, that was their duty. They were his subjects. They lived by his favour. Yet how disloyal they were! A country inhabited by such shameless people must soon have gone to ruin. Of course, as the story says, "it is sweet to live". Who does not love life? Who does not dislike to die? But no brave man - no loyal man even - should so much as think about his life when duty requires him to give it.'

'But', said Midzuguchi, who had joined us a little too late to hear the beginning of the narration, 'perhaps Admetus was actuated by filial piety. Had I been Admetus, and found no one among my subjects willing to die for me, I should have said to my wife: Dear wife, I cannot leave my father alone now, because he has no other son, and his grandsons are still too young to be of use to him. Therefore, if you love me, please die in my place.'

'You do not understand the story', said Yasukochi. 'Filial piety did not exist in Admetus. He wished that his father should have died for him.'

'Ah'! exclaimed the apologist in real surprise, 'that is not a nice story, teacher!'

'Admetus', declared Kawabuchi, 'was everything which is bad. He was a hateful coward, because he was afraid to die: he was a tyrant, because he wanted his subjects to die for him; he was an unfilial son because he wanted his old father to die in his place; and he was an unkind husband, because he asked his wife - a weak woman with little children - to do what *he* was afraid to do as a man. What could be baser than Admetus?'

'But Alkestis', said Iwai, 'Alkestis was all that is good. For she gave up her children and everything - even like the Buddha [*Shaka*] himself. Yet she was very young. How true and brave! The beauty of her face might perish like a spring-blossoming, but the beauty of her act should be remembered for a thousand times a thousand years. Eternally her soul will hover in the universe. Formless she is now; but it is the Formless who teach us more kindly than our kindest living teachers - the soul of all who have done pure, brave, wise deeds.'

'The wife of Admetus', said Kumamoto, inclined to austerity in his judgements, 'was simply obedient. She was not entirely blameless. For, before her death, it was her highest duty to have severely reproached her husband for his foolishness. And this she did not do - not at least as our teacher tells the story.'

'Why Western people should think that story beautiful', said Zaitsu, 'is difficult for us to understand. There is much in it which fills us with anger. For some of us cannot but think of our parents when listening to such a story. After the Revolution of Meiji, for a time, there was much suffering. Often perhaps our parents were hungry; yet we always had plenty of food. Sometimes they could scarcely get money to live; yet we were educated. When we think of all it cost them to educate us, all the trouble it gave them to bring us up, all the love they gave us, and all the pain we caused them in our foolish childhood, then we think we can never, never do enough for them. And therefore we do not like that story of Admetus.'

The bugle sounded for recess. I went to the parade-ground to take a smoke. Presently a few students joined me, with their rifles and bayonets - for the next hour was to be devoted to military drill. One said: 'Teacher, we should like another subject for composition - not *too* easy.'

I suggested: 'How would you like this for a subject: What is most difficult to understand.'

'That', said Kawabuchi, 'is not hard to answer - the correct use of English prepositions.'

'In the study of English by Japanese students - yes', I answered. 'But I did not mean any special difficulty of that kind. I meant to write your ideas about what is most difficult for all men to understand.'

'The universe'? queried Yasukochi. 'That is too large a subject.'

'When I was only six years old', said Orito, 'I used to wander along the seashore, on fine days, and wonder at the greatness of the world. Our home was by the sea. Afterwards I was taught that the problem of the universe will at last pass away, like smoke.'

'I think', said Miyakawa, 'That the hardest of all things to understand is why men live in the world. From the time a child is born, what does he do? He eats and drinks; he feels happy and sad; he sleeps at night; he awakes in the morning. He is educated; he grows up; he marries; he has children; he gets old; his hair turns first grey and then white; he becomes feebler and feebler, and he dies.

'What does he do all his life? All his real work in this world is to eat and to drink, to sleep and to rise up; since, whatever be his occupation as a citizen, he toils only that he may be able to continue doing this. But for what purpose does a man really come into the world? Is it to eat? Is it to drink? Is it to sleep? Every day he does exactly the same thing, and yet he is not tired! It is strange.

'When rewarded he is glad; when punished, he is sad. If he becomes

251

rich, he thinks himself happy. If he becomes poor, he is very unhappy. Why is he glad or sad according to his condition? Happiness and sadness are only temporary things. Why does he study hard? No matter how great a scholar he may become, what is there left of him when he is dead? Only bones.'

Miyakawa was the merriest and wittiest in his class; and the contrast between his joyous character and his words seemed to me almost startling. But such swift glooms of thought - especially since Meiji - not infrequently make apparition in quite young Oriental minds. They are fugitive as shadows of summer clouds; they mean less than they would signify in Western adolescence; and the Japanese lives not by thought, nor by emotion, but by duty. Still, they are not haunters to encourage.

'I think', said I, 'a much better subject for you all would be the Sky: the sensations which the sky creates in us when we look at it on such a day as this. See how wonderful it is!'

It was blue to the edge of the world, with never a floss of cloud. There were no vapours on the horizon; and very far peaks, invisible on most days, now massed into the glorious light, seemingly diaphanous.

Then Kumashiro, looking up to the mighty arching, uttered with reverence the ancient Chinese words:

'*What thought is so high as It is? What mind is so wide?*'

'Today', I said, 'is beautiful as any summer day could be - only that the leaves are falling, and the *semi* are gone.'

'Do you like *semi*, teacher?' asked Mori.

'It gives me great pleasure to hear them', I answered. 'We have no such cicadae in the West.'

'Human life is compared to the life of a *semi*', said Orito - '*utsuzemi no yo*. Brief as the song of the *semi* all human joy is, and youth. Men come for a season and go, as do the *semi*.'

'There are no *semi* now', said Yasukochi; 'perhaps the teacher thinks it is sad.'

'I do not think it sad', observed Noguchi. 'They hinder us from study. I hate the sound they make. When we hear that sound in summer, and are tired, it adds fatigue to fatigue so that we fall asleep. If we try to read or write, or even think, when we hear that sound we have no more courage to do anything. Then we wish that all those insects were dead.'

'Perhaps you like the dragon-flies', I suggested. 'They are flashing all around us; but they make no sound.'

'Every Japanese likes dragon-flies', said Kumashiro. 'Japan, you know, is called Akitsusu, which means the Country of the Dragon-fly.'

We talked about different kinds of dragon-flies; and they told me of one I had never seen - the *shōro-tombo*, or 'Ghost dragon-fly', said to have some strange relation to the dead. Also they spoke of the *yamma* - a very large kind of dragon-fly, and related that in certain old songs the samurai were called *yamma*, because the long hair of a young warrior used to be tied up into a knot in the shape of a dragon-fly.

A bugle sounded; and the voice of the military officer rang out: '*Atsumar É*'! (fall in!) But the young men lingered an instant to ask:

'Well, what shall it be, teacher - that which is most difficult to understand?'

'No', I said, 'the Sky.'

And all that day the beauty of the Chinese utterance haunted me, filled me like an exaltation:

What thought is so high as It is? What mind is so wide?

5

There is one instance in which the relation between teachers and students is not formal at all - one precious survival of the mutual love of other days in the old *samurai* schools. By all the aged Professor of Chinese is reverenced; and his influence over the young men is very great. With a word he could calm any outburst of anger; with a smile he could quicken any generous impulse. For he represents to the lads their ideal of all that was brave, true, noble, in the elder life - the Soul of Old Japan.

His name, signifying 'Moon-of-Autumn', is famous in his own land. A little book has been published about him, containing his portrait. He was once a *samurai* of high rank belonging to the great clan of Aidzu. He rose early to positions of trust and influence. He has been a leader of armies, a negotiator between princes, a statesman, a ruler of provinces - all that any knight could be in the feudal era. But in the intervals of military or political duty he seems to have always been a teacher. There are few such teachers. There are few such scholars. Yet to see him now, you would scarcely believe how much he was once feared - though loved - by the turbulent swordsmen under his rule. Perhaps there is no gentleness so full of charm as that of the man of war noted for sternness in his youth.

When the Feudal System made its last battle for existence, he heard the summons of his lord, and went into that terrible struggle in which even the women and little children of Aidzu took part. But courage and the sword alone could not prevail against the new methods of war; the power of Aidzu was broken; and he, as one of the leaders of that power, was long a political prisoner.

But the victors esteemed him; and the Government he had fought against in all honour took him into its service to teach the new generations. From younger teachers these learned Western science and Western languages. But he still taught that wisdom of the Chinese sages which is eternal, and loyalty, and honour, and all that makes the man.

Some of his children passed away from his sight. But he could not feel alone; for all whom he taught were as sons to him, and so reverenced him. And he became old, very old, and grew to look like a god - like a *kami-sama*.

The *kami-sama* in art bear no likeness to the Buddhas. These more ancient divinities have no down-cast gaze, no meditative impassiveness. They are lovers of Nature; they haunt her fairest solitudes, and enter into the life of her trees, and speak in her waters, and hover in her winds. Once upon the earth they lived as men; and the people of the land are their posterity. Even as divine ghosts, they remain very human, and of many dispositions. They are the emotions, they are the sensations of the

253

living. But as figuring in legend and the art born of legend, they are mostly very pleasant to know. I speak not of the cheap art which treats them irreverently in these sceptical days, but of the older art explaining the sacred texts about them. Of course such representations vary greatly. But were you to ask what is the ordinary traditional aspect of a *kami*, I should answer: 'An ancient smiling man of wondrously gentle countenance, having a long white beard, and all robed in white with a white girdle.'

Only that the girdle of the aged Professor was of black silk, just such a vision of Shinto he seemed when he visited me the last time.

He had met me at the college, and had said: 'I know there has been a congratulation at your house; and that I did not call was not because I am old or because your house is far, but only because I have been long ill. But you will soon see me.'

So one luminous afternoon he came, bringing gifts of felicitation - gifts of the antique high courtesy, simple in themselves, yet worthy a prince: a little plum-tree, every branch and spray one snowy dazzle of blossoms; a curious and pretty bamboo vessel full of wine; and two scrolls bearing beautiful poems - texts precious in themselves as the work of a rare calligrapher and poet; otherwise precious to me, because written by his own hand. Everything which he said to me I do not fully know. I remember words of affectionate encouragement about my duties - some wise, keen advice - a strange story of his youth. But all was like a pleasant dream; for his mere presence was a caress, and the fragrance of his flower-gift seemed as a breathing from the Takama-no-hara. And as a *kami* should come and go, so he smiled and went, leaving all things hallowed. The little plum-tree has lost its flowers: another winter must pass before it blooms again. But something very sweet still seems to haunt the vacant guest-room; perhaps only the memory of that divine old man - perhaps a spirit ancestral, some Lady of the Past, who followed his steps all viewlessly to our threshold that day, and lingers with me awhile, just because he loved me.

Footnotes:

1. This essay was written early in 1894. Since then, the study of French and of German has been made optional instead of obligatory, and the Higher School course considerably shortened, by a wise decision of the late Minister of Education, Mr Inouye. It is to be hoped that measures will eventually be taken to render possible making the study of English also optional. Under existing conditions the study is forced upon hundreds who can never obtain any benefit from it.

LAFCADIO'S FAREWELL

Sayonara!

A land where sky and earth so strangely intermingle that what is reality may not be distinguished from what is illusion - that all seems a mirage, about to vanish. For me, alas! it is about to vanish forever.

The little steamer shrieks again, puffs, backs into midstream, turns from the long white bridge. And as the grey wharves recede, a long *Aaaaaaaaaa* rises from the uniformed ranks, and all the caps wave, flashing their Chinese ideographs of brass. I clamber to the roof of the tiny deck cabin, wave my hat, and shout in English: 'Good-by, good-by'! And there floats back to me the cry: '*Manzai, manzai*'! [Ten thousand years to you! ten thousand years!] But already it comes faintly from far away. The packet glides out of the river-mouth, shoots into the blue lake, turns a pine-shadowed point; and the faces, and the voices, and the wharves, and the long white bridge have become memories.

Still for a little while looking back, as we pass into the silence of the great water, I can see, receding on the left, the crest of the ancient castle, over grand shaggy altitudes of pine, and the place of my home, with its delicious garden, and the long blue roofs of the schools. These, too, swiftly pass out of vision. Then only faint blue water, faint blue mists, faint blues and greens and greys of peaks looking through varying distance, and beyond all, towering ghost white into the east, the glorious spectre of Daisen.

And my heart sinks a moment under the rush of those vivid memories which always crowd upon one the instant after parting - memories of all that make attachment to places and to things. Remembered smiles; the morning gathering at the threshold of the old *yashiki* to wish the departing teacher a happy day; the evening gathering to welcome his return; the dog waiting by the gate at the accustomed hour; the garden with its lotus-flowers and its cooing of doves; the musical boom of the temple bell from the cedar groves; songs of children at play; afternoon shadows upon many-tinted streets; the long lines of lantern-fires upon festal nights; the dancing of the moon upon the lake; the clapping of hands by the river shore in salutation to the Izumo sun; the endless merry pattering of *geta* over the windy bridge: all these and a hundred other happy memories revive for me with almost painful vividness, while the far peaks, whose names are holy, slowly turn away their blue shoulders, and the little steamer bears me, more and more swiftly, ever farther and farther from the Province of the Gods.

Reverie

It has been said that men fear death much as the child cries at entering the world, being unable to know what loving hands are waiting to receive it. Certainly this comparison will not bear scientific examination. But as a happy fancy it is beautiful, even for those to whom it can make no religious appeal whatever - those who must believe that the individual mind dissolves with the body, and that an eternal continuance of personality could only prove an eternal misfortune. It is beautiful, I think, because it suggests, in so intimate a way, the hope that to larger knowledge the Absolute will reveal itself as mother-love made infinite. The imagining is Oriental rather than Occidental; yet it accords with a sentiment vaguely defined in most of our Western creeds. Through ancient grim conceptions of the Absolute as Father, there has gradually been infused some later and brighter dream of infinite tenderness - some all-transfiguring hope created by the memory of Woman as Mother; and the more that races evolve towards higher things, the more Feminine becomes their idea of a God.

Conversely, this suggestion must remind even the least believing that we know of nothing else, in all the range of human experience, so sacred as mother-love - nothing so well deserving the name of divine. Mother-love alone could have enabled the delicate life of thought to unfold and to endure upon the rind of this wretched little planet: only through that supreme unselfishness could the nobler emotions ever have found strength to blossom in the brain of man; only by help of mother-love could the higher forms of trust in the Unseen ever have been called into existence.

But musings of this kind naturally lead us to ask ourselves emotional questions about the mysteries of Whither and Whence. Must the evolutionist think of mother-love as a merely necessary result of material affinities - the attraction of the atom for the atom? Or can he venture to assert, with ancient thinkers of the East, that all atomic tendencies are shapen by one eternal moral law, and that some are in themselves divine, being manifestations of the Four Infinite Feelings?... What wisdom can decide for us? And of what avail to know our highest emotions divine, since the race itself is doomed to perish? When mother-love shall have wrought its uttermost for humanity, will not even that uttermost have been in vain?

At first thought, indeed, the inevitable dissolution must appear the blackest of imaginable tragedies - tragedy made infinite! Eventually our planet must die: its azure ghost of air will shrink and pass, its seas dry up, its very soil perish utterly, leaving only a universal waste of sand and stone - a withered corpse of a world. Still for a time this mummy will turn about the sun, but only as the dead moon wheels now across our nights, one face forever in scorching blaze, the other in icy darkness. So will it circle, blank and bald as a skull; and like a skull will it bleach and crack and crumble, ever drawing nearer and yet more near to the face of its flaming parent, to vanish suddenly at last in the cyclonic lightning of his breath. One by one the remaining planets must follow. Then will the mighty star himself begin to fail - to flicker with ghastly changing colours - to crimson towards his death. And finally the monstrous fissured cinder of him, hurled into some colossal sun-pyre, will be dissipated into vapour more tenuous than the dream of the dream of a ghost....

What, then, will have availed the labour of the life that was - the life effaced without one sign to mark the place of its disparition in the illimitable abyss? What, then, the worth of mother-love, the whole dead world of human tenderness, with its sacrifices, hopes, memories, its divine delights and diviner pains, its smiles and tears and sacred caresses, its countless passionate prayers to countless vanished gods?

Such doubts and fears do not trouble the thinker of the East. They disturb chiefly because of old wrong habits of thought, and the consequent blind fear of knowing that what we have so long called Soul belongs, not to Essence, but to Form.... Forms appear and vanish in perpetual succession; but the Essence alone is Real. Nothing real can be lost, even in the dissipation of a million universes. Utter destruction, everlasting death - all such terms of fear have no correspondence to any truth but the eternal law of change. Even forms can perish only as waves pass and break: they melt but to swell anew - nothing can be lost....

In the nebulous haze of our dissolution will survive the essence of all that has ever been in human life - the units of every existence that was or is, with all the affinities, all their tendencies, all their inheritance of forces making for good or evil, all the powers amassed through myriad generations, all energies that ever shaped the strength of races; and times innumerable will these again be orbed into life and thought. Transmutations there may be; changes also made by augmentation or diminution of affinities, by subtraction or addition of tendencies; for the dust of us will then have been mingled with the dust of other countless worlds and of their peoples. But nothing essential can be lost. We shall inevitably bequeath our part to the making of the future cosmos - to the substance out of which another intelligence will slowly be evolved. Even as we must have inherited something of our psychic being out of numberless worlds dissolved, so will future humanities inherit, not from us alone, but from millions of planets still existing.

For the vanishing of our world can represent, in the disparition of a universe, but one infinitesimal detail of the quenching of thought: the peopled spheres that must share our doom will exceed for multitude the visible lights of heaven.

Yet those countless solar fires, with their viewless millions of living planets, must somehow re-appear: again the wondrous Cosmos, self-born as self-consumed, must resume its sidereal whirl over the deeps of the eternities. And the love that strives forever with death shall rise again, through fresh infinitudes of pain, to renew the everlasting battle.

The light of the mother's smile will survive our sun; the thrill of her kiss will last beyond the thrilling of stars; the sweetness of her lullaby will endure in the cradle-songs of worlds yet unevolved. The tenderness of her faith will quicken the fervour of prayers to be made to the hosts of another heaven, to the gods of a time beyond Time. And the nectar of her breasts can never fail: that snowy stream will still flow on, to nourish the life of some humanity more perfect than our own, when the Milky Way that spans our night shall have vanished forever out of Space.

EXTRACTS FROM LAFCADIO HEARN'S LETTERS

To Basil Hall Chamberlain

Extracts from Lafcadio Hearn's letters to Basil Hall Chamberlain, Professor of Japanese Language at the Imperial University of Tokyo.

(i)

KUMAMOTO

14 January 1893

DEAR CHAMBERLAIN - Your delightful lines came this morning, and I waited only till after class to have this chance of chatting about something very close to my heart. I have just sent away an article about it - under the rather misleading title, 'The Japanese Smile'.

259

Your lines about Lowell almost put him into my room, and I think I can hear him talk. Now for some presumption. He is so much larger a man than I, that I would feel it presumption to differ with him on any point if I did not remember that in the psychological world a man may grow too tall to see anything near him clearly. Now first for my present position. Of course no thinker can ignore Lowell's book. The idea is too powerful, too scientific, and too well sustained not to demand the utmost respect and study. I have given both. The result is that I must *fully accept* his idea as a discovery. The point on which I struggled longest was Spencer's statement that the 'highest individuation must coincide with the greatest mutual dependence' - that evolutionary progress is 'at once towards the greatest separateness and the greatest union'. This point was hard for me to accept because, in view of other studies I made, hard for me to understand. Now understanding it, taking it as a conviction into my mind, nothing remains but to accept Lowell's view.

But still we are not at one. This is because his standpoint of pure science is too high to allow of that intimacy which means soul sympathy. I have tried to study from the bottom what he has observed from the top. Now, to me, the most beautiful, the most significant, the most attractive point of Japanese character, is revealed by the very absence of that personality to which Mr Lowell's book points as an Oriental phenomenon. I do not mean the fact *in itself*, but that which it signifies. What it signifies was very, very hard for me to understand. I could not understand some points until after a weary study of the Chinese classics. Others I understood, by guess, from passages in the *Kojiki* - in old poems, in Buddhist texts. Most of what I understand, however, I learned from mixing in the life of the people, observing, watching, questioning, wondering. Of course even now my knowledge is trifling. Still, it teaches me this:

(1) That the lack of personality is to a great extent voluntary, and that this fact is confirmed by the appearance of personality, strongly and disagreeably marked, where the social and educational conditions are new, and encourage selfishness.

(2) That every action of Japanese life in the old Japan, from prince to peasant, was religiously regulated by the spirit of self-repression for the sake of the family, the community, the nation - and that the so-called impersonality signifies the ancient moral tendency to self-sacrifice for duty's sake.

And this, here badly expressed, confirms my often avowed belief that on the moral side the old Japanese civilisation was as far in advance of the Western, as it was materially behind it. This advance was gained at some considerable sacrifice to character and mental evolution. But the loss does not signify that the moral policy was wrong. It signifies only that it was too much in the direction of mutual dependence. It was the highest possible morality from any high religious standpoint - Christian or pagan - the sacrifice of self for others. But it was in advance of the time. The indications are that the highly selfish and cunning, as well as the unselfish and frank qualities of man are necessary to the preservation of society and its development; and that in a civilisation based upon the Occidental plan, the former qualities are still much more valuable to a community than the latter. But an ideally perfect state would be the Oriental form of Confucian government, with Japanese morals, unstiffened by ultra conservatism, stimulating the development of the higher emotions and repressing the ignoble self only. It is just to such a state that we hope to attain in the unknown future. I think we have thrown Japan morally backwards a thousand years; she is going to adopt our vices (which are much too large for her). I agree with Percival Lowell, but I also agree with Viscount Torio (a wonderful thinker), and I venture the opinion that both views are reconcilable. It does not follow because we have cultivated mental and physical force to the highest pitch so far known, that our methods of cultivation are natural and right, or that we may not have ultimately to abandon all our present notions about the highest progress and the highest morality. Personally I think we are dead wrong, but that's another matter.

And now, begging pardon for so long a howl about abstracts - let me talk about my book. I have written to the firm *asking them to make it still larger*. What insolence! But I offered to sacrifice all commissions, payments, and even remuneration for articles. To me the all important point is to get out a thoroughly sympathetic book, without morbidness, just enough fun to keep in tone with modern thought. I hope I shall succeed. If not, I must try another publisher, rather than cut down the book. But I don't want another publisher. They are the Macmillans of America, beautiful printers, and essentially a *literature* firm. If I had Lowell's genius and Lowell's independence, how happy I should be. He can go where he likes, see what he likes, write what he likes and make beautiful books. I am heavily handicapped even in competing with writers as much below Lowell as he is above me.

I like a rainy day, too, with a purring stove in the room, and some writing to do.

My best wishes ever,

LAFCADIO HEARN

(ii)

17 January 1893

DEAR CHAMBERLAIN - I'm writing just because I feel lonesome; isn't that selfish? However, if I can amuse you at all, you will forgive me. You have been away a whole year, so perhaps you would like to hear some impressions of mine during that time. Here goes.

The illusions are forever over; but the memory of many pleasant things remains. I know much more about the Japanese than I did a year ago; and still I am far from understanding them well. Even my own little wife is somewhat mysterious still to me, though always in a lovable way. Of course a man and woman know each other's hearts; but outside of personal knowledge, there are race-tendencies difficult to understand. Let me tell one. In Oki we fell in love with a little *samurai* boy, who was having a hard time of it, and we took him with us. He is now like an adopted son - goes to school and all that. Well, I wished at first to pet him a little, but I found that was not in accordance with custom, and that even the boy did not understand it. At home, I therefore scarcely spoke to him at all; he remained under the control of the women of the house. They treated him kindly - though I thought coldly. The relationship I could not quite understand. He was never praised, and rarely scolded. A perfect code of etiquette was established between him and all the other persons in the house, according to degree and rank. He seemed extremely cold-mannered, and perhaps not even grateful - that was, so far as I could see. Nothing seemed to move his young placidity; whether happy or unhappy his mien was exactly that of a stone Jizō. One day he let fall a little cup and broke it. According to custom, no one noticed the mistake, for fear of giving him pain. Suddenly I saw tears streaming down his face. The muscles of the face remained quite smilingly placid as usual, but even the will could not control tears. They came freely. Then everybody laughed, and said kind things to him, till he began to laugh too. Yet that delicate sensitiveness no one like me could have guessed the existence of.

But what followed surprised me more. As I said he had been (in my idea) distantly treated. One day he did not return from school for three hours after the usual time. Then to my great surprise the women began to cry - to cry passionately. I had never been able to imagine alarm for the boy could have affected them so. And the servants ran all over town in real, not pretended, anxiety to find him. He had been taken to a teacher's house for something relating to school matters. As soon as his voice was heard at the door, everything was quiet, cold, and amiably polite again. And I marvelled exceedingly.

Sensitiveness exists in the Japanese to an extent never supposed by the foreigners who treat them harshly at the open ports. In Izumo I knew a case of a maid servant who received a slight rebuke with a smile, and then quietly went out and hung herself. I have notes of many curious suicides of a similar sort. And yet the Japanese master is never brutal or cruel. How Japanese can serve a certain class of foreigners at all, I can't understand. Possibly they do not think of them (the foreigners) as being exactly human beings, but rather *oni*, or at best *Tengu*.

Well, here is another thing. My cook wears a smiling, healthy, rather pleasing face. He is a good-looking young man. Whenever I used to think of him I thought of the smile, I saw a mask before me merry as one of those little masks of Oho-kumi-nushi-no-kami they sell at Mionoseki. One day I looked through a little hole in the *shoji*, and saw him alone. The face was not the same face. It was thin and drawn and showed queer lines worn by old hardship. I thought, 'He will look just like that when he is dead'. I went in, and the man was all changed - young and happy again - nor have I ever seen that look of trouble in his face since. But I know when he is alone he wears it. He never shows his *real* face to me; he wears the mask of happiness as an etiquette.

Do you remember that awful Parisian statue, a statue of which I forget the name, though the name might be Society? A beautiful white woman bends smiling above you in stone. A witchery is that smile of hers. After admiring her a while face to face, you turn about her, to see more of the artist's work. And then, lo and behold! the face you looked upon turns out not to be a face at all; it was a Masque; you now see the real head thrown back, in a distortion of unutterable pain. I think such an Oriental statue might also be made. This Orient knows not our deeper pains, nor can it even rise to our larger joys; but it has its pains. Its life is not so sunny as might be fancied from its happy aspect. Under the smile of its toiling millions there is suffering bravely hidden and unselfishly borne; and a lower intellectual range is counter-balanced by a childish sensitiveness to make the suffering balance evenly in the eternal order of things.

Therefore I love the people very much, more and more the more I know them.

Conversely I detest with unspeakable detestation the frank selfishness, the apathetic vanity, the shallow vulgar scepticism of the New Japan - the New Japan that prates its contempt about Tempo times, and ridicules the dear old man of the pre-Meiji era, and that never smiles, having a heart as hollow and bitter as a dried lemon.

And with this, I say good-night.

Ever most truly,

LAFCADIO HEARN

(iii)

19 January 1893

DEAR CHAMBERLAIN -...I know your own sentiments about free opinion, but there are social questions. In my preface I have taken the ground that Japan has nothing to gain by Christianity. If you think that is all right as a private opinion, I'll let it stand. If you think my heterodoxy could reflect in any way unfavourably upon the mention of yourself in the work, I'll strike out, or modify the preface. Still, I really think just what I say; the Japanese are better than the Christians, and Christianity only seems to corrupt their morals. I haven't gone that far in the book; but I am quite sure my opinions, so far as present things go, are not much out of the truth.

Fiske and others cling to the name Christianity with the desperation of drowning men; it is only a name. Our Western faith is far higher than the thing called Christianity. Our ethics have outgrown it, and burst their clothing of dogma. Our social evils are unaffected by it, except for the worse. We had to give up the legends of Genesis, the various traditions of Scriptural authorship, the belief in miracles, the belief in inspiration, the belief in vicarious sacrifice, the belief in the divinity of Christ, the belief in hell and heaven, the belief in the Father - the belief in everything but the Holy Ghost. That is advanced Unitarianism, I believe. I'm afraid, like Ruskin, of the Holy Ghost; the Lord and Giver of Life, that we don't know anything about, except as He 'wells up in consciousness'. But what is left of Christianity? Why, nothing whatever essentially of Christ. And just as surely as everything else has gone, so surely the very name must go at last. To the thinkers of a higher and more rational faith in the future, the very name - recalling so much that is horrible in human history - will be discarded because of its exclusiveness, its narrowness, and its memories

263

of blood and fire. (There's heresy for you!)

I should find living away from all Europeans rather hard, if it were not for the little world I have made around me. Some of it lingers in Matsue: but there are nearly twelve here to whom I am Life and Food and other things. However intolerable anything else is, at home I enter into my little smiling world of old ways and thoughts and courtesies, where all is soft and gentle as something seen in sleep. It is so soft, so intangibly gentle and lovable and artless, that sometimes it seems a dream only; and then a fear comes that it might vanish away. It has become Me. When I am pleased, it laughs; when I don't feel jolly, everything is silent. Thus, light and vapoury as its force seems, it is a moral force, perpetually appealing to conscience. I cannot imagine what I should do away from it. It is better to enter some old Buddhist cemetery here, than moulder anywhere else. For one may at least vaguely hope the realisation of the old Buddhist saying: 'The relation of father and child is but one life only; yet that of husband and wife is for two, and that of master and servant for three.' You know the verse, of course.

Very faithfully,

LAFCADIO HEARN

(iv)

23 January 1893

DEAR CHAMBERLAIN - With a penetration peculiarly your own, you have probed my weak point (one which your criticism makes me feel aware of for the first time strongly). Yes; I have got out of touch with Europe altogether, and think of America when I make comparisons. At nineteen years of age, after my people had been reduced from riches to poverty by an adventurer - and before I had seen anything of the world except in a year of London among the common folk - I was dropped moneyless on the pavement of an American city to begin life. Had a rough time. Often slept in the street, etc., worked as a servant, waiter, printer, proof-reader, hack-writer, gradually pulled myself up. I never gave up my English citizenship. But I had eighteen years of American life, and so got out of touch with Europe. For the same reason, I had to work at literature through American vehicles. That is no matter, however, because it has only been within the last few years that I learned to master my instrument a little - language. My first work was awfully florid. I have a novel, *Chita*, written in 1886, though not published for two or three years later, which I am now ashamed of. Self-control was the hardest thing to learn. Now I have got on far enough not to be afraid to offer work to an English publisher. Your offer of an introduction is of the highest importance possible. As for the book I think there is no doubt the publishers will yield. But I would like to try my next luck with an English firm, very much....

You tell me about your difficulty in literary composition - perhaps I can make suggestion. I do not know your method, and everybody has his own. But I think I know your difficulty - that it is also my own in Japan. Composition becomes difficult only when it becomes work - that is, literary labour without a strong inspirational impulse or an emotional feeling behind it. Now, in Japan, after my first experiences are over, I can't imagine anybody having either an inspiration or a strong emotion. The atmosphere is soporific, grey, without electricity. Therefore work has to be forced. I never write without painfully forcing myself to do it.

Now there are two ways of forced work. The first is to force thought by concentration. This is fatiguing beyond all expression - and I think injurious. I can't do it. The second way is to force the *work* only, and let the thought develop itself. This is much less fatiguing, and gives far better results - sometimes surprising results that are mistaken for inspiration.

I go to work in this way. The subject is before me; I can't bother even thinking about it. That would tire me too much. I simply arrange the notes, and write down whatever part of the subject most pleases me first. I write hurriedly without care. Then I put the MS aside for the day, and do something else more agreeable. Next day I read over the pages written, correct, and write them all over again. In the course of doing this, quite mechanically new thoughts come up, errors make themselves felt, improvements are suggested. I stop. Next day, I rewrite the third time. This is the test time. The result is a great improvement usually - but not perfection. I then take clean paper, and begin to make the final copy. Usually this has to be done twice. In the course of four to five rewritings, the whole thought reshapes itself, and the whole style is changed and fixed. The work has done itself, developed, grown; it would have been very different had I trusted to the first thought. But I let the thought define and crystallise itself.

Perhaps you will say this is too much trouble. I used to think so. But the result is amazing. The average is five perfect pages a day, with about two or three hours work. By the other method one or two pages a day are extremely difficult to write. Indeed I do not think I could write one perfect page a day, by thinking out everything as I write. The mental strain is too much. The fancy is like a horse that goes well without whip or spur, and refuses duty if either are used. By petting it and leaving it free, it surpasses desire. I know when the page is fixed by a sort of focussing it takes - when the first impression has returned after all corrections more forcibly than at first felt, and in half the space first occupied. Perhaps you have done all this in prose, as you must have done it in other work; but if you have not, you will be astonished at the relief it gives. My whole book was written thus. Of course it looks like big labour to rewrite every page half a dozen times. But in reality it is the least possible labour. To those with whom writing is almost an automatic exertion, the absolute fatigue is no more than that of writing a letter. The rest of the work *does itself*, without your effort. It is like spiritualism. Just move the pen, and the ghosts do the wording, etc. I am writing this only as a letter to you. It makes so many pages. If I were writing it for print, I would rewrite at least five times - with the result of putting the same thoughts much more forcibly in half the space. Then again, I keep the thing going like a conjurer's balls. The first day's five pp. are recopied the second, and another five written; the third day the first five are again recopied, and another five written. There is always matter ahead, though, I never recopy more than the first five, at one time. When these are finished, then I begin the second five. The average is five per day, 150 pp. per month. Another important thing is to take the most agreeable part of the subject first. Order is of no earthly consequence, but a great hindrance. The success of this part gives encouragement, and curiously develops the idea of the relative parts.

Well, perhaps, I have been telling you something you know more about than I; but comparing notes is always good, and often a help. And now for another subject.

There is a queer custom in Izumo which may interest you. When a wedding takes place in the house of an unpopular man in the country, the young men of the village carry a roadside statue of Jizō into the *zashiki*, and announce the coming of the god. (This is especially done with an avaricious farmer, or a stingy family.) Food and wine are demanded for the god. The members of the family must come in, salute the deity, and give all the sake and food demanded while any remains in the house. It is dangerous to refuse; the young peasants would probably wreck the house. After this, the statue is carried back again to its place. The visit of Jizō is much dreaded. It is never made to persons who are liked. In the cities this is not done, but stones are thrown into the house in heaps. Such an action is an expression of public opinion almost as strong as that of our Western charivari.

Ever faithfully,

LAFCADIO HEARN

... English self-suppression is certainly a marvellous quality. Yet it is something so different from this Eastern self-control. Its pent-up vital force moreover finds vent in many ways unknown to the Orient, and foreign to its character. And lastly; is it not considerably one-sided? Is it not confined to the outer repression of everything suggesting weakness or affection - not to the masking of other feelings? Think of Heine's Englishman, with a black halo of spleen cutting against the sunny Italian sky! But, jest aside, see the faces of London (I remember them still) or the faces of any English crowd. There is such pain and passion there. Again, the extraordinary mobility and development of the facial muscles, shows something totally different to the Buddhist jihi-calm of these Japanese masks. If we could draw a line at all I would say it lies here: We suppress the amiable facial expression, and expose the aggressive and the sorrowful and the painful feelings; while the Japanese cultivate the former, even as a mask, and suppress, in physiognomical play, everything representing the latter. Of course the peculiar nakedness of the American face greatly exaggerates the harder side of physiognomy, as we know it in Europe. America is the country of terrible faces: Fourier ought to have lived in it before writing his chapter on the physiognomy of the *civilisés*. One other thing in the way of opposites, I think, is that we suppress certain forms of action more than their expression by physiognomy; while the Japanese repress the facial exhibition more than the action which would be the ultimate possible result of the feeling in question. A Western man would (unless belonging to a very artificial class of society) be apt to look serious before killing himself. But even the average Japanese would smile more pleasantly, and act more kindly than usual, just before cutting his throat or lying down in front of a railway train. Hard and fast lines, however, are difficult to draw. Nothing is so hazardous as to attempt to make any general statement - and yet no temptation is stronger.

Ever with best wishes,

LAFCADIO HEARN

(v)

22 January 1893

DEAR CHAMBERLAIN - I predicted a letter from Nagasaki; but the prediction I found too difficult to fulfil. In fact I fled away from Nagasaki, and propose to relate to you the history of my adventures, or some of them.

I left Kumamoto on the morning of the 20th, alone, en route for Nagasaki via Hyakkwan. From Kumamoto to Hyakkwan is about one and one-half hours by *jinricksha*. A dirty little country village in a sea of ricefields, is Hyakkwan. The people are simple and good. I found one of my students there studying Chinese. Then I took a boat for the steamer. The boat was a broken-nosed boat.

The boat left the creek and wriggled over a sea, still as the silent sea of Coleridge's poem, unto the distance of four *ri*. It was tiresome. Then it stopped and waited; and for more than an hour I watched the water surface sinuously moving with a queer motion as of reticulated stuffs being pulled in opposite directions, network of ripples above network of ripples. There was nothing else to watch. At last I saw an inverted comma on the edge of the sky. It came nearer. Finally I heard a scream of steam that filled my soul with joy. But it turned out to be the wrong steamer. I waited one more hour in that boat, and the right steamer appeared.

Except for the Oki steamer I never became familiar with such an instrument of torture. Her name was the *Taiko Maru*. She was built only for *kimono* or *yukata*, and for the squatting position. The heat was that of the drying room of a steam-laundry. There was nothing to drink but tea. I slept on the *tatami*, comfortably, with my head on a pillow of leather paper stamped with the curious figure of an elephant-headed Karashishi. Had I donned Japanese clothes instead of a duck suit, I would have been comfortable. But as I was going to a European hotel, I dressed according to the code - for which I was very sorry later on.

We reached Nagasaki at 3 am, the blackest hour. A coolie promised to take me to the hotel, but took me a mile away from it and then said he did not know where it was. I took my baggage from him, and found a belated *kurumaya* to take me to the hotel. It was locked up. I put my shoulder against the gate, and it opened and I went up steps between heights of clipped shrubbery and ranks of flower pots filled with ornamental plants into a piazza, full of rocking-chairs and lamps and silence. There

I waited for sunrise. Sunrise over the bay was really lovely; I saw strips of gold, like those of the old ballads. And at last the house woke up and I got a room.

But it was too hot to stay in the hotel. A dead heat, worse than any tropical heat I ever felt, and getting worse as the sun rose. I hired a *kuruma* and rushed about. I saw the beautiful city in the most beautiful light possible; I climbed the hills; I visited the new metal *torii*. Let me assure you that it is very ugly - that *torii*; it is the ugliest I ever saw in Japan. It is monstrously shaped, looks top-heavy, has no grace, and is of a sooty stove-colour. Whoever made the design ought to be killed with the edge of the sword.

Then I got breakfast and went out again. The sum of my impressions was that Nagasaki is the prettiest seaport I ever saw, full of picturesqueness and quaintness - made for artists to etch and for photographers to photograph. But I could not buy anything I wanted, or find anything I wished to find in a Western line. Very few foreigners - and no books - nothing to pick up - no supplies to be had except in large quantities.

As the day grew hotter, I began to grieve exceedingly that I had put on a duck suit, and had gone to the Bellevue Hotel. Comfort inside of Western clothes and Western architecture in such heat was out of the question. Not even in Venezuela, in the hottest hours of the afternoon, did I ever feel such heat. In the hotel I heard the guests say they could not sleep for the heat. There was nothing for it except iced drinks at twenty-five cents. I drank about four yen worth, and was angry with all the world, because I could not strip or be comfortable. By six o'clock I determined to flee away. The heat was hell - and though I like heat, the combination of heat and stupid convention is something beyond my power of endurance. If I had to wear European clothes and live in a European house in such heat for one week, I should go crazy or die. I resolved to flee away from Nagasaki at once.

In a Japanese hotel one can always be comfortable and naked. In a Japanese hotel everything you want to buy is found for you. In a Japanese hotel arrangements are made to take you anywhere you want to go. In a Japanese hotel they buy your tickets for you, and accompany you to the steamer or railroad. But in the beastly Western hotels, nobody will even answer a question. There is nobody to ask, except depraved Japanese servants who understand no language when asked to take any trouble. I got a *kuruma* and went to a Japanese steamship company, and begged them, in my bad Japanese, to get me outside of Nagasaki as quick as possible. To my surprise they understood and sympathised with me, and promised to send for me at 3 am. I waited in the hotel till the heat became so atrocious that even the mosquitoes had not strength to bite - then I tried to go out. But men wearing shirt-tails asked me if I 'wanna nice girl' - so I went back again, and sat in the stifling verandah until 3 am. Then the Japanese Company sent a man and a sampan for me, and took me away. And I blessed them therefor.

Got out of the harbour by half-past three, on the *Kinrin Maru* (an old acquaintance), with a ticket for Misumi. From Misumi I was told a small steamer would take me to Hyakkwan. Got to Misumi at 9 am. But there was no small steamer that day.

At Misumi there is a hotel, the Urashimaya, built and furnished in Western style, as much superior to the Nagasaki hotel as the sun is superior to a farthing candle. Also a very beautiful woman, graceful as a dragon-fly, with a voice like the tinkling of a crystal wind-bell, took care of me, hired *kurumaya*, gave me a splendid breakfast, and charged me for all the entertainment only forty *sen* .

She understood my Japanese, and talked to me, and I felt like a soul suddenly reborn in the heart of a luminous lotus-flower in the garden of Paradise. Also all the maidens of the hotel seemed to me *tennin* - since I had just escaped from the most frightful place of sojourn that exists in this world. And summer mists bathed sea and hills and all distant things - a world of divinely soft blue, the blue of iridescent mother-of-pearl. There were a few white clouds dreaming in the sky; and they threw long white trembling lights on the water. And I dreamed of Urashima. The small soul of me drifted out over that summer sea, steeped in all the blue light - and in the fairy boat there was a maiden standing, more beautiful than the blue light itself, and softer, and sweeter; and she said to me in a voice that seemed to come from a thousand summers back, 'Now we will go to my father's palace, the Dragon Palace under the waves of the South.' But I said, 'No; I must go home to Kumamoto; I have telegraphed, you see.' 'Then you will pay the *kurumaya* only seventy-five *sen*', she made answer, 'and you can come back again when you wish, because you will not open the box.' And in this day-dream there came to me the interpretation of the divine old story; and I learned the mystery of it and the meaning. I put the box into my heart of hearts, and went away.

Hours I watched the blue world, and wondered at the loveliness of it, and thought of the old Gods and their ways - though along the road ran a line of telegraph poles. And upon all the telegraph top wires sat rows of little white-breasted birds. I saw they always sat with their heads towards the road. They watched us passing without fear. I counted hundreds. Not one sat with its tail to the road - not even one. All seemed waiting for something. I kept on counting them till I fell asleep in the *kuruma* , and floated away somewhere in a phantom-boat; and the daughter of the Dragon-King stood over me and smiled and said, 'You will pay the *kurumaya* only seventy-five *sen*'....

Drums awoke me - peasants in all the villages invoking the rain. No rain; only white clouds - ghosts of clouds that died a thousand summers ago - or perhaps that summer mist that escaped from Urashima's box. (Really he was foolish to open the box. I remember opening such a box long, long ago. Therefore my soul became old.) Always the birds in rows on the telegraph wires, and not even one with its tail turned to the road. There were picturesque scenes. Nagahama village was pretty. It possesses a great spring at the foot of a hill. There boys and girls were bathing together. I stopped to look at them. A young girl lifted a bucket of cold water to give the runner to drink, and her light dress opening with the effort showed the ripeness of a youth sweet as fruit before it has become too soft. Always beating of drums at every village for rain.

The *kurumaya* deserts me. Is succeeded by a fraud. I discharge the fraud in the middle of rice fields and tramp on alone, carrying my own baggage. Kumamoto is still three and one half *ri* distant. The little birds watch me from the telegraph wires. Extraordinary *semi* - quite different from those of Izumo - cry piteously and utter plaintive squeals when seized by little boys. Of course it is like squealing with one's feet instead of with one's mouth. But being directed by will, and for the purpose of exciting compassion, the squeal is equally pathetic.

Then I find a good *kurumaya* and proceed. I get home as the shadows lengthen. The sun has flayed my hands, and I have eaten nothing since nine o'clock, and I have not been in bed for three days, and I have not a dry thread on me. But I am home again, and therefore supremely happy. Nagasaki exists for me only as an evil dream of a hotel in hell, with the seven deadly sins for waiters. Certainly I shall never see it again. It is the hardest place to go to, or to escape from, in the whole world. When I was in it Kumamoto seemed to me displaced by magic to the distance of 100,000 miles, beyond long successions of typhoons and mountain ranges. I am again in a *yukata* - upon *tatami* - in real Japan. Of my trip I have nevertheless some pleasant recollections - and a pretty fan, representing mountains and summer-sea, and bearing the name 'Urashimaya'. At sight of it the vision and the dream return. I will often see them again; for the box will never be opened. But I was obliged to disobey the daughter of the Dragon-God in one thing; I paid the *kurumaya* - one yen and twenty-five *sen*. Had they only known they could have made me pay one hundred and twenty-five yen.

'How much', my wife asks me, 'would you accept on condition of spending a week more in the Bellevue Hotel, Nagasaki?'

'Surely', I answer, 'no sum earthly. Only the promise of perpetual youth in the palace of the Dragon-God for a thousand years, or a transportation to the Paradise of Amida Buddha.'

Ever with best regards,

LAFCADIO HEARN

16 August 1893

DEAR CHAMBERLAIN - I have been a little neglectful, because of my reverie about Urashima, called 'The Dream of a Summer Day', which I am now sending to Boston. Many, many thanks for your kindness in having the text looked at for me. And do you know, the beauty of that word Elysium greatly grew as I contemplated *Horai*, and felt that it could never be made to convey any idea to an English reader, and that only the Greek word could render the idea of ghostly happiness properly?...

The great plague of summer nights here is insects. So came the goblins about Saint Anthony. Two curious beetles, one of which is shaped hexagonally, are especially tormenting, as they produce when alarmed the most atrocious conceivable smell. On the other hand, the singing insects are wonderful. A cricket called *junta* is very musical here, more than in Izumo, and really seems to talk. Other creatures at night sing like birds.

One of these is cooked and eaten by *geisha* to make their voices sweet.

Ever most sincerely,

LAFCADIO HEARN

(vi)

11 October 1893

DEAR CHAMBERLAIN - I am thinking it is time to write you - though there is no news. Suppose I write you of one day of my life as a sample. I don't see why I shouldn't - though I would not write it to anybody else on either side the world.

Morning, 6 am - The little alarm clock rings. Wife rises and wakes me, with the salutation *de rigueur* of old *samurai* days. I get myself into a squatting posture, draw the never-extinguished *hibachi* to the side of the *futons*, and begin to smoke. The servants enter, prostrate themselves, and say good morning to the *danna-sama*, and proceed to open the *tō*. Meanwhile in the other chambers the little oil lamps have been lighted before the tablets of the ancestors, and the Buddhist (not the Shinto) deities - and prayers are being said, and offerings to the ancestors made. (Spirits are not supposed to eat *the food* offered them - only to absorb some of its living essence. Therefore the offerings are very small.) Already the old men are in the garden, saluting the rising sun, and clapping their hands, and murmuring the Izumo prayers. I stop smoking, and make my toilet on the *engawa*.

7 am - Breakfast, very light - eggs and toast. Lemonade with a spoonful of whiskey in it; and black coffee. Wife serves; and I always make her eat a little with me. But she eats sparingly, as she must afterwards put in an appearance at the regular family breakfast. Then *kurumaya* comes. I begin to put on my *yofuku*. I did not at first like the Japanese custom - that the wife should give each piece of clothing in regular order, see to the pockets, etc.; I thought it encouraged laziness in a man. But when I tried to oppose it, I found I was giving offence and spoiling pleasure. So I submit to the ancient rule.

7.30 am - All gather at the door to say *sayonara*; but the servants stand outside, according to the new custom requiring the servants to stand when the master is in *yofuku*. I light a cigar - kiss a hand extended to me (this is the only imported custom), and pass to the school.

(*Blank of 4 to 5 hours.*)

Returning, at the call of the *kurumaya*, all come to the door again as before, to greet me with the *O-Kaeri*; and I have to submit to aid in undressing, and in putting on the *kimono, obi*, etc. The kneeling-cushion and *hibachi* are ready. There is a letter from Chamberlain San, or Mason San. Dinner.

The rest eat only when I am finished: because there are two *ukyo*, but I am the worker. The principle is that the family supporter's wants are first to be considered - though in other matters he does not rank first. For instance, the place of honour when sitting together is always by age

271

and parentage. I then take the fourth place, and wife the fifth. And the old man is always then served the first.

During the repast there is a sort of understanding that the rest of the family and the servants are not to be disturbed without necessity. There is no rule; but the custom I respect. So I never go into that part of the house unnecessarily till they are finished. There is also some etiquette about favourite places, which is strictly observed.

3 pm 4. - If very hot, everybody sleeps - the servants sleeping by turns. If cool and pleasant, all work. The women make clothes. The men do all kinds of little things in the garden and elsewhere. Children come to play. The *Asahi Shimbun* arrives.

6 pm - Bath hour.

6.30 - 7.30 - Supper.

8 pm - Everybody squats round the *hako-hibachi* to hear the *Asahi Shimbun* read, or to tell stories. Sometimes the paper does not come - then curious games are played, in which the girls join. The mother sews at intervals. One game is very original. A piece of string is tied in a large loop and a number of little loops and ends are made with short pieces of string. Then the large loop is spread on a velvet *zabuton*, so as to form the outline of the face of Otafuku. Blindfolded, then, the players must put the other loose ends and bits of string inside the circle, so as to make the rest of the face. But this is hard to do, and every mistake produces extraordinary comicalities. But if the night is very fine, we sometimes go out - always taking turns so that the girls get their share of the outing. Sometimes the theatre is the attraction. Sometimes there are guests. I think the greatest joy, though, is the discovery and purchase of odd or pretty things in some lamp-lit shop at night. It is brought home in great triumph, and all sit round it in a circle to admire. My own evening, however, is generally passed in writing. If guests come for me, the rest of the family remains invisible till they go away - except wife, that is, if the guests are important. Then she sees to their comfort. Ordinary guests are served only by the girls.

As evening wanes, the turn of the *kami-sama* comes. During the day, they received their usual offerings; but it is at night the special prayers are made. The little lamps are lighted; and each of the family in turn, except myself, say the prayers and pay reverence. These prayers are always said standing, but those to the *hotoke* are said kneeling. Some of the prayers are said for me. I was never asked to pray but once - when there was grief in the house; and then I prayed to the gods, repeating the Japanese words one by one as they were told to me. The little lamps of the *kami* are left to burn themselves out.

All wait for me to give the signal of bed-time - unless I should become so absorbed in writing as to forget the hour. Then I am asked if I am not working too hard. The girls spread the futons in the various rooms; and the *hibachi* are replenished, so that we - i.e., I and the men only - may smoke during the night if we wish. Then the girls prostrate themselves with an *o-yasumi*! and all becomes quiet.

Sometimes I read till I fall asleep. Sometimes I keep on writing with a pencil in bed - but always, according to ancient custom, the little wife asks *pardon for being the first to go to sleep*. I once tried to stop the habit - thinking it too humble. But after all it is pretty - and is so set into the soul that it could not be stopped. And this is an ordinary day in outline. Then we sleep.

Faithfully ever,

LAFCADIO HEARN

(vii)

14 December 1893

DEAR CHAMBERLAIN - What you said in your last letter about the effect of darkness upon you in childhood, haunted me: I thought I would revert to it another time. And now that about one hundred compositions have been corrected, I can find a chance to chat about it.

You specified nothing: I understand the feeling itself was vague - like many other feelings of childhood of which the indefiniteness itself is a fear - a sort of mysterious depression of which you could not yourself have told the cause. (This I also remember - but it became coupled with other unpleasant sensations of which I shall speak presently.) It seems to me these feelings of earliest childhood - so intense and yet so vague - are the weirdest in all human experience, and that for the best of reasons: *they are really ghostly*. Not of our own experience are these; they [are] of the dead - of the vanished generations behind us; and I am not sure but that our pleasures are equally weird at that age. I remember crying loudly at an air played upon the piano, in the midst of a fashionable gathering; and I remember people (long buried) whose names I have quite forgotten, making their voices and faces kind, and trying to coax me to tell what was the matter. Naturally I could not tell; I can only vaguely guess now; I know the emotions stirred within my child-heart were not me - but of other lives. But *then* I had to give a reason: so I lied. I said I was thinking of my uncle who was dead (though I never really cared for him at all). Then I got petting, the cake, and wondered, young as I was, how I had been able to deceive.

Have you not noticed how utterly the psychologists have failed to explain the fear that comes in dreams? The suspension of will-power is given as an explanation; but that will not do, because there is frequently loss of will-power in dreams unaccompanied by the *real* fear of nightmare. The real fear of nightmare is greater than any fear possible to experience in waking moments; it is the highest possible form of mental suffering; it is so powerful that were it to last more than a few instants it would cause death; and it is so intimately linked to feelings of which we know nothing in waking hours - feelings not belonging to life at all - that we cannot describe it. It is certainly well that we cannot. Now I have long fancied that this form of fear also is explainable only by the inheritance of ancestral memories - not any one painful experience, but the multitudinous fears of a totally unknown past, which the gods have otherwise mercifully enabled us to forget. The memories themselves are indeed gone - only the sensations of them remain, stir into life at vague moments of sleep, and especially in the sleep of sickness, when the experiences of real life grow faintest in recollection.

Well, when I was a child, bad dreams took for me real form and visibility. In my waking hours *I saw* them. They walked about noiselessly and made hideous faces at me. Unhappily I had no mother then - only an old grandaunt who never had children of her own, and who hated superstition. If I cried for fear in the dark, I only got whipped for it; but the fear of ghosts was greater than the fear of whippings - *because I could see the ghosts*. The old lady did not believe me; but the servants did, and used to come and confort me by stealth. As soon as I was old enough to be sent to a child-school, I was happier - because, though badly treated there, I had companions at night who were not ghosts. Gradually the phantoms passed - I think when I was about ten or eleven I had ceased to fear. It is only in dreams now that the old fear ever comes back.

Now I believe in ghosts. Because I saw them? Not at all. I believe in ghosts, though I disbelieve in souls. I believe in ghosts because there are no ghosts now in the modern world. And the difference between a world full of ghosts and another kind of world, shows us what ghosts mean - and gods.

The awful melancholy of that book of Pearson's may be summed up in this, I think - 'The Aspirational has passed forever out of life'. It is horribly true. What made the aspirational in life? Ghosts. Some were called gods, some demons, some angels; they changed the world for man - they gave him courage and purpose and the awe of Nature that slowly changed into love; they filled all things with a sense and motion of invisible life; they made both terror and beauty.

There are no ghosts, no angels and demons and gods: all are dead. The world of electricity, steam, mathematics, is blank and cold and void. No man can even write about it. Who can find a speck of romance in it? What are our novelists doing? Crawford must write of Italy or India or ancient Persia; Kipling of India; Black of remote Scotch country life; James lives only as a marvellous psychologist, and he has to live and make his characters live on the Continent; Howells portrays the ugliest and harshest commonplaces of a transient democracy. What great man is writing, or can write of fashionable society anything worth reading, or of modern middle life, or of the poor of cities - unless after the style of 'Ginx's Baby'? No! those who write must seek their material in those parts of the world where ghosts still linger - in Italy, in Spain, in Russia, in the old atmosphere of Catholicism. The Protestant world has become bald and cold as a meeting-house. The ghosts are gone; and the results of their departure prove how real they were. The Cossacking of Europe might have one good result - that of bringing back the ghosts - with that Wind of the Spirit which moves the ocean of Russian peasant life for the gathering storm.

Sometimes I think of writing a paper to be called 'The Vanishing of the Gods'.

Perhaps you are tired of theories. But I want to speak of one thing more - *a theoriser*, a beautiful French boy of seventeen, whose name was Henry Charles Reade. He died at seventeen. Friends who loved him collected his boyish poems, and printed them in a little book, seven or eight years ago. One of these poems expresses a sensation only a psychologist of power could explain. It relates to what Spencer tells us is relative to all antecedent experience. I offer my own 'overdone' translation of it - because I have not the original. The original was more simple, and in all respects worthy of a better rendering; but the idea is as follows:

I think that God resolved to be
    Ungenerous when I came one earth,
And that the heart *He* gave to me
    Was old already ere my birth.
He placed within my childish breast
    A worn-out heart - to save expense! -
A heart long tortured by unrest
    And torn by passion's violence.
Its thousand tender scars proclaim
    A thousand episodes of woe: -
And yet I know not how it came
    By all those wounds which hurt it so!
Within its chambers linger hosts
    Of passion-memories never mine -
Dead fires - dreams faded out - the ghosts
    Of suns that long have ceased to shine.
Perfumes, deliriously sweet,
    Of loves that I have never known,
It holds - and burns with maddening heat
    For beauty I may never own.
O weirdest fate! - O hopeless woe!
    Anguish unrivalled! - peerless pain! -
To wildly love - and never know
    The object wildly loved in vain!

    Certainly the lad who could write such a poem at sixteen might have been a poet if he lived - don't you think so?

LAFCADIO HEARN

(viii)

10 June 1894

DEAR CHAMBERLAIN - Today I could not stand it any longer. I dismissed my class abruptly for the first time, and went home to write a letter of resignation. After having written it, I tore it up, and went, for the first time in my life, to the house of Sakurai (he has a brother professor in the university), the headmaster. He is civilised, having been educated in France; and I felt some confidence in him, because he allows no one to be familiar with him. I could not find him in his house: he was at an archery club. I sat down, or knelt down, in the archery shed, and looked at all those Oriental impassive faces, and my courage began to ooze away. Perhaps you don't know what it is to want to say something very private, and find your man for the time being part of a public in nowise interested in you - rather the reverse. But I stuck it out, saying now or never; and after the archery asked to see the gentleman privately. Happily no one else understands French. I went to his house, and conversed with him very guardedly - mentioning no names, but simply giving my three years' experience of discomfort. He smiled and seemed to understand, thought a little, became suddenly impassive, and said: 'You are generally liked - they are not polite and courteous; and besides Japanese are cold. You have no friend, I know; but I am your well-wisher, and I keep your confidence. If there be anything very disagreeable, come to me and tell me frankly, and I'll settle it as well as I can. As for your contract, that oversight was only due to your being so long here, that we forgot to ask you. When the director comes back, we settle that.' I said: 'I am no longer interested in staying; I am only interested in being able to go away on good terms.' I think he understands exactly what I refer to, and I think he will hold his peace to all but the director. The director dislikes the person I am troubled by, and there may be found a way to get rid of him. But the headmaster, who is a perfect gentleman, would not like me even to think he understood; and I believe we talked in riddles all the time. However, I have more courage now to finish the three weeks left.

Yet Lowell says the Japanese have no individuality! I wish he had to teach here for a year, and he would discover some of the most extraordinary individuality he ever saw. There are eccentrics and personalities among the Japanese as with us: only, they show less quickly on the surface. No man can make a sweeping general statement about Japanese character in a negative sense, without finding out his mistake later. It is only by degrees, however, that one finds out they have just as much difference among them as any Orientals. But physiologically and conventionally these are less perceptible at first sight.

Won't you think me a crank, writing all this stuff? But it is part of the record of a disillusioned enthusiast. You remember my first letters from Izumo. *Quantum matatus ab illo*! The iron - Japanese iron - has entered into my soul -

And thro' the body of the Knight
  He made cauld iron gae, gae,
  He made cauld iron gae!

Ever,

LAFCADIO HEARN

(ix)

YOKOHAMA, 15 July 1894

DEAR CHAMBERLAIN - This is a very bad letter, because written under difficulties. I hope to run up to 19 Akasaka Daimachi tomorrow, for a couple of days.

I have been intimately acquainted with Mason for more than a million years, and understand, I think, just why you like each other. Mason is what Goethe would have called 'a beautiful soul'. I have been to his charming little home, and felt quite in Paradise there, and love everything and everybody in it. We passed today at Kamakura swimming and indulging in debaucheries of beefsteak, whiskey and lemonade, gin and ginger ale and beer. His son was with us - and I like the little man very much; we soon became friends. Well, you understand how very, very delightful things were. I should not trust myself to say exactly what I felt about our holiday. We are to take a trip together presently.

Coming out of my solitude of nearly five years to stand on the deck of the *Kobe Maru* on the 10th, I felt afraid, I saw myself again among giants. Everything seemed huge, full of force, dignity, massive potentialities divined but vaguely. A sudden sense of the meaning of that civilisation I had been so long decrying and arguing against, and vainly rebelling against, came upon me crushingly. In another few hours I had new friends.

The first man I spoke to was an engineer. He and I felt each other at once. He had been, like myself, a wanderer - had seen Mt Everest from a bungalow in Nepal, and studied many things.

The twin bits of our race-souls touched at once. What no Japanese could feel, that rough square man knew, and he seemed to me a deity, or a demi-deity - and I felt like one about to worship Western gods.

Another day, and I was in touch with England again. How small suddenly my little Japan became! - how lonesome! What a joy to feel the West! What a great thing is the West! What new appreciations of it are born of isolation! What a horrible place the school! - I was a prisoner released from prison after five years' servitude!

Then I stopped thinking. For I saw my home, the lights of its household gods, and my boy reaching out his little hands to me - and all the simple charm and love of old Japan. And the fairy-world seized my soul again, very softly and sweetly, as a child might catch a butterfly.

Still, I am rather inclined to look forward to Tokyo. I can't dislike it any more. I have seen Mason's home, so Tokyo seems to me very beautiful after all. What queer experiences these! - how they make a man feel himself a creature of the forces of life, moved and moulded by that which is outside of himself!

How would it be were I here for a couple of years? Just now, you know, I seem to be in Scandinavia. Never did I see so many blond men with accipitrine noses, berserker eyebrows, etc. I did not know how fair Englishmen were till now. I give up many notions. I must write of disillusions, and speak respectfully of the open ports.

Faithfully,

LAFCADIO HEARN

Excuse this letter. The room is awfully hot, and I'm writing on a washstand.

(x)

TOKYO, 17 July 1894

DEAR CHAMBERLAIN - The banks were inaccessible for three days after my arrival in Yokohama, and it was only yesterday afternoon (Monday) that I was able to wind up my little business in Yokohama, and wire to Toda. (By the way, the bank manager, a very nice fellow - after giving me a lecture for not having settled the business a year ago - practically made me a present of fifty yen. I don't think bankers are such terrible people after all. Certainly no American banker would have done it - at least not for an insignificant school-teacher.)

Well, now for what would have been written last night had I not been very tired.

On the way from Shimbashi, I stopped at Hasegawa's, gave him two stories, and liked him. At your house all was in waiting for me; but the dog first made my acquaintance - running before to the gate. He is now watching my every movement as I write, and we are good friends.

Mr Toda is too kind, and takes too much trouble for me. He was not in at the moment I came - but making preparations for me on the strength of the telegram. He speaks English - which is delightful, as I can express all my wants. The charm of the home lacks but one thing - your presence; but I am not selfish enough to wish you to leave the mountains even for a day while this prodigious heat lasts. (I like heat; but I doubt if many do; and the heat in Tokyo is tropical.) I can't yet write my impressions about 19 - as I am still confused with kindnesses. Only - that delightful casket in the room upstairs with the medallion on top enclosing a picture of some structure that might have been the stately pleasure dome of Kubla Khan - what a fairy-thing it is!...

And now for confessions. I am glad my paper on *jiujutsu* was not published; and I am grateful to the gods for having been obliged to visit Tokyo and Yokohama. The *jiujutsu* paper must be remodelled; and my ideas of the open ports reconstructed, repaired, renovated, and decorated. I have received from the gods inspiration for a paper - the Romance of the Open Ports - or, perhaps, the morality of the open ports. If I had Michelet's divine gift of uttering tender surprises, I could startle the world with a paper on the ideas that came to me the other day. Perhaps there are illusions among them, too. But, after all, what are all high ideals but illusions, and all high thought and sentiment lives by them, and ascends by them, as by those golden fairy-ladders of legend - whereof each step vanishes as quickly as the foot passes it? Really, I was totally unfitted to make any judgements about the ports when I left them. I had had my ugly experiences with American business men and American tricksters, who played the role of friends for a purpose; I had seen infinitely too much of the black side of life as a journalist of long standing; I was uncomfortably situated and had Hinton in my thoughts as a colonial type. In short, I had seen nothing which I ought to have seen. Then, by contrast, the caressing atmosphere into which I entered on going to Izumo - where secret orders had been given 'to make the foreigner happy' - affected my judgement still more. Now comes the turn. The hospitable openness, the sympathies, and the abnegations light up for me all at once.

But here is the principal fact that impressed me about the moral question - *entre nous*: for I don't want anybody else to get on the track of the idea till I develop it.

Morality is not shown by any unavoidable obedience to codes - indeed, it's often shown in the breaking of them. It is shown best, I think, when men, in defiance of traditions, conventions, and prejudices - without any obligation, and in utter disregard of their own interests - follow the guiding of their hearts on the path of what they feel to be eternally right and true. Race prejudice and cruelty *do* exist: they exist everywhere a little; and the unfortunate quality of goodness is that it remains invisible and silent. Love and generosity do not get themselves talked about: they never 'advertise' - as Kipling would say. And, indeed, the fact that they are taken as a matter of course suggests their commonness. In connection with all this, there is a beautiful subject - requiring very delicate handling - that has never been touched. What of the numbers who have given up England, France, Italy — all the large Western life - all that made them, and all that must in silent hours pull at their heart-strings as the sea pulls at the soul of a boy - for pure love of duty? Never again will they dwell with their kindred - never visit the scenes they dream of in sick hours, when the Past floats back to say, hand in hand with the Shadow of Death - 'We are waiting, Come'! They have wealth; they have no obstacles or laws to hinder them. Only moral obligations they need not perforce obey. But even these have little to do with the matter. It is simply love - purified affection, from which every atom of selfishness has been sifted out ages ago. In the brief time since I got on the *Kobe Maru* I have learned so many astonishing things, that it really seems to me I must have been guilty of blasphemies in other days - may the gods forgive my ignorance! - And then the tales of prejudice! Numbers have given their whole lives and brains and means not merely to do what is right and good, but what is extraordinary and generous to the uttermost limit of their human capacity. My imaginary hard-fisted and cold-hearted businessmen of the colonies vanish away - phantoms only; and in their places what warm human realities appear! Really there is a vast romance to be written here in a few words - with help of thoughts and illustrations from evolutional philosophy. How you should smile to compare this letter with other letters written long ago! But in a few years more, how will I be writing to you again? Truly we have not permanent opinions until our mental growth is done. The opinions we have are simply lent us for a while by the gods - at compound interest.

Really, I must try later to get into this exiled Western life, and love it, and study it, and tell all the beautiful things there are in it, leaving that which is not beautiful to be related by its enemies.

'Read *all* my books'!! - I haven't been able to read anything yet. I may be able to take a few glimpses at some one corner of this wilderness of good things. I will read the titles, though, as knowing what you have may help me later to pick up for you something you have not.

Mason and I project a trip to Nagano for a few days. I will leave my valise with your kind Toda, and seek Zenkoji - whither all the dead must go before their journey to the Meido. Mason is a man awfully fond of movement. I could not live as he has to do. Had I such a sweet little home in Tokyo, nothing could pull me out of it except at vast intervals of time. He needs exercise, however, and reminds me of a Targui (the plural 'Touareg(s)' is always used by the papers, in spite of the books about that extraordinary race). You know they are very tall fair men with blue eyes (when the race is pure.) 'They can be known far off by their walk - *long and measured, like the stride of the ostrich.'*

Ever with best regards and - but I can't thank you on paper for all this, you know! I shall try to revenge myself at some future day -

LAFCADIO HEARN

(xi)

11 September 1894

DEAR CHAMBERLAIN - Glad to get even a line in from you - though it has not brought me as good news of you as I could wish. Perhaps it is only the unsettled weather: the clear autumn may bring back strength.

I was interested by Lowell's letter. Since I first read of Schiaparelli's discovery, I had always wondered why different astronomers could not agree on the character of the so-called canals - many pronouncing them double, others single. Lowell would seem really to have hit the cause. - What are the canals? *Are* they canals, or only the lines of a monstrous planetary breaking-up?

I have just sent off another sketch, 'A Wish Fulfilled' - the story of one day of a Japanese soldier.

Lord! Lord! what *is* morality? Nature's law - the cosmic law - is struggle, cruelty, pain - everything religion declares essentially immoral. The bird devours the fly, the cat the bird. Everything has been shaped, evolved, developed by atrocious immorality. Our lives are sustained only by murder. Passions are given, which, if satisfied, would stifle the earth with population, were there not other passions of cruelty and avarice to counteract them. Perhaps it is the higher morality that the strong races should rob the weak - deprive them of liberties and rights - compel them to adopt beastly useless conventions - insult their simple faith - force upon them not the higher pleasures but the deeper pains of an infinitely more complicated and more unhappy civilisation.

There certainly is no answer to this. It is contrary to all our inborn feelings of right. But what is that feeling? Only the necessary accompaniment of a social state. Does it correspond to any supreme law of the universe? - or is it merely relative? We *know* it is relative; we don't know anything about the ultimate laws. The God of the Universe may be a Devil, only mocking us with contradictions - forcing us through immeasurable pain to supreme efforts which are to end in nothing but the laughter of skulls in a world's dust. Who knows? - We are only what we can't help being.

From remote time all my ancestors were in the army. Yet to kill the fly that buzzes round me as I write this letter seems to me wrong. To give pain knowingly, even to one whom I dislike, gives more pain to myself. Psychology tells me the why - the origin of the feeling. But not by any such feeling is the world ruled - or will so be ruled for incalculable time. Such dispositions are counted worthless and weak, and are unfitted for the accomplishment of large things. Yet all religions teach the cultivation of the very qualities that ruin us. Clever men always follow the forms and laugh at the spirit. Out of all this enormous and unspeakably cruel contradiction, what is to come? A golden age, some say. But what good will that do us? - and what good will it do any one - since it must pass according to inevitable laws? I understand the laws, their results. But what is their meaning? What is right? What is wrong? Why should there be laws at all?

(I must try to get James Hinton's '*Mystery of Pain*', to see if he can throw any light on the matter.)

We are all tired of Kumamoto. I must try to get out of it this year or next year. I am almost certain, however, that I had better go to America for a time. One does not isolate oneself from the Aryan race without paying the penalty. You could not know what it means, unless you had borne it long; the condition is unspeakable. You say I work well. If I did not, I should go insane, or become a prey to nervous disease. Perhaps the suffering has been good in this - that it has forced me to literary discipline which I could not otherwise have obtained. To write three volumes in five years (for my new book is almost done) really means a good deal - teaching besides. But Kumamoto, what with earthquakes, robbers, and thunderstorms, is my realisation of a prison in the bottom of hell. I would be glad of half the salary with half as much more peace of mind.

Is it selfish to tell you my feelings? It would be, perhaps, if you were feeling gloriously well, but as you also have some trouble - perhaps more suffering from illness than you ever speak of - you will have the grim comfort of knowing that one not sick at all thinks of your existence as the seventh heaven - as the life of Haroun Al Raschid - as the luxury of the most fortunate of the fortunate khalifs of Bagdad.

Faithfully, with best wishes,

LAFCADIO HEARN

LAFCADIO HEARN'S 'AT A RAILWAY STATION'

A Case Of Sympathetic Understanding
Of The Inner Life Of Japan

by

PROFESSOR HIRAKAWA SUKEHIRO

Lafcadio Hearn's name does not appear at all in Edwin Reischauer's *United States and Japan*. It appears once in Akira Iriye's *Across the Pacific*, and merely as that of a foreign professor who gained the respect of Japanese students. It seems that Hearn is completely ignored by the post-Pacific war generation of American students of Japan. If Hearn is still remembered in American academic circles, it is by some literary historians: in the *Literary History of the United States*, edited by Robert Spiller *et al.* (1948), Harry Levin describes Hearn as a 'civilised nomad', using Hearn's own designation. Van Wyck Brooks, a more sympathetic critic, gives a detailed description of Hearn's characteristics in his *The Confident Years* (1952). Four good monographs have been written in the United States in the last two decades: a biography by Elizabeth Stevenson (1961), a study of Hearn as critic and thinker by Beongcheon Yu (1964), an analysis of Hearn's literary achievements by Arthur Kunst (1969), and a Ph.D. thesis by Margaret McAdow Lazar (1977) which discusses the problem of interpretation of life within one ethnic group to an audience of another.[1]

---

*This paper was given at the Woodrow Wilson International Center for Scholars, Smithsonian Institution, Washington, D.C. 19 July, 1978.

But to Japanese readers these Hearn studies by American scholars of American literature have a common defect: they lack intelligent understanding as soon as they enter the last fourteen years of Hearn's literary activities in Japan. Though these years are the most important, they are treated rather briefly. The reverse may also be true of Hearn studies by Japanese scholars: they limit their perspectives to Hearn's Japanese years without paying sufficient attention to his formative years in Europe (1850-69), in America (1869-87), or in the French West Indies (1887-89).

But what is interesting about Hearn is his respective reputations as a writer in America and Japan. Towards the turn of the century Hearn benefited in the West from the first fascination with Japan as an emerging nation that defeated China (1895) and Russia (1905). Even after Hearn's death (1904) his works were popular in the West. They could be found in family libraries all over the world. Until the early 1930s Japanese travellers abroad were often accosted by those who had read and loved his writings. But, according to Arthur Kunst, 'the great Pacific war with Japan in the 1940s seemed for a time to have obliterated Hearn from the American consciousness, a kind of guilt over a youthful infatuation. The misleading notion of Hearn as a spokesman for Japan left him without literary defences when Japan and things Japanese became enemy.'[2]

Since then Hearn's reputation has not recovered; after the war a whole new generation of competent interpreters of Japan replaced him. Hearn has finally become an example not to be imitated by serious students of Japan: 'He never made great progress in spoken or written Japanese... and he committed errors that would have been impossible had he possessed command of the language' (Marius Jansen: 'Lafcadio in Japan').[3] The present-day American Japanologists are proud of their academic achievement. They are conscious of being successors to the British Japanologists of former days. They hold in high regard the opinions voiced by Basil Hall Chamberlain, the British dean of Western scholars on Japan and Hearn's one-time friend and mentor in Japan. In the last (1939) edition of his *Things Japanese*, Chamberlain added an acrimonious remark to the article about Lafcadio Hearn:

'He saw details very distinctly while incapable of understanding them as a whole. Not only was this the case mentally but also physically. Blind of one eye, he was extremely short-sighted of the other. On entering a room his habit was to grope all around, closely examining wallpaper, the backs of books, pictures, curios, and other ornaments. Of these he could have drawn up an exact catalogue; but he had never properly seen either the horizon or the stars.'

Chamberlain's deprecation was a fatal blow. It is curious, but people seemed to forget that the same Chamberlain had praised Hearn half a century before ('Never perhaps was scientific accuracy of detail married to such tender and exquisite brilliancy of style'). Hearn's writings are today so discredited among American Japan specialists that if a young student quotes Hearn sympathetically, he is almost certain to be criticised by his academic advisers and considered a belated romanticist unfit for serious scholarship. There is, however, no problem at all with quoting the authoritative Chamberlain. For example, the first of the well-known five-volume series on Japan's modernisation, published by Princeton University Press, opens with a quotation from Chamberlain's *Things Japanese*:

'To have lived through the transition stage of modern Japan makes a man feel preternaturally old; for here he is in modern times ... and yet he can himself distinctly remember the Middle Ages.'[4]

Although experiences of the same kind were shared by Hearn, it is not proper for an American Japanologist to quote his observations.

The situation is, however, different in Japan, where Hearn's reputation is still increasing. Already in the 1930s Albert Mordell noted: 'It is singular that Japan should be the place of publication and the first to welcome these volumes in English.' 'These volumes' were articles written by Hearn during his early newspaper days in America. The sixteen-volume *Writings of Lafcadio Hearn*, originally published by Houghton Mifflin Co., were recently reprinted by Rinsen Co. in Kyoto. Apart from Japanese translations of Hearn's collected writings - which contain twice as many articles as the original sixteen-volume work - the English texts themselves are today more widely read in Japan than in the United States or in Great Britain. Earl Miner explains the curious phenomenon, in his *Japanese Traditions in British and American Literature*, in the following way:

'It is also significant that he idealised the people of Japan and their culture, not simply or blindly, but in the terms in which the Japanese themselves like to think they excel. The Japanese ideals were close to his own - or he never would have become a Japanese subject under the conditions he did - and he communicates them to the Western reader with a fine fervour. This fact accounts for a situation with which the West is not too well acquainted, Hearn's continuous popularity in Japan. A nation which found somewhat to its embarrassment that it was far behind in what the West liked to think was civilisation was naturally happy to find itself praised for what it was, rather than blamed for what it failed to succeed in becoming; and later, in this century, when the Japanese found they had become rather too drably the Westernised nation which they had once sought to be, it was pleasant for them to be able to return to his praise in the hope that what he saw was still basically true, after all. In a sense, the Japanese have fallen prey to a foreign exoticising of themselves.'[5]

If Japanese continue to read Hearn solely because of their narcissistic tendencies, Hearn's continuous popularity in Japan is deplorable. It is true that without the desire to see and to feel an artistically and psychologically satisfying past, Hearn's appeal could never have existed in Japan. But there are other simpler explanations for Japanese attachment to Hearn. His English is easy for Japanese students to understand. Japanese junior and senior high school students read with pleasure ghostly stories retold by Hearn. These *Kwaidan* are more artistic and more ghostly in Hearn's English versions than in the Japanese originals. Hearn's realistic descriptions of a Matsue day in the 1890s have a nostalgic charm, because no Japanese writer of the time paid attention to the life of the common people in a provincial town. Moreover, Hearn taught with impressive success at the Imperial University of Tokyo (1896-1903). From his earlier experience in Matsue (1890-91) and Kumamoto (1891-1894), he had come to know a great deal about Japanese students. His lectures, which contain many references to Japanese literature, were adapted to the Japanese student's way of thinking and feeling. He was a professor of comparative literature *avant la lettre*. But the lectures were at the same time the consummation of his American newspaper writings. In the United States he wrote extensively about French, American, and other literature and reviewed books. In Tokyo, as well as in New Orleans, Hearn had to find an outlet for his critical intelligence: first his letters, then his lectures served his inner need well. Before coming to Japan, Hearn was the best translator of French literature in the United States; his constant reference to the contribution of foreign elements to the English character and literature was stimulating to Japanese students of the Meiji era, for some of whom the sole purpose of literary study was to create a new Japanese literature.

Reading Hearn's lectures some twenty years later, Edmund Gosse confessed that he was struck by the vigour of his analysis and the delicacy of his taste:

'These lectures are marked by an almost naïve simplicity. We seem to be returning in them to the infancy of criticism, where everything is good or bad, beautiful or ugly. But this does not detract from their merit, which depends on their freshness, their artless enthusiasm, and also on the vigour with which impressions independently made on the enthusiasm of the lecturer are passed on to his audience.'...[6]

It is difficult to deny that Hearn is an excellent interpreter of Western literature in Japan. This is a matter easy for Englishmen or Americans to judge. But what of Hearn's interpretations of the Japanese mind to Westerners? This is the point which I try to explore in this paper, examining the short story 'At a Railway Station' and using some Japanese materials which have remained unnoticed by American Hearn scholars.

The difficulty of mutual comprehension

Some of you may ask if Hearn was really an American writer. It is indeed very difficult to give him a proper place in a simple framework of the history of a national literature. The unusual nature of his career resists the literary historian's neat classification. Hearn was born in 1850 on an Ionian island of an Anglo-Irish father, surgeon and officer in one of Queen Victoria's regiments, and a Greek mother. He was raised in Dublin and educated in France and England. He spent almost twenty years in America (Cincinnati and New Orleans) and in the French West Indies before coming to Japan in 1890. He married a Japanese, obtained Japanese citizenship, and after fourteen years of diligent work died in 1904 in Tokyo. But his having been a Japanese citizen does not necessarily mean that Hearn, alias Koizumi Yakumo, is a Japanese writer. He wrote in English. His stories and essays were written for English-speaking readers. Hearn's best contributions appeared in the *Atlantic Monthly*. When he wrote 'we', he meant 'we Westerners'. Through his publications he belonged to the American literary world. In this sense Hearn was an American writer.

But his assumption of the Japanese name Koizumi Yakumo was somewhat different from Christian missionaries assuming Oriental names. Free from a religious or secular sense of mission, Hearn was extremely gifted at seeing through the eyes of others. He was of the opinion that those who would study impartially the life and thought of the Orient must also study those of the Occident from the Oriental point of view. The results of such a comparative attitude are in no small degree retroactive. What is interesting about Hearn is that he was, according to his character and his faculty of perception, affected to a greater or lesser degree by those Japanese influences to which he submitted himself. His penetrating analysis of the Japanese smile derives from such an experience. In an article collected in *Glimpses of Unfamiliar Japan*, Vol. II, he said: 'It is, possibly, by long sojourn among a people less gravely disposed that we (Westerners) can best learn our own temperament.' Here Hearn is talking about English gravity and Japanese levity; in other words, the Japanese speak of the 'angry faces' of the Westerners, and the Westerners speak with strong contempt of the Japanese smile. Hearn illustrates the difficulty of mutual understanding with a personal experience of his. After having lived for nearly three years in the interior of Japan, he returned to English life for a few days at the open port of Kobe. He writes in 'The Japanese Smile':

> To hear English once more spoken by Englishmen touched me more than I could have believed possible; but this feeling lasted only for a moment. My object was to make some necessary purchases. Accompanying me was a Japanese friend, to whom all that foreign life was utterly new and wonderful, and who asked me this curious question: "Why is it that the foreigners never smile? You smile and bow when you speak to them; but they never smile. Why?"
>
> 'The fact was, I had fallen altogether into Japanese habits and ways, and had got out of touch with Western life; and my companion's question first made me aware that I had been acting somewhat curiously. It also seemed to me a fair illustration of the difficulty of mutual comprehension between the two races.' 7.

'At a Railway Station': Fiction and truth

Hearn was a literary artist, but he did not write plays, poetry or novels during his Japanese years. It is difficult to accommodate his writings, such as 'The Japanese Smile', within the context of literary history. These essays should be considered 'Japanese studies'. But Hearn did not seek knowledge just for the sake of information. He tried to use Japanese materials for the sake of his artistic aspirations. He could not stay safely within the limits prescribed by the rules of a discipline.

We can recognise in Hearn's writings two dominant strains: that of stylistic artistry and that of cultural interpretation. Sometimes he sacrifices the accuracy of the latter for the sake of his aesthetic need. This tendency must be particularly repugnant to the Japan specialists of the later generations. But Hearn at his best is superb: his mastery of illustration serves remarkably well as a tool of cultural interpretation. Hearn should not be judged separately as a literary artist without inventive capacity or as a Japan interpreter without scientific discipline. He should be evaluated in his own terms. As an example of a happy blending of the two dominant strains in Hearn's work, I quote 'At a Railway Station', a very short story also marked by an almost naïve simplicity.

Kokoro

1

AT A RAILWAY STATION

Seventh day of the sixth Month;

twenty-sixth of Meiji

Yesterday a telegram from Fukuoka announced that a desperate criminal captured there would be brought for trial to Kumamoto today, on the train due at noon. A Kumamoto policeman had gone to Fukuoka to take the prisoner in charge.

Four years ago a strong thief entered some house by night in the Street of the Wrestlers, terrified and bound the inmates, and carried away a number of valuable things. Tracked skilfully by the police, he was captured within twenty-four hours - even before he could dispose of his plunder. But as he was being taken to the police station he burst his bonds, snatched the sword of his captor, killed him, and escaped. Nothing more was heard of him until last week.

Then a Kumamoto detective, happening to visit the Fukuoka prison, saw among the toilers a face that had been four years photographed upon his brain.

'Who is that man'? he asked the guard.

'A thief', was the reply - 'registered here as Kusabe.'

The detective walked up to the prisoner and said:

'Kusabe is not your name. Nomura Teichi, you are needed in Kumamoto for murder.'

The felon confessed all.

I went with a great throng of people to witness the arrival at the station. I expected to hear and see anger; I even feared possibilities of violence. The murdered officer had been much liked; his relatives would certainly be among the spectators; and a Kumamoto crowd is not very gentle. I also thought to find many police on duty. My anticipations were wrong.

The train halted in the usual scene of hurry and noise - scurry and clatter of passengers wearing *geta* - screaming of boys wanting to sell Japanese newspapers and Kumamoto lemonade. Outside the barrier we waited for nearly five minutes. Then, pushed through the wicket by a police sergeant, the prisoner appeared - a large, wild-looking man, with head bowed down, and arms fastened behind his back. Prisoner and guard both halted in front of the wicket; and the people pressed forward to see - but in silence. Then the officer called out:

'Sugihara San! Sugihara O-Kibi! Is she present?'

A slight, small woman standing near me, with a child on her back, answered, '*Hai*'! and advanced through the press. This was the widow of the murdered man; the child she carried was his son. At a wave of the officer's hand the crowd fell back, so as to leave a clear space about the prisoner and his escort. In that space the woman with the child stood facing the murderer. The hush was of death.

Not to the woman at all, but to the child only, did the officer then speak. He spoke low, but so clearly that I could catch every syllable:

'Little one, this is the man who killed your father four years ago. You had not yet been born; you were in your mother's womb. That you have no father to love you now is the doing of this man. Look at him - [here the officer, putting a hand to the prisoner's chin, sternly forced him to lift his eyes] - look well at him, little boy! Do not be afraid. It is painful; but it is your duty. Look at him!'

Over the mother's shoulder the boy gazed with eyes widely open, as in fear; then he began to sob; then tears came; but steadily and obediently he still looked - looked - looked - straight into the cringing face.

The crowd seemed to have stopped breathing.

I saw the prisoner's features distort; I saw him suddenly dash himself down upon his knees despite his fetters, and beat his face into the dust, crying out the while in a passion of hoarse remorse that made one's heart shake:

'Pardon! Pardon! Pardon me, little one! That I did - not for hate was it done, but in mad fear only, in my desire to escape. Very, very wicked I have been; great unspeakable wrong have I done you! But now for my sin I go to die. I wish to die; I am glad to die! Therefore, O little one, be pitiful! forgive me!'

The child still cried silently. The officer raised the shaking criminal; the dumb crowd parted left and right to let them by. Then, quite suddenly, the whole multitude began to sob. And as the bronzed guardian passed, I saw what I had never seen before - what few men ever see - what I shall probably never see again - the tears of a Japanese policeman.

The crowd ebbed, and left me musing on the strange morality of the spectacle. Here was justice unswerving yet compassionate - forcing knowledge of a crime by the pathetic witness of its simplest result. Here was desperate remorse, praying only for pardon before death. And here was a populace - perhaps the most dangerous in the Empire when angered - comprehending all, touched by all, satisfied with the contrition and the shame, and filled, not with wrath, but only with the great sorrow of the sin - through simple deep experience of the difficulties of life and the weaknesses of human nature.

But the most significant, because the most Oriental, fact of the episode was that the appeal to remorse had been made through the criminal's sense of fatherhood - that potential love of children which is so large a part of the soul of every Japanese.

There is a story that the most famous of all Japanese robbers Ishikawa Goemon, once by night entering a house to kill and steal, was charmed by the smile of a baby which reached out hands to him, and that he remained playing with the little creature until all chance of carrying out his purpose was lost.

It is not hard to believe this story. Every year the police records tell of compassion shown to children by professional criminals: Some months ago a terrible murder case was reported in the local papers - the slaughter of a household by robbers. Seven persons had been literally hewn to pieces while asleep; but the police discovered a little boy quite unharmed, crying alone in a pool of blood; and they found evidence unmistakable that the men who slew must have taken great care not to hurt the child.

This is a very touching story and is also a remarkable observation of the Japanese mind. I suppose that the author himself found the story very well written, and that must be the reason he put 'At a Railway Station' at the beginning of his book *Kokoro*. Hearn was a seasoned journalist and knew how to arrange his articles. *Kokoro*, his third book on Japan, was published in 1895. Hearn himself explained the title:

> 'The papers composing this volume treat of the inner rather than of the outer life of Japan - for which reason they have been grouped under the title *Kokoro* (heart). Written with the above character, this word signifies also mind, in the emotional sense.'...

The timing of the publication was extremely good. It was the year when Japan won victory over China, and the West began to be interested in Japan and the Japanese mentality. That must be the reason the book was translated into nine or ten European languages.[8]

First I should refer to Hearn's exoticism, which, in my opinion, is not a main feature of his Japanese studies. In this story some exotic touches are found in expressions such as 'Seventh day of the sixth Month; - twenty-six of Meiji' which corresponds to 7 June, 1893. 'The Street of the Wrestlers' is a literal translation of *Sumō-machi*. The author chose this street for the exotic flavour of its name, because the actual crime was not committed in *Sumō-machi*, but on an Amakusa island. The expression 'a strong thief' - which I do not believe to be in English or American usage - is a literal translation of *gōzoku* or *gōtō*, which means a burglar. The expression reminds us of a letter Hearn sent to a helper: 'If I ask you to translate something, *please never try to translate a Japanese IDIOM by an English IDIOM*, that would be no use to me. Simply translate the words *exactly* however funny it seems.'[9] Sometimes Hearn is so close to customs and words that Japanese readers recognise behind Hearn's English expressions Japanese realities which are not always familiar to American or English readers. (In this case *gō* means strong and *zoku* means thief.)

One should never forget that Hearn was a newspaperman in Cincinnati (in 1872 on the *Enquirer*, and in 1875 on the *Commercial*) and in New Orleans in 1878 on the *Item* and in 1881 on the *Times Democrat*.) He was a skilful reporter and very interested in crime. Writing newspaper reports was a good exercise for him as he had wished to become a good story-teller.

In this story Hearn first exposes factual data. The second part of the story is more personal and more concrete in sense-appealing details. The same process has been repeatedly exploited since the time of Boccaccio: the literary genre of *novella* and the journalistic genre of *news* belong to the same pattern. Hearn had already used the same method in many of his earlier criminal reportages such as 'The Violent Cremation'; this Cincinnati *Enquirer* article was said to have confirmed Hearn in his role as the *Enquirer's* sensational reporter.

The scene at the railway station appeals strongly to readers' sensitivities. Hearn wrote in the first-person 'I' in order to strengthen the sense of immediacy. He went with a great throng of people to witness the arrival of the criminal at Kumamoto station. Hearn employs description only once: 'the train halted in the usual scene of hurry and noise - scurry and clatter of passengers wearing *geta* - screaming of boys wanting to sell

Japanese newspapers and Kumamoto lemonade.' By capturing the colour and flurry of sounds typical at the train station, the reporter is able to dramatise the unusual 'hush' as 'of death' of the following scene. (Hearn repeats the same technique when he depicts a village railway station in 'Red Bridal':[10]

> The early morning train from Kyoto was in; the little station was full of hurry and noise - the clattering of *geta*, humming of converse, and fragmentary cries of village boys selling cakes and luncheons: "*Kwashi yoros - ! Sushi yoros! - Bento yoros - "*!

This is also the only description of a scene in detail just before the double suicide of the young lovers who lie down across the inside rail.

Hearn expected to see anger: he even feared the possibility of violence such as he had witnessed in his American days. For example 'Almost a Riot',[11] a story that appeared in the Cincinnati *Enquirer* more than twenty years earlier (24 August, 1873), depicts a mob and besieged policemen. Consciously or unconsciously Hearn was compelled to compare the Japanese attitude with the American attitude. He was afraid of a lynching, but the crowd's reaction was quite different. Hearn described the scene with the accuracy of someone who was present on the spot. Hearn heard the policeman calling: 'Sugihara San! Sugihara O-Kibi'! And Hearn saw a slight, small woman, standing near him, with a child on her back, who answered '*Hai*'. When the policeman spoke to the child, he spoke low, but so clearly that Hearn, a foreigner, could catch every syllable. Moreover, Hearn saw the scene before his eyes. He writes three times 'I saw': 'I saw the prisoner's features distort; I saw him suddenly dash himself down upon his knees,' and 'I saw what I had never seen before - the tears of a Japanese policeman.'

Margaret McAdow Lazar, in her Ph.D. thesis, says (p. 244): '"At a Railway Station" is based on an episode from Hearn's experience.... Using the first person, he tells of what he saw the previous day.'

Mrs Lazar takes the word 'yesterday' with which the story begins for the truth. Though she had spent a year in Tokyo at International Christian University, she did not refer to Japanese studies on Lafcadio Hearn. Dr Kunst, author of the article 'Lafcadio Hearn's Use of Japanese Sources', seems to know rather little of his subject. Beong-cheon Yu, who is supposed to have a native understanding of Eastern thought, has not treated the problem of fiction and truth. In short, American studies on Hearn have been conducted by American scholars of American literature, and Hearn's Japanese works have not always been adequately studied.

On the other hand, American scholars of Japan have not paid much attention to Hearn. Hearn is not reliable as a Japanologist; his knowledge of Japanese is said to be poor. It is true that some of his letters written in Japanese were published, but his son was so ashamed of the quality of his father's Japanese that he emended them.

It is true that Hearn could not read Japanese texts mingled with Chinese characters, but it is also true that his wife Setsuko could not speak or read English. Consequently, the communication between husband and wife was conducted exclusively in Japanese - a pidgin Japanese, perhaps, but the important point to notice is that it was still in Japanese that the communication was made.

Though utterly unknown to American students of Hearn, 'At a Railway Station' was written on the basis of a newspaper article. Hearn, a newspaper reporter in his American days, was interested in journalism in Japan also. He asked his wife and his father-in-law to read Japanese newspaper articles aloud to him. Though incapable of reading Japanese texts himself, Hearn, a linguistically gifted man with considerable experiences of a folklorist, could well gather the meaning and contexts of Japanese newspapers if difficult passages were explained or paraphrased by his wife or father-in-law. Maruyama Manabu, a Japanese scholar and native of Kumamoto, has checked Japanese newspapers of the twenty-sixth year of Meiji and found in the *Kyūshū Nichinichi Shimbun* of 22 April, 1893,[12] an article describing the arrival in Kumamoto of a criminal, Ōbuchi Suejirō. He arrived, not from the greater and better known city of Fukuoka but from Saga, at Ikeda Station, Kumamoto, Friday, 20 April. (Does the date at the head of the story, 'Seventh day of the six month', mean then that the story was written after seven weeks of incubation?) The murdered policeman's real name was not Sugihara but Miyazaki.

In his Kumamoto days (1891-94) Hearn was busily engaged in teaching at the Kumamoto Governmental College (Kumamoto Daigo Kōtō Chū-gakkō). He taught twenty-seven hours a week, and he had classes on Friday until late in the afternoon. So it is not possible that he himself went to the station to witness the arrival of the criminal on the twentieth of April. The newspaper article is very long, so I will omit the details of the prisoner's crimes, which were much more complicated and different from those succinctly described by Hearn. Hearn just simplified them, for what was important for Hearn to describe was not the details of the crimes. What he wanted to convey to Western readers was the Japanese heart, *kokoro*, the Japanese mind in the emotional sense. So Hearn focused his attention - and his readers' attention - on the scene outside the wicket of the railway station. The literal translation of the *Kyūshū Nichinichi Shimbun* reads as follows:

The policeman in charge stopped the prisoner, took off the prisoner's hat, and turned to the family of the dead Miyazaki, saying:
'"Look at this man. It is he who killed Mr Miyazaki seven years ago. This man is the criminal who killed your husband; this man is the criminal who killed your father. Your heart must be burning with resentment, but it is now time for you to resign yourselves to fate."

'The widow and the mother, recalling the days past, could not look at the prisoner's face any more, knelt down on the spot and shamelessly cried in the presence of others. Touched by the sight, spectators also wiped tears from their eyes. The son of Miyazaki (who had been in his mother's womb when his father was killed, and is now seven years old) did not know what the problem was. A look of wonderment appeared on his face, as he watched his mother and his grandmother weep. Then the policeman addressed the child:

'"Because you were in your mother's womb, you did not know it. But this is the burglar[13] who ran away, killing Mr Miyazaki, your father. Look at his face. Take a good look at his face."

'Though he was young, the child, hearing that this was the bad man, murderer of his father, raised his eyes and gazed with indignation at the face of the criminal, and shed tears in spite of himself. A hush fell over the crowd as they viewed the scene, and the usually tearless policeman coughed to conceal his emotion. The criminal himself blinked his eyes and said:

"'You are the bereaved family of Mr Miyazaki. Although I put him to the sword in my desire to escape, I had no grudge or hatred against him. I was able to flee from the city, Kumamoto, at that time, but the Way of Heaven could not be challenged. I am now arrested to my great shame, and am soon to be hanged at the gallows. You may think that I am a hateful, loathsome wretch; but talk is of no use now. I am going to be fairly punished and justice will be done, so please don't be worried any more."

'The policeman then placed the hat on the prisoner and took him away to the prison.'

It is beyond my ability to translate into English the Kabuki-like melodramatic style of the original article. Though it was written in a somewhat old-fashioned Japanese, it has a human touch which still appeals to readers. Now let me explain some details which Hearn modified on purpose. Through the modifications we can see and evaluate Hearn's technique as a story writer.

The time of the crime, which was originally committed seven years earlier, is now changed to four years earlier. Consequently, the child who actually was seven years old becomes four years old. This age of four rather than seven is an important change. According to the original Japanese newspaper, the boy of seven was standing beside his mother and his grandmother. In his fictitious account Hearn had the mother carry her son on her back. The pick-a-back of small children was a typical Japanese habit, but mothers cannot carry boys of seven. (By the way, Hearn in one of his other stories based on Japanese newspaper articles, 'A Living God',[14] made the hero older by several tens of years; because in the story he wanted to emphasise the wisdom of an old man.) By making the mother carry her child on her back, Hearn dramatised the scene of the confrontation with the culprit. The railway station where the widow with the boy stood facing the murderer reminds us of a scene in a film or in a television drama. It is a close-up scene. According to the *Kyūshū Nichinichi Shimbun*, the widow and her mother-in-law had been informed beforehand of the arrival of the prisoner. But Hearn omitted the mother-in-law. He tried to focus attention on the solitary widow ('a slight, small woman') and her only child. There was a more significant change: in the original newspaper article it was not the murderer but the widow and the mother of Miyazaki who dashed themselves down upon their knees and cried in the presence of others.

Some may feel that this kind of analytical comment destroys the beautiful image created by Hearn; and some may have confirmed the impression that what Hearn wrote about Japan is a poem, a fiction, not the truth. However, in the case of 'At a Railway Station', the changes Hearn made are, in my opinion, quite permissible. I would like to distinguish between the notions of fact and truth - *jijitsu* and *shinjitsu*. In dealing with Japanese materials Hearn has two objectives to accomplish: he must catch the Japanese mind in the material itself and he must write a work of art which can stand on its own merits. Hearn the artist modified some facts in order to give a unified impression: in the story the culprit dashes himself upon his knees - this fictitious action may be justified if we take into consideration what he said in a passion of hoarse remorse. His falling on his knees and his words are in complete harmony. Hearn changed some details in order to make the readers feel and understand more intensely what the Japanese mind is, what the Japanese common people's sentiment is. Hearn the reporter tried to convey to Western readers the truth about Japanese *kokoro*. It may be true that in many of Hearn's writings he embellished some features of Japanese characteristics. But still I believe that in short stories like this Hearn was a good reporter.

Arthur Kunst, incidentally, makes in his book a typically American mistake. He thinks that the breathless Kumamoto 'crowd' in tears are at the brink of violence. If they were so, Kunst's evaluation[15] would be quite correct: 'The remarkable thing about "At a Railway Station" is how little difference would be made by placing the story in Cincinnati or in St Pierre.' What is remarkable about the story is that the Japanese crowd's reaction is quite different from what Hearn anticipated. The story may be accepted as evidence of what Reischauer asserts in his book *The Japanese*: 'A true case of lynching, so far as I know, has never occurred in Japan.' Kunst is extremely critical of *Kokoro*:

'As the title suggests ("Heart"), Hearn is still striving for that elusive "inner" Japan, a vain quest which vitiates more than half of the fifteen pieces; the increasing stultification of Hearn's stories, or the waste of his time in didactic speculation, is compensated for by works which are good *despite* his intentions.'[16]

Quite different in tone is a critical appreciation written by Hugo von Hofmannsthal.[17] I would like to quote a passage:

'"At a Railway Station" is an anecdote, almost a trivial anecdote, not exempt from sentimentality. But it was written by one who knew how to write, and what is more, it was felt beforehand by one who knew how to feel.'

It is true that, like many of Hearn's writings. 'At a Railway Station' is not exempt from Victorian sentimentality. But it is also true that Hearn was a sensitive reporter who knew how to write and how to feel. He was a rare Westerner who could take part in the daily existence of the common people of Japan and could think with their thoughts.

At this point we must refer to the talent shown in his previous interpretations of Creole culture: he was extremely skilful at ferreting out its ethnic characteristics. In his Martinique days he learned their patois: his knowledge of French helped him in this case. While in Japan, Hearn was too busily engaged in teaching and writing. He could not read Japanese newspaper articles which use not only a Japanese syllabary system but also many Chinese characters. However, this disability does not necessarily disqualify him as a shrewd interpreter of the inner life of Japan. He applied the methods of folkloric research with which he had become comfortable. I imagine scenes in the Koizumi family where Hearn listened carefully to the voice of his wife Setsuko. The *Descriptive Catalogue of the Hearniana in the Hearn Library of the Toyama University* shows that Hearn had a vast collection of books concerning folklore, ethnology, and anthropology. He knew how to collect legends and stories, and he had already been successful at interpreting life within one ethnic group to an audience of another in his American days. As a reporter for the Cincinnati newspapers he had written a series of sketches of the life of the blacks who lived along the Ohio River levee. They are said to be the only picture Americans have of the life of blacks in a border city in the post-Civil War period. In Matsue and Kumamoto, too, as a folklorist, Hearn energetically collected materials, but he made little attempt to present them as they were, except for songs of children, proverbs, and some other materials. He had strong artistic aspirations so he preferred instead to select those with a 'weird beauty', like ghost stories or those which contained revelations of cultural character, like the stories collected in *Kokoro*. Hearn, who had earned his daily bread with the pen, knew quite well that so long as interpretative and artistic elements did not merge harmoniously, ethnic studies as such would not be accepted by American publishers.

According to the recollections of his wife, 'Omoidenoki', Hearn always asked her to read as if she herself were telling the story, with the sentiments in her own voice. When he listened to Setsuko reading the Kyushu newspaper article, for example, he must have noticed delicate changes in her voice. Through the tones of her voice Hearn could understand what kinds of emotions the Japanese felt towards the widow, towards the child, and also towards the shaking criminal. The sob which Hearn mentioned in the story was, perhaps, the sob of his wife Setsuko. She must have been touched to tears when reading the newspaper for her husband. Hearn thus could envision the actual scene through his mind's eye. One secret of Hearn's success lies in the collaboration of husband and wife. I might also add that the less cultivated the wife, the better. The genuine emotion of the common people of Japan could be transmitted without any cultural bias. One of the touching episodes in Setsuko's recollection is a follows. Once, asked about a poem in the (eighth-century anthology) *Manyōshū*, Setsuko could not give an answer. She apologised for her ignorance and wept that she was of no help to him. Hearn took his wife to his bookshelves and showed her many of his writings. 'How was it possible for me to write so many books? I owe you everything; I have written all these books, listening to your stories.' And he added: '*Anata gakumon aru toki, watashi kono hon kakemasen. Anata gakumon nai toki, watashi kakemashita.*' ('If you were learned, I could not have written these books; because you were not learned, I could write them.')

In his American days Hearn was one of the best translators of French literature. In Japan he could not translate Japanese material word for word. Neither would Hearn make a literal translation of Japanese police news. He rather enjoyed recreating his own stories. In America he was already a writer of twice-told tales (*Stray Leaves from Strange Literature; Some Chinese Ghosts*). He wanted to make works of art out of raw material of little literary value. He improved Japanese ghost stories in his English adaptation. His only failure among them was 'Of A Promise Kept', in which he tried to 'improve' an Ueda Akinari story: the original is too perfect to be rewritten in a new form.

In 'At a Railway Station', Hearn even tried to add some general observations about the cultural and religious background of the event. After he had heard the story and after the emotion had subsided, Hearn mused on the strange morality of the spectacle:

'Here was justice unswerving yet compassionate - here was a populace, comprehending all, touched by all, satisfied with the contrition and the shame, and filled, not with wrath, but only with the great sorrow of the sin - through simple deep experience of the difficulties of life and the weaknesses of human nature.'

Lafcadio Hearn is known for his accuracy of detail; he is dogmatic and clumsy in generalisation. But in this story, even though there is a kind of idealisation of certain Japanese characteristics, his grasp of the Buddhistic sentiment among Kumamoto people seems essentially correct. More than eighty years later, Edwin Reischauer writes along the same lines in his *The Japanese* (1977):

'Where Westerners may feel unmitigated indignation, contempt, or condemnation, Japanese are most likely to emphasise extenuating circumstances and the pitifulness of the miscreant.... (The post-crime attitude of the culprit, that is, his degree of penitence is taken into consideration).'[18]

One might say that in Hearn's treatment there is a sort of dramatisation. It may be a defect, but scholarly works which give us abstract conclusions without providing any concrete examples lack appeal and charm. Embellished or not, 'At a Railway Station' has a strong appeal to the Japanese. Dr Takeo Doi, in his *The Anatomy of Dependence*, a book highly appreciated by American Japanologists, quotes the story to illustrate the Japanese attitude towards feelings of guilt.[19] (I am, however, afraid that Doi is in error in believing that 'At a Railway Station' is a true story. He makes another error when he carries the interpretation one step further: 'One may surely say that besides feeling sorry for the child the criminal here had also awoken to a sense of his own wretchedness. He was, in a sense, identifying with the child.' Some psychiatrists' conjectures are more fictitious than writers' imaginations.)

To those Americans who have visited an industrialised Japan, Hearn's Japan is a world of the past. They cannot recognise in today's Japan the features which Hearn described in his twelve volumes of Japanese writings. To them, therefore, Hearn's continuous charm to some Japanese is an enigma, and it is sometimes a source of irritation. However, although the outer life of Japan has changed greatly, the inner life remains relatively unchanged. Hearn himself knew the anthropologist's definition of culture: 'the pattern which gives standards to people living in a specific area, or the pattern by which people living in that area gain a sense of identity.' Culture in this broader sense cannot change so easily: the core personality of the Japanese, the Japanese mind, has, therefore, been rather the same. This explains in part Hearn's continuous fascination for some Japanese. They get the impression that what Hearn wrote about their 'inner life' is intimately true. Earl Miner is correct in his remark that Hearn idealised the people of Japan and their culture in the terms in which the Japanese themselves like to think they excel: Hearn, by paying attention to Setsuko's voice, could capture the moral reactions of the Japanese to an event. In the case of 'At a Railway Station' there were already certain elements of idealism and didacticism in the original newspaper article; the story was, therefore, doubly idealised, first by the Japanese reporter and second by Setsuko and Lafcadio.

A love-hate relationship

There is, however, another motive in Hearn which urged him to write idealised pictures of Old Japan. Hearn had a strong dislike for certain aspects of Western civilisation. Basil Hall Chamberlain, after praising many good qualities of the author of *Glimpses of Unfamiliar Japan, Out of the East, Kokoro*, and other writings, adds the following remark in his *Things Japanese*:

> 'Our only quarrel is with some of Lafcadio Hearn's judgements: in righting the Japanese, he seems to us continually to wrong his own race. The objectionable character in his stories is too apt to be a European.'

As the product of a love-hate relationship between the West and Japan, Hearn is an interesting case. The principal reason Hearn was so happy in his early Japanese days in Matsue was that he had spent unhappy years in Britain and the United States. He found that he fitted into life in Matsue better than anywhere else he had lived. Small of stature (5 feet 3 inches high), and dark like the Japanese, Hearn felt he blended well with his environment. To Chamberlain he wrote that in coming to Japan he felt he had escaped from the 'pressure of ten atmospheres into a perfectly normal medium'. 'Ten atmospheres' is his exaggeration, but there is some truth in what he wrote, and the Japanese in the United States quite well understand what Hearn meant by the expression. Aggressiveness, which is a vice in Japan, is a virtue in the United States; human relations are much softer in Japan. In the differently civilised city of Matsue, Hearn, a well-paid foreign teacher, enjoyed a degree of social acceptance he had not experienced before.

However, when we try to analyse the cultural observation which Hearn attached to 'At a Railway Station', we must go one step further and take a look at his frustrated childhood: Lafcadio Hearn was a son 'begotten almost by accident'.[20] Charles Bush Hearn, an officer of the British occupation army, fell in love with a native girl from an Ionian island. They married after a first child was born. When Patrick Lafcadio Hearn, their second child, was two years old, the boy and his Greek mother, who did not speak English, moved to Dublin. Charles Bush Hearn went away to a Caribbean island with his regiment. The boy's mother could not communicate with her husband's relatives. Some four years later the boy's father decided, one-sidedly, to terminate his marriage to the Greek girl while she was away in Greece giving birth to Lafcadio's brother. Charles Bush Hearn married again, and Lafcadio was confided to the care of his great aunt.

Lafcadio would never forgive his father for this disloyalty to his mother; he never would acknowledge that he inherited anything from him. In a letter to his brother James, Lafcadio mentioned their father briefly:

'I suspect I do not love him.... The soul in me is not of him.' But of their mother he wrote almost emphatically:

> 'Whatever there is good in me... came from that dark race soul of which we know so little. My love of right, my hate of wrong, my admiration for what is beautiful or true, my capacity for faith in man or woman, my sensitiveness to artistic things, which gives me whatever little *success I have* - even that language power... came from Her.'[21]

In America, he abandoned the name 'Patrick' his Anglo-Irish father had selected and used 'Lafcadio', derived from Lefcadia, the name of his natal island. In sum, the quarrels between the parents, his mother's flight from Dublin, and the general instability of the family had a permanent effect on a sensitive child.

In his Cincinnati days, Hearn wrote a series of articles about mediums and spiritualists in a local newspaper. They were cheerfully contemptuous of spiritualists. But in the last article, appearing on 25 January, 1874, Patrick Lafcadio Hearn himself spoke through a medium with the spirit of his father who had died seven years before:

> 'I am your father, P -.'
> 'Have you any word for me?'
> 'Yes.'
> 'What is it?'
> 'Forgive me' - in a long whisper.
> 'I have nothing to forgive.'
> 'You have, indeed' - very faintly.
> 'What is it?'
> 'You know well' - distinctly....
> 'I wronged you; forgive me' - a loud, distinct whisper.
> 'I do not consider that you have.'
> 'It would be better not to contradict the spirit,' interrupted the medium, 'until it has explained matters.'
> 'I do not wish to contradict the spirit in the sense you imply', answered the reporter. '*I thoroughly understand the circumstances alluded to*; but I wish to explain that I have long ceased to consider it as a wrong done me.'[22]

This is a very strange document, because Hearn, the reporter, wrote it without caring how little the readers would understand. Elizabeth Stevenson comments as follows: '[In this article] Hearn looked back towards childhood and said goodbye to it. He never completely succeeded in exorcising the past, but this was an almost unconscious attempt to do so.'[23]

The special attention Hearn paid to the relationship between parents and children in Japan derives from his sentiment and conviction that there is something different in Japan. In the last observation attached to 'At a Railway Station', Hearn comments on the 'potential love of children which is so large a part of the soul of every Japanese'. I am not very sure if Hearn's comment is relevant in the context, but I am sure that this comment reflected the traumatic experience of being abandoned by his father at the tender age of six. Once wounded in childhood, Hearn was extremely sensitive about man's sense of fatherhood.

In the original *Kyūshū Nichinichi* newspaper article, the police officer first addressed the widow and the mother of the murdered policeman and then, after a time, turned to the child. However, in his story Hearn modified the scene as follows:

'The hush was of death.

Not to the woman at all, but to the child only, did the officer then speak.'

It is true that in Japan conversations are oftentimes conducted, not directly between a man and a woman, but indirectly through a child. Katharine Sansom, in her *Living in Tokyo*, made a remark of the same nature:

'There is a legend from the latter half of the nineteenth century, when Christian missionaries and teachers of the English and German languages began to come to Japan, that they needed only to push their babies' perambulators before them into any town or village to be made immediately welcome.'[24]

Hearn must have noticed the Japanese tendency to first address the child, and used it. But the fact that in this story the appeal to remorse had been made in that manner reflected how keenly Hearn was pre-occupied with the problem of man's sense of fatherhood. As Hearn strongly condemned his father's attitude towards his children, so he magnified, by way of contrast, the Oriental compassion shown to children. However, the expression 'Oriental' used by Hearn in the story is not an exact term. The only Asian country Hearn ever lived in was Japan. So Hearn should have used the word 'Japanese' instead of 'Oriental'. But what Hearn wanted to say about Japan is that there is something different which does not exist in the Occident. By way of contrast he insisted on the Oriental - that is, the non-Occidental aspect of the episode. Consciously or unconsciously, the conclusion of 'At a Railway Station' became an indirect accusation against his British father, who had been the cause of so many miseries during his childhood and youth.

By the way, it was in Kumamoto that Lafcadio Hearn became a father at the age of forty-three. It was November of the same twenty-sixth year of Meiji that a son was born. Hearn was deeply moved by the birth; he was a man who could not expect to marry in the United States: he was poor, short in stature, blind in one eye, and extremely shy. He was practically ostracised from Cincinnati for having lived with a coloured girl. The birth of a son was something beyond his expectation, and, deeply touched, he wrote his joy in a letter addressed to his friend Hendrick, adding the following reflection:

'Then I thought with astonishment of the possibility that men could be cruel to women who bore their children; and the world seemed very dark for a moment.'

It is clear what Hearn had in mind: the cruelty of his father towards his mother. After the birth of the son, whom he named Kazuo - because the pronunciation was rather similar to Cadio of Lafcadio - he made up his mind to obtain Japanese citizenship. The reason was a financial consideration. Hearn was very careful about his property. When he was a child he was heir to a considerable fortune, but it fell fraudulently into the hands of a relative and was lost. As a husband eighteen years older than his wife, he wished all his property to be left to his wife and to his children after his death. At that time of unequal treaties, however, if a Westerner died, his property went automatically to his Western relatives. It was basically because of these financial considerations that Lafcadio Hearn became a Japanese with the name of Koizumi Yakumo.

This was also the beginning of his alienation from the European communities of Yokohama, Tokyo, and Kobe. Hearn was considered a bizarre character who had 'gone native'. Hearn, in turn, was extremely critical of those Westerners who, in the open ports, lived with Japanese mistresses.

When translating the passage I quoted earlier from 'The Japanese Smile' into Japanese, I expressed Hearn's friend's words in feminine speech. I do so on purpose, because I am convinced that the friend who accompanied Hearn was his wife. But Hearn was so afraid of his American readers' reaction that he hid the fact. Not wishing to wound his female readers' sensitivities, Hearn avoided mentioning that he had a Japanese wife. He felt obliged to be equivocal on this point. His wife appears very often in his essays and sketches, but he referred to her just as a friend who accompanied him or, more often, as an old man-servant with the name of Manyemon. Today readers may laugh at his timid precaution. But I wish to call your attention to the racism in America which greatly influenced American interpretations of Japan and the Japanese. When Americans are fair in their dealings with Japanese-Americans, then Americans are friendly towards Japan. When not, then their attitude towards Japan often follows suit. There must be a relationship between American attitudes towards other ethnic groups within American society and American attitudes towards other nations. To translate Hearn's companion's conversation into masculine or feminine speech may seem a trifling matter, but this kind of detail is still significant.

The feelings Westerners residing in Japan harboured towards inter-racial marriages can be conjectured from the article on 'Eurasians' in B. H. Chamberlain's *Things Japanese*:

> 'Eurasians. Half-castes are often called Eurasians, from their being half-Europeans and half-Asiatics or Asians. Eurasians usually resemble the Japanese mother rather than the European father, in accordance with the general physiological law whereby the fair parent gives way to the dark. The time that has elapsed since Japanese Eurasians began to be numerous is not long enough to inform us whether this mixed race will endure, or whether, as so often happens in such cases, it will die out in the third or fourth generations.'

I don't think the Koizumi family, which is now in the third and fourth generation, has a good feeling towards the writer of such an article. The pseudo-scientific nature of Chamberlain's article confirms again the impression that even scholars are not exempt from the prejudices or basic presuppositions of their time, as so often happens in such studies.

Police behaviour in Japan

I would like to add one last comment. What is often overlooked but very relevant to today's problem is the accuracy of Hearn's observations. An example is his description of Japanese police-public relations, which have fundamentally not changed very much. In 1976 a very interesting comparative study was published: *Forces of Order: Police Behaviour in Japan and the United States* by David H. Bayley, (University of California Press). The description of Japanese policemen is summarised by a reviewer, Thomas Rohlen, as follows:

'Japanese patrolmen are hard-working, proud of their job and social status, well trained, and highly professional. In dealings with the public they are not high-handed. They are used to bending the law in the direction of tolerance when the offence is minor and the offender repentant. They have a view of human nature and society that accepts fallibility and weakness and credits social disadvantage and personal misfortune with causing people to go astray. This perspective gives rise to an active police role in ameliorating social conditions; it tempers interactions with boisterous, ill-behaved, and frantic citizens; and it gives the police on the scene, arbiters of a world gone awry, a moral role analogous to that of teacher or parent.'[25]

All these features recently observed by Bayley were so well described by Hearn some eighty-five years ago. This police paternalism might be repugnant to some people. But frankly speaking, if I compare Japanese police-public relations with American police-public relations, I prefer Japanese policemen. Even though most Japanese do not appreciate how safe a world they live in, the FBI knows that the rate of robbery in the United States in the year 1975 was one hundred and four times as high as in Japan. Women in New York City today are ten times more likely to be raped than they are in Tokyo.

I would like to mention that authority in every country at its lowest level is in many ways symbolic of its culture. American cops are symbolic of American culture. Nothing testifies so eloquently to the continuity of Russian culture as Soviet police practice. I pay much respect to Lafcadio Hearn, who could look at Japanese society from the bottom. Even in the midst of Japan's student turmoil in the 1960s, when the tension between students and police was high, 'At a Railway Station' made a strong impression on students. Hearn's *Kokoro*, written for American readers of three or four generations ago, has still its charm, appeal, and truth.

Tokyo University is said to have been rather rude and inconsiderate to Lafcadio Hearn, ousting him after six years and seven months' service. I hope it is not entirely devoid of meaning that a faculty member of the university, who still feels grateful to Hearn in many ways, has tried to evaluate him again in the light of recent scholarship. Hearn may be a minor writer, but for those of us who are interested in the love-hate relationship between Japan and the United States, Hearn's writings are still very suggestive.

Footnotes:

1. Elizabeth Stevenson, *Lafcadio Hearn*. New York: Macmillan Co., 1961; Beongcheon Yu, *An Ape of Gods: The Art and Thought of Lafcadio Hearn*. Detroit: Wayne State University Press, 1964: Arthur E. Kunst, *Lafcadio Hearn*. New York: Twayne Publishers. Inc., 1969; Margaret McAdow Lazar, *The Art of Lafcadio Hearn: A Study of His Literary Development*. Xerox University Microfilms, 1977.

2. Kunst, *Lafcadio Hearn*, p. 126.
3. Marius Jansen, 'Lafcadio in Japan', *University* (A Princeton Magazine). Winter 1963-64, Number 19, pp. 22-27.
4. *Changing Japanese Attitudes Toward Modernisation*, ed. by M. Jansen, p. 7. The quotation was by John Hall.
5. Earl Miner, *Japanese Traditions in British and American Literature*. Princeton Univ. Press, 1958, p. 64.
6. Edmund Gosse, *Silhouettes*, p. 226.
7. Hearn, 'The Japanese Smile', *Writings*, VI, p. 357. The origin of the essay can be traced back to his review of an English book, *The Philosophy of Laughter and Smiling* by C. Vasey.
8. *Kokoro* was translated into German, French, Danish, Finnish, Spanish, Italian, Hungarian, Polish, Russian, and Dutch, according to *Lafcadio Hearn, A Bibliography* by P.D. Perkins, 1934.
9. Hearn, letter to Adzukizawa, Feb. 27, 1892. These letters are collected in Maruyama's studies on Hearn. See note 12.
10. Hearn, 'Red Bridal', *Writings*, VII, p.211.
11. 'Almost a Riot' is reprinted in *Barbarous Barbers* edited by Nishizaki, Hokuseido Press, Tokyo.
12. Maruyama's studies on Hearn (in Japanese) have recently been reprinted in *Maruyama Manabu Senshū, Bungaku-hen*, Furukawa Shoten, Tokyo, 1976.
13. The original word used in the *Kyūshū Nichinichi Shimbun* is *gōzoku* strong thief.
14. Hearn, 'A Living God', *Writings*, V111, pp 3-23. As for Hearn's use of Japanese sources, see Hirakawa's study in *Koizumi Yakumo Sakuhinshū*, vol. 111, pp. 295-314. Kawade Shobō Shinsha, Tokyo, 1977.
15. Kunst, *Lafcadio Hearn*, p. 92.
16. Kunst, *Lafcadio Hearn*, p. 92.
17. Hofmannsthal, *Prosa II*, pp. 104-107. I would like to quote in more detail from the original: '... Ja, wahrhaftig, das Herz der Dinge ist in diesen fünfzehn Kapiteln, und indem ich ihre Titel überlese, sehe ich ein, dass es ebenso unmöglich ist, von ihrem Inhalt eine genaue Vorstellung zu geben als von einem neuen Parfum, als von dem Klang einer Stimme, die der andere nicht gehört hat. Ja, nicht einmal die künstlerische Form, in der diese Kunstwerke einer unvergleichlichen Feder konzentriert sind, wusste ich richtig zu bezeichnen. Da ist das Kapitel, das die Überschrift trägt: "Auf einer Eisenbahn-station". Es ist eine kleine Anekdote. Eine beinahe triviale Anekdote. Eine Anekdote, die nicht ganz frei von Sentimentalität ist. Nur freilich von einem Menschen geschrieben, der schreiben kann, und vorher von einem Menschen gefühlt, der fühlen kann.'
18. Edwin Reischauer, *The Japanese*, Belknap, Harvard, 1977, p. 142.
19. Takeo Doi, *The Anatomy of Dependence*, Kōdansha International, pp. 51-52.
20. The interpretation was by Elizabeth Stevenson.
21. Quoted in Tinker: *Lafcadio Hearn's American Days*, p. 325.
22. Hearn, *Occidental Gleanings I*, p. 32.
23. Elizabeth Stevenson, *Lafcadio Hearn*, p. 40.
24. Katharine Sansom is the second wife of Sir George Sansom. Her *Living in Tokyo* was published in New York in 1937 by Harcourt, Brace & Co. In her remark (p. 175) she further adds: 'And certainly it is true that if an infant were to search the universe for an agreeable place to be born into, he could not do better than choose Japan, for they adore children here, and ill-usage of them and crimes against them are very rare.' Japanese, having had little to do with raising livestock, got the habit of raising children as if they were plants. Japanese parents did not know the use of rods against their children.
25. Thomas Rohlen's book review appeared in *The Journal of Japanese Studies*, vol. 3, no. 2, Summer, 1977.

Supplementary Comment on the Lafcadio Hearn Paper

(at the Woodrow Wilson International Centre for Scholars, 19 July 1978)

Before summarising my paper above, I would like to situate Lafcadio Hearn in the wider context of Japanese-American relationship, and I would like to refer to some features of Hearn which distinguish him from American Japan specialists of later generations.

The importance of Japanese-American relations is obvious. The United States and Japan stand first and third in the world in economic production, respectively, and fourth and sixth in population. Between Japan and the United States there has grown up the largest trans-regional trade the world has ever known. But as the United States and Japan have different backgrounds, intellectual and cultural contacts are not very close. There is a sort of imbalance not only in trade but also in cultural relations: the attention the Japanese give to what is going on in the United States is much greater than the attention Americans give to what is going on in Japan. The United States occupies the largest part of foreign news columns in Japanese newspapers, but Japan appears not so often in American newspapers or on American television. We have the impression that looking from the Japanese side of the Pacific the United States is large and near, as if the Japanese looked at the United States through a telescope. But looking from the American side, Japan is small and far away, as if Americans looked at Japan through the same telescope, but from the other end of it. This kind of imbalance in attention is to a certain degree inevitable. For many countries, European and Asian, the United States is the most important country. But the reverse is not always true. There are many important countries for the United States, but none of them is the most important. Neither a Western European country, nor a Latin American country, nor Japan can exclusively monopolise American attention. This inevitable imbalance in attention is, I think, the principal cause of the present day love-hate relationship between the United States and other countries around the world.

But in the case of Japanese-American relations the problem is serious because of the differing cultural backgrounds. And here I have to say something about the role played by American Japan specialists who are working in the State Department or in various universities, because these Japan experts are instrumental in promoting good or bad images of Japan. The United States has a lot of excellent Japan specialists. I much admire the spectacular development of Japanese studies in this country since World War II, and I have much enjoyed the intellectual companionship of Japan specialists such as Ronald Morse and professors at Princeton, Maryland, and other universities. It is my honour and pleasure to have Professor Earl Miner and Ronald Morse as the discussants for my paper, although Ron Morse told me that he would kill me today by his comments.

I have much admiration for American Japanese studies, but I have some criticisms too. The day before yesterday I discussed or disputed with Ron Morse over the telephone about my paper, and I have made up my mind to attack the American Japanologists first before being killed. One thing which surprised me in this country is that Japan experts, though they are of very good quality, have rather little influence outside their academic circles. American Japanologists very often stick together, read their papers among themselves. Their publications have a limited readership. Oftentimes their books sell more in Japanese translation than in their American originals. Some people explain that American Japan experts stick together because they have been influenced by the Japanese groupishness: as Japanese tend to stick together, so American Japan scholars stick together under the ominous Japanese influence. Even though there may be a bit of truth in the remark, I think there may be other explanations.

Whatever the reason is, American Japanologists' influence outside their academic circles is very limited. The distorted image of the Japanese created by the single best-seller, *Shōgun*, is, to my regret, far more influential than many serious Japanese studies published by American university presses.

But there have been some exceptional American interpreters of things Japanese, whose influence goes beyond academic circles. Ambassador Reischauer is an example. His book *The Japanese* was on the list of best-sellers for many weeks. Ruth Benedict's *The Chrysanthemum and the Sword* sold well immediately after World War II, and long before, towards the turn of the century, Lafcadio Hearn made Japan known to the West. At that time Hearn was considered to be the only Westerner who understood Old Japan. But Hearn is today forgotten in the English-speaking countries. In my paper I have tried to evaluate him again, by analysing objectively one of his stories, 'At a Railway Station'. My paper is an attempt at interpretation of the story, Hearn's technique of twice-told stories, his application of folkloristic methods, and his peculiar love-hate relationship with Japan and the Occident. My justification in taking up Lafcadio Hearn is that he is still very popular in Japan. A new Japanese translation of his selected writings was published last year in Tokyo.

The reason why I chose Hearn as one of my subjects of study is rather simple. Subjectively, I very much like some of his stories for their gem-like quality, some of his interpretative essays for their insights, and some of his sketches for their realistic descriptions of the common people of Meiji Japan. Objectively, Hearn is in Japan the best known of foreign writers who have ever come to Japan. To many Japanese Hearn is a symbol of true appreciation of the Japanese character. You may say that Hearn's writings have dated. But compared to other Americans who came to Japan from the middle of the nineteenth century through the middle of the twentieth century, Hearn's position is distinctly high. Percival Lowell's books such as *The Soul of The Far East*, Henry Adams' letters from Japan, have much less appeal today than they had at the time of their publication. I'll try to explain some of Percival Lowell's method. His is the way of jumping at some general idea or theory, enunciated as a theorem, and argue down from it deductively. His personality and impersonality theory of the difference between Western and Far Eastern folk is a case in point. The idea may contain a measure of truth, but the problem with Percival Lowell is that the idea became an *idée fixe*, and I think that little, if anything, is gained by declaring Japanese 'impersonal' or by declaring Westerners 'individualistic'. Lowell's method is rather barren. But the stereotyped distinction of personality and impersonality theory still persists, and I have sometimes been surprised to hear some of my colleagues at the Centre repeat it.

But this type of approach from the top has repeatedly been used: instead of the dichotomy Personality-Impersonality, Ruth Benedict introduced the notion of Guilt culture and Shame culture, another dichotomy. Even if this dichotomy of hers contains a measure of truth, I still very much doubt the basic assumption of Ruth Benedict that guilt culture is superior to shame culture. Japanese-Americans are very proud of the fact that their crime rate is the lowest among ethnic groups in this country. If their shame culture prevents Japanese-Americans from committing crimes, shame culture is a good thing.

Then what was the method used by Lafcadio Hearn? Hearn was well aware of the fundamental difference between Lowell and himself. As Hearn had had no university education, he had some complexes and paid respects to Lowell's scientific mind. But Hearn determined not to 'do anything in Lowell's line'. Hearn said in a letter that 'to read Lowell's *The Soul of the Far East* after a year-and-a-half in Japan was quite different from reading it in America.' He said the same thing about Pierre Loti. Before coming to Japan he was enthusiasic about Loti's writings, and translated some of them for New Orleans newspapers. But Hearn was not a superficial impressionist. His method was something he had learned as a newspaper reporter. If Percival Lowell and his followers observed the Japanese from the top, Hearn tried to observe the Japanese people from the bottom. Moreover, he applied consciously some methods of folkloristic investigation. I think that in this approach lies the secret of his enduring popularity in Japan. As he had done before in Louisiana and in the French West Indies, in Japan too he paid attention to folk-lore: songs of children, proverbs, superstitions, ghost stories, customs and manners of the common people, and popular beliefs.

When we pay attention to what Hearn had done in his American days we understand much better his Japanese writings. There are so many parallels in what he had done in America as an apprentice to what he did in Japan as a literary craftsman who knows his *métier*. For example, in New Orleans he described the voices of itinerant vendors of the 1870s in an article entitled 'Voices of Dawn'. In Matsue again he paid attention to voices of Japanese itinerant vendors, and by so doing compared his Japanese experience with his previous American and European experiences. And what is interesting about Hearn is that he was affected by the Japanese influences to which he submitted himself; he not only tried to study the life and thought of the Orient but also tried to see those of the Occident from the Oriental point of view. This attitude was rather rare among Westerners of the time. Americans are often urged to study foreign countries and culture, the usual reason given being the need to overcome parochialism and to broaden horizons. These are main purposes to be sure, but there is another aspect which is equally important, though very often overlooked: foreign travel is a means of learning about oneself and one's society. What is distinctive in one's own world, too familiar usually to be recognised, becomes obvious by comparison with the lives of others. Hearn's studies are interesting in this sense, too. And here I have to refer to some characteristics of American Japanese studies conducted by American experts who came to Japan together with the Occupation. As you know, most American studies on Japan began with World War II and the American Occupation of Japan.

Most of these American studies of contemporary Japan have been concerned primarily with Japan's changing aspects, pointing to the 'feudal' and 'modern' elements as representing different or opposing qualities. The heyday of this kind of approach came during the occupation years of reforms. The goal adopted by General MacArthur and his American staff was the uprooting of feudal elements from Japanese society, and the goal was shared by many Japanese social scientists. The tendency towards such an approach is still prevalent among Japanese Marxists and perhaps among American scholars too. It was their thesis that any phenomena which seem peculiar to Japan, not having been found in Western society, can be labelled 'feudal' or 'pre-modern' elements and are to be regarded as contradictory or obstructive to the modernisation or democratisation of Japan. Under such views there is an unfounded assumption that when it is completely modernised Japanese society will or should become the same as that of the West. The proponents of such views, including many American idealists of various types - missionaries, teachers, and reformers - are interested in uprooting the so-called feudal elements in Japanese society.

But the contemporary scene has changed dramatically. A quarter of a century ago, scholars spoke of Japan's economic crisis as endemic. But Japan's economic problems have been transformed by a period of spectacular industrial growth, and the Japanese have recovered confidence in their traditional ways of life. To the eyes of many Japanese, therefore, American and Japanese criticisms of Japan immediately after the war have dated. The Japanese are today more and more conscious that modernisation is different from Westernisation. The assumption that universal laws of historical progression require that every country change according to the model shown by the so-called advanced countries such as Great Britain, France, or the United States is no longer valid, and many Japanese, I for one, are more positively interested today in the traditional aspects of Japanese culture. I may give you the following explanation as a kind of figure of speech: the Japanese language has much changed with the introduction of new words and foreign expressions, but the grammatical structure itself has not changed. Japanese society, too, has much changed with the introduction of many reforms and many new elements. But fundamental modes of human relations have not greatly changed since the mythological times of the *Kojiki*.

Until recently, not only in Japan but also in various parts of the world, people were convinced of the truth of laws of human development. Herbert Spencer's laws of human development had a strong impact not only in the United States but also in Japan and China, and I think Spencer with his universal laws of historical progression was the forerunner of Marxism in the Far East. My opinion is that Spencer prepared the soil in Japan and China in which Marxism with its universal laws of historical development took root easily and deeply.

Lafcadio Hearn, although he was a romantic anti-materialist, was, as a child of his time, under the strong influence of Herbert Spencer. The influence is most conspicuous in Hearn's last book, *Japan - An Attempt at Interpretation*. Among his writings this was the most widely read in America and went through several editions and many impressions. But to my judgement this is his worst book. He was dogmatic and clumsy at theorising. So when he tried to synthesise his views on Japan, he was not very skilful. The book was vitiated by the overwhelming influence of Spencerian postulates. Books which depend too much on abstract theoretical considerations date more rapidly than books which depend on observations of concrete details. Books are like cities: as there are some cities which become old gracefully (such as New Orleans), so there are books which become old gracefully. Some of Hearn's stories are now old-fashioned, but they have become old gracefully. I am afraid, however, that many American studies of Japan, products of the Ph.D. industry, will become old like some huge buildings in American slums: they have to be demolished in the course of time. Among Hearn's qualities I prefer his literary craftsmanship. I very much admire his faculty of perception, what he called 'soul sympathy'. I don't say that all of his writings are interesting. But some of his writings are still very suggestive, and as an example I have chosen the story 'At a Railway Station'. As American scholars of American literature have not paid attention to Japanese studies on Lafcadio Hearn, I have tried to analyse the story, using the Japanese newspaper material discovered by a Japanese scholar some forty years ago. (By the way, the Japanese scholar, Maryuama Manabu, who began his academic career as an English literature professor, ended his career as a folklorist. The shift in his career was due to the influence of his Hearn studies. The charm of Hearn the folklorist was such that Maruyama switched his academic discipline in the middle of his life.)

As to the content of the story 'At a Railway Station' I don't think I have to give you any further explanation: Hearn himself concludes the story by indicating what he thinks the episode reveals about Japanese psychology. The outright expression of emotion is typical of the Japanese, but the feelings displayed by the crowd, the policeman, and the murderer are not. Behind the peculiar Japanese avoidance of public emotional display there is the sensitivity of the people. The way of achieving emotional justice instinctively taken by the police officer in shaming the criminal before the victim's son is precisely emotion of the simplest and purest sort, and Hearn comments on 'that potential love of children which is so large a part of the soul of every Japanese'. As Hearn's story is different from the original newspaper article, we cannot guarantee the veracity of his conclusion. But Hearn, a skilful writer, illustrated the same truth with two additional episodes. The episode of Ishakawa Goemon, the greatest of the Japanese robbers, a legendary figure from the sixteenth century, was cited to confirm the accuracy of Hearn's analysis. Goemon once by night, entering a house to kill and steal, was charmed by the smile of a baby; he kept playing with the baby and went away without stealing anything. Hearn could use the episode because he had found it while gathering Japanese folk-lore.

I have to say something about Hearn's dislike of certain aspects of Western civilisation. In the latter half of the last century there were many American artists who wanted to flee from the United States. But Hearn, the immigrant, could not have returned. He knew what he had fled from in England. That must be the reason he went in search of a new chance first to the French West Indies and then to Japan. His dislike of his British father, his dislike of industrial civilisation, and especially his dislike of Christian missionaries gave him new perspectives. Many Americans who have come to Japan for other purposes than that of tourism and of business were those Americans with a strong sense of mission. This was the case not only with missionaries but also with admirals, generals, and ambassadors, such as Commodore Perry, General MacArthur òr Mrs Vining, tutor to the Crown Prince. Lafcadio Hearn was a rare American who was free from this sort of sense of mission. If Hearn had a sense of mission, it was how to achieve artistry with new ethnic materials.

You may say that Hearn's literary use of ethnological materials is not very correct. He operated under what present-day folklorists now regard as a misconception of the nature of oral narrative. Hearn felt an artistic impulse to 'improve' the rough and unpolished oral tales into forms of written literature. I know that the oral style is different from literary style, but it is missing the point to criticise Hearn for what he did not want to do. He wanted to be a literary artist. He used folkloristic materials to realise his literary ambitions. At any rate, in the case of 'At a Railway Station' I don't think that anyone could criticise Hearn for having used a newspaper article for a literary purpose. Hofmannsthal, a shrewd critic, once remarked that Hearn's story is a product of journalistic activities, but of the best quality. I think that Lafcadio Hearn is one of the most sympathetic reporters that the United States has ever sent to Japan.

Ron Morse told me that I should have taken up other stories than 'At a Railway Station'. But I like it. You may call me a sentimental Japanese. It is true that Hearn sometimes lapses into sentimentality in many of his stories and essays. But I think that in works of art the intellectual approach should be complemented by the emotional approach. The secret of Hearn's appeal lies in the combination, and in this sense 'At a Railway Station' is very well written. But I have another extrinsic reason for taking up the story. The story, as you have seen, deals with a Japanese policeman. Japanese police, especially the Japanese military police, had a very bad reputation during the 1930s and 40s. So for someone like David Bayley, an American police expert, who went several years ago to Japan to study her police behaviour on the spot, everything was a surprise. As he put it, Japan is a heaven for cops. Crime rates are low in Japan, and police-public relations are incredibly good in Japanese cities as well as in her countryside. All these findings amazed him. But these relations had already been well described by Lafcadio Hearn. For someone like me who is interested in basic modes of human relations, in the persistence of social structure, in the basic value orientation of the Japanese, Hearn's writings are very suggestive. Hearn has an instinct for finding in legends and in daily events the permanent archetypes of human experience - therein lies the secret of his power to move us, and he knows which tales to choose and which details to emphasise.

Before ending I would like to apply Hearn's own standard of criticism to his writings. Hearn said, in a lecture given at Tokyo University: 'If there is one authority that a writer can trust as "the greatest of critics" it is the public' - not the public of a day or a generation, but the public of many generations, the consensus of national opinion or of the opinion of mankind about a book that has been subjected to the awful test of time. This opinion of mankind, Hearn admits, may not be so articulate as the opinion of a trained critic, since it is based upon feeling rather than upon thinking. It only says 'we like this'. Yet there is no judgement so sure as this opinion for the simple reason that it is 'the outcome of an enormous experience'. Subjected to the awful test of time, Lafcadio Hearn as an American writer is almost forgotten, but Japanese national opinion, based upon feeling rather upon thinking, continues to say 'we like Hearn'. Hearn, alias Koizumi Yakumo, has today definitely become a Japanese writer.

Postscript

During my stay in Washington I have had some contacts with Youth for Understanding, an organisation which sends American high school students to various foreign countries and in exchange receives in American families boys and girls coming from abroad for a period varying from two months to one year. American students after having passed happy days in Japan come back to the United States and tell their parents and friends about their Japanese experiences with much excitement. But their parents and friends, knowing very little of Japan, do not respond properly to their enthusiasm. They either repeat some clichés and stereotypes or show little interest in what the young returnees from Japan tell them. Frustrated, these American returnees from Japan begin to stick together and exchange their various and common experiences of Japan among themselves. This is what the Youth for Understanding official told me. It is the same with American Japan specialists or with Japanese residing in America. People stick together so long as they share a common cultural heritage - or, more precisely, people stick together so long as others cannot share their particular cultural heritage; and without exaggeration I can say that the common denominators of the Japanese culture are rather different from those of American culture. If it is difficult for American returnees from Japan and for American Japan specialists to explain correctly what the characteristics of Japanese culture are, then it would be much more difficult for someone like me who has come to this country for the first time. But as my explanations differ considerably from those usually given by American Japan specialists, these papers and comments may be of some interest to readers.